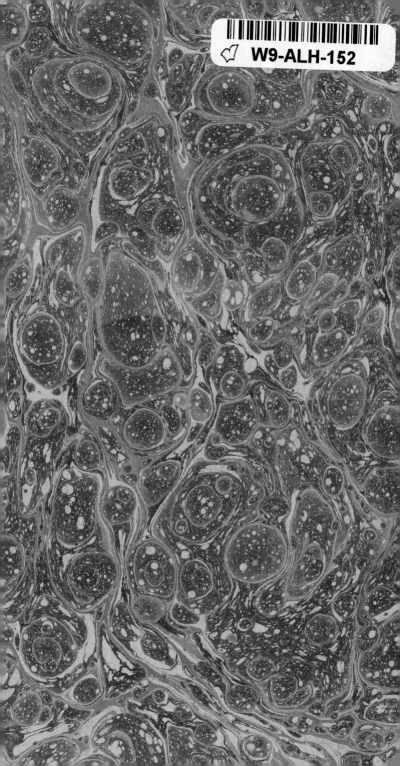

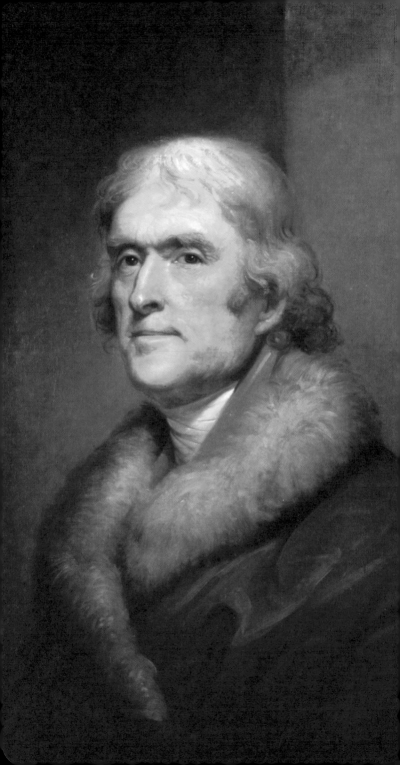

THE JEFFERSON BIBLE

—.—

The Life and Morals of Jesus of Nazareth
Extracted Textually from the Gospels
in Greek, Latin, French & English

—.—

BY THOMAS JEFFERSON

—.—

SMITHSONIAN EDITION

with Essays by Harry R. Rubenstein,
Barbara Clark Smith & Janice Stagnitto Ellis

—.—

SMITHSONIAN BOOKS
Washington, D.C.

Smithsonian Books titles may be purchased for educational,
business, or sales promotional use. For information, please write:
Special Markets Department, Smithsonian Books,
P.O. Box 37012, MRC 513, Washington, DC 20013-7012

Library of Congress CIP Data
Jefferson, Thomas, 1743–1826.
[Life and morals of Jesus of Nazareth]
The Jefferson Bible : the life and morals of Jesus of Nazareth extracted
textually from the Gospels in Greek, Latin, French & English /
by Thomas Jefferson ; with essays by Harry R. Rubenstein,
Barbara Clark-Smith, and Janice Stagnitto Ellis. — Smithsonian ed.
p.   cm.
English, French, Greek, and Latin.
Originally published: Washington, D.C. : U.S. G.P.O., 1904.
With new essays.
Includes bibliographical references and index.
ISBN 978-1-58834-312-3 (alk. paper)
1. Jesus Christ—Rationalistic interpretations. 2. Bible. N.T. Gospels—
Criticism, interpretation, etc. 3. Jesus Christ—Biography—Sources,
Biblical. 4. Jesus Christ—Teachings. 5. Jesus Christ—History of
doctrines—18th century. 6. Jesus Christ—History of doctrines—19th
century. 7. Bible. N.T. Gospels—Criticism, interpretation, etc.—History—
18th century. 8. Bible. N.T. Gospels—Criticism, interpretation, etc.—
History—19th century. I. Bible. N.T. Gospels. Polyglot. 2011. II. Title.
BT304.95.J44 2011
232.9—dc23

2011017356

11 12 13 14 15 16 · 5 4 3 2

Printed in China though Oceanic Graphic Printing, Inc.

Frontispiece:
Portrait of Thomas Jefferson (1743–1826)
by Rembrandt Peale, ca. 1805

Illustration and production credits are listed
on the last page of this volume.

CONTENTS

FOREWORD

—— · ——

Brent D. Glass

The Elizabeth MacMillan Director
National Museum of American History

FOR HIS TOMBSTONE AT MONTICELLO, THOMAS JEFFERSON LEFT specific instructions on how he wanted to be remembered: as "Author of the Declaration of American Independence / of the Statute of Virginia for religious freedom / and the Father of the University of Virginia." Although he omitted any reference to his years of public service, including two terms as president of United States, no one can quarrel with the legacy that he valued most. Jefferson championed the ideals of the Age of Enlightenment—the primacy of human reason and individual conscience, the cause of human rights, and the importance of public education.

In the decade before his death in 1826, Jefferson left other intriguing clues for future historians who would try to unravel his complex and often contradictory thoughts and actions. On the bottom of his portable writing desk, the desk on which he had drafted the Declaration of Independence, he attached a note in 1825 that reads, "Politics, like religion, has its superstitions. These, gaining strength with time, may, one day give imaginary value to this relic, for its association with the birth of the Great Charter of our Independence." He understood that this desk, now one of the treasures of the National Museum of American History, would become a powerful symbol of the ideas that shaped our country's formative years. The ideas that were "self-evident" to Jefferson and his colleagues were the concepts of individual rights and equality, ideas based not on superstition but on human reason.

Jefferson's Bible—*The Life and Morals of Jesus of Nazareth*—offers further evidence of the personal philosophy that guided his public life. Any discussion about Jefferson's religious beliefs must reference this extraordinary text as a primary source. He began assembling this book while he

6

served as president, although he did not complete the project until 1820. It was a private enterprise known to only a few close associates. By removing all references to superstition and the supernatural, Jefferson made clear his admiration of Jesus as a great teacher and moral philosopher while, at the same time, reaffirming his belief in and commitment to the power of reason as the basis for understanding life and the natural world.

Since the Smithsonian Institution acquired Jefferson's Bible in 1895, the book's condition has become increasingly fragile, and public access has been limited. In recent years, however, the need to preserve and present this unique treasure offered the National Museum of American History a rare opportunity. We undertook a complex and challenging conservation initiative that will ensure its preservation for future generations and bring the preserved book to a wider audience through exhibitions, a website, and this publication.

The National Museum of American History was able to conserve and exhibit Jefferson's Bible through a public-private partnership—generous gifts from Peter and Rhondda Grant, Brenton Halsey, Charles and Cammy Bryan, and other contributors, and a grant from the Smithsonian's Fund for Collection Care and Preservation. These funds complemented the efforts of a dedicated team of scholars and conservators led by Harry Rubenstein and Janice Stagnitto Ellis. Through their work, Jefferson's Bible will take its place with his portable writing desk as twin reminders of the private and public life of one of America's greatest leaders, a complex and influential man who defined his own times and continues even today to shape our understanding of what it means to be an American.

Acknowledgments

It is with great gratitude that we thank the many individuals and institutions that have supported this publication and the conservation project that has made it possible. We are indebted to Director Brent Glass and Associate Director David Allison of the National Museum of American History for all their continual support and encouragement of this project. This publication also relied heavily on the support of many members of the museum staff, including William L. Bird, Grace Boone, Nan Card, Nanci Edwards, Karen Garlick, Lisa Kathleen Graddy, Joycinna Graves, Kay Habeger, Debra Hashim, Valeska Hilbig, Michael Johnson, Amy Karazsia, Janice Lilja, Melinda Machado, Sara Murphy, and Margaret Webster.

The project is indebted to Richard Strauss and the entire staff of the Smithsonian Photographic Services, American History Division, and especially Hugh Talman, whose beautiful photographs of the volume's individual pages made this facsimile possible. This publication would not have happened without the indispensable work of studying and conserving Jefferson's original volume. We thank the dedicated staff, fellows, and interns of the NMAH Department of Preservation Services, including Richard Barden, Laura A. Bedford, Sarah Naomi Emerson, Sunae Park Evans, Valeria Orlandini, Emily S. Rainwater, Beth Richwine, and Suzanne Thomassen-Krauss.

Many individuals and institutions around the country also generously offered their advice and guidance, including Jeff Speakman, Jennifer Giaccai, Mehdi Moini, and Harriet Beaubien from the Smithsonian's Museum Conservation Institute; Pamela Henson, Courtney Esposito, John Dillaber, and Nora Lockshin, Smithsonian Institution Archives; Martin Kalfatovic and David Holbert, Smithsonian Institution Libraries; Grace Cohen Grossman, Skirball Cultural Center; Susan Stein and the Thomas Jefferson Foundation at Monticello; Peter S. Onuf, Corcoran Department of History, University of Virginia; Michael F. Suarez, S.J., Rare Book School, University of Virginia; Heather Riser, Albert and Shirley Small Special Collections Library, University of Virginia; Eliza Gilligan, University of Virginia Library; Lois Olcott Price, Joan Irving, and Richard Wolbers, Wintherthur/University of Delaware Art Conservation Program; Donald Richie and Tamara Elliot, United States Senate; Jana Dambrogio, Mark Ormsby, and Morgan Zinsmeister, National Archives and Records Administration; Renate Mesmer, Folger Shakespeare Library; Cathleen Baker, University of Michigan; and Yasmeen Khan and Julie Biggs, Library of Congress.

Special thanks to Carolyn Gleason and Christina Wiginton of Smithsonian Books and Marie Koller of Smithsonian Media for their wonderful work in shaping and producing this volume. We are most grateful to Duke Johns for his careful editorial work and to our outstanding designer Robert L. Wiser for embracing the intricacies of this project with gusto. David Li of Oceanic Graphic Printing was instrumental in identifying the modern materials and methods most in keeping with Jefferson's original choices.

Finally, we would like to express our deepest thanks to our families, who have shared this project with us in many ways: Daniel Bluestone, David J. Ellis, and Anne L. Pierce.

MORALS
OF
JESUS

History of the Jefferson Bible

Harry R. Rubenstein & Barbara Clark Smith

In the year 1820, Thomas Jefferson completed a project that he had long planned. Twelve years earlier he had resisted countless calls that he seek a third term as president and had retired from public life to his home at Monticello. Now, at seventy-seven years of age, Jefferson constructed a book that he entitled *The Life and Morals of Jesus of Nazareth*. Assembling excerpts from the four gospels of the New Testament, he rearranged them to tell a chronological and edited story of Jesus's life, parables, and moral teaching. Jefferson cut from printed texts in four different languages— English, French, Latin, and Greek. We may picture him in the crowded room he called his "cabinet," working at his table and donning his spectacles as evening approached. He pasted the extracts he had chosen on blank pages of paper, laying them in four columns across the pages so as to allow immediate comparison among the different language versions of each Bible verse. When finished, he sent his pages to a Richmond bookbinder, who stitched them together in a red leather binding adorned with gold tooling.

Commonly referred to today as "the Jefferson Bible," the resulting book was small: 8¼ inches tall and just under 5 inches wide. In those pages, Jefferson sought to clarify and distill Jesus's teachings, which he believed to provide "the most sublime and benevolent code of morals which has ever been offered to man." He rid the gospel message of those aspects that appeared to him as "contrary to reason," leaving behind only the "authentic" story of Jesus. Readers of *The Life and Morals of Jesus* can trace Jefferson's inclusions and exclusions, the parts of the gospels he considered

Opposite: Gold-tooled spine of Jefferson's volume

"diamonds" of wisdom, and the parts that he discarded and indecorously likened to "a dunghill." The red leather book now resides in the Smithsonian's National Museum of American History, which holds it in trust for the people of the nation. This new edition of Jefferson's *The Life and Morals of Jesus* presents digitized images of the pages of Jefferson's "little volume," which the Smithsonian has conserved in order to stabilize its condition, so that it may continue to be accessible for future generations.

———

In *The Life and Morals of Jesus*, we gain insight into just what teachings Jefferson prized from the four gospels. He created his book not for publication but for his own use only. "I never go to bed without an hour, or half an hour's previous reading of something moral," he told a physician who inquired about his habits of daily life. Jefferson's library included volumes of moral teaching from classical philosophers, recent works by European thinkers, and multiple editions of the Bible. Yet *The Life and Morals of Jesus* may often have been his choice for such readings, providing thoughts and reflections—in Jefferson's own words—"whereon to ruminate in the intervals of sleep." The pages of this volume thus allow readers to approach Jefferson not as a revolutionary or a president, but as a private man.

Such access to Jefferson's religious sentiments is a privilege that was denied to most of his contemporaries. Jefferson was famously reticent about his convictions. No one insisted more firmly than he did on the privacy of religion, that each individual's belief was a matter of concern only for the individual and for God. So sacred did Jefferson hold the individual's private relationship with the Creator that he purposefully chose not to influence the beliefs even of his own family. Jefferson's grandchildren reported to Henry Randall, a nineteenth-century biographer, that when they asked him about his beliefs, Jefferson revealed little. On this subject each of them, he counseled, must consult conscience and reason to reach his or her own conclusions. Nor did he generally discuss his opinions beyond the family circle: "I not only write nothing about religion," he once told a correspondent, "but rarely permit myself to speak of it."

Behind this stance lay impersonal logic as well as painful personal experience. Jefferson reasoned that God intended to reserve the matter of belief to individuals to resolve. After all, while kings and their bishops might force outward religious observance from their subjects, history showed that inward conviction was another matter: "No man can conform his faith to the dictates of another. The life and essence of religion consists in the internal persuasion or belief of the mind." The nature of men's minds—varied, idiosyncratic, prone to a diversity of faiths and practices—testified to the Creator's intentions.

Jefferson's experience more than confirmed his dedication to the privacy of belief. He suffered from strident, bitter, and very public attacks on his supposed views on religion. His early political writings—pamphlets about the imperial crisis of the 1770s and the Declaration of Independence itself—spoke of God as the Creator. Shortly after independence, however, when Jefferson proposed that the state of Virginia disestablish the Anglican Church, he encountered fierce opposition from Anglican clergy and others who favored the alliance of church and state. His opponents sought to defend existing Anglican privileges, including economic support by means of public taxes and the commitment of government authority to restricting gatherings of dissenters from the established faith. Disestablishment, Jefferson later recalled, caused "the severest conflicts in which I have ever been engaged."

Indeed, ending legal privilege for religion was an integral part of Jefferson's revolution. Other Americans would wage war on the battlefield, but Jefferson's battles would take place in Williamsburg, the capital of Virginia. In 1777 Jefferson left the Continental Congress and declined a post presenting American interests in France. Instead he chose to serve in the Virginia House of Delegates. There Jefferson quickly became chair of a legislative committee charged with revising the laws of the commonwealth. The revision involved more than removing the official imprimatur of George III; it would introduce substantive changes in "the principles, morals, and manners" of the people. There was urgency, Jefferson believed, because the upsurge in popular activism that accompanied the war would soon decline. "The shackles, therefore, which shall not be knocked off at the conclusion of this war, will remain on us long," he concluded. In a postwar America, privileged and conservative men would reinstate restrictions on popular liberty. Such restrictions would "be made heavier and heavier, till our rights shall revive or expire in a convulsion." He hoped to make use of a small window of opportunity.

Establishing religious freedom was thus one part of Jefferson's larger project of prompting Virginia to shed its monarchical past. Over the next several years, the Committee to Revise the Laws introduced more than 120 bills, some major and some minor, aimed together at composing, in Jefferson's words, "a system by which every fibre would be eradicated of antient or future aristocracy and a foundation laid for a government truly republican." To prevent a future aristocracy, Jefferson sought to end the practice of primogeniture, which worked to concentrate property in the hands of a privileged few. These changes would promote the division of property across the generations. At the same time, he moved to make new lands in the western areas of the state freely accessible to the free, white, poor population. He also proposed a public system of education, using tax dollars to found schools and to fund promising scholars whose families were too poor to underwrite an education.

In Jefferson's mind, the bill for religious freedom was a critical step toward transforming colonial Virginia into a republican society. Looking at history, he saw established church hierarchies working arm-in-arm with monarchs and aristocrats to restrict free inquiry, control belief, and enjoin unquestioned obedience on the common people. After all, the historian Peter Onuf reminds us, established religion "was *everywhere* in Jefferson's world," and often it worked "to prop up corrupt and tyrannical regimes." Although he liked and respected various individual clergymen, Jefferson saw the organized and established clergy as prone to what he called "priestcraft," which distorted the true teachings of the Bible. In Virginia he had witnessed the authority of government being used to suppress gatherings for worship by Presbyterians, Baptists, and others and to threaten dissenting preachers with the force of law. He had seen respected professors at the College of William and Mary forced into reticence about their liberal and "rational" beliefs, in an institution officially limited to those who subscribed to the thirty-nine articles of the Anglican faith.

In 1786 a bill finally made its way through the Virginia House of Delegates. The law guaranteed Presbyterians, Baptists, and other sects in Virginia the freedom to worship, stating, "No man shall be compelled to frequent or support any religious worship place, or ministry whatsoever, nor shall be enforced, restrained, molested or burthened in his body or goods, nor shall otherwise suffer on account of his religious opinions or belief." With this provision, the law moved beyond protecting the rights of dissenters to include those of deists, skeptics, and those with no religion at all. It clearly showed the stamp of Jefferson's authorship.

Jefferson later hailed the Virginia Statute for Religious Freedom as among his greatest contributions, but its success also created bitter enemies and a broad public readiness to see its author as hostile not only to religious establishments but to religion itself. Critics seized on Jefferson's comments on church and state in his *Notes on the State of Virginia*, first published in France in 1784. In

Notes Jefferson argued that neither unorthodoxy nor outright disbelief posed any threat to a society. "It does me no injury for my neighbor to say there are twenty gods or no God. It neither picks my pocket nor breaks my leg," he wrote. Predictably, perhaps, the phrase suggested to some readers more than a simple dissent from orthodoxy. Jefferson increasingly found himself charged with being an infidel, atheist, or worse—not only unchristian but anti-Christian in his aspirations.

In the face of these public denunciations, Jefferson stood on principle. He refused to counter such charges in a public speech or published essay: "I am ... averse to the communication of my religious tenets to the public, because it would countenance the presumption of those who have endeavored to draw them before that tribunal." Individuals should simply not admit that their religious beliefs were other people's business. "It behooves every man who values liberty of conscience for himself, to resist invasions of it in the case of others; or their case may be, by change of circumstances, become his own," he argued. "It behooves him, too, in his own case to give no example of concession, betraying the common right of independent opinion, by answering questions of faith, which the laws have left between God and himself." Yet Jefferson's silence stimulated ever more unfettered speculations about his beliefs.

For Jefferson, these political attacks were experienced in concert with his exploration of Christian principles. *The Life and Morals of Jesus* represents the culmination of conversations and correspondence that took place between Jefferson and an extraordinary circle of colleagues and friends over the span of several decades. Those conversations, in turn, were a part of an international flowering of scientific experiment and rational inquiry that marked the eighteenth century. Participants in the Enlightenment applied the critical force of human reason to test received knowledge about the natural, social, and moral worlds. As the scientific method uncovered laws of the physical world, so human reason might fathom the laws of human nature and human institutions of society and government. Jefferson and many of his correspondents embraced the exhilarating prospect of liberating their contemporaries' minds from inherited misconceptions and superstitions. Thus the English scientist and theologian Joseph Priestley (1733–1804) was thankful to live in an era of "the gradual diffusion of intellectual light, and a better aspect of things in a moral respect than has ever appeared in the world before." Jefferson joined with Priestley and others in seeking to establish humanity's moral duties and determine the role of religion in promoting them. The man who sat at Monticello and perused the gospels for the parts amenable to reason shared his search for a rational Christianity with others of his generation.

A key participant in these conversations with Jefferson was Dr. Benjamin Rush (1746–1813), the Philadelphia physician, scientist, and humanitarian who represented Pennsylvania in the Continental Congress during the Revolution and in the convention that propounded the U.S. Constitution in 1787. By the 1790s, Rush was an imposing figure, a professor of medicine, a renowned practitioner, and an active force in humanitarian efforts to end African American slavery, promote temperance, and mitigate the harsh punishments inflicted on criminals in society. Late in the decade, when Jefferson was serving in Philadelphia as vice president, the two men sometimes sat together into the evening, mulling aspects of moral philosophy and Christianity. The discussion must sometimes have been contentious, for it uncovered stark differences of opinion. Rush himself was deeply religious, raised in the evangelical "New Light" Presbyterian tradition that had swept the Middle Atlantic provinces since the 1730s. His faith laid emphasis on one's personal and emotional communion with God, the importance of fellowship among believers, and reliance on the Bible rather than on the teachings of learned clergymen.

Portrait of Benjamin Rush (1746–1813) by Thomas Sully, ca. 1813

Rush never considered scientific advances or the tools of human reason to conflict with his piety. "The truths of Christianity," he wrote, "dwell alike in the mind of the Deity, and reason and religion are equally the offspring of his goodness." Since God had given humankind knowledge through revelation as well as through the application of reason, it followed that the truths disclosed by one would prove harmonious with the truths revealed by the other.

Like Jefferson, Rush promoted freedoms for dissenting sects and the abolition of all religious tests for citizenship, voting, and office holding. Watching Philadelphia's grand procession to celebrate the U.S. Constitution in 1788, he described his own delight. He saw a profoundly "American parade ... where a rabbi walked with arms linked between a Catholic priest and a Protestant clergyman." This symbolic gesture underscored a great virtue of the U.S. Constitution: it opened "all its power and offices alike not only to every sect of Christians but to worthy men of every religion." Unlike Jefferson, however, Rush believed that religious conviction among the populace was necessary to the republican society that he envisioned for the United States. "I have always considered Christianity as the strong ground of Republicanism," he wrote Jefferson in 1800; only Christian faith and Christian morals, however bolstered and clarified by reason, could steady the nation's course and secure the promise of the Revolution for future generations.

Jefferson and Rush remained friends and correspondents, united by their common commitment to free inquiry and to a republican future for their nation. Convinced that his friend was too secular in his thinking, Rush encouraged him to formulate his beliefs in writing. Jefferson promised he would take on that task, and over the next several years the two friends reminded each other in correspondence that this pledge was still to be fulfilled. Jefferson surely had ample excuses for delay. As the presidential election of 1800 approached, he wrote to Rush: "I promised you a letter on Christianity, which I have not forgotten. On the contrary, it is because I have reflected on it, that I find much more time necessary for it than I can at present dispose of." In other words, as he considered the project carefully, Jefferson found that it would take more thought than he had first imagined.

At the same time, Jefferson's campaign for the presidency redoubled his opponents' acrimonious attacks. The election turned into a bitter contest between the Jeffersonian Republicans and the Federalists supporting John Adams, and religion played a prominent role. Established clergymen retained the position they had enjoyed prior to the Revolution in several New England states. The Presbyterian and Congregational churches remained established by law in Connecticut and Massachusetts, respectively. Clergymen of these denominations still received support from state taxpayers and backing from state authorities. Jefferson's views on the separation of church and state threatened their privileged position. Together with their Federalist allies, they spread fears of Jefferson's alleged opposition to all Christianity.

Some clergymen warned their parishioners that they should hide their Bibles if Jefferson became president, and that such an electoral outcome might bring down God's wrath on the new republic. The Reverend William Linn, who had served as president of Queen's College (now Rutgers University), proclaimed in a widely distributed pamphlet that "the election of any man avowing the principles of Mr. Jefferson would . . . destroy religion, introduce immorality and loosen all the bonds of society."

These attacks had hardly died down following the election, when President Jefferson came under a new wave of public criticism for his association with the pamphleteer and revolutionary Thomas Paine. That renowned patriot hero returned to the United States in 1802, after fifteen tumultuous years of pursuing reform and revolution in England and France. Jefferson invited Paine to stay for

Miniature portrait of Thomas Paine (1737–1809) by John Trumbull, 1788, given as a gift from the artist to Jefferson

Portrait of Joseph Priestley (1733–1804) by Rembrandt Peale, 1801

several weeks at the presidential mansion in Washington. Yet many Americans now condemned Paine as the ungodly author of *The Age of Reason*, which powerfully argued Paine's deist beliefs in God as maker, while rejecting the divinity of Jesus and denouncing clerical power. The Federalist press vilified Paine as "so notorious a drunkard" and "so impious a buffoon" that it ill became the president, as the "highest officer in the union," to offer his "cooperation" with the man. Critics associated Jefferson with Paine's most unpopular views on Christianity as a way to lessen the Republican president's public support. Such attacks did not move Jefferson to mount a public defense, but they may have reinforced his determination to fulfill his promise to Rush in order to crystallize, articulate, and record his convictions.

Other developments and other correspondents also shaped Jefferson's views. Joseph Priestley, the preeminent Anglo-American scientist and a leading theologian, had published *An History of the Corruptions of Christianity* in England in 1782. He held that science would demystify the world and ultimately undermine the political and religious authorities who promoted superstition to maintain their "undue and usurped authority." As he surveyed the history of Christian precepts and church doctrine, Priestley concluded that Jesus's original teachings had been much distorted. He accepted the gospel accounts of miracles, and belief in the resurrection formed "the very cornerstone" of his faith. Nonetheless, many Christian doctrines—the Trinity, the virgin birth, original sin, and predestination, among others—found a place on Priestley's list of "corruptions." He believed such teachings prevented people from understanding and embracing Christian faith and that authorities multiplied the mysteries of religion and promulgated superstitions. By so doing, they clouded the minds of the laity; they convinced the common people that they needed learned authorities in order to understand their duties to God and one another. "You are told that matters of the state and church are of great mystery into which you should not delve," Priestley wrote. He advised his readers to ignore such strictures. Neither government nor religion lay beyond the reach of common reason.

Priestley became an anathema to many of his compatriots for his unitarian ideas, criticisms of the established church, and admiration of the revolution taking place in France. He and his family suffered denunciation and threats of violence. In 1791 rioters in Birmingham, England, destroyed several dissenting chapels and nearly thirty houses belonging to dissenting families, including Priestley's home. Jefferson, Rush, and other Americans quickly came to Priestley's support. Encouraged by his American colleagues, he immigrated to the United States in 1794.

Priestley's work suggested to Jefferson another way to approach the text of the Bible. In March 1803 Priestley sent his recently published *Socrates and Jesus Compared* to the president. This comparative approach to the moral philosophies of the two historic teachers provided Jefferson with a model for putting down his own thoughts. The result was Jefferson's "Syllabus of an Estimate of the merit of the doctrines of Jesus, compared with those of others," which he sent off to Rush "as the only discharge of my promise I can probably ever execute."

In the "Syllabus" Jefferson divided the development of moral thought into three sections. First were the principles promulgated by "the most esteemed" of ancient Greek and Roman philosophers and sects; second were the moral principles of the biblical Jews; third came the teachings of Jesus of Nazareth, seen as a reformer to the Jewish world. In brief, Jefferson credited philosophers such as Socrates, Pythagoras, Cicero, and Seneca with teaching their followers to govern their passions. Yet he considered the ancients' views of social life, their accounts of "our duties to others," to be sorely undeveloped. Judaism had contributed "the belief in one only God," or deism. Nonetheless,

Jefferson had little regard for the social ethics of the Jews of biblical times, and he indicted their stance toward other nations as lacking in benevolence. In this context, Jefferson concluded that Jesus of Nazareth had challenged and reformed the Judaism of his day. Advising his followers to love their neighbors, Jesus had extended a code of ethics beyond the individual's outer life, or the mere performance of social obligations, to encompass each person's inner state. Equally important, Jesus had made the moral duties of affection, benevolence, and philanthropy incumbent on "all mankind." Here Jefferson focused on the universality of the Christian code of ethics, its equal claim on all individuals that they live as brethren with their fellows.

The "Syllabus" thus described humankind's moral progress. At the same time, it also expressed Jefferson's view that the New Testament itself provided only an imperfect transmission of the finest of Jesus's teachings. Jesus had not written his teachings himself, and his disciples, Jefferson believed, had been largely illiterate and unsophisticated men. In addition, Jesus had faced the crushing opposition of the learned and powerful of his day, who suppressed his message as they cut short his life. Well after Jesus's lifetime, powerful interests found their own advantage "in sophisticating and perverting the simple doctrines he taught." Like Priestley's work, then, the "Syllabus" laid emphasis on the corruptions of Jesus's contributions to human ethics.

As Jefferson explained his beliefs to Rush, "They are the result of a life of enquiry and reflection, and very different from that anti-Christian system, imputed to me by those who know nothing of my opinions. To the corruptions of Christianity, I am indeed opposed; but not to the genuine precepts of Jesus himself. I am a Christian, in the only sense in which he wished any one to be; sincerely attached to his doctrines, in preference to all others; ascribing to himself every human excellence, and believing he never claimed any other." Denying the divinity of Jesus, Jefferson credited him with bringing the highest moral wisdom to the world. No divinity was necessary, either for the reformer of Jewish beliefs or for any other human being. Morality arose not from revelation or inspiration, but rather from the dictates of nature and reason.

Besides sending the "Syllabus" to Rush, Jefferson sent copies to his two daughters and at least two members of his cabinet. Though he did not mean the "Syllabus" for publication, he was confident that it was a document to be shared by his loyal inner circle. It clearly expressed his views on religion and countered his critics' charges against him. Equally important, it was a statement that upheld, in Jefferson's mind, that he was a true Christian.

Jefferson also sent a copy of the "Syllabus" to Priestley, hoping to enlist the great man in pursuing a study along similar lines. When Priestley accepted the charge, Jefferson hailed his decision: "I rejoice that you have undertaken the task of comparing the moral doctrines of Jesus with those of the ancient philosophers," he wrote. "You are so much in possession of the whole subject, that you will do it easier and better than any other person living." Despite that opinion, Jefferson went on to give the theologian a bit of advice. Priestley should first distinguish Jesus's moral teaching, in his own words, from the evangelists and then leave all else aside. Jefferson mentioned that he himself had ordered English and Greek editions of the New Testament, planning to extract "morsels of morality, and paste them on the leaves of a book." Now, however, he would leave the project to "better hands."

It is not certain whether Priestley ever saw Jefferson's letter. He died on February 4, 1804, shortly after it was posted. The task of extracting "morsels of morality" thus fell back on the president. He worked on the project at the end of the day in the executive mansion, and he limited himself to the two English editions he had ordered. He cut out selected passages and pasted the text into a blank book. As he recalled years later, "It was the work of 2. or 3.

nights only at Washington, after getting thro' the evening task of reading the letters and papers of the day." By March 10, 1804, the forty-six-page volume had been completed. Jefferson entitled the work *The Philosophy of Jesus of Nazareth extracted from the account of his life and doctrines as given by Matthew, Mark, Luke and John. Being an abridgement of the New Testament for the use of the Indians unembarrassed with matters of fact or faith beyond the level of their comprehensions.*

Historians debate what Jefferson meant by referring to "Indians" in his subtitle. He wrote to John Adams, "I have performed this operation for my own use." But might Jefferson have briefly considered its publication? Other scholars suggest that the subtitle served as a subterfuge, a way to deflect criticism from the orthodox in case *The Philosophy of Jesus* ever fell into public hands. Still others detect in the reference an inside joke; perhaps Jefferson's "Indians" were his Federalist opposition and clerical critics, whose "level of . . . comprehensions" Jefferson might wish to impugn. Whatever Jefferson's original intentions, *The Philosophy of Jesus* remained private. In the following years, this volume—lost after Jefferson's death—was one that Jefferson read over in the evenings in search of moral insights.

Whether dissatisfied with his compilation or seeing it as only the initial step, in 1805 Jefferson ordered two additional copies of the New Testament in English and two in French. The volumes, however, would remain unclipped on his bookshelves for many years. The duties of the presidency and numerous other projects drew his attention in other directions.

It was in retirement at Monticello that Jefferson returned to his project on the teachings of Jesus. Again, it was the result of an old friend's urging. In their waning years Jefferson and John Adams renewed their friendship and, in 1812, began a historic correspondence. The exchanges covered a broad sweep of topics, from their personal lives to politics, their presidencies, and religion. The two men found distance from their earlier partisan conflicts and substantial commonality in their views. Adams shared Jefferson's concern about the continuing influence of the wealthy and well-born: "Your aristocrats are the most difficult animals to manage of anything in the whole theory and practice of government. They will not suffer themselves to be governed. They not only exert all their own subtlety, industry and courage, but they employ the commonalty to knock to pieces every plan and model that the most honest architects in legislation can invent to keep them within bounds." With established churches still strong in Massachusetts and Connecticut, Adams likewise worried about their partisan and self-interested influence on politics and society. The man raised in the Congregationalist Church also shared his doubts about the prevailing orthodoxy. "You will say I am no Christian," Adams wrote to Jefferson as he confided those doubts. Jefferson said no such thing, of course, but rather shared a copy of his "Syllabus" with his correspondent. Adams's positive response rekindled Jefferson's enthusiasm for his previous endeavor.

By 1816 Jefferson was writing to a few friends that he was considering revising *The Philosophy of Jesus*, and he suggested that "to this Syllabus and Extract, if a history of his life can be added, written with the same view of the subject, the world will see, after the fogs shall be dispelled, in which for 14 centuries he has been inveloped by Jugglers to make money of him, when genuine character shall be exhibited, which they have dressed up in the rags of an Imposter, the world, I say, will at length see the immortal merit of this first of human Sages." So *The Life and Morals of Jesus* would go beyond *The Philosophy of Jesus* to include the biographical account that Jefferson gleaned from the evangelists' unreliable narratives.

In 1819 he took up the project in earnest. He assembled the different language versions of the New Testaments that

Portrait of John Adams (1735–1826) by Gilbert Stuart, 1823–24

he had ordered while serving as president. Selecting those passages that he believed were uncorrupted by misunderstandings, fabrications, and time, he cut them out and carefully glued them onto loose pages. As scholars reconstruct the events, by 1820 Jefferson had finished the project and sent his pages to Frederick A. Mayo, a Richmond bookbinder. Even though Jefferson had discussed this endeavor with several of his closest friends over the years, he never shared or directly discussed the final product with any of them. He left no explanation of his decisions regarding what to include and what to reject.

Nonetheless, the completed work reflects the goals that Jefferson had set out to accomplish. Left behind in the source material were those elements that he could not support through reason, that he believed were later embellishments, or that seemed superfluous or repetitious across the Four Evangelists' accounts. Absent are the annunciation, the resurrection, the water being turned to wine, and the multitudes fed on five loaves of bread and two fishes. It essentially offers what the title indicates: a distillation of the teachings of Jesus the moral reformer, combined with what Jefferson accepted as the historical facts pertaining to Jesus the man.

Although the phrase "Jefferson's Bible" became attached to *The Life and Morals of Jesus* long after Jefferson's time, in this respect it is an apt and accurate phrase. "I am of a sect by myself, as far as I know," he told a correspondent in 1819. This then *was* Thomas Jefferson's Bible; it contained the one form of Christianity—however misshapen it appeared to others—that Jefferson believed.

The act of cutting apart the New Testament to create something fresh and new was an ambitious, even audacious, initiative. Yet this revision of the gospels shared a common spirit with Jefferson's earlier revision of Virginia laws. Together they confirm one contemporary's view of Jefferson's character: the Virginian, remarked the journalist William Duane, was "the greatest rubber off of dust" that he had ever encountered. On these projects, as in the rest of his life, Jefferson displayed an extraordinary lack of reverence toward the authorities of the past. Here is the paradox noted by historian Joyce Appleby: "Jefferson distinguished himself from his contemporaries by opposing the mindless transfer of laws, ideas—even words—from one generation to another. The true Jeffersonian legacy is to be hostile to legacies."

To Jefferson, no tradition was so sacred as to escape reconsideration in the light of new discoveries and the progress of knowledge. The acts of Parliament, the English common law, and the Bible itself must be read through the lens of enlightened human reason, then changed as reason might dictate. His efforts toward revision of the laws and his revision of the gospels shared a common impulse, a drive to separate the true from the corrupt, the wheat from the chaff, or the diamonds from the dung.

———

The Life and Morals of Jesus remained in the family's hands after Jefferson's death. Its existence may have been known only to a few of his surviving acquaintances. The first known public notice of the book appeared in Henry S. Randall's three-volume biography, *The Life of Thomas Jefferson*, published in 1858. Randall had learned of Jefferson's project from a mention in his subject's correspondence, although he never saw the book itself. With the permission of Thomas Jefferson Randolph, Jefferson's oldest grandson, Randall obtained and included in his biography a listing of the passages that Jefferson had assembled for his volume. Still, as long as the book stayed with the family, it remained largely unknown.

The Life and Morals of Jesus would not find its way into public hands until 1895, when Cyrus Adler, the librarian of the Smithsonian Institution, purchased the volume from Carolina Randolph, the daughter of Randolph. Adler's interest in the book dated back to 1886, when, as a student of Semitic studies at Johns Hopkins University, he became

Portrait of Cyrus Adler (1863–1940)
while serving as Smithsonian librarian, ca. 1890

acquainted with the Cohen family of Baltimore. Dr. Joshua I. Cohen had assembled a significant library of Hebraica and Judaica, and the family granted Adler the opportunity to catalog the collection.

In Cohen's library Adler found two copies of the New Testament, from which many passages had been carefully removed. Printed notes pasted on the inside covers of the two books described Jefferson's project and provided provenance for the Testaments. An inscription from Cohen testified, "This and the Corresponding vol. are the identical copies alluded to in the above article. They were purchased by me at the sale of Dr. Macaulay's Medical library, by whom they had been bought at the sale of Mr. Jefferson's Library." Adler decided that the two volumes Jefferson had used to create *The Life and Morals of Jesus* fell outside the scope of his cataloging project. Intrigued by his discovery, however, Adler tried unsuccessfully to locate Jefferson's completed work.

Years later, now the Smithsonian Institution's librarian and serving as a curator of world religions, Adler renewed his search. The 1895 Cotton States International Exposition in Atlanta had invited the Smithsonian to showcase its holdings at the fair. The Smithsonian department of Oriental Antiquities and Historic Religious Ceremonials chose to display objects in its collections that would be "illustrative of the Bible." Adler, now tasked with organizing an exhibition on biblical antiquities, resumed his search for Jefferson's missing compilation of biblical extracts. He discovered that the book now belonged to Carolina Randolph, great-granddaughter of Thomas Jefferson. In 1895 Adler persuaded her to sell the volume to the National Museum for $400.

In its first public display at the exposition, *The Life and Morals of Jesus* was presented along with the fauna, flora, and antiquities of biblical Palestine and ancient and modern translations of the Bible and the New Testament. The volume exhibited under the title "Thomas Jefferson's Bible" was the final object for public view, presented—as Jefferson would have perhaps approved—as the culmination of the entire exhibition.

With Jefferson's volume now available, interest in the work increased. In 1902 Congressman John F. Lacey of Iowa introduced a resolution for the printing of a facsimile of the volume along with an introduction by Adler. News that both houses of Congress had adopted the resolution soon prompted a protest that Jefferson himself might have anticipated. The Presbyterian Ministers' Association made a formal complaint, arguing that, by stripping Jesus of his divinity, the work constituted an assault upon the commonly received views of the church. Yet Lacey, a devout Christian, had been inspired by Jefferson's book. He responded, "No one that examines this little volume, whether he be saint or sinner, will rise from his perusal without having a loftier idea of the teachings of our Savior." Congress seriously considered rescinding the resolution but decided to go forward. The Government Printing Office had each page photographed, and in 1904 it published Jefferson's full text for the first time. The office distributed 9,000 copies to the two chambers of Congress. In following years, newly elected senators each received a copy of the book on the day they swore their oath of office, a tradition that did not end until the books ran out in the 1950s. The distribution of these copies prompted numerous commercial printings. In the course of the twentieth century, Jefferson's private book at last circulated among a broad public audience.

In 1920, a century after Jefferson had completed *The Life and Morals of Jesus*, the book and its English sources were reunited. Adler, retired from the Smithsonian, received notice from Bertha Cohen that the family wished to donate the two New Testaments that Adler had discovered many years before. Now they would appear along with *The Life and Morals of Jesus*, on display in the Smithsonian's Arts and Industry Building. A delighted Adler put the family in contact with the museum's curators. On June 14, 1920, Cohen presented the two tattered volumes to the Smithsonian. It seems fitting that all three books now reside in a national museum dedicated to "the increase and diffusion of knowledge."

The Life and Morals of Jesus is the work of Jefferson's own hands and a product of his distinctive intellect. Intended as a private work, it offers insight into the individual who created it, the thought of his times, and the American Revolution. It can be read as a historical document that illuminates the new nation, and it remains a thoughtful examination of the New Testament, composed by a brilliant American mind.

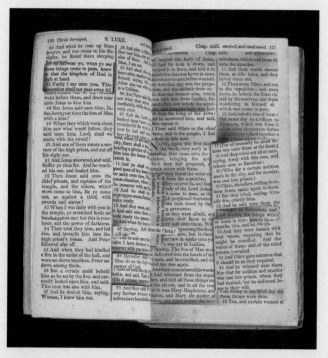

English-edition New Testament source book illustrates that Jefferson literally extracted the passages he wished to include.

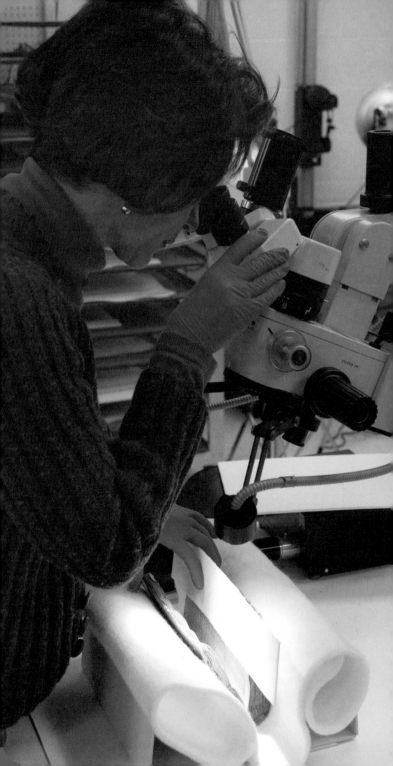

CONSERVATION

—— · ——

Janice Stagnitto Ellis

WHEN THOMAS JEFFERSON'S GREAT-GRANDDAUGHTER, Carolina Randolph, sold *The Life and Morals of Jesus of Nazareth* to Smithsonian Institution librarian Cyrus Adler in 1895, he had a plan for it. Miss Randolph and her family had kept this book out of the public eye for more than sixty-five years after Jefferson's death, but the time had come to let it be seen. She chose to entrust this closely held family treasure, Jefferson's "little volume," to a national venue, where it became a national treasure.

In 1904 the Government Printing Office had black-and-white photographs made of each page in order to publish a photolithographic facsimile edition of the book. These photographs now serve as the first documentation of the physical condition of *The Life and Morals of Jesus of Nazareth*, eighty-four years after Jefferson made it. They reveal that, by 1904, the pages had already begun to tear at the edges from handling and use. Several page openings, including those at pages 38 and 77, were severely darkened, probably from exposure to natural light, gaslight, and their pollutants while the artifact was on display. Over the next hundred years, following the emerging profession of artifact conservation, the Smithsonian Institution reduced the public display of the book, limiting its access to protect it from the ordinary attrition of age and use, but time worsened its condition nonetheless. Eventually the museum considered it too fragile for exhibition and limited even scholarly access. Once again, Jefferson's volume became an inaccessible treasure.

In 2009 the Smithsonian's National Museum of American History (NMAH) committed to making *The Life and*

——

Opposite: Microscopic examination of the Jefferson Bible prior to repair

Morals of Jesus of Nazareth accessible again and embarked
upon conserving and scanning the book's individual pages.
Four NMAH conservators assembled to preserve Jefferson's Bible. The Smithsonian's Museum Conservation Institute, Smithsonian Institution Libraries, and numerous
consultants from the National Archives and Records
Administration, Library of Congress, Winterthur/Univer-
sity of Delaware, University of Virginia, and others provided additional expertise. Conservation scientists tested
the materials. Scholars and conservators provided historical, bibliographic, and treatment insight. In order to meet
the museum's priority of exhibition and scholarly use,
conservators needed to make the artifact usable again
without causing further damage. To achieve this result,
they needed to define the artifact's condition, determine its
chemical and physical instability, implement a conservation
treatment to stabilize it, produce a preservation scan, and
create a baseline from which future conservators could
monitor its condition over time.

Preparing the book for conservation treatment and exhibition was a painstaking process. And Jefferson's creation is
no ordinary book. Unlike other early nineteenth-century
books, it was not printed by a single printer on one type of
paper and brought to a bookbinder to be bound. It is more
like a scrapbook. Created by Jefferson's own hand sometime
between 1819 and 1820, it was made up from multiple clippings removed from other printed Bibles and glued to the
front and back of each leaf in forty-three paper folios. These
clippings were arranged so densely that, at first glance, each
page resembles a single imprint. A close examination reveals
the seventy-seven-year-old Jefferson's mental and physical
skills: a practical demonstration of his meticulous hand-
work, his tidiness and planning, his strategic and near-
surgical approach to "extracting" clippings from his source
books, and his careful attention to detail.

To make *The Life and Morals of Jesus of Nazareth*,
Jefferson purchased two copies each of three New Testament

translations. The Greek and Latin translations are printed together in Wingrave's 1794 London edition of Leusden's Greek Testament; the English translation is from Jacob Johnson's Philadelphia 1804 edition of the King James New Testament; and the French is from Ostervald's Paris 1802 edition of the New Testament. He needed two copies of each so that he could cut passages from the fronts and backs of pages.

He purchased blank paper, most likely "royal" size, which measured 19 by 24 inches. Each royal sheet was cut down into six pieces measuring 9½ by 8 inches. These were folded in half to produce pages measuring 8 inches tall by 4¾ inches wide. Jefferson drew a center-divide ruling line on the front and back of each page. He made tiny pencil hatch marks on these ruling lines to indicate the upper margins of the pages. (On page 7, just above the pencil mark, a single curly reddish hair protrudes from beneath the upper left corner of verse 15.) Then he carefully glued the New Testament cutouts onto his blank paper beginning at the pencil mark. He arranged the text on either side of the ruling line in two vertical columns per page, so that on each double-page spread one can read the same text in four columns: Greek and Latin on the left-hand page; French and English on the right. He handwrote page numbers and notes in the margins and made corrections to his mistakes or the publishers' when needed. For example, he added an omitted verse to the English margin on page 40 and corrected a translation error by changing the word "out" to "up" on an English verse on page 5, Luke 6:12. On page 64 he edited Matthew 24:38 by cutting out the word "as" in the verse that begins "For as in the days," revealing an intellectual focus as sharp as the knife he used to remove the offending word.

Page 22 reveals that, just above Matthew 13, Jefferson had accidentally cut off text at the far right edge of a clipping. But he then aligned and glued a replacement fragment in place with such precision that only the darkening caused by the extra adhesive under the fragment gives the mistake away.

Using iron-gall ink mixed at home from commercially available ink powders, he wrote abbreviations in the margins to indicate the gospel and chapter number: a cross stroke on the letter "M" indicated "Mt" for Matthew, "Mr" for Mark, and "L" and "J" for Luke and John. He frequently started the quill stroke for each diminutive initial capital in the center of the letter, leaving a small tail in the middle of each, before moving his quill to the ascending stroke.

Rather than send the completed forty-three folios to his favorite bookbinder, Joseph Milligan, who was in the twilight of his career, Jefferson sent them to a new book-binder in Richmond: Frederick August Mayo. Two years earlier, on November 30, 1818, Jefferson wrote in his first letter to Mayo that "I am particular in my bindings and have hitherto been obliged to send my choice books to Milligan in Georgetown because I have found no workman in America but him who can give me such as the London and Paris bindings, besides the good taste with which he works. [A] book bound by him is as heavy as a piece of metal while the common bindings of this country are so spongy, that after a book has been opened, it will never shut close again." Mayo obliged with a binding that held the pages firmly immobile.

To bind it to Jefferson's liking, Mayo compensated the folds of the folios with extra paper stubs that increased the spine's bulk to equal that of the center of the page where Jefferson had glued the clippings. Mayo then added end leaves and Stormont pattern marbled flyleaves and sewed them together on four sewing supports, three folios at a time, to create a text block. He sewed pale blue- and rose-colored silk endbands to the head and tail, lined the spine with layers of heavyweight paper, and laced-on the front and back boards. He covered the book "tight back," gluing the leather directly to the spine linings, using full-leather, straight-grain red morocco, a goat skin laboriously steeped, slaked, pounded, stretched, and processed for more

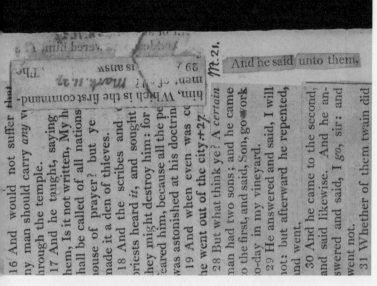

Jefferson identified this folded clipping on the foredge of page 56 by writing on the back in iron-gall ink.

than sixty days and tanned with sumac. It was the finest-quality, most expensive leather available. He embellished the leather binding with gold tooling on the covers, spine, board edges, and turn-ins, and placed his binder's ticket on the inside of the front cover.

Jefferson wrote a separate, two-page index listing all the passages in the entire book. At some later point, the index was glued inside the book between the front cover and the marble flyleaf.

Nearly two centuries later, the original Mayo binding remained intact. But exposure to oxygen, humidity, and light had caused the Jefferson Bible's paper to become rigid. The glue Jefferson had used to adhere the clippings had hardened (it contains both starch and protein). The paper became inflexible and brittle from the glue's acidity. Humidity caused the paper to become distorted, and it had cracked at the hills and valleys. Mayo's binding also damaged Jefferson's paper. The robustly lined tight-back spine could barely

Restricted opening before treatment shows
the binding's inflexible spine and stubs.

flex. As the book was opened, the paper just beyond the stubs became the hinging point rather than the spine. When the paper became brittle with age, the stubs caused the forty-three folios to break. Opening the book wider than thirty degrees caused damage because neither the paper nor the binding had enough remaining flexibility.

To decide on a conservation treatment for the Jefferson Bible, conservators needed to understand all the risks and anticipate how to avoid them. With the Jefferson Bible, this was a complex task, because it is made from many different types of materials that affect the physical and chemical stability of each other and the whole. There are twelve different papers (the blank folio paper; six source book papers; maps; end leaves; stubs; marbled paper; and the index). Two types of adhesive were used to glue the clippings on the paper (starch and animal glue). There are seven printing inks (six source books and maps). At least four different iron-gall inks are included (ruling lines, page numbers, marginalia, and for the index). These inks were made from different proportions of the most common ingredients ("vitriol" iron sulfate, oak galls, water, and gum arabic) from recipe to recipe or from batch to batch. The resulting aging characteristics, chemical stability, and solubility of the inks vary considerably.

With so many materials, often a solution to one problem would exacerbate another. For this reason, aqueous (water) treatment of the paper was ruled out. Nonaqueous alkalization solutions, commonly used to buffer acidic paper, would not have addressed the chemical needs of the other materials such as the iron-gall inks, and they were also ruled out. Ultimately, the complexity of the materials was too great for every type of chemical conservation treatment considered.

Conservation also required layers of decision making beyond simply identifying materials. For example, when investigating all the iron-gall inks in the volume, the conservators questioned where one recipe or batch ended and another began. The conservators needed to determine the most useful locations for analytical tests when iron-gall inks, paper, and adhesives varied significantly over one hundred pages. They observed that Jefferson had used a draftsman's tool called a divider to gently score the ruling lines on the pages before inking them. They debated whether the weakness in the center of each ruled page resulted from the physical damage made by the draftsman's tool, chemical damage from the acidic iron-gall ink eating into the paper, or the combination of both.

Even the proposed change of Frederick Mayo's book-binding needed special consideration. Hannah French, a noted scholar of bookbinding history, described the binding as a masterpiece in her 1986 book, *Bookbinding in Early America*. Museum curators questioned how to maintain the integrity of the original craftsman bookbinder's master-piece while addressing the needs of the Jefferson document bound inside.

The most compelling need of *The Life and Morals of Jesus of Nazareth* was repairing the physical damage that the binding structure had caused to the brittle paper. Without addressing the binding, the artifact would remain too fragile to ever use again. Ninety-eight percent of the book pages had either cracked or been partially torn by the stubs. The book was disbound to improve the flexibility of the Mayo binding and change the stub design. Although the original stubbed binding design had served the text block well enough when the book's paper was young and flexible, it did not serve the old, stiff paper.

To remedy the tight binding, conservators first took the book apart, keeping the leather cover intact but separating it from the bound text block, removing the restrictive spine linings beneath and snipping the sewing inside the pages so that they could be separated once again into forty-three loose folios. Every scrap removed from the original binding was saved for future research. The disbound pages were dry-cleaned and physically repaired using *Tosa tengujo*

Adhesive failure caused some
clippings to delaminate.

Weakness at the ruling line
resulted in occasional tearing.

Japanese paper, Berlin tissue, and a reversible adhesive. The repaired pages were digitally photographed using a Hasselblad H4D-50 50 megapixel DSLR camera and a Zeiss 120 macro lens, producing the first complete color images ever taken of the artifact. The folios were resewn not with the original stubs, which were numbered and saved, but with new, more flexible paper. The text block was resewn through the original sewing holes, using unbleached linen thread in an unsupported sewing stitch sewn through a linen spine lining material. The original silk endbands were sewn back in place, and the original red morocco covers and spine were reused. The resulting treatment provided the book with the needed flexibility while using materials and techniques sympathetic with the original artifact.

To address the chemical stabilization of the volume, the conservation treatment plan also included the design and manufacture of a long-term protective enclosure. Organic materials such as paper and leather degrade fastest when exposed to light, oxygen, and moisture. The protective enclosure reduces the book's exposure to these hazards as well as environmental fluctuations and pollutants.

In 2011, with the conservation treatment of *The Life and Morals of Jesus of Nazareth* completed, the National Museum of American History once again is able to present Carolina Randolph's gift to a wide audience, through exhibitions, this facsimile reproduction, and digital images. The preservation project not only has made the volume more accessible but also provided new insights into how it was constructed and, through materials analysis, provided a baseline description of the book's physical and chemical state, thereby enabling future conservators to monitor its condition with accuracy. For the first time, scholars and the general public alike can access this treasure in intimate detail. Jefferson's little volume is now simultaneously safely accessible to everyone and safely preserved at the Smithsonian.

Removing spine linings from text block after cover has been detatched

Selected Bibliography

Adams, Dickinson W., ed., and Ruth W. Lester, asst. ed. *Jefferson's Extracts from the Gospels: "The Philosophy of Jesus" and "The Life and Morals of Jesus."* The Papers of Thomas Jefferson, 2nd ser. Princeton: Princeton University Press, 1983.

Adler, Cyrus. *I Have Considered the Days.* Philadelphia: Jewish Publication Society of America, 1945.

Appleby, Joyce. "Introduction: Jefferson and His Complex Legacy." In *Jeffersonian Legacies*, edited by Peter S. Onuf. Charlottesville: University Press of Virginia, 1993.

Braden, Bruce, ed. *"Ye will say I am no Christian": The Thomas Jefferson/John Adams Correspondence on Religion, Morals, and Values.* Amherst, NY: Prometheus Books, 2006.

Church, Forrest. "The Gospel according to Thomas Jefferson." In *The Jefferson Bible: The Life and Morals of Jesus of Nazareth.* Boston: Beacon Press, 1989.

Cunningham, Noble E., Jr. *In the Pursuit of Reason: The Life of Thomas Jefferson.* Baton Rouge: Louisiana State University Press, 1987.

D'Elia, Donald J. "Benjamin Rush: Philosopher of the American Revolution." *Transactions of the American Philosophical Society.* New series, vol. 64, part 5. 1974.

Ellis, Joseph J. *American Sphinx: The Character of Thomas Jefferson.* New York: Vintage, 1998.

Ferling, John. *Adams vs. Jefferson: The Tumultuous Election of 1800.* New York: Oxford University Press, 2004.

French, Hannah D. *Bookbinding in Early America: Seven Essays on Masters and Methods.* Worcester, MA: Worcester American Antiquarian Society, 1986.

Grossman, Grace Cohen, with Richard Eighme Ahlborn. *Judaica at the Smithsonian: Cultural Politics as Cultural Model.* Washington, DC: Smithsonian Institution Press, 1997.

Jefferson, Thomas. *Autobiography of Thomas Jefferson*, with an introduction by Dumas Malone. New York: G. P. Putnam's Sons, n.d.

———. *Notes on the State of Virginia.* Ed. with an introduction and notes by William Peden. New York: W. W. Norton, 1972.

Keane, John. *Tom Paine: A Political Life.* Boston: Little, Brown, 1995.

Onuf, Peter S. "Jefferson's Religion: Priestcraft, Enlightenment, and the Republican Revolution." In *The Mind of Thomas Jefferson.* Charlottesville: University Press of Virginia, 2007.

Paine, Thomas. *The Age of Reason.* Secaucus, NJ: Citadel Press, 1974.

Peterson, Merrill, and Robert C. Vaughan, eds. *The Virginia Statute for Religious Freedom: Its Evolution and Consequences in American History.* Cambridge: Cambridge University Press, 1988.

Randall, Henry S. *The Life of Thomas Jefferson.* 3 vols. New York: Derby and Jackson, 1858.

Schofield, Robert E. *The Enlightened Joseph Priestley: A Study of His Life and Work from 1773 to 1804.* University Park: Pennsylvania State University Press, 2004.

A Table

of the Texts ~~of this Extract~~ narrative from the Evangelists, ~~employed in this Narrative~~ and of the order of their arrangement.

Luke. 2. 1 — 7. Joseph & Mary go to Bethlehem, where Jesus is born

    21. 39. he is circumcised & named & they return to Nazareth

    40. 42 — 48. 51. 52. at 12 years of age he accompanies his parents to Jerusalem and returns.

L. 3. 1. 2. Mk. 1. a M. 3. 4. 5. 6. John baptises in Jordan.

M. 3. 13. Jesus is baptised. L. 3. 23. at 30 years of age.

J. 2. 12 — 16. drives the traders out of the temple.

J. 3. 22. M. 4. 12. Mk. 6. 17 — 28. he goes, baptises but retires into Galilee on the death of John

~~Mk.~~ Mk. 1. 21. 22. he teaches in the Synagogue.

M. 12. 1 — 5. 9 — 12. Mk. 2. 27. M. 12. 14. 15. explains the Sabbath.

L. 6. 12 — 17. call of his disciples.

M. 5. 1 — 12. L. 6. 24. 25. 26. M. 5. 13 — 47. L. 6. 34. 35. 36. M. 6. 1. — 34. 7. 1.

L. 6. 38. M. 7. 3 — 20. 12. 35. 36. 37. 7. 24 — 29. the Sermon in the Mount

M. 8. 1. Mk. 6. 6. M. 11. 28. 29. 30. exhorts.

L. 7. 36 — 46. a woman anointeth him.

Mk. 3. 31 — 35. L. 12. 1 — 7. 13 — 15 precepts

L. 12. 16. — 21. parable of the rich man.

    22 — 48. 54. 59. L. 13. 1 — 5 precepts.

L. 13. 6 — 9. parable of the fig tree.

L. 11. 37 — 46. 52. 53. 54. precepts.

M. 13. 1 — 9. Mk. 4. 10. M. 13. 18 — 23. parable of the Sower.

Mk. 4. 21. 22. 23. precepts. M. 13. 24 — 30. 36 — 52. parable of the Tares

Mk. 4. 26 — 34. L. 9. 57 — 62. L. 5. 27 — 29. Mk. 2. 15 — 17 precepts

L. 5. 36 — 39. parable of new wine in old bottles.

M. 13. 53 — 57 a prophet hath no honor in his own country.

M. 9. 36 Mk. 6. 7 M. 10. 5. 6. 9 — 18. 23. 26 — 31. Mk 6. 12. 30. mission, instrns, return apace

J. 7. 1. Mk. 7. 1 — 5. 14 — 24. M. 18. 1 — 4. 7 — 9. 12 — 17. 21 — 22. 5 precepts.

M. 18. 23. — 35. parable of the wicked servant.

Mt. 26. 14—16. Judas undertakes to point out Jesus.

17—20. L. 22. 24—27. J. 13. 2. 4—17. 21—26. 31. 34. 35. Mt. 26. 31. 33

L. 22. 33—34. Mt. 26. 35—45: precepts to his disciples, ~~washes their feet~~ trou-
-ble of mind and prayer.

J. 18. 1—3. Mt. 26. 49—50. Judas conducts the officers to Jesus.

J. 18. 4—8. Mt. 26. 50—52. 55. 56. Mk. 14. 51. 52. Mt. 26. 57. J. 18. 15. 16. 18. 17
J. 18. 25. 26. 27. Mt. 26. 75. J. 18. 19—23. Mk. 14. 55—61.
L. 22. 67. 68. 70. Mk. 14. 63—65: he is arrested & carried
before Caiaphas the High priest & is condemned.

J. 18. 28—31. 33—38. L. 23. 5. Mt. 27. 13. is then carried to Pilate.

L. 23. 6—12. who sends him to Herod.

L. 23. 13—16. Mt. 27. 15—23. 26. recieves him back, scourges and
delivers him to execution.

Mt. 27. 27. 29—31. 3—8. L. 23. 26—32. J. 19. 17—24. Mt. 27. 39—43.
L. 23. 39—41. 34. J. 19. 25—27. Mt. 27. 46—55. 56. his crucifixion,
death and burial.

J. 19. 31—34. 38—42. Mt. 27. 60. his burial.

The

Life and Morals

of

Jesus of Nazareth

Extracted textually

from the Gospels

in

Greek, Latin

French & English.

Κεφ. β'. 2.

1 Ἐγένεῖο δὲ ἐν ταῖς ἡμέραις ἐκείναις, ἐξῆλθε δόγμα παρὰ Καίσαρ@ Αὐγύςυ, ἀπογράφεσθαι πᾶσαν τὴν οἰκεμένην.

2 (Αὕτη ἡ ἀπογραφὴ πρώτη ἐγένεῖο ἡγεμονεύον@ τῆς Συρίας Κυρηνίυ.)

3 Καὶ ἐπορεύονῖο πάνῖες ἀπογράφεσθαι, ἕκας@ εἰς τὴν ἰδίαν πόλιν.

4 Ἀνέβη δὲ κ Ἰωσὴφ ἀπὸ τῆς Γαλιλαίας, ἐκ πόλεως Ναζαρὲτ, εἰς τὴν Ἰεδαίαν, εἰς πόλιν Δαβὶδ, ἥτις καλεῖται Βηθλεεμ, (διὰ τὸ εἶναι αὐτὸν ἐξ οἴκ κ παῖριᾶς Δαβὶδ,)

* 5 ‡ Ἀπογράψασθαι ‡ σὺν Μαριὰμ τῇ ‡ μεμνησευμένη αὐτῷ γυναικὶ, ὄση ‡ ἐγκύῳ.

6 Ἐγένεῖο δὲ ἐν τῷ εἶναι αὐτὲς ἐκεῖ, ἐπλήσθησαν αἱ ἡμέραι τοῦ τεκεῖν αὐτήν.

* 7 Καὶ ἔτεκε τὸν υἱὸν αὐτῆς τὸν πρωτότοκον, κ ‡ ἐσπαργάνωσεν αὐτὸν, κ ‡ ἀνέκλινεν αὐτὸν ἐν τῇ ‡ φάτνῃ· διότι ἐκ ἦν αὐτοῖς τόπ@ ἐν τῷ ‡ καῖαλύμαῖι.

21 Καὶ ὅτε ἐπλήσθησαν ἡμέραι ὀκτὼ τοῦ περιῖεμεῖν τὸ παιδίον, κ ἐκλήθη τὸ ὄνομα αὐτῦ Ἰησῦς.

39 Καὶ ὡς ἐτέλεσαν ἅπανῖα τὰ καῖὰ τὸν νόμον Κυρίε, ὑπέςρεψαν εἰς τὴν Γαλιλαίαν, εἰς τὴν πόλιν αὐτῶν Ναζαρέτ.

40 Τὸ δὲ παιδίον ηὔξανε, κ ἐκραῖαιῦῖο πνεύμαῖι, πληρέμενον σοφίας.

42 Καὶ ὅτε ἐγένεῖο ἐτῶν δώδεκα, ἀναβάνῖων αὐτῶν εἰς Ἱεροσόλυμα καῖὰ τὸ ἔθ@ τῆς ἑορτῆς·

43 Καὶ ῖελειωσάνῖων τὰς ἡμέρας, ἐν τῷ ὑποςρέφειν αὐτὲς, ὑπέμεινεν Ἰησὲς ὁ παῖς ἐν Ἱερεσαλήμ· κ ἐκ ἔγνω Ἰωσὴφ κ ἡ μήτηρ αὐτῦ.

* 44 ‡ Νομίσονῖες δὲ αὐτὸν ἐν τῇ ‡ συνοδίᾳ εἶναι, ἦλθον ἡμέρας ὁδὸν· κ ‡ ἀνεζήῖεν αὐτὸν ἐν τοῖς ‡ συγγενέσι κ ἐν τοῖς ‡ γνωςοῖς.

45 Καὶ μὴ εὑρόνῖες αὐτὸν, ὑπέςρεψαν εἰς Ἱερεσαλὴμ, ζηῖῦνῖες αὐτόν.

CAPUT II.

1 FActum est antem in diebus illis, exiit edictum à Cæsare Augusto, describi omnem habitatam.

2 Hæc descriptio prima facta est præside Syriæ Cyrenio.)

3 Et ibant omnes describi, unusquisque in propriam civitatem.

4 Ascendit autem & Joseph à Galilæa, ex civitate Nazaret, in Judæam, in civitatem David, quæ vocatur Bethlehem, propter esse ipsum ex domo & familia David,

5 Describi cum Maria desponsata sibi uxore, existente prægnante.

6 Factum est autem in esse eos ibi, impleti sunt dies parere ipsam.

7 Et peperit filium suum primogenitum, & fasciavit eum, & reclinavit eum in præsepi: quia non erat eis locus in diversorio.

21 Et quando impleti sunt dies octo circumcidendi puerulum, & vocatum est nomen ejus JESUS,

39 Et ut persecerunt omnia quæ secundum legem Domini, reversi sunt in Galilæam in civitatem suam Nazaret.

40 At puer crescebat, & corroborabatur spiritu, plenus sapientia:

42 Et quum factus esset annorum duodecim, ascendentibus illis in Hierosolyma, secundum consuetudinem festi,

43 Et consummantibus dies, in reverti ipsos, remansit Jesus puer in Hierusalem: & non cognovit Joseph & mater ejus.

44 Existimantes autem illum in comitatu esse, venerunt diei iter: & requirebant eum in cognatis, & in notis.

45 Et non invenientes eum, regressi sunt in Hierusalem, quærentes eum.

The Roman empire taxed.

En ce tems-là, on publia un Edit de la part de César-Auguste, pour faire un dénombrement des habitans de toute la terre.

2. Ce dénombrement se fit, avant que Quirinus fût Gouverneur de Syrie.

3. Ainsi tous alloient pour être enregistrés, chacun dans sa ville.

4. Joseph aussi monta de Galilée en Judée, de la ville de Nazareth, à la ville de David, nommé Beth-léhem, parce qu'il étoit de la maison et de la famille de David;

5. Pour être enregistrés avec Marie son épouse, qui étoit enceinte.

6. Et pendant qu'ils étoient là, le tems auquel elle devoit accoucher arriva.

7. Et elle mit au monde son Fils premier-né, et elle l'emmaillotta, et le coucha dans une crèche, parce qu'il n'y avoit point de place pour eux dans l'hôtellerie.

21. Quand les huit jours furent accomplis pour circoncire l'enfant, il fut appelé JESUS,

39. Et après qu'ils eurent accompli tout ce qui est ordonné par la Loi du Seigneur, ils retournèrent en Galilée, à Nazareth, qui étoit leur ville.

40. Cependant l'enfant croissoit et se fortifioit en esprit, étant rempli de sagesse.

42. Et quand il eut atteint l'âge de douze ans, ils montèrent à Jérusalem, selon la coutume de la fête.

43. Lorsque les jours *de la fête* furent achevés, comme ils s'en retournoient, l'enfant Jésus demeura dans Jérusalem; et Joseph et sa mère ne s'en aperçurent point.

44. Mais pensant qu'il étoit en la compagnie de ceux qui faisoient le voyage avec eux, ils marchèrent une journée, et ils le cherchèrent parmi *leurs* parens et ceux de leur connoissance;

45. Et ne le trouvant point, ils retournèrent à Jérusalem, pour l'y chercher.

AND it came to pass in those days, that there went out a decree from Cesar Augustus, that all the world should be taxed.

2 (And this taxing was first made when Cyrenius was governor of Syria.)

3 And all went to be taxed, every one into his own city.

4 And Joseph also went up from Galilee, out of the city of Nazareth, into Judea, unto the city of David, which is called Beth-lehem (because he was of the house and lineage of David,)

5 To be taxed with Mary his espoused wife, being great with child.

6 And so it was, that, while they were there, the days were accomplished that she should be delivered

7 And she brought forth her firstborn son, and wrapped him in swaddling-clothes, and laid him in a manger; because there was no room for them in the inn.

21 And when eight days were accomplished for the circumcising of the child, his name was called JESUS,

39 And when they had performed all things, according to the law of the Lord, they returned into Galilee, to their own city Nazareth.

40 And the child grew, and waxed strong in spirit, filled with wisdom;

42 And when he was twelve years old, they went up to Jerusalem, after the custom of the feast.

43 And when they had fulfilled the days, as they returned, the child Jesus tarried behind in Jerusalem; and Joseph and his mother knew not *of it.*

44 But they supposing him to have been in the company, went a day's journey; and they sought him among *their* kinsfolk and acquaintance.

45 And when they found him not, they turned back again to Jerusalem, seeking him.

46 Καὶ ἐγένετο, μεθ' ἡμέρας τρεῖς εὗρον αὐτὸν ἐν τῷ ἱερῷ καθεζόμενον ἐν μέσῳ τῶν διδασκάλων, κỳ ἀκούοντα αὐτῶν, κỳ ἐπερωτῶντα αὐτάς.

* 47 ‡ Ἐξίςαντο δὲ πάντες οἱ ἀκούοντες αὐτῷ, ἐπὶ τῇ συνέσει κỳ ταῖς ‡ ἀποκρίσεσιν αὐτῷ.

48 Καὶ ἰδόντες αὐτὸν ἐξεπλάγησαν. Καὶ πρὸς αὐτὸν ἡ μήτηρ αὐτῷ εἶπε· Τέκνον, τί ἐποίησας ἡμῖν ὅτως; ἰδὲ ὁ πατήρ σε κἀγὼ ὀδυνώμενοι ἐζητᾶμέν σε.

52 Καὶ Ἰησᾶς προέκοπτε σοφία κỳ ἡλικία,

* 1 ᾿ΕΝ ἔτει δὲ † πεντεκαιδεκάτῳ τῆς † ἡγεμονίας Τιβερίε Καίσαρ@, ‡ ἡγεμονεύοντ@· Ποντίε Πιλάτε τῆς Ἰεδαίας, κỳ † τετραρχῶντ@· τῆς Γαλιλαίας Ἡρώδε, Φιλίππε δὲ τῷ ἀδελφῷ αὐτῷ τετραρχῶντ@· τῆς Ἰτεραίας κỳ Τραχωνίτιδ@· χώρας, κỳ Λυσανίε τῆς Ἀβιλήνης τετραρχῶντ@·,

2 Ἐπ' Ἀρχιερέων Ἄννα κỳ Καϊάφα,

4 Ἐγένετο Ἰωάννης βαπτίζων ἐν τῇ ἐρήμῳ,

4 Αὐτὸς δὲ ὁ Ἰωάννης εἶχε τὸ ἔνδυμα αὐτοῦ ἀπὸ τριχῶν καμήλου, κỳ ζώνην δερματίνην περὶ τὴν ὀσφὺν αὐτοῦ· ἡ δὲ τροφὴ αὐτοῦ ἦν ἀκρίδες κỳ μέλι ἄγριον.

5 Τότε ἐξεπορεύετο πρὸς αὐτὸν Ἱεροσόλυμα, κỳ πᾶσα ἡ Ἰουδαία, κỳ πᾶσα ἡ περίχωρ@· τοῦ Ἰορδάνου.

6 Καὶ ἐβαπτίζοντο ἐν τῷ Ἰορδάνῃ ὑπ' αὐτοῦ,

13 Τότε παραγίνεται ὁ Ἰησᾶς ἀπὸ τῆς Γαλιλαίας ἐπὶ τὸν Ἰορδάνην πρὸς τὸν Ἰωάννην, τοῦ βαπτισθῆναι ὑπ' αὐτὸ.

23 Καὶ αὐτὸς ἦν ὁ Ἰησᾶς ὡσεὶ ἐτῶν τριάκοντα ἀρχόμεν@·,

12 Μετὰ τᾶτο κατέβη εἰς Καπερναὰμ, αὐτὸς κỳ ἡ μήτηρ αὐτῷ, κỳ οἱ ἀδελφοὶ αὐτῷ κỳ οἱ μαθηταὶ αὐτῷ· κỳ ἐκεῖ ἔμειναν ἐ πολλὰς ἡμέρας.

---

46 Et factum est, post dies tres invenerunt illum in templo sedentem in medio doctorum, & audientem illos, & interrogantem eos.

47 Stupebant autem omnes audientes eum, super intelligentia & responsis ejus.

48 Et videntes ipsum, attoniti fuerunt: Et ad illum mater ejus dixit: Fili, quid fecisti nobis sic? ecce pater tuus & ego dolentes quærebamus te.

52 Et Jesus proficiebat sapientia, & ætate,

1 IN anno autem quinto decimo imperii Tiberii Cæsaris, præsidente Pontio Pilato Judææ, & tetrarcha Galilææ Herode, Philippo autem fratre ejus tetrarcha Iturææ, & Trachonitidis regionis, & Lysania Abilenæ tetrarcha,

2 Sub principibus Sacerdotum Anna & Caiapha,

4 Fuit Joannes baptizans in deserto.

4 Ipse autem Joannes habebat indumentum suum è pilis cameli, & zonam pelliceam circa lumbum suum: esca autem ejus erat locustæ & mel silvestre.

5 Tunc exibat ad eum Hierosolyma, & omnis Judæa, & omnis circum vicinia Jordanis.

6 Et baptizabantur in Jordane ab eo,

13 Tunc accedit Jesus à Galilæa ad Jordanem ad Joannem, baptizari ab eo.

23 Et ipse erat Jesus quasi annorum triginta incipiens

12 Post hoc descendit in Capernaum, ipse & mater ejus, & fratres ejus, & discipuli ejus, & ibi manserunt non multis diebus.

46. Et au bout de trois jours, ils le trouvèrent dans le Temple, assis au milieu des Docteurs, les écoutant et leur faisant des questions.

47. Et tous ceux qui l'entendoient étoient ravis de sa sagesse et de ses réponses.

48. Quand *Joseph et Marie* le virent, ils furent étonnés ; et sa mère lui dit : *Mon* enfant, pourquoi as-tu ainsi agi avec nous ? Voilà ton père et moi qui te cherchions étant fort en peine.

51. Il s'en alla ensuite avec eux, et vint à Nazareth, et il leur étoit soumis.

52. Et Jésus croissoit en sagesse, en stature, et en grace.

LA quinzième année de l'empire de Tibère César, Ponce Pilate étant Gouverneur de la Judée, Hérode étant Tétrarque de la Galilée, Philippe son frère, Tétrarque de l'Iturée et de la province de la Trachonite, et Lysanias, Tétrarque d'Abilène ;

2. Anne et Caïphe étant Souverains Sacrificateurs,

4. Jean baptisoit dans le désert,

4. Ce Jean avoit un habit de poils de chameau, et une ceinture de cuir autour de ses reins, et sa nourriture étoit des sauterelles et du miel sauvage.

5. Alors ceux de Jérusalem, et de tout le pays des environs du Jourdain, venoient à lui.

6. Et ils étoient baptisés par lui dans le Jourdain,

13. Alors Jésus vint de Galilée au Jourdain vers Jean, pour être baptisé par lui.

23. Et Jésus étoit *alors* âgé d'environ trente ans,

12. Après cela, il descendit à Capernaüm, avec sa Mère, ses Frères, et ses Disciples ; et ils n'y demeurèrent que peu de jours ;

---

46 And it came to pass, that after three days they found him in the temple, sitting in the midst of the doctors, both hearing them, and asking them questions. **L. 2.**

47 And all that heard him were astonished at his understanding and answers.

48 And when they saw him, they were amazed: and his mother said unto him, Son, why hast thou thus dealt with us? behold, thy father and I have sought thee sorrowing.

51 And he went down with them, and came to Nazareth, and was subject unto them:

52 And Jesus increased in wisdom and stature.

NOW in the fifteenth year of the reign of Tiberius Cesar, Pontius Pilate being governor of Judea, and Herod being tetrarch of Galilee, and his brother Philip tetrarch of Iturea and of the region of Trachonitis, and Lysanias the tetrarch of Abilene; **L 3**

2 Annas and Caiaphas being the high priests,

4 John did baptize in the wilderness, **Mk. 1.**

4 And the same John had his raiment of camels' hair, and a leathern girdle about his loins; and his meat was locusts and wild honey. **M. 3**

5 Then went out to him Jerusalem, and all Judea, and all the region round about Jordan.

6 And were baptized of him in Jordan,

13 Then cometh Jesus from Galilee to Jordan unto John, to be baptized of him. **M. 3.**

23 And Jesus himself began to be about thirty years of age, **L. 3.**

12 After this he went down to Capernaum, he, and his mother, and his brethren, and his disciples; and they continued there not many days. **J. 2.**

3

13 Καὶ ἐγγὺς ἦν τὸ πάσχα τῶν Ἰεδαίων, κỳ ἀνέβη εἰς Ἱεροσόλυμα ὁ Ἰησῦς.

* 14 Καὶ εὗρεν ἐν τῷ ἱερῷ τὰς πωλῦντας ‡ βόας κỳ πρόβατα κỳ περιστεράς, κỳ τὰς † κερματιςὰς καθημένες.

* 15 Καὶ ποιήσας † φραγέλλιον ἐκ ‡ σχοινίων, πάντας ἐξέβαλεν ἐκ τῦ ἱερῦ, τά τε πρόβατα κỳ τὰς βόας κỳ τῶν κολλυβιςῶν ἐξέχεε τὸ † κέρμα, κỳ τὰς τραπέζας ἀνέςρεψε·

* 16 Καὶ τοῖς τὰς περιςερὰς πωλῦσιν εἶπιν· Ἄρατε ταῦτα ἐντεῦθεν· μὴ ποιεῖτε τὸν οἶκον τῦ πατρός με οἶκον † ἐμπορείω.

22 Μετὰ ταῦτα ἦλθεν ὁ Ἰησῦς, κỳ οἱ μαθηταὶ αὐτῦ εἰς τὴν Ἰεδαίαν γῆν κỳ ἐκεῖ διέτριβε μετ' αὐτῶν κỳ ἐβάπτιζεν.

12 Ἀκούσας δὲ ὁ Ἰησῦς ὅτι Ἰωάννης παρεδόθη, ἀνεχώρησεν εἰς τὴν Γαλιλαίαν.

17 Αὐτὸς γὰρ ὁ Ἡρώδης, ἀποςείλας ἐκράτησε τὸν Ἰωάννην, κỳ ἔδησεν αὐτὸν ἐν τῇ φυλακῇ, διὰ Ἡρωδιάδα τὴν γυναῖκα Φιλίππε τῦ ἀδελφῦ αὐτῦ, ὅτι αὐτὴν ἐγάμησεν.

18 Ἔλεγε γὰρ ὁ Ἰωάννης τῷ Ἡρώδῃ· Ὅτι ἐκ ἔξεςί σοι ἔχειν τὴν γυναῖκα τῦ ἀδελφῦ σε.

19 Ἡ δὲ Ἡρωδιὰς ἐνεῖχεν αὐτῷ, κỳ ἤθελεν αὐτὸν ἀποκτεῖναι· κỳ ἐκ ἠδύνατο·

20 Ὁ γὰρ Ἡρώδης ἐφοβεῖτο τὸν Ἰωάννην, εἰδὼς αὐτὸν ἄνδρα δίκαιον κỳ ἅγιον, κỳ συνετήρει αὐτόν· κỳ ἀκούσας αὐτῦ, πολλὰ ἐποίει, κỳ ἡδέως αὐτῦ ἤκυε.

21 Καὶ γενομένης ἡμέρας εὐκαίρε, ὅτε Ἡρώδης τοῖς γενεσίοις αὐτῦ δεῖπνον ἐποίει τοῖς μεγιςᾶσιν αὐτῦ, κỳ τοῖς χιλιάρχοις, κỳ τοῖς πρώτοις τῆς Γαλιλαίας,

22 Καὶ εἰσελθούσης τῆς θυγατρὸς αὐτῆς τῆς Ἡρωδιάδος, κỳ ὀρχησαμένης, κỳ ἀρεσάσης τῷ Ἡρώδῃ κỳ τοῖς συνανακειμένοις, εἶπεν ὁ βασιλεὺς τῷ κορασίω· Αἴτησόν με ὃ ἐὰν θέλης, κỳ δώσω σοι.

23 Καὶ ὤμοσεν αὐτῇ· Ὅτι ὃ ἐάν με αἰτήσης, δώσω σοι, ἕως ἡμίσας τῆς βασιλείας μυ.

---

13 Et prope erat Pascha Judæorum, & ascendit Hierosolymam Jesus.

13 Et invenit in templo vendentes boves, & oves, & columbas, & numularios sedentes.

15 Et faciens flagellum ex funiculis omnes ejecit ex templo, & oves & boves: & numulariorum effudit monetam, & mensas subvertit.

16 Et columbas vendentibus dixit: Auferte ista hinc: ne facite domum patris mei domum mercatûs.

22 Post hæc venit Jesus & discipuli ejus in Judæam terram: & illic morabatur cum eis, & baptizabat.

12 Audiens autem Jesus quod Joannes traditus esset, secessit in Galilæam:

17 Ipse enim Herodes mittens prehendit Joannem, & vinxit eum in custodia, propter Herodiadem uxorem Philippi fratris sui, quia eam duxerat.

18 Dicebat enim Joannes Herodi: Quod non licet tibi habere uxorem fratris tui.

19 At Herodias insidiabatur illi: & volebat eum occidere, & non poterat.

20 Nam Herodes metuebat Joannem, sciens eum virum justum & sanctum: & conservabat eum, & audiens eum, multa faciebat, & suaviter eum audiebat.

21 Et facta die opportuna, quum Herodes natalitiis suis cœnam faciebat principibus suis, & tribunis, & primis Galilææ:

22 Et ingressa filia ipsius Herodiadis, & saltante, & placente Herodi & unà recumbentibus ait rex puellæ: Pete a me quicquid velis, & dabo tibi.

23 Et juravit illi: Quia quicquid petieris, dabo tibi, usque dimidium regni mei.

13. Car la Pâque des Juifs étoit proche ; et Jésus monta à Jérusalem.

14. Il trouva dans le Temple des gens qui vendoient des taureaux, des brebis et des pigeons, avec des changeurs qui y étoient assis.

15. Et ayant fait un fouet de petites cordes, il les chassa tous du Temple, et les brebis et les taureaux ; il répandit la monnoie dès changeurs, et renversa leurs tables ;

16. Et il dit à ceux qui vendoient les pigeons : Otez tout cela d'ici, et ne faites pas de la Maison de mon Père, une maison de marché.

22. Après cela, Jésus s'en alla en Judée avec ses Disciples, et il y demeura avec eux, et y baptisoit.

12. Or, Jésus ayant appris que Jean avoit été mis en prison, se retira dans la Galilée.

17. Car Hérode avoit envoyé prendre Jean, et l'avoit fait lier dans la prison, à cause d'Hérodias, femme de Philippe son frère, parce qu'il l'avoit épousée.

18. Car Jean disoit à Hérode : Il ne t'est pas permis d'avoir la femme de ton frère.

19. C'est pourquoi Hérodias lui en vouloit, et elle désiroit de le faire mourir ; mais elle ne pouvoit,

20. Parce qu'Hérode craignoit Jean, sachant que c'étoit un homme juste et saint ; il le consideroit, il faisoit même beaucoup de choses selon ses avis, et il l'écoutoit avec plaisir.

21. Mais un jour vint à propos, auquel Hérode faisoit le festin du jour de sa naissance, aux Grands de sa cour, aux officiers de ses troupes, et aux principaux de la Galilée.

22. La fille d'Hérodias étant entrée, et ayant dansé, et ayant plu à Hérode et à ceux qui étoient à table avec lui, le Roi dit à la jeune fille : Demande-moi ce que tu voudras, et je te le donnerai.

23. Et il le lui jura, disant : Tout ce que tu me demanderas, je te le donnerai, jusqu'à la moitié de mon Royaume.

J.2.
13 And the Jews' passover was at hand; and Jesus went up to Jerusalem,

14 And found in the temple those that sold oxen, and sheep, and doves, and the changers of money, sitting:

15 And, when he had made a scourge of small cords, he drove them all out of the temple, and the sheep, and the oxen; and poured out the changers' money, and overthrew the tables;

16 And said unto them that sold doves, Take these things hence; make not my Father's house an house of merchandise.

J.3.
22 After these things came Jesus and his disciples into the land of Judea; and there he tarried with them, and baptized.

M. A.
12 Now, when Jesus had heard that John was cast into prison, he departed into Galilee:

M. 6.
17 For Herod himself had sent forth, and laid hold upon John, and bound him in prison for Herodias' sake, his brother Philip's wife; for he had married her.

18 For John had said unto Herod, It is not lawful for thee to have thy brother's wife.

19 Therefore Herodias had a quarrel against him, and would have killed him; but she could not:

20 For Herod feared John, knowing that he was a just man, and an holy, and observed him; and when he heard him, he did many things, and heard him gladly.

21 And when a convenient day was come, that Herod, on his birthday, made a supper to his lords, high captains, and chief estates of Galilee;

22 And when the daughter of the said Herodias came in and danced, and pleased Herod, and them that sat with him, the king said unto the damsel, Ask of me whatsoever thou wilt, and I will give it thee.

23 And he sware unto her, Whatsoever thou shalt ask of me, I will give it thee, unto the half of my kingdom.

4

24 Ἡ δὲ ἐξελθῦσα, εἶπε τῇ μηῆρὶ αὐτῆς· Τί αἰτήσομαι; Ἡ δὲ εἶπε· Τὴν κεφαλὴν Ἰωάννε τῦ βαπλιςῦ.

25 Καὶ εἰσελθῦσα εὐθέως μετὰ σπυδῆς πρὸς τὸν βασιλέα, ᾐτήσαλο, λέγυσα. Θέλω ἵνα μοι δῷς ἐξ αὐτῆς ἐπὶ πίνακι τὴν κεφαλὴν Ἰωάννε τῦ Βαπλιςῦ.

26 Καὶ περίλυπ☉ γενόμεν☉ ὁ βασιλεὺς, διὰ τοὺς ὅρκες κ᾽ τοὺς συνανακειμένες οὐκ ἠθέλησεν αὐτὴν ἀθετῆσαι.

* 27 Καὶ εὐθέως ‡ ἀποςείλας ὁ ‡ βασιλεὺς ‡ σπεκυλάτωρα, ‡ ἐπέταξεν ‡ ἐνεχθῆναι τὴν κεφαλὴν αὐτοῦ.

* 28 Ὁ δὲ ἀπελθὼν ‡ ἀπεκεφάλισεν αὐτὸν ἐν τῇ φυλακῇ· κ᾽ ἤνεγκε τὴν κεφαλὴν αὐτοῦ ἐπὶ πίνακι, κ᾽ ἔδωκεν αὐτὴν τῷ κορασίῳ· κ᾽ τὸ κοράσιον ἔδωκεν αὐτὴν τῇ μηῆρὶ αὐτῆς.

24 Illa verò egreſſa, dixit matri ſuæ : Quid petam? Illa verò ait : Caput Joannis Baptiſtæ.

25 Et ingreſſa ſtatim cum ſtudio ad regem, petivit, dicens : Volo ut mihi des ex ipſa in diſco caput Joannis Baptiſtæ.

26 Et contriſtatus factus rex, propter juramenta, & ſimul diſcumbentes, non voluit eam rejicere.

27 Et ſtatim mittens rex ſpeculatorem, injunxit afferri caput ejus. Ille autem abiens decollavit eum in carcere :

28 Et attulit caput ejus in diſco, & dedit illud puellæ, & puella dedit illud matri ſuæ.

29 Et

21 Καὶ εἰσπορεύονlαι εἰς Καπερναύμ· κ᾽ εὐθέως τοῖς σάββασιν εἰσελθὼν εἰς τὴν συναγωγὴν, ἐδίδασκε.

22 Καὶ ἐξεπλήσσονlο ἐπὶ τῇ διδαχῇ αὐτῦ· ἦν γὰρ διδάσκων αὐτὺς ὡς ἐξυσίαν ἔχων, κ᾽ ἐχ ὡς οἱ γραμμαλεῖς.

21 Et ingrediuntur in Capernaum : & ſtatim Sabbatis ingreſſus in ſynagogam, docebat.

22 Et percellebantur ſuper doctrina ejus : Erat enim docens eos quaſi auctoritatem habens, & non ſicut Scribæ.

Κεφ. ιβ'. 12.

1 ἘΝ ἐκείνῳ τῷ καιρῷ ἐπορεύθη ὁ Ἰησῦς τοῖς Σάββασι διὰ τῶν σπορίμων· οἱ δὲ μαθηlαὶ αὐτῦ ἐπείνασαν, κ᾽ ἤρξανlο τίλλειν ςάχυας, κ᾽ ἐσθίειν.

2 Οἱ δὲ Φαρισαῖοι ἰδόνlες, εἶπον αὐτῷ· Ἰδὺ, οἱ μαθηlαί σε ποιῦσιν ὃ ἐκ ἔξεςι ποιεῖν ἐν σαββάτῳ.

3 Ὁ δὲ εἶπεν αὐτοῖς· Οὐκ ἀνέγνωlε τί ἐποίησε Δαβὶδ, ὅτε ἐπείνασεν αὐτὸς, κ᾽ οἱ μετ᾽ αὐτῦ;

4 Πῶς εἰσῆλθεν εἰς τὸν οἶκον τῦ Θεῦ, κ᾽ τὺς ἄρτυς τῆς προθέσεως ἔφαγεν, ὃς ἐκ ἐξὸν ἦν αὐτῷ φαγεῖν, ἐδὲ τοῖς μεῖ᾽ αὐτῦ, εἰ μὴ τοῖς ἱερεῦσι μόνοις;

5 Ἢ ἐκ ἀνέγνωlε ἐν τῷ νόμῳ, ὅτι τοῖς Σάββασιν οἱ ἱερεῖς ἐν τῷ ἱερῷ τὸ Σάββατον βεβηλῦσι, κ᾽ ἀναίτιοί εἰσι;

CAPUT XII.

1 IN illo tempore abiit Jeſus Sabbatis per ſata : at diſcipuli ejus eſurierunt, & cœperunt vellere ſpicas, & manducare.

2 Verum Phariſæi videntes, dixerunt ei : Ecce diſcipuli tui faciunt quod non licet facere in Sabbato.

3 Ille verò dixit eis : Non legiſtis quid fecerit David, quando eſuriit ipſe & qui cum eo?

4 Quomodo intravit in domum Dei, & panes propoſitionis comedit, quos non licitum erat ei edere, neque his qui cum eo, niſi Sacerdotibus ſolis?

5 Aut non legiſtis in lege, quia Sabbatis Sacerdotes in ſacro Sabbatum violant, & inculpati ſunt?

24 And she went forth, and said unto her mother, What shall I ask? and she said, The head of John the Baptist.

25 And she came in straightway with haste unto the king, and asked, saying, I will that thou give me, by and by in a charger, the head of John the Baptist.

26 And the king was exceeding sorry; yet for his oath's sake, and for their sakes which sat with him, he would not reject her.

27 And immediately the king sent an executioner, and commanded his head to be brought: and he went and beheaded him in the prison;

28 And brought his head in a charger, and gave it to the damsel: and the damsel gave it to her mother.

21 And they went into Capernaum; and straightway on the sabbath-day, he entered into the synagogue, and taught.

22 And they were astonished at his doctrine: for he taught them as one that had authority, and not as the scribes.

AT that time Jesus went on the sabbath-day through the corn; and his disciples were an hungered, and began to pluck the ears of corn, and to eat.

2 But when the Pharisees saw it, they said unto him, Behold, thy disciples do that which is not lawful to do upon the sabbath-day.

3 But he said unto them, Have ye not read what David did when he was an hungered, and they that were with him;

4 How he entered into the house of God, and did eat the shew-bread, which was not lawful for him to eat, neither for them which were with him, but only for the priests?

5 Or, have ye not read in the law, how that on the sabbath-days, the priests in the temple profane the sabbath, and are blameless?

---

24. Et étant sortie, elle dit à sa mère : Que demanderai-je ? Et sa mère lui dit : Demande la tête de Jean-Baptiste.

25. Et étant incontinent rentrée avec empressement vers le Roi, elle lui fit sa demande, et lui dit : Je voudrois que tout à l'heure tu me donnasses dans un bassin la tête de Jean-Baptiste.

26. Et le Roi en fut triste ; cependant, à cause du serment, et de ceux qui étoient à table avec lui, il ne voulut pas la refuser.

27. Et il envoya incontinent un de ses gardes, et lui commanda d'apporter la tête de Jean.

28. Le garde y alla, et lui coupa la tête dans la prison ; et l'ayant apportée dans un bassin, il la donna à la jeune fille, et la jeune fille la présenta à sa mère.

21. Ensuite ils entrèrent à Capernaüm ; et Jésus étant d'abord entré dans la Synagogue le jour du Sabbat, il y enseignoit,

22. Et ils étoient étonnés de sa doctrine, car il les enseignoit comme ayant autorité, et non pas comme les Scribes.

EN ce tems-là, Jésus passoit par des blés un jour de Sabbat ; et ses Disciples ayant faim, se mirent à arracher des épis, et à en manger.

2. Les Pharisiens voyant cela, lui dirent : Voilà tes Disciples qui font ce qu'il n'est pas permis de faire le jour du Sabbat.

3. Mais il leur dit : N'avez-vous pas lu ce que fit David ayant faim, tant lui que ceux qui étoient avec lui :

4. Comment il entra dans la maison de Dieu, et mangea les pains de proposition, dont il n'étoit pas permis de manger, ni à lui, ni à ceux qui étoient avec lui, mais aux seuls Sacrificateurs ?

5. Ou n'avez-vous pas lu dans la Loi, que les Sacrificateurs, au jour du Sabbat, violent le Sabbat dans le Temple, sans être coupables ?

9 Καὶ μεταβὰς ἐκεῖθεν, ἦλθεν εἰς τὴν συναγωγὴν αὐτῶν.

10 Καὶ ἰδοὺ, ἄνθρωπος ἦν τὴν χεῖρα ἔχων ξηράν· καὶ ἐπηρώτησαν αὐτὸν, λέγοντες· Εἰ ἔξεστι τοῖς σάββασι θεραπεύειν; ἵνα κατηγορήσωσιν αὐτῷ.

11 Ὁ δὲ εἶπεν αὐτοῖς· Τίς ἔσται ἐξ ὑμῶν ἄνθρωπος, ὃς ἕξει πρόβατον ἕν, καὶ ἐὰν ἐμπέσῃ τοῦτο τοῖς σάββασιν εἰς βόθυνον, οὐχὶ κρατήσει αὐτὸ καὶ ἐγερεῖ;

12 Πόσῳ οὖν διαφέρει ἄνθρωπος προβάτου; ὥστε ἔξεστι τοῖς σάββασι καλῶς ποιεῖν.

27 Καὶ ἔλεγεν αὐτοῖς· Τὸ σάββατον διὰ τὸν ἄνθρωπον ἐγένετο, οὐχ ὁ ἄνθρωπος διὰ τὸ σάββατον.

14 Οἱ δὲ Φαρισαῖοι συμβούλιον ἔλαβον κατ' αὐτοῦ ἐξελθόντες, ὅπως αὐτὸν ἀπολέσωσιν.

15 Ὁ δὲ Ἰησοῦς γνοὺς ἀνεχώρησεν ἐκεῖθεν· καὶ ἠκολούθησαν αὐτῷ ὄχλοι πολλοί, καὶ ἐθεράπευσεν αὐτοὺς πάντας.

* 12 Ἐγένετο δὲ ἐν ταῖς ἡμέραις ταύταις, ἐξῆλθεν εἰς τὸ ὄρος προσεύξασθαι· καὶ ἦν † διανυκτερεύων ἐν τῇ προσευχῇ τοῦ Θεοῦ.

13 Καὶ ὅτε ἐγένετο ἡμέρα, προσεφώνησε τοὺς μαθητὰς αὐτοῦ· καὶ ἐκλεξάμενος ἀπ' αὐτῶν δώδεκα, οὓς καὶ ἀποστόλους ὠνόμασε·

14 (Σίμωνα, ὃν καὶ ὠνόμασε Πέτρον, καὶ Ἀνδρέαν τὸν ἀδελφὸν αὐτοῦ, Ἰάκωβον καὶ Ἰωάννην, Φίλιππον καὶ Βαρθολομαῖον·

15 Ματθαῖον καὶ Θωμᾶν, Ἰάκωβον τὸν τοῦ Ἀλφαίου, καὶ Σίμωνα τὸν καλούμενον Ζηλωτήν·

16 Ἰούδαν Ἰακώβου, καὶ Ἰούδαν Ἰσκαριώτην, ὃς καὶ ἐγένετο προδότης·)

* 17 Καὶ καταβὰς μετ' αὐτῶν, ἔστη ἐπὶ † τόπου † πεδινοῦ, καὶ ὄχλος μαθητῶν αὐτοῦ, καὶ πλῆθος πολὺ τοῦ λαοῦ ἀπὸ πάσης τῆς Ἰουδαίας καὶ Ἱερουσαλήμ, καὶ τῆς παραλίου Τύρου καὶ Σιδῶνος, οἳ ἦλθον ἀκοῦσαι αὐτοῦ, καὶ ἰαθῆναι ἀπὸ τῶν νόσων αὐτῶν·

---

9 Et transiens inde, venit in synagogam eorum.

10 Et ecce homo erat manum habens aridam, & interrogabant eum, dicentes, Si licet Sabbatis curare? ut accusarent eum.

11 Ipse autem dixit illis, Quis erit ex vobis homo qui habebit ovem unam, & si ceciderit hæc Sabbatis in foveam, nonne apprehendet eam & exiget?

12 Quanto igitur præstat homo ove? Itaque licet Sabbatis bona facere.

27 Et dicebat eis: Sabbatum propter hominem factum est, non homo propter Sabbatum.

14 At Pharisæi consilium ceperunt adversus eum, exeuntes, ut eum perderent.

15 At Jesus cognoscens, recessit inde: & sequutæ sunt eum turbæ multæ, & curavit eos omnes:

12 Factum est autem in diebus illis, exiit in montem orare: & erat pernoctans in oratione Dei.

13 Et quum factus esset dies, advocavit discipulos suos: & eligens ex ipsis duodecim, quos & Apostolos nominavit.

14 Simonem, quem & nominavit Petrum, & Andream fratrem ejus, Jacobum & Joannem, Philippum & Bartholomæum!

15 Matthæum & Thomam, Jacobum Alphæi, & Simonem vocatum Zeloten.

16 Judam Jacobi, & Judam Iscariotem, qui & fuit traditor.

17 Et descendens cum illis, stetit in loco campestri, & turba discipulorum ejus, & multitudo copiosa plebis ab omni Judæa, & Hierusalem, & maritima Tyri & Sidonis, qui venerunt audire eum, & sanari à languoribus suis:

9 And when he was departed thence, he went into their synagogue:

10 And, behold, there was a man which had *his* hand withered. And they asked him, saying, Is it lawful to heal on the sabbath-days? that they might accuse him.

11 And he said unto them, What man shall there be among you, that shall have one sheep, and if it fall into a pit on the sabbath-day, will he not lay hold on it, and lift *it* out?

12 How much then is a man better than a sheep? Wherefore it is lawful to do well on the sabbath-days.

Mk. 2.

27 And he said unto them, The sabbath was made for man, and not man for the sabbath:

M. 12.

14 Then the Pharisees went out, and held a council against him, how they might destroy him.

15 But when Jesus knew *it*, he withdrew himself from thence: and great multitudes followed him,

L. 6.

12 And it came to pass in those days, that he went up into a mountain to pray, and continued all night in prayer to God.

13 And when it was day, he called *unto him* his disciples; and of them he chose twelve, whom also he named Apostles;

14 Simon, (whom he also named Peter,) and Andrew his brother, James and John, Philip and Bartholomew,

15 Matthew and Thomas, James *the son* of Alpheus, and Simon called Zelotes,

16 And Judas *the brother* of James, and Judas Iscariot, which also was the traitor.

17 And he came down with them, and stood in the plain; and the company of his disciples, and a great multitude of people out of all Judea and Jerusalem, and from the sea-coast of Tyre and Sidon, which came to hear him,

---

9. Étant parti de-là, il vint dans leur synagogue.

10. Et il y trouva un homme qui avoit une main sèche; et ils lui demandèrent, pour avoir lieu de l'accuser : Est-il permis de guérir dans les jours de Sabbat?

11. Et il leur dit, Qui sera celui d'entre vous, qui ayant une brebis, si elle tombe au jour du Sabbat dans une fosse, ne la prenne et ne l'en retire?

12. Et combien un homme ne vaut-il pas mieux qu'une brebis? Il est donc permis de faire du bien dans les jours de Sabbat.

27. Puis il leur dit : Le Sabbat a été fait pour l'homme, et non pas l'homme pour le Sabbat.

14. Là-dessus les Pharisiens étant sortis, délibérèrent entr'eux comment ils le feroient périr.

15. Mais Jésus connoissant *cela*, partit de-là, et une grande multitude le suivit.

12. En ce tems-là, *Jésus* alla sur une montagne pour prier; et il passa toute la nuit à prier Dieu.

13. Et dès que le jour fut venu il appela ses Disciples, et il en choisit douze d'entr'eux qu'il nomma Apôtres.

14. *Savoir*, Simon, qu'il nomma aussi Pierre, et André son frère, Jacques et Jean, Philippe et Barthelemi;

15. Matthieu et Thomas, Jacques *fils* d'Alphée, et Simon appelé le Zélé;

16. Jude, *frère* de Jacques et Judas Iscariot, qui fut celui qui le trahit.

17. Etant ensuite descendu avec eux, il s'arrêta dans une plaine, avec la troupe de ses Disciples, et une grande multitude de peuple de toute la Judée et de Jérusalem, et de la *contrée* maritime de Tyr et de Sidon, qui étoient venus pour l'entendre.

ΚΕΦ. ε΄ 5. — CAPUT V.

1 Ἰδὼν δὲ τοὺς ὄχλους, ἀνέβη εἰς τὸ ὄρος, ᾗ καθίσαντος αὐτοῦ προσῆλθον αὐτῷ οἱ μαθηταὶ αὐτοῦ.

2 Καὶ ἀνοίξας τὸ ςόμα αὐτοῦ, ἐδίδασκεν αὐτοὺς, λέγων·

3 Μακάριοι οἱ πτωχοὶ τῷ πνεύματι· ὅτι αὐτῶν ἐςὶν ἡ βασιλεία τῶν οὐρανῶν.

4 Μακάριοι οἱ πειθοῦντες· ὅτι αὐτοὶ παρακληθήσονται.

5 Μακάριοι οἱ πραεῖς· ὅτι αὐτοὶ κληρονομήσουσι τὴν γῆν.

6 Μακάριοι οἱ πεινῶντες ᾗ διψῶντες τὴν δικαιοσύνην· ὅτι αὐτοὶ χορτασθήσονται.

7 Μακάριοι οἱ ἐλεήμονες· ὅτι αὐτοὶ ἐλεηθήσονται.

8 Μακάριοι οἱ καθαροὶ τῇ καρδίᾳ· ὅτι αὐτοὶ τὸν Θεὸν ὄψονται.

* 9 ‡ Μακάριοι οἱ † εἰρηνοποιοί· ὅτι αὐτοὶ υἱοὶ Θεοῦ κληθήσονται.

10 Μακάριοι οἱ δεδιωγμένοι ἕνεκεν δικαιοσύνης· ὅτι αὐτῶν ἐςιν ἡ βασιλεία τῶν οὐρανῶν.

11 Μακάριοί ἐςε ὅταν ὀνειδίσωσιν ὑμᾶς ᾗ διώξωσι, ᾗ εἴπωσι πᾶν πονηρὸν ῥῆμα καθ᾽ ὑμῶν, ψευδόμενοι, ἕνεκεν ἐμοῦ.

12 Χαίρετε ᾗ ἀγαλλιᾶσθε· ὅτι ὁ μισθὸς ὑμῶν πολὺς ἐν τοῖς οὐρανοῖς· οὕτω γὰρ ἐδίωξαν τοὺς προφήτας τοὺς πρὸ ὑμῶν.

1 Videns autem turbas, ascendit in montem : & sedente eo, advenerunt illi discipuli ejus.

2 Et aperiens os suum, docebat eos, dicens :

3 Beati pauperes spiritu, quoniam ipsorum est regnum cælorum.

4 Beati lugentes, quia ipsi consolabuntur.

5 Beati mites, quoniam ipsi hæreditabunt terram.

6 Beati esurientes & sitientes justitiam, quoniam ipsi saturabuntur.

7 Beati misericordes, quoniam ipsi misericordiâ afficientur.

8 Beati mundi corde, quoniam ipsi Deum videbunt.

9 Beati pacifici, quoniam ipsi filii Dei vocabuntur.

10 Beati persecutione affecti propter justitiam, quoniam ipsorum est regnum cælorum.

11 Beati estis quum maledixerint vos, & persecuti fuerint, & dixerint omne malum verbum adversum vos, mentientes, propter me.

12 Gaudete & exultate, quoniam merces vestra multa in cælis, sic enim persequuti sunt Prophetas qui ante vos.

---

24 Πλὴν οὐαὶ ὑμῖν τοῖς πλουσίοις· ὅτι ἀπέχετε τὴν παράκλησιν ὑμῶν.

* 25 ‡ Οὐαὶ ὑμῖν οἱ ‡ ἐμπεπλησμένοι· ὅτι πεινάσετε. Οὐαὶ ὑμῖν οἱ ‡ γελῶντες ᾗ νῦν· ὅτι ‡ πενθήσετε ᾗ κλαύσετε.

26 Οὐαὶ ὑμῖν ὅταν καλῶς ὑμᾶς εἴπωσι πάντες οἱ ἄνθρωποι· κατὰ ταῦτα γὰρ ἐποίουν τοῖς ψευδοπροφήταις οἱ πατέρες αὐτῶν.

24 Veruntamen væ vobis divitibus, quia habetis consolationem vestram.

25 Væ vobis impleti : quia esurietis. Væ vobis ridentes nunc : quia lugebitis & flebitis.

26 Væ quum benedixerint vobis homines : secundum hæc enim faciebant pseudoprophetis patres eorum.

---

13 Ὑμεῖς ἐςε τὸ ἅλας τῆς γῆς· ἐὰν δὲ τὸ ἅλας μωρανθῇ, ἐν τίνι ἁλισθήσεται· εἰς οὐδὲν ἰσχύει ἔτι, εἰ μὴ βληθῆναι ἔξω, ᾗ καταπατεῖσθαι ὑπὸ τῶν ἀνθρώπων.

14 Ὑμεῖς ἐςε τὸ φῶς τοῦ κόσμου, Οὐ δύναται πόλις κρυβῆναι ἐπάνω ὄρους κειμένη.

13 Vos estis sal terræ ; si autem sal infatuatum sit, in quo sal etur ? ad nihilum valet ultra, si non ejici foras, & conculcari, ab hominibus.

14 Vos estis lux mundi : non potest civitas abscondi supra montem posita.

CHAPITRE V.

Sermon sur la Montagne.

Jésus voyant tout ce peuple, monta sur une montagne ; et s'étant assis, ses Disciples s'approchérent de lui.

2. Et ouvrant sa bouche, il les enseignoit, en disant :

3. Heureux les pauvres en esprit; car le Royaume des cieux est à eux.

4. Heureux ceux qui pleurent ; car ils seront consolés.

5. Heureux les débonnaires ; car ils hériteront la terre.

6. Heureux ceux qui sont affamés et altérés de la justice ; car ils seront rassasiés.

7. Heureux les miséricordieux ; car ils obtiendront miséricorde.

8. Heureux ceux qui ont le cœur pur ; car ils verront Dieu.

9. Heureux ceux qui procurent la paix ; car ils seront appelés enfans de Dieu.

10. Heureux ceux qui sont persécutés pour la justice ; car le Royaume des cieux est à eux.

11. Vous serez heureux, lorsqu'à cause de moi on vous dira des injures, qu'on vous persécutera , et qu'on dira faussement contre vous toute sorte de mal.

12. Réjouissez-vous alors , et tressaillez de joie, parce que votre récompense sera grande dans les cieux ; car on a ainsi persécuté les Prophètes qui ont été avant vous.

24. Mais malheur à vous, riches; parce que vous avez déjà reçu votre consolation.

25. Malheur à vous , qui êtes rassasiés ; parce que vous aurez faim. Malheur à vous , qui riez maintenant ; car vous vous lamenterez et vous pleurerez !

26. Malheur à vous , lorsque tous les hommes diront du bien de vous ; car leurs pères en faisoient de même des faux Prophètes.

13. Vous êtes le sel de la terre ; mais si le sel perd sa saveur, avec quoi le salera-t-on ? Il ne vaut plus rien qu'à être jeté dehors, et à être foulé aux pieds par les hommes.

14. Vous êtes la lumière du monde : Une ville située sur une montagne ne peut être cachée.

AND seeing the multitudes, he went up into a mountain: and when he was set, his disciples came unto him:

2 And he opened his mouth, and taught them, saying,

3 Blessed *are* the poor in spirit : for their's is the kingdom of heaven.

4 Blessed *are* they that mourn : for they shall be comforted.

5 Blessed *are* the meek : for they shall inherit the earth.

6 Blessed *are* they which do hunger and thirst after righteousness : for they shall be filled.

7 Blessed *are* the merciful : for they shall obtain mercy.

8 Blessed *are* the pure in heart : for they shall see God.

9 Blessed *are* the peace-makers : for they shall be called the children of God.

10 Blessed *are* they which are persecuted for righteousness' sake : for their's is the kingdom of heaven.

11 Blessed *are* ye when *men* shall revile you, and persecute *you*, and shall say all manner of evil against you falsely, for my sake.

12 Rejoice, and be exceeding glad ; for great *is* your reward in heaven: for so persecuted they the prophets which were before you.

24 But woe unto you that are rich ! for ye have received your consolation.

25 Woe unto you that are full ! for ye shall hunger. Woe unto you that laugh now ! for ye shall mourn and weep.

26 Woe unto you when all men shall speak well of you ! for so did their fathers to the false prophets.

13 Ye are the salt of the earth : but if the salt have lost his savour, wherewith shall it be salted : it is thenceforth good for nothing, but to be cast out, and to be trodden under foot of men.

14 Ye are the light of the world. A city that is set on an hill cannot be hid.

15 Οὐδὲ καίουσι λύχνον, κỳ τι
θέασιν αὐτὸν ὑπὸ τὸν μόδιον, ἀλλ᾽
ἐπὶ τὴν λυχνίαν, κỳ λάμπει πᾶσι
τοῖς ἐν τῇ οἰκίᾳ.

16 Οὕτω λαμψάτω τὸ φῶς ὑ-
μῶν ἔμπροσθεν τῶν ἀνθρώπων, ὅπως
ἴδωσιν ὑμῶν τὰ καλὰ ἔργα, κỳ δο-
ξάσωσι τὸν πατέρα ὑμῶν τὸν ἐν
τοῖς οὐρανοῖς.

17 Μὴ νομίσητε ὅτι ἦλθον καταλῦσαι τὸν νόμον, ἢ τὰς προφήτας· οὐκ
ἦλθον καταλῦσαι, ἀλλὰ πληρῶσαι.

· 18 ‡ Ἀμὴν γὰρ λέγω ὑμῖν, ἕως
ἂν παρέλθῃ ὁ οὐρανὸς κỳ ἡ γῆ, † ἰῶτα
‡ ἓν ‡ ἢ μία ‡ κεραία οὐ μὴ
‡ παρέλθῃ ἀπὸ τοῦ ‡ νόμου, ἕως
ἂν πάντα γένηται.

19 Ὃς ἐὰν οὖν λύσῃ μίαν τῶν
ἐντολῶν τούτων τῶν ἐλαχίςων, κỳ
διδάξῃ οὕτω τοὺς ἀνθρώπους, ἐλά-
χις⊙ κληθήσεται ἐν τῇ βασιλείᾳ
τῶν οὐρανῶν· ὃς δ᾽ ἂν ποιήσῃ κỳ διδάξῃ οὗτ⊙ μέγας κληθήσεται ἐν
τῇ βασιλείᾳ τῶν οὐρανῶν.

20 Λέγω γὰρ ὑμῖν, ὅτι ἐὰν μὴ
περισσεύσῃ ἡ δικαιοσύνη ὑμῶν
πλεῖον τῶν Γραμματέων κỳ Φαρισαίων, οὐ μὴ εἰσέλθητε εἰς τὴν
βασιλείαν τῶν οὐρανῶν.

21 Ἠκούσατε ὅτι ἐῤῥέθη τοῖς
ἀρχαίοις· Οὐ φονεύσεις· ὃς δ᾽ ἂν
φονεύσῃ, ἔνοχ⊙ ἔςαι τῇ κρίσει.

* 22 Ἐγὼ δὲ λέγω ὑμῖν, ὅτι
πᾶς ὁ † ὀργιζόμεν⊙ τῷ ἀδελφῷ
αὐτοῦ ‡ εἰκῆ, ἔνοχος ἔςαι τῇ κρίσει·
ὃς δ᾽ ἂν ‡ εἴπῃ τῷ ἀδελφῷ αὐτοῦ
† ῥακά ἔνοχ⊙ ἔςαι τῷ συνεδρίῳ· ὃς
δ᾽ ἂν εἴπῃ ‡ μωρὲ, ‡ ἔνοχ⊙ ἔςαι
εἰς τὴν ‡ γέενναν τοῦ ‡ πυρός.

23 Ἐὰν οὖν προσφέρῃς τὸ δῶρόν σου
ἐπὶ τὸ θυσιαςήριον, κἀκεῖ μνησθῇς,
ὅτι ὁ ἀδελφός σου ἔχει τι κ.λα σοῦ,

* 24 Ἄφες ἐκεῖ τὸ δῶρόν σου ἔμπροσθεν τοῦ θυσιαςηρίου, κỳ ὕπαγε,
πρῶτον † διαλλάγηθι τῷ ἀδελφῷ
σου, κỳ τότε ἐλθὼν πρόσφερε τὸ
‡ δῶρόν σου.

---

15 Neque accendunt lucer-
nam, & ponunt eam sub me-
dio, sed super candelabrum, &
lucet omnibus in domo.

16 Sic luceat lux vestra coram
hominibus, ut videant vestra
pulchra opera, & glorificent Patrem vestrum qui in cælis.

17 Ne putetis quod veni dif-
solvere legem, aut Prophetas;
non veni dissolvere, sed adim-
plere.

18 Amen quippe dico vobis,
donec prætereat cælum & terra,
jota unum, aut unus apex non
præteribit à lege, donec omnia
fiant.

19 Qui ergo solverit unum
mandatorum istorum minimorum, & docuerit sic homines,
minimus vocabitur in regno cælorum : qui autem fecerit & docuerit, hic magnus vocabitur in
regno cælorum.

20 Dico enim vobis, quòd si
non abundaverit justitia vestra
plus Scribarum & Pharisæorum,
non intrabitis in regnum cælorum.

21 Audistis quia pronunciatum est antiquis : Non occides:
qui autem occiderit, obnoxius
erit judicio.

22 Ego autem dico vobis, quia
omnis irascens fratri suo imme-
ritò, obnoxius erit judicio : qui
autem dixerit fratri suo Raca,
obnoxius erit confessui : qui autem dixerit fatue, obnoxius erit
in gehennam ignis.

23 Si ergo offers munus tuum
ad altare, & ibi recordatus fueris, quia frater tuus habet aliquid adversum te, ·

24 Relinque ibi munus tuum
ante altare, & vade, prius recon-
ciliare fratri tuo, & tunc veniens
offer munus tuum.

15. Et on n'allume point une chandelle pour la mettre sous un boisseau , mais *on la met* sur un chandelier , et elle éclaire tous ceux qui *sont* dans la maison.

16. Que votre lumière luise ainsi devant les hommes , afin qu'ils voient vos bonnes œuvres, et qu'ils glorifient votre Père qui *est* dans les cieux.

17. Ne pensez point que je sois venu abolir la Loi ou les Prophètes ; je suis venu, non pour les abolir , mais pour les accomplir.

18. Car je vous dis en vérité , que jusqu'à ce que le ciel et la terre passent, il n'y aura rien dans la Loi qui ne s'accomplisse , jusqu'à un seul iota , et à un seul trait de lettre.

19. Celui donc qui aura violé l'un de ces plus petits commandemens, et qui aura ainsi enseigné les hommes, sera estimé le plus petit dans le Royaume des cieux ; mais celui qui les aura observés et enseignés, celui-là sera estimé grand dans le Royaume des cieux.

20. Car je vous dis , que si votre justice ne surpasse celle des Scribes et des Pharisiens , vous n'entrerez point dans le Royaume des cieux.

21. Vous avez entendu qu'il a été dit aux Anciens : Tu ne tueras point ; et celui qui tuera sera punissable par les Juges.

22. Mais moi , je vous dis , que quiconque se met en colère contre son frère , sans cause , sera puni par les Juges ; et celui qui dira à son frère, Racha, sera puni par le Conseil ; et celui qui lui dira, Fou, sera punissable par la géhenne du feu.

23. Si donc tu apportes ton offrande à l'autel , et que là tu te souviennes que ton frère a quelque chose contre toi ;

24. Laisse là ton offrande devant l'autel, et va-t-en premièrement te réconcilier avec ton frère; et, après cela, viens et offre ton offrande.

15 Neither do men light a candle, and put it under a bushel, but on a candlestick, and it giveth light unto all that are in the house.

16 Let your light so shine before men, that they may see your good works, and glorify your Father which is in heaven.

17 Think not that I am come to destroy the law, or the prophets: I am not come to destroy, but to fulfil.

18 For verily I say unto you, Till heaven and earth pass, one jot or one tittle shall in no wise pass from the law, till all be fulfilled.

19 Whosoever, therefore, shall break one of these least commandments, and shall teach men so, he shall be called the least in the kingdom of heaven: but whosoever shall do, and teach *them*, the same shall be called great in the kingdom of heaven.

20 For I say unto you, That except your righteousness shall exceed *the righteousness* of the scribes and Pharisees, ye shall in no case enter into the kingdom of heaven.

21 Ye have heard that it was said by them of old time, Thou shalt not kill; and, whosoever shall kill, shall be in danger of the judgment:

22 But I say unto you, That whosoever is angry with his brother without a cause, shall be in danger of the judgment: and whosoever shall say to his brother, Raca, shall be in danger of the council: but whosoever shall say, Thou fool, shall be in danger of hell fire.

23 Therefore, if thou bring thy gift to the altar, and there rememberest that thy brother hath aught against thee;

24 Leave there thy gift before the altar, and go thy way; first be reconciled to thy brother, and then come and offer thy gift.

8

25 Ἴσθι † εὐνοῶν τῷ ‡ ἀντιδίκῳ σου ‡ ταχὺ, ἕως ὅτου εἶ ἐν τῇ ὁδῷ μετ' αὐτοῦ μήποτέ σε παραδῷ ὁ ἀντίδικ☉ τῷ ‡ κριτῇ, καὶ ὁ κριτής σε παραδῷ τῷ ὑπηρέτῃ, καὶ εἰς φυλακὴν βληθήσῃ.

26 Ἀμὴν λέγω σοι, οὐ μὴ ἐξέλθῃς ἐκεῖθεν ἕως ἂν ἀποδῷς τὸν ἔσχατον κοδράντην.

27 Ἠκούσατε ὅτι ἐρρήθη τοῖς ἀρχαίοις· Οὐ μοιχεύσεις·

28 Ἐγὼ δὲ λέγω ὑμῖν, ὅτι πᾶς ὁ βλέπων γυναῖκα πρὸς τὸ ἐπιθυμῆσαι αὐτῆς, ἤδη ἐμοίχευσεν αὐτὴν ἐν τῇ καρδίᾳ αὐτοῦ.

29 Εἰ δὲ ὁ ὀφθαλμός σου ὁ δεξιὸς σκανδαλίζει σε, ἔξελε αὐτὸν, καὶ βάλε ἀπὸ σοῦ συμφέρει γάρ σοι, ἵνα ἀπόληται ἓν τῶν μελῶν σου, καὶ μὴ ὅλον τὸ σῶμά σου βληθῇ εἰς γέενναν.

30 Καὶ εἰ ἡ δεξιά σου χεὶρ σκανδαλίζει σε, ἔκκοψον αὐτὴν, καὶ βάλε ἀπὸ σοῦ· συμφέρει γάρ σοι, ἵνα ἀπόληται ἓν τῶν μελῶν σου, καὶ μὴ ὅλον τὸ σῶμά σου βληθῇ εἰς γέενναν·

31 Ἐρρήθη δὲ ὅτι ὃς ἂν ἀπολύσῃ τὴν γυναῖκα αὐτοῦ, δότω αὐτῇ ἀποστάσιον·

32 Ἐγὼ δὲ λέγω ὑμῖν, ὅτι ὃς ἂν ἀπολύσῃ τὴν γυναῖκα αὐτοῦ, παρεκτὸς λόγου πορνείας, ποιεῖ αὐτὴν μοιχᾶσθαι· καὶ ς ἐὰν ἀπολελυμένην γαμήσῃ, μοιχᾶται.

33 Πάλιν ἠκούσατε ‡ ὅτι † ἐρρήθη τοῖς ‡ ἀρχαίοις· Οὐκ † ἐπιορκήσεις, ἀποδώσεις δὲ τῷ Κυρίῳ τοὺς ὅρκους σου.

34 Ἐγὼ δὲ λέγω ὑμῖν, μὴ ὀμόσαι ὅλως· μήτε ἐν τῷ οὐρανῷ, ὅτι θρόν☉ ἐστὶ τοῦ Θεοῦ·

35 Μήτε ἐν τῇ γῇ, ὅτι ὑποπόδιόν ἐστι τῶν ποδῶν αὐτοῦ· μήτε εἰς

---

25 Esto benesentiens adversario tuo cito, dum es in via cum eo: ne forte te tradat adversarius judici, & judex te tradat ministro; & in custodiam conjiciaris.

26 Amen dico tibi, non exies inde, donec reddas novissimum quadrantem.

27 Audistis quia pronunciatum est antiquis: Non moechaberis.

28 Ego autem dico vobis, quia omnis conspiciens mulierem ad concupiscendum eam, jam moechatus est eam in corde suo.

29 Si autem oculus tuus dexter scandalizat te, erue eum, & projice abs te: confert enim tibi ut pereat unum membrorum tuorum, & non totum corpus tuum conjiciatur in gehennam.

30 Et si dextera tua manus scandalizat te, abscinde eam, & projice abs te: confert enim tibi ut pereat unum membrorum tuorum, & non totum corpus tuum conjiciatur in gehennam.

31 Pronunciatum est autem, quod quicumque absolverit uxorem suam, det ei repudium.

32 Ego autem dico vobis, quia quicunque absolverit uxorem suam, exceptâ ratione fornicationis, facit eam moechari: & qui absolutam duxerit, adulterat.

33 Iterum audistis quia pronunciatum est antiquis: Non perjurabis: reddes autem Domino juramenta tua.

34 Ego autem dico vobis, non jurare omninò, neque in caelo, quia thronus est Dei:

35 Neque in terra, quia scabellum est pedum ejus: neque

25. Accorde-toi au plutôt avec ta partie adverse, pendant que tu es en chemin avec elle, de peur que ta partie adverse ne te livre au Juge, et que le Juge ne te livre au Sergent, et que tu ne sois mis en prison.

26. Je te dis en vérité, que tu ne sortiras pas de là, jusqu'à-ce que tu aies payé le dernier quadrain.

27. Vous avez entendu qu'il a été dit aux Anciens : Tu ne commettras point adultère.

28. Mais moi, je vous dis, que quiconque regarde une femme pour la convoiter, il a déjà commis l'adultère avec elle dans son cœur.

29. Que si ton œil droit te fait tomber *dans le péché*, arrache-le, et jette-le loin de toi ; car il vaut mieux pour toi qu'un de tes membres périsse, que si tout ton corps étoit jeté dans la géhenne.

30. Et si ta main droite te fait tomber *dans le péché*, coupe-la, et jette-la loin de toi ; car il vaut mieux pour toi qu'un de tes membres périsse, que si tout ton corps étoit jeté dans la géhenne.

31. Il a été dit aussi : Si quelqu'un répudie sa femme, qu'il lui donne la lettre de divorce.

32. Mais moi, je vous dis, que quiconque répudiera sa femme, si ce n'est pour cause d'adultère, il l'expose à devenir adultère; et que quiconque se mariera à la femme qui aura été répudiée, commet un adultère.

33. Vous avez encore entendu qu'il a été dit aux Anciens : Tu ne te parjureras point ; mais tu t'acquitteras envers le Seigneur de ce que tu auras promis avec serment.

34. Mais moi, je vous dis : Ne jurez point du tout ; ni par le ciel, car c'est le trône de Dieu :

35. Ni par la terre, car c'est son

---

25 Agree with thine adversary quickly, whilst thou art in the way with him ; lest at any time the adversary deliver thee to the judge, and the judge deliver thee to the officer, and thou be cast into prison.

26 Verily I say unto thee, Thou shalt by no means come out thence, till thou hast paid the uttermost farthing.

27 Ye have heard that it was said by them of old time, Thou shalt not commit adultery :

28 But I say unto you, That whosoever looketh on a woman, to lust after her, hath committed adultery with her already in his heart.

29 And if thy right eye offend thee, pluck it out, and cast *it* from thee : for it is profitable for thee, that one of thy members should perish, and not *that* thy whole body should be cast into hell.

30 And if thy right hand offend thee, cut it off, and cast *it* from thee : for it is profitable for thee, that one of thy members should perish, and not *that* thy whole body should be cast into hell.

31 It hath been said, Whosoever shall put away his wife. let him give her a writing of divorcement :

32 But I say unto you, That whosoever shall put away his wife, saving for the cause of fornication, causeth her to commit adultery : and whosoever shall marry her that is divorced, committeth adultery.

33 Again, ye have heard that it hath been said by them of old time, Thou shalt not forswear thyself, but shalt perform unto the Lord thine oaths :

34 But I say unto you, Swear not at all : neither by heaven; for it is God's throne :

35 Nor by the earth : for it is his

9

Ἱεροσόλυμα, ὅτι πόλις ἐςὶ τοῦ μεγάλου βασιλέως·

36 Μήτε ἐν τῇ κεφαλῇ σου ὀμόσῃς, ὅτι οὐ δύνασαι μίαν τρίχα λευκὴν ἢ μέλαιναν ποιῆσαι.

37 Ἔςω δὲ ὁ λόγ☉· ὑμῶν, Ναὶ ναὶ, Οὒ οὒ· τὸ δὲ περισσὸν τούτων, ἐκ τοῦ πονηροῦ ἐςιν.

38 Ἠκούσατε ὅτι ἐῤῥέθη· Ὀφθαλμὸν ἀντὶ ὀφθαλμοῦ, ⁊ ὀδόντα ἀντὶ ὀδόντ☉.

39 Ἐγὼ δὲ λέγω ὑμῖν, μὴ ἀντιςῆναι τῷ πονηρῷ· ἀλλ᾽ ὅςις σε ῥαπίσει ἐπὶ τὴν δεξιάν σου σιαγόνα, ςρέψον αὐτῷ ⁊ τὴν ἄλλην.

40 Καὶ τῷ θέλοντί σοι κριθῆναι, ⁊ τὸν χιτῶνά σου λαβεῖν, ἄφες αὐτῷ ⁊ τὸ ἱμάτιον.

* 41 Καὶ ‡ ὅςις σε ‡ ἀγγαρεύσει ‡ μίλιον ἕν, ὕπαγε μετ᾽ αὐτοῦ δύο.

42 Τῷ αἰτοῦντί σε δίδου ⁊ τὸν θέλοντα ἀπὸ σοῦ δανείσασθαι μὴ ἀποςραφῇς.

43 Ἠκούσατε ὅτι ἐῤῥέθη· Ἀγαπήσεις τὸν πλησίον σου, ⁊ μισήσεις τὸν ἐχθρόν σου.

44 Ἐγὼ δὲ λέγω ὑμῖν, ἀγαπᾶτε τοὺς ἐχθροὺς ὑμῶν, εὐλογεῖτε τοὺς καταρωμένους ὑμᾶς, καλῶς ποιεῖτε τοὺς μισοῦντας ὑμᾶς, ⁊ προσεύχεσθε ὑπὲρ τῶν ἐπηρεαζόντων ὑμᾶς ⁊ διωκόντων ὑμᾶς·

45 Ὅπως γένεσθε υἱοὶ τοῦ πατρὸς ὑμῶν τοῦ ἐν οὐρανοῖς, ὅτι τὸν ἥλιον αὐτοῦ ἀνατέλλει ἐπὶ πονηροὺς ⁊ ἀγαθοὺς, ⁊ βρέχει ἐπὶ δικαίους ⁊ ἀδίκους.

46 Ἐὰν γὰρ ἀγαπήσητε τοὺς ἀγαπῶντας ὑμᾶς, τίνα μισθὸν ἔχετε; οὐχὶ ⁊ οἱ τελῶναι τὸ αὐτὸ ποιοῦσι;

47 Καὶ ἐὰν ἀσπάσησθε τοὺς ἀδελφοὺς ὑμῶν μόνον, τί περισσὸν ποιεῖτε; οὐχὶ ⁊ οἱ τελῶναι οὕτω ποιοῦσιν;

---

in Hierosolyma, quia civitas est magni regis:

36 Neque in capite tuo juraveris, quia non potes unum capillum album aut nigrum facere.

37 Sit autem sermo vester, Etiam, etiam, Non, non : quod autem abundans his, à malo est.

38 Audistis quia pronunciatum est : Oculum pro oculo, & dentem pro dente.

39 Ego autem dico vobis, non obsistere malo : sed quicumque te percusserit in dexteram tuam maxillam, verte illi & aliam.

40 Et volenti tibi judicium parari, & tunicam tuam tollere, dimitte ei & pallium.

41 Et quicunque te angariaverit milliare unum, vade cum illo duo.

42 Petenti te, da : & volentem à te mutuare, ne avertaris.

43 Audistis quia pronunciatum est, Diliges proximum tuum, & odio habebis inimicum tuum.

44 Ego autem dico vobis, Diligite inimicos vestros, benedicite maledicentes vos : benefacite odientibus vos, & orate pro infestantibus vos, & infectantibus vos.

45 Ut sitis filii Patris vestri qui in cælis, quia solem suum producit super malos et bonos, & pluit super justos & injustos.

46 Si enim dilexeritis diligentes vos, quam mercedem habetis? nonne & publicani idem faciunt?

47 Et si salutaveritis fratres vestros tantum, quid abundans facitis? nonne & publicani sic faciunt?

marchepied, ni par Jérusalem, car c'est la ville du grand Roi.

36. Ne jure pas non plus par ta tête ; car tu ne peux faire devenir un seul cheveu blanc ou noir.

37. Mais que votre parole soit, Oui, Oui, Non, Non ; ce qu'on dit de plus vient du malin.

38. Vous avez entendu qu'il a été dit : œil pour œil, et dent pour dent.

39. Mais moi, je vous dis, de ne pas résister à celui qui vous fait du mal ; mais si quelqu'un te frappe à la joue droite, présente-lui aussi l'autre.

40. Et si quelqu'un veut plaider contre toi, et t'ôter ta robe, laisse-lui encore l'habit.

41. Et si quelqu'un te veut contraindre d'aller une lieue avec lui, vas-en deux.

42. Donne à celui qui te demande, et ne te détourne point de celui qui veut emprunter de toi.

43. Vous avez entendu qu'il a été dit : Tu aimeras ton prochain, et tu haïras ton ennemi.

44. Mais moi, je vous dis : Aimez vos ennemis, bénissez ceux qui vous maudissent, faites du bien à ceux qui vous haïssent, et priez pour ceux qui vous outragent et qui vous persécutent ;

45. Afin que vous soyez enfans de votre Père qui est dans les cieux ; car il fait lever son soleil sur les méchans et sur les bons, et il fait pleuvoir sur les justes et sur les injustes.

46. Car si vous n'aimez que ceux qui vous aiment, quelle récompense en aurez-vous ? les péagers même n'en font-ils pas autant ?

47. Et si vous ne faites accueil qu'à vos frères, que faites-vous d'extraordinaire ? Les péagers même n'en font-ils pas autant ?

footstool : neither by Jerusalem ; for it is the city of the great King :

36 Neither shalt thou swear by thy head ; because thou canst not make one hair white or black.

37 But let your communication be, Yea, yea ; Nay, nay : for whatsoever is more than these cometh of evil.

38 Ye have heard that it hath been said, An eye for an eye, and a tooth for a tooth :

39 But I say unto you, That ye resist not evil : but whosoever shall smite thee on thy right cheek, turn to him the other also.

40 And if any man will sue thee at the law, and take away thy coat, let him have thy cloak also.

41 And whosoever shall compel thee to go a mile, go with him twain.

42 Give to him that asketh thee ; and from him that would borrow of thee, turn not thou away.

43 Ye have heard that it hath been said, Thou shalt love thy neighbour, and hate thine enemy :

44 But I say unto you, Love your enemies, bless them that curse you, do good to them that hate you, and pray for them which despitefully use you, and persecute you ;

45 That ye may be the children of your Father which is in heaven : for he maketh his sun to rise on the evil and on the good, and sendeth rain on the just and on the unjust.

46 For if ye love them which love you, what reward have ye ? do not even the publicans the same ?

47 And if ye salute your brethren only, what do ye more than others ? do not even the publicans so ?

10

34 Καὶ ἐὰν δανείζητε παρ᾽ ὧν ἐλπίζετε ἀπολαβεῖν, ποία ὑμῖν χάρις ἐστί; καὶ γὰρ οἱ ἁμαρτωλοὶ ἁμαρτωλοῖς δανείζουσιν, ἵνα ἀπολάβωσι τὰ ἴσα.

35 ‡ Πλὴν ‡ ἀγαπᾶτε τοὺς ‡ ἐχθροὺς ὑμῶν, καὶ ‡ ἀγαθοποιεῖτε, καὶ δανείζετε ‡ μηδὲν ‡ ἀπελπίζοντες· καὶ ἔσται ὁ μισθὸς ὑμῶν πολὺς, καὶ ἔσεσθε υἱοὶ τοῦ ὑψίστου· ὅτι αὐτὸς ‡ χρηστός ἐστιν ἐπὶ τοὺς ‡ ἀχαρίστους καὶ ‡ πονηρούς.

36 Γίνεσθε οὖν οἰκτίρμονες, καθὼς καὶ ὁ πατὴρ ὑμῶν οἰκτίρμων ἐστί.

Κεφ. ϛ´. 6.

1 Προσέχετε τὴν ἐλεημοσύνην ὑμῶν μὴ ποιεῖν ἔμπροσθεν τῶν ἀνθρώπων, πρὸς τὸ θεαθῆναι αὐτοῖς· εἰ δὲ μήγε, μισθὸν οὐκ ἔχετε παρὰ τῷ πατρὶ ὑμῶν τῷ ἐν τοῖς οὐρανοῖς.

2 Ὅταν οὖν ποιῇς ἐλεημοσύνην, μὴ σαλπίσῃς ἔμπροσθέν σου, ὥσπερ οἱ ὑποκριταὶ ποιοῦσιν ἐν ταῖς συναγωγαῖς καὶ ἐν ταῖς ῥύμαις, ὅπως δοξασθῶσιν ὑπὸ τῶν ἀνθρώπων· Ἀμὴν λέγω ὑμῖν, ἀπέχουσι τὸν μισθὸν αὐτῶν.

3 Σοῦ δὲ ποιοῦντος ἐλεημοσύνην, μὴ γνώτω ἡ ἀριστερά σου τί ποιεῖ ἡ δεξιά σου·

4 Ὅπως ᾖ σου ἡ ἐλεημοσύνη ἐν τῷ κρυπτῷ· καὶ ὁ πατήρ σου ὁ βλέπων ἐν τῷ κρυπτῷ, αὐτὸς ἀποδώσει σοι ἐν τῷ φανερῷ.

5 Καὶ ὅταν προσεύχῃ, οὐκ ἔσῃ ὥσπερ οἱ ὑποκριταί· ὅτι φιλοῦσιν ἐν ταῖς συναγωγαῖς καὶ ἐν ταῖς γωνίαις τῶν πλατειῶν ἑστῶτες προσεύχεσθαι, ὅπως ἂν φανῶσι τοῖς ἀνθρώποις· Ἀμὴν λέγω ὑμῖν, ὅτι ἀπέχουσι τὸν μισθὸν αὐτῶν.

6 Σὺ δὲ ὅταν προσεύχῃ, εἴσελθε εἰς τὸ ταμιεῖόν σου, καὶ κλείσας τὴν θύραν σου, πρόσευξαι τῷ πατρί σου τῷ ἐν τῷ κρυπτῷ· καὶ ὁ πατήρ σου ὁ βλέπων ἐν τῷ κρυπτῷ, ἀποδώσει σοι ἐν τῷ φανερῷ.

7 ‡ Προσευχόμενοι δὲ μὴ † βαττολογήσητε, ὥσπερ οἱ ‡ ἐθνικοί· ‡ δοκοῦσι γὰρ ὅτι ἐν τῇ † πολυλογίᾳ αὐτῶν ‡ εἰσακουσθήσονται.

8 Μὴ οὖν ὁμοιωθῆτε αὐτοῖς· οἶδε γὰρ ὁ πατὴρ ὑμῶν, ὧν χρείαν ἔχετε, πρὸ τοῦ ὑμᾶς αἰτῆσαι αὐτόν.

- 34 Et si mutuum dederitis à quibus speratis recipere, quæ vobis gratia est? Etenim peccatores peccatoribus fœnerantur, ut recipiant æqualia.

35 Veruntamen diligite inimicos vestros, & benefacite, & mutuum date nihil desperantes: & erit merces vestra multa, & eritis filii Altissimi: quia ipse benignus est super ingratos & malos.

36 Estote ergo misericordes, sicut & Pater vester misericors est.

CAPUT VI.

1 Attendite misericordiam vestram non facere ante homines, ad spectari eis: si autem non, mercedem non habetis apud Patrem vestrum qui in cælis.

2 Cum ergo facis eleemosynam, ne tuba clanxeris ante te, sicut hypocritæ faciunt in synagogis & in vicis, ut glorificentur ab hominibus: amen dico vobis, excipiunt mercedem suam.

3 Te autem faciente eleemosynam, nesciat sinistra tua quid faciat dextera tua.

4 Ut sit tua eleemosyna in secreto: & Pater tuus videns in secreto, ipse reddet tibi in manifesto.

5 Et quum ores, non eris sicut hypocritæ: quia amant in synagogis, & in angulis platearum stantes orare, ut appareant hominibus, amen dico vobis, quod excipiunt mercedem suam.

6 Tu autem cum ores, intra in cubiculum tuum, & claudens ostium tuum, ora Patrem tuum qui in secreto: & Pater tuus conspiciens in secreto, reddet tibi in apparenti.

7 Orantes autem ne inania loquamini, sicut ethnici, arbitrantur enim quod in multiloquio suo exaudientur.

8 Ne igitur assimilemini eis: novit enim Pater vester quorum usum habetis, ante vos petere eum.

34 And if ye lend *to them* of whom ye hope to receive, what thank have ye? for sinners also lend to sinners, to receive as much again.

35 But love ye your enemies, and do good, and lend, hoping for nothing again: and your reward shall be great, and ye shall be the children of the Highest: for he is kind unto the unthankful, and *to* the evil.

36 Be ye, therefore, merciful, as your Father also is merciful.

TAKE heed that ye do not your alms before men, to be seen of them: otherwise ye have no reward of your Father which is in heaven.

2 Therefore, when thou doest *thine* alms, do not sound a trumpet before thee, as the hypocrites do in the synagogues, and in the streets, that they may have glory of men. Verily I say unto you, They have their reward.

3 But when thou doest alms, let not thy left hand know what thy right hand doeth:

4 That thine alms may be in secret: and thy Father, which seeth in secret, himself shall reward thee openly.

5 And when thou prayest, thou shalt not be as the hypocrites *are:* for they love to pray standing in the synagogues, and in the corners of the streets, that they may be seen of men. Verily I say unto you, They have their reward.

6 But thou, when thou prayest, enter into thy closet; and, when thou hast shut thy door, pray to thy Father which is in secret; and thy Father which seeth in secret, shall reward thee openly.

7 But when ye pray, use not vain repetitions, as the heathen *do:* for they think that they shall be heard for their much speaking.

8 Be not ye, therefore, like unto them: for your Father knoweth what things ye have need of, before ye ask him.

---

34. Et si vous ne prêtez qu'à ceux de qui vous espérez de recevoir, quel gré vous en saura-t-on? puisque les gens de mauvaise vie prêtent aussi aux gens de mauvaise vie, afin d'en recevoir la pareillle.

35. C'est pourquoi, aimez vos ennemis, faites du bien, et prêtez sans en rien espérer, et votre récompense sera grande, et vous serez les enfans du très-hant; parce qu'il est bon envers les ingrats et les méchans.

36. Soyez donc miséricordieux, comme aussi votre père est miséricordieux.

PRENEZ garde de ne pas faire votre aumône devant les hommes, afin d'en être vu; autrement vous n'en aurez point de récompense de votre Père qui *est* aux cieux.

2. Quand donc tu feras l'aumône, ne fais pas sonner la trompette devant toi, comme font les hypocrites, dans les Synagogues et dans les rues, afin qu'ils *en* soient honorés des hommes. Je vous dis en vérité, qu'il reçoivent leur récompense.

3. Mais quand tu fais l'aumône, que la main gauche ne sache pas ce que fait ta droite.

4. Afin que ton aumône se fasse en secret; et ton Père qui *te* voit dans le secret, te le rendra publiquement.

5. Et quand tu prieras, ne fais pas comme les hypocrites; car ils aiment à prier en se tenant debout dans les Synagogues et aux coins des rues, afin d'être vus des hommes. Je vous dis en vérité, qu'ils reçoivent leur récompense.

6. Mais toi, quand tu pries, entre dans ton cabinet; et ayant fermé la porte, prie ton père qui *est* dans ce *lieu* secret; et ton père qui te voit dans le secret, te récompensera publiquement.

7. Or, quand vous priez, n'usez pas des vaines redites comme les Païens; car ils croient qu'ils seront exaucés en parlant beaucoup.

8. Ne leur ressemblez donc pas; car votre Père sait de quoi vous avez besoin, avant que vous *le* lui demandiez.

9 Οὕτως οὖν προσεύχεσθε ὑμεῖς· ΠΑΤΕΡ ἡμῶν ὁ ἐν τοῖς οὐρανοῖς· ἁγιασθήτω τὸ ὄνομά σου·

10 Ἐλθέτω ἡ βασιλεία σου· γενηθήτω τὸ θέλημά σου, ὡς ἐν οὐρανῷ, κỳ ἐπὶ τῆς γῆς.

11 Τὸν ἄρτον ἡμῶν τὸν ἐπιούσιον δὸς ἡμῖν σήμερον.

12 Καὶ ἄφες ἡμῖν τὰ ὀφειλήματα ἡμῶν, ὡς ͳ ἡμεῖς ἀφίεμεν τοῖς ὀφειλέταις ἡμῶν.

13 Καὶ μὴ εἰσενέγκῃς ἡμᾶς εἰς πειρασμὸν, ἀλλὰ ῥῦσαι ἡμᾶς ἀπὸ τοῦ πονηροῦ· ὅτι σοῦ ἐςιν ἡ βασιλεία, κỳ ἡ δύναμις, κỳ ἡ δόξα εἰς τοὺς αἰῶνας· ἀμήν.

14 Ἐὰν γὰρ ἀφῆτε τοῖς ἀνθρώποις τὰ παραπτώματα αὐτῶν, ἀφήσει κỳ ὑμῖν ὁ πατὴρ ὑμῶν ὁ οὐράνιος·

15 Ἐὰν δὲ μὴ ἀφῆτε τοῖς ἀνθρώποις τὰ παραπτώματα αὐτῶν, οὐδὲ ὁ πατὴρ ὑμῶν ἀφήσει τὰ παραπτώματα ὑμῶν.

16 Ὅταν δὲ νηςεύητε, μὴ γίνεσθε, ὥσπερ οἱ ὑποκριταὶ, σκυθρωποί· ἀφανίζουσι γὰρ τὰ πρόσωπα αὐτῶν, ὅπως φανῶσι τοῖς ἀνθρώποις νηςεύοντες· ἀμὴν λέγω ὑμῖν, ὅτι ἀπέχουσι τὸν μισθὸν αὐτῶν.

17 Σὺ δὲ νηςεύων ἄλειψαί σου τὴν κεφαλὴν, κỳ τὸ πρόσωπόν σου νίψαι·

18 Ὅπως μὴ φανῇς τοῖς ἀνθρώποις νηςεύων, ἀλλὰ τῷ πατρί σου τῷ ἐν τῷ κρυπτῷ· κỳ ὁ πατήρ σου ὁ βλέπων ἐν τῷ κρυπτῷ, ἀποδώσει σοι ἐν τῷ φανερῷ.

* 19 Μὴ ‡ θησαυρίζετε ὑμῖν ‡ θησαυροὺς ἐπὶ τῆς ‡ γῆς, ὅπου ‡ σὴς κỳ ‡ βρῶσις ‡ ἀφανίζει, κỳ ὅπου ‡ κλέπται ‡ διορύσσουσι κỳ ‡ κλέπτουσι·

20 Θησαυρίζετε δὲ ὑμῖν θησαυροὺς ἐν οὐρανῷ, ὅπου οὔτε σὴς οὔτε βρῶσις ἀφανίζει, κỳ ὅπου κλέπται οὐ διορύσσουσιν οὐδὲ κλέπτουσιν.

21 Ὅπου γάρ ἐςιν ὁ θησαυρὸς ὑμῶν, ἐκεῖ ἔςαι κỳ ἡ καρδία ὑμῶν.

22 Ὁ λύχνⷦ τοῦ σώματός ἐςιν ὁ ὀφθαλμός· ἐὰν οὖν ὁ ὀφθαλμός σου ἁπλοῦς ᾖ, ὅλον τὸ σῶμά σου φωτεινὸν ἔςαι.

---

9 Sic ergo orate vos : Pater noster qui in cælis, sanctificetur nomen tuum.

10 Adveniat regnum tuum : Fiat voluntas tua, sicut in cælo, & in terra.

11 Panem nostrum supersubstantialem da nobis hodie.

12 Et dimitte nobis debita nostra, sicut & nos dimittimus debitoribus nostris.

13 Et ne inferas nos in tentationem, sed libera nos à malo. Quoniam tuum est regnum, & potentia, & gloria in secula. Amen.

14 Si enim dimiseritis hominibus lapsus eorum, dimittet & vobis Pater vester cælestis.

15 Si autem non dimiseritis hominibus lapsus ipsorum, nec Pater vester dimittet lapsus vestros.

16 Quum autem jejunatis, ne fiatis sicut hypocritæ, obtristati; obscurant enim facies suas; ut appareant hominibus jejunantes, amen dico vobis, quia recipiunt mercedem suam.

17 Tu autem jejunans, unge tuum caput, & faciam tuam lava:

18 Ut ne appareas hominibus jejunans, sed Patri tuo qui in secreto : & Pater tuus videns in secreto, reddet tibi in manifesto.

19 Ne thesaurizate vobis thesauros in terra, ubi ærugo & tinea exterminat, & ubi fures perfodiunt, & furantur.

20 Thesaurizate autem vobis thesauros in cælo, ubi neque ærugo, neque tinea exterminat, & ubi fures non effodiunt, nec furantur.

21 Ubi enim est thesaurus vester, ibi erit & cor vestrum.

22 Lucerna corporis est oculus; si igitur oculus tuus simplex fuerit, totum corpus tuum lucidum erit.

9. Vous donc, priez ainsi : Notre Père qui *es* aux cieux, ton nom soit sanctifié ;

10. Ton règne vienne ; ta volonté soit faite sur la terre comme au ciel ;

11. Donne-nous aujourd'hui notre pain quotidien ;

12. Pardonne-nous nos péchés, comme aussi nous pardonnons à ceux qui nous ont offensés ;

13. Et ne nous abandonne point à la tentation, mais délivre-nous du malin. Car à toi appartient le règne, la puissance, et la gloire à jamais : Amen.

14. Si vous pardonnez aux hommes leurs offenses, votre Père céleste vous pardonnera aussi *les vôtres* ;

15. Mais si vous ne pardonnez pas aux hommes leurs offenses, votre Père ne vous pardonnera pas non plus les vôtres.

16. Et quand vous jeûnez, ne prenez pas un air triste comme les hypocrites ; car ils se rendent le visage tout défait, afin qu'il paroisse aux hommes qu'ils jeûnent.

17. Mais toi, quand tu jeûnes, oins ta tête et lave ton visage ;

18. Afin qu'il ne paroisse pas aux hommes que tu jeûnes, mais *seulement* à ton Père qui *est* en secret ; et ton Père qui *te* voit dans le secret, te récompensera publiquement.

19. Ne vous amassez pas des trésors sur la terre, où les vers et la rouille gâtent tout, et où les larrons percent et dérobent ;

20. Mais amassez-vous des trésors dans le ciel, où les vers ni la rouille ne gâtent rien, et où les larrons ne percent ni ne dérobent point ;

21. Car où est votre trésor, là sera aussi votre cœur.

22. L'œil est la lumière du corps. Si donc ton œil est sain, tout ton corps sera éclairé ;

9 After this manner, therefore, pray ye: Our Father which art in heaven; Hallowed be thy name.

10 Thy kingdom come. Thy will be done in earth, as *it is* in heaven.

11 Give us this day our daily bread.

12 And forgive us our debts, as we forgive our debtors.

13 And lead us not into temptation; but deliver us from evil: For thine is the kingdom, and the power, and the glory, for ever. Amen.

14 For if ye forgive men their trespasses, your heavenly Father will also forgive you:

15 But if ye forgive not men their trespasses, neither will your Father forgive your trespasses.

16 Moreover, when ye fast, be not as the hypocrites, of a sad countenance: for they disfigure their faces, that they may appear unto men to fast. Verily I say unto you, They have their reward.

17 But thou, when thou fastest, anoint thine head, and wash thy face;

18 That thou appear not unto men to fast, but unto thy Father which is in secret: and thy Father, which seeth in secret, shall reward thee openly.

19 Lay not up for yourselves treasures upon earth, where moth and rust doth corrupt, and where thieves break through and steal:

20 But lay up for yourselves treasures in heaven, where neither moth nor rust doth corrupt, and where thieves do not break through nor steal:

21 For where your treasure is, there will your heart be also.

22 The light of the body is the eye: if, therefore, thine eye be single, thy whole body shall be full of light.

23 Ἐὰν δὲ ὁ ὀφθαλμός σου πονηρὸς ᾖ, ὅλον τὸ σῶμά σου σκοτεινὸν ἔςαι. Εἰ οὖν τὸ φῶς τὸ ἐν σοὶ, σκότ⊙ ἐςὶ, τὸ σκότ⊙ πόσον;

24 Οὐδεὶς δύναται δυσὶ κυρίοις δουλεύειν. ἢ γὰρ τὸν ἕνα μισήσει, κỳ τὸν ἕτερον ἀγαπήσει· ἢ ἑνὸς ἀνθέξεται, κỳ τοῦ ἑτέρου καταφρονήσει· οὐ δύνασθε Θεῷ δουλεύειν κỳ μαμμωνᾷ.

25 Διὰ τοῦτο λέγω ὑμῖν, μὴ μεριμνᾶτε τῇ ψυχῇ ὑμῶν, τί φάγητε κỳ τί πίητε· μηδὲ τῷ σώματι ὑμῶν, τί ἐνδύσησθε· οὐχὶ ἡ ψυχὴ πλεῖόν ἐςι τῆς τροφῆς, κỳ τὸ σῶμα τοῦ ἐνδύματ⊙;

26 Ἐμβλέψατε εἰς τὰ πετεινὰ τοῦ οὐρανοῦ, ὅτι οὐ σπείρουσιν, οὐδὲ θερίζουσιν, οὐδὲ συνάγουσιν εἰς ἀποθήκας, κỳ ὁ πατὴρ ὑμῶν ὁ οὐράνιος τρέφει αὐτά· οὐχ ὑμεῖς μᾶλλον διαφέρετε αὐτῶν;

27 Τίς δὲ ἐξ ὑμῶν μεριμνῶν δύναται προσθεῖναι ἐπὶ τὴν ἡλικίαν αὐτοῦ πῆχυν ἕνα;

* 28 Καὶ περὶ ἐνδύματ⊙ τί μεριμνᾶτε; † καταμάθετε τὰ ‡ κρίνα τοῦ ‡ ἀγροῦ ‡ πῶς ‡ αὐξάνει· οὐ ‡ κοπιᾷ, ‡ οὐδὲ ‡ νήθει·

29 Λέγω δὲ ὑμῖν, ὅτι οὐδὲ Σολομὼν ἐν πάσῃ τῇ δόξῃ αὐτοῦ περιεβάλετο ὡς ἓν τούτων.

* 30 Εἰ δὲ τὸν ‡ χόρτον τοῦ ἀγροῦ, σήμερον ὄντα, κỳ ‡ αὔριον εἰς ‡ κλίβανον βαλλόμενον, ὁ Θεὸς ‡ οὕτως ‡ ἀμφιέννυσιν, οὐ πολλῷ μᾶλλον ὑμᾶς, ὀλιγόπιςοι;

31 Μὴ οὖν μεριμνήσητε, λέγοντες· Τί φάγωμεν, ἢ τί πίωμεν, ἢ τί περιβαλώμεθα;

32 Πάντα γὰρ ταῦτα τὰ ἔθνη ἐπιζητεῖ· οἶδε γὰρ ὁ πατὴρ ὑμῶν ὁ οὐράνι⊙, ὅτι χρῄζετε τούτων ἁπάντων.

33 Ζητεῖτε δὲ πρῶτον τὴν βασιλείαν τοῦ Θεοῦ, κỳ τὴν δικαιοσύνην αὐτοῦ, κỳ ταῦτα πάντα προςτεθήσεται ὑμῖν.

34 Μὴ οὖν μεριμνήσητε εἰς τὴν αὔριον· ἡ γὰρ αὔριον μεριμνήσει τὰ ἑαυτῆς· ἀρκετὸν τῇ ἡμέρᾳ ἡ κακία αὐτῆς· 29. † 3.

---

23 Si autem oculus tuus malus fuerit, totum corpus tuum tenebrosum erit. si ergo lumen quod in te, tenebræ sunt, tenebræ quantæ?

24 Nemo potest duobus dominis servire : aut enim unum oderit, & alterum diliget : aut unum amplexabitur, & alterum despiciet. non potestis Deo servire & mammonæ.

25 Propter hoc dico vobis, ne anxiemini animæ vestræ, quid manducetis, & quid bibatis : neque corpori vestro, quid induamini. nonne anima plus est escâ, & corpus indumento?

26 Inspicite in volatilia cæli, quoniam non seminant, neque metunt, neque congregant in horrea, & Pater vester cælestis pascit illa, nonne vos magis excellitis illis?

27 Quis antem ex vobis anxiatus potest adjicere ad staturam suam cubitum unum?

28 Et circa vestimentum quid anxiamini? Observate lilia agri quomodo augentur : non satigantur, neque nent.

29 Dico autem vobis, quoniam nec Salomon in omni gloria sua amictus est sicut unum istorum.

30 Si autem fœnum agri hodie existens, & cras in clibanum injectum, Deus sic circumornat, non multò magis vos, exiguæ fidei?

31 Ne igitur anxiemini, dicentes : Quid manducabimus, aut quid bibemus, aut quid circumamiciemur?

32 Omnia enim hæc gentes inquirunt. Novit enim Pater vester cælestis quod opus habetis horum omnium.

33 Quærite autem primùm regnum Dei, & justitiam ejus, & hæc omnia adponentur vobis.

34 Ne igitur anxiemini in cras : nam cras curabit sua ipsins : sufficiens diei malitia sua.

23. Mais si ton œil est mauvais, tout ton corps sera ténébreux. Si donc la lumière qui est en toi n'est *que* ténèbres, combien seront grandes ces ténèbres !

24. Nul ne peut servir deux maîtres ; car ou il haïra l'un, et aimera l'autre ; ou il s'attachera à l'un, et méprisera l'autre. Vous ne pouvez servir Dieu et Mammon.

25. C'est pourquoi je vous dis : Ne soyez point en souci de votre vie, de ce que vous mangerez, ou de ce que vous boirez ; ni pour votre corps, de quoi vous serez vêtus. La vie n'est-elle pas plus que la nourriture ; et le corps plus que le vêtement ?

26. Regardez les oiseaux de l'air ; car ils ne sèment, ni ne moissonnent, ni n'amassent *rien* dans des greniers, et votre Père céleste les nourrit : N'êtes-vous pas beaucoup plus excellens qu'eux ?

27. Et qui est-ce d'entre vous, qui, par son souci, puisse ajouter une coudée à sa taille ?

28. Et pour ce qui est du vêtement, pourquoi en êtes-vous en souci ? Apprenez comment les lis de champs croissent ; ils ne travaillent ni ne filent.

29. Cependant, je vous dis, que Salomon même, dans toute sa gloire, n'a point été vêtu comme l'un d'eux.

30. Si donc Dieu revêt ainsi l'herbe des champs, qui est aujourd'hui, et qui demain sera jetée dans le four, ne vous *revêtira-t-il* pas beaucoup plutôt, ô gens de petite foi ?

31. Ne soyez donc point en souci, disant : Que mangerons-nous ? que boirons-nous ? Ou de quoi serons-nous vêtus ?

32. Car ce sont les Païens qui recherchent toutes ces choses ; et votre Père céleste sait que vous avez besoin de toutes ces choses-là.

33. Mais cherchez premièrement le Royaume de Dieu et sa justice, et toutes ces choses vous seront données par-dessus.

34. Ne soyez donc point en souci pour le lendemain ; car le lendemain aura soin de ce qui le regarde : A chaque jour suffit sa peine.

23 But if thine eye be evil, thy whole body shall be full of darkness. If, therefore, the light that is in thee be darkness, how great *is* that darkness ?

24 No man can serve two masters : for either he will hate the one, and love the other ; or else he will hold to the one, and despise the other. Ye cannot serve God and mammon.

25 Therefore I say unto you, Take no thought for your life, what ye shall eat or what ye shall drink ; nor yet for your body, what ye shall put on. Is not the life more than meat, and the body than raiment ?

26 Behold the fowls of the air : for they sow not, neither do they reap, nor gather into barns ; yet your heavenly Father feedeth them. Are ye not much better than they ?

27 Which of you, by taking thought, can add one cubit unto his stature ?

28 And why take ye thought for raiment ? Consider the lilies of the field how they grow : they toil not, neither do they spin ;

29 And yet I say unto you, That even Solomon in all his glory was not arrayed like one of these.

30 Wherefore, if God so clothe the grass of the field, which to day is, and to morrow is cast into the oven, *shall he* not much more *clothe* you ? O ye of little faith ;

31 Therefore, take no thought, saying, What shall we eat ? or, What shall we drink ? or, Wherewithal shall we be clothed ?

32 (For after all these things do the Gentiles seek :) for your heavenly Father knoweth that ye have need of all these things.

33 But seek ye first the kingdom of God, and his righteousness ; and all these things shall be added unto you.

34 Take therefore no thought for the morrow : for the morrow shall take thought for the things of itself. Sufficient unto the day *is* the evil thereof.

Κεφ. ζ´. 7.

CAPUT VII.

1 ΜΗ κρίνετε, ἵνα μὴ κρι-
θῆτε.

1 NE judicate, ut non judi-
cemini.

2 Ἐν ᾧ γὰρ κρίματι κρίνετε,
κριθήσεσθε· κ᾽ ἐν ᾧ μέτρῳ με-
τρεῖτε, ἀντιμετρηθήσεται ὑμῖν.

2 In quo enim judicio judica-
veritis, judicabimini : & in
qua mensurâ mensi fueritis, re-
metietur vobis.

* 3 Β Δίδοτε, κ᾽ δοθήσεται ὑ-
μῖν· ‡ μέτρον καλὸν, † πεπιε-
σμένον κ᾽ ‡ σεσαλευμένον κ᾽ † ὑ-
περεκχυνόμενον δώσουσιν εἰς τὸν
‡ κόλπον ὑμῶν·

3 Β Date, & dabitur vobis :
Mensuram bonam, confertam,
& coagitatam, & super fluen-
tem dabunt in sinum vestrum :

3 Τί δὲ βλέπεις τὸ κάρφ⊙· τὸ
ἐν τῷ ὀφθαλμῷ τοῦ ἀδελφοῦ σου,
τὴν δὲ ἐν τῷ σῷ ὀφθαλμῷ δοκὸν
οὐ κατανοεῖς;

3 Quid autem intueris festucam
quæ in oculo fratris tui, at in tuo
oculo trabem non animadvertis?

4 Ἢ πῶς ἐρεῖς τῷ ἀδελφῷ σου·
Ἄφες· ἐκβάλω τὸ κάρφ⊙· ἀπὸ τοῦ
ὀφθαλμοῦ σου· κ᾽ ἰδοὺ ἡ δοκὸς ἐν
τῷ ὀφθαλμῷ σου;

4 Aut quomodo dices fratri
tuo : Sine ejiciam festucam de
oculo tuo, & ecce trabs in oculo
tuo ?

* 5 ‡ Ὑποκριτὰ, ἔκβαλε πρῶτον τὴν ‡ δοκὸν ἐκ τοῦ ὀφθαλμοῦ
σου, κ᾽ τότε διαβλέψεις ἐκβαλεῖν
τὸ ‡ κάρφ⊙· ἐκ τοῦ ὀφθαλμοῦ
τοῦ ἀδελφοῦ σου.

5 Hypocrita, ejice primùm
trabem de oculo tuo, & tunc
intueberis ejicere festucam de
oculo fratris tui.

6 Μὴ δῶτε τὸ ἅγιον τοῖς κυσὶ,
μηδὲ βάλητε τοὺς μαργαρίτας ὑ-
μῶν ἔμπροσθεν τῶν χοίρων· μήποτε καταπατήσωσιν αὐτοὺς ἐν
τοῖς ποσὶν αὐτῶν, κ᾽ στραφέντες
ῥήξωσιν ὑμᾶς.

6 Ne detis sanctum canibus,
neque mittatis margaritas vestras ante porcos, ne forte con-
culcent eas in pedibus suis, &
conversi dirumpant vos.

7 Αἰτεῖτε, κ᾽ δοθήσεται ὑμῖν·
ζητεῖτε, κ᾽ εὑρήσετε· κρούετε, κ᾽
ἀνοιγήσεται ὑμῖν.

7 Petite, & dabitur vobis :
quærite, & invenietis : pulsate,
& aperietur vobis.

8 Πᾶς γὰρ ὁ αἰτῶν λαμβάνει,
κ᾽ ὁ ζητῶν εὑρίσκει, κ᾽ τῷ κρούοντι
ἀνοιγήσεται.

8 Omnis enim petens acci-
pit : & quærens invenit, &
pulsanti aperietur.

9 Ἢ τίς ἐστιν ἐξ ὑμῶν ἄνθρω-
π⊙·, ὃν ἐὰν αἰτήσῃ ὁ υἱὸς αὐτοῦ
ἄρτον, μὴ λίθον ἐπιδώσει αὐτῷ;

9 Aut quis est ex vobis homo,
quem si petierit filius suus panem, nunquid lapidem dabit ei ?

10 Καὶ ἐὰν ἰχθὺν αἰτήσῃ, μὴ
ὄφιν ἐπιδώσει αὐτῷ;

10 Et si piscem petierit, nunquid serpentem dabit ei ?

* 11 Εἰ οὖν ὑμεῖς, πονηροὶ ὄντες,
‡ οἴδατε ‡ δόματα ‡ ἀγαθὰ διδόναι
τοῖς τέκνοις ὑμῶν, πόσῳ μᾶλλον ὁ
πατὴρ ὑμῶν ὁ ἐν τοῖς οὐρανοῖς, δώσει ἀγαθὰ τοῖς αἰτοῦσιν αὐτόν;

11 Si ergo vos mali existen-
tes, nôstis data bona dare filiis
vestris, quanto magis Pater vester qui in cælis, dabit bona petentibus se ?

12 Πάντα οὖν ὅσα ἂν θέλητε
ἵνα ποιῶσιν ὑμῖν οἱ ἄνθρωποι, οὕτω
κ᾽ ὑμεῖς ποιεῖτε αὐτοῖς· οὗτ⊙·
γάρ ἐστιν ὁ νόμ⊙· κ᾽ οἱ προφῆται.

12 Omnia ergo quæcumque
vultis ut faciant vobis homines,
ita & vos facite illis. Hæc enim
est Lex & Prophetæ.

CHAPITRE VII.

Fin du Sermon sur la Montagne.

NE jugez point, afin que vous ne soyez point jugés.

2. Car on vous jugera du même jugement que vous aurez jugé ; et on vous mesurera de la même mesure que vous aurez mesuré *les autres.*

38. Donnez, et on vous donnera; on vous donnera dans le sein une bonne mesure, pressée et secouée, et qui se répandra par-dessus;

3. Et pourquoi regardes-tu une paille qui *est* dans l'œil de ton frère ; tandis que tu ne vois pas une poutre qui *est* dans ton œil ?

4. Ou comment dis-tu à ton frère, permets que j'ôte cette paille de ton œil, toi qui a une poutre dans le tien ?

5. Hypocrite, ôte premièrement de ton œil la poutre, et alors tu penseras à ôter la paille hors de l'œil de ton frère.

6. Ne donnez point les choses saintes aux chiens, et ne jetez point vos perles devant les pourceaux ; de peur qu'ils ne les foulent à leurs pieds, et que se tournant ils ne vous déchirent.

7. Demandez, et on vous donnera ; cherchez, et vous trouverez ; heurtez, et on vous ouvrira.

8. Car quiconque demande, reçoit ; et qui cherche, trouve ; et l'on ouvre à celui qui heurte.

9. Et qui sera même l'homme d'entre vous qui donne une pierre à son fils, s'il lui demande du pain ?

10. Et s'il lui demande du poisson, lui donnera-t-il un serpent?

11. Si donc, vous, qui êtes mauvais, savez bien donner à vos enfans des bonnes choses, combien plus votre Père qui est dans les cieux, donnera-t-il des biens à ceux qui *les* lui demandent.

12. Toutes les choses que vous voulez que les hommes vous fassent, faites-*les*-leur aussi de même ; car c'est là la Loi et les Prophètes.

JUDGE not, that ye be not judged.

2 For with what judgment ye judge, ye shall be judged: and with what measure ye mete, it shall be me~ ured to you again.

38 Give, and it shall be given unto you ; good measure, pressed down, and shaken together, and running over, shall men give into your bosom.

3 And why beholdest thou the mote that is in thy brother's eye, but considerest not the beam that is in thine own eye ?

4 Or how wilt thou say to thy brother, Let me pull out the mote out of thine eye ; and, behold, a beam *is* in thine own eye ?

5 Thou hypocrite ! first cast out the beam out of thine own eye ; and then shalt thou see clearly to cast out the mote out of thy brother's eye.

6 Give not that which is holy unto the dogs ; neither cast ye your pearls before swine, lest they trample them under their feet, and turn again and rend you.

7 Ask, and it shall be given you ; seek, and ye shall find ; knock, and it shall be opened unto you:

8 For every one that asketh, receiveth ; and he that seeketh, findeth ; and to him that knocketh, it shall be opened.

9 Or what man is there of you, whom if his son ask bread, will he give him a stone ?

10 Or if he ask a fish, will he give him a serpent?

11 If ye then, being evil, know how to give good gifts unto your children, how much more shall your Father, which is in heaven, give good things to them that ask him ?

12 Therefore all things whatsoever ye would that men should do to you, do ye even so to them : for this is the law and the prophets.

13 ‡ Εἰσέλθετε διὰ τῆς ‡ ςενῆς πύλης· ὅτι † πλατεῖα ἡ ‡ πύλη, κỳ ‡ εὐρύχωρ⊙ ἡ ‡ ὁδὸς ἡ ‡ ἀπάγυσα εἰς τὴν ‡ ἀπώλειαν, κỳ πολλοί εἰσιν οἱ εἰσερχόμενοι δι' αὐτῆς·

14 Ὅτι ςενὴ ἡ πύλη, κỳ τεθλιμμένη ἡ ὁδὸς ἡ ἀπάγουσα εἰς τὴν ζωὴν, κỳ ὀλίγοι εἰσὶν οἱ εὑρίσκοντες αὐτήν.

15 Προσέχετε δὲ ἀπὸ τῶν ψευδοπροφητῶν, οἵτινες ἔρχονται πρὸς ὑμᾶς ἐν ἐνδύμασι προϐάτων, ἔσωθεν δέ εἰσι λύκοι ἅρπαγες.

16 Ἀπὸ τῶν καρπῶν αὐτῶν ἐπιγνώσεσθε αὐτούς. Μήτι συλλέγουσιν ἀπὸ ἀκανθῶν ςαφυλὴν, ἢ ἀπὸ τριϐόλων σῦκα;

17 Οὕτω πᾶν δένδρον ἀγαθὸν καρποὺς καλοὺς ποιεῖ· τὸ δὲ σαπρὸν δένδρον καρποὺς πονηροὺς ποιεῖ.

18 Οὐ δύναται δένδρον ἀγαθὸν καρποὺς πονηροὺς ποιεῖν, οὐδὲ δένδρον σαπρὸν καρποὺς καλοὺς ποιεῖν.

19 Πᾶν δένδρον μὴ ποιοῦν καρπὸν καλὸν, ἐκκόπτεται, κỳ εἰς πῦρ βάλλεται.

20 Ἄραγε ἀπὸ τῶν καρπῶν αὐτῶν ἐπιγνώσεσθε αὐτούς.

35 Ὁ ἀγαθὸς ἄνθρωπ⊙ ἐκ τῦ ἀγαθῦ θησαυρῦ τῆς καρδίας ἐκϐάλλει τὰ ἀγαθά· κỳ ὁ πονηρὸς ἄνθρωπ⊙ ἐκ τῦ πονηρῦ θησαυρῦ ἐκϐάλλει πονηρά.

36 Λέγω δὲ ὑμῖν, ὅτι πᾶν ῥῆμα ἀργὸν, ὃ ἐὰν λαλήσωσιν οἱ ἄνθρωποί, ἀποδώσουσι περὶ αὐτῦ λόγον ἐν ἡμέρᾳ κρίσεως.

37 Ἐκ γὰρ τῶν λόγων σε δικαιωθήσῃ, κỳ τ λόγων σε καταδικασθήσῃ.

24 Πᾶς οὖν ὅςις ἀκούει μου τοὺς λόγους τούτους, κỳ ποιεῖ αὐτοὺς, ὁμοιώσω αὐτὸν ἀνδρὶ φρονίμῳ, ὅςις ᾠκοδόμησε τὴν οἰκίαν αὐτῦ ἐπὶ τὴν πέτραν·

25 Καὶ κατέϐη ἡ βροχὴ, κỳ ἦλθον οἱ ποταμοὶ, κỳ ἔπνευσαν οἱ ἄνεμοι, κỳ προσέπεσον τῇ οἰκίᾳ ἐκείνῃ, κỳ οὐκ ἔπεσε· τεθεμελίωτο γὰρ ἐπὶ τὴν πέτραν.

---

13 Intrate per angustam portam, quia lata porta & spatiosa via ducens ad perditionem, & multi sunt ingredientes per eam.

14 Quia angusta porta, & stricta via ducens ad vitam, & pauci sunt invenientes eam.

15 Attendite verò à falsis prophetis, quia veniunt ad vos in indumentis ovium, intrinsecùs autem sunt lupi rapaces.

16 A fructibus eorum agnoscetis eos. Nunquid colligunt à spinis uvam, aut de tribulis ficum?

17 Sic omnis arbor bona fructus bonos facit: at cariosa arbor fructus malos facit.

18 Non potest arbor bona fructus malos facere, neque arbor cariosa fructus pulchros facere.

19 Omnis arbor non faciens fructum pulchrum, exscinditur, & in ignem injicitur.

20 Itaque ex fructibus eorum agnoscetis eos.

35 Bonus homo de bono thesauro cordis ejicit bona: & malus homo de malo thesauro ejicit mala.

36 Dico autem vobis, quòd omne verbum otiosum quod loquuti fuerint homines, reddent de eo rationem in die judicii.

37 Ex enim verbis tuis justificaberis, & ex verbis tuis condemnaberis.

24 Omnis ergo quicunque audit mea verba hæc, & facit ea, assimilabo illum viro prudenti, qui ædificavit domum suam super petram.

25 Et descendit pluvia & venerunt flumina & flaverunt venti, & procuberunt domui illi, & non cecidit: fundata erat enim super petram.

13 Enter ye in at the strait gate; for wide is the gate, and broad is the way, that leadeth to destruction, and many there be which go in thereat:

14 Because strait is the gate, and narrow is the way, which leadeth unto life, and few there be that find it.

15 Beware of false prophets, which come to you in sheep's clothing, but inwardly they are ravening wolves.

16 Ye shall know them by their fruits. Do men gather grapes of thorns, or figs of thistles?

17 Even so, every good tree bringeth forth good fruit; but a corrupt tree bringeth forth evil fruit.

18 A good tree cannot bring forth evil fruit, neither can a corrupt tree bring forth good fruit.

19 Every tree that bringeth not forth good fruit is hewn down, and cast into the fire.

20 Wherefore by their fruits ye shall know them.

35 A good man, out of the good treasure of the heart, bringeth forth good things: and an evil man, out of the evil treasure, bringeth forth evil things.

36 But I say unto you, That every idle word that men shall speak, they shall give account thereof in the day of judgment.

37 For by thy words thou shalt be justified, and by thy words thou shalt be condemned.

24 Therefore whosoever heareth these sayings of mine, and doeth them, I will liken him unto a wise man, which built his house upon a rock:

25 And the rain descended, and the floods came, and the winds blew, and beat upon that house; and it fell not: for it was founded upon a rock.

---

13. Entrez par la porte étroite ; car la porte large et le chemin spacieux mènent à la perdition, et il y en a beaucoup qui y entrent.

14. Mais la porte étroite, et le chemin étroit mènent à la vie, et il y en a peu qui le trouvent.

15. Gardez-vous des faux Prophètes, qui viennent à vous en habits de brebis, mais qui au dedans sont des loups ravissans.

16. Vous les reconnoitrez à leurs fruits : Cueille-t-on des raisins sur des épines, ou des figues sur des chardons ?

17. Ainsi tout arbre qui est bon porte de bons fruits ; mais un mauvais arbre porte de mauvais fruits.

18. Un bon arbre ne peut porter de mauvais fruits, ni un mauvais arbre porter de bons fruits.

19. Tout arbre qui ne porte point de bons fruits, est coupé et jeté au feu.

20. Vous les connoitrez donc à leurs fruits.

21. Ceux qui me disent : Seigneur, Seigneur, n'entreront pas tous au Royaume des cieux ; mais celui-là seulement qui fait la volonté de mon Père qui est dans les cieux.

22. Plusieurs me diront en ce jour-ci : Seigneur, Seigneur, n'avons-nous pas prophétisé en ton nom ? N'avons-nous pas chassé les Démons en ton nom ? Et n'avons-nous pas fait plusieurs miracles en ton nom ?

23. Alors, je leur dirai ouvertement : Je ne vous ai jamais connus : Retirez-vous de moi, vous qui faites métier d'iniquité.

24. Quiconque donc entend ces paroles que je dis, et les met en pratique, je le comparerai à un homme prudent, qui a bâti sa maison sur le roc.

25. Et la pluie est tombée, les torrens se sont débordés, et les vents ont soufflé, et sont venus fondre sur cette maison-là ; elle n'est point tombée, car elle étoit fondée sur le roc.

26 Καὶ πᾶς ὁ ἀκούων μου τοὺς λόγους τούτους, ᾗ μὴ ποιῶν αὐτοὺς ὁμοιωθήσεται ἀνδρὶ μωρῷ, ὅ-τις ᾠκοδόμησε τὴν οἰκίαν αὐτοῦ ἐπὶ τὴν ἄμμον·

‡ 27 Καὶ ‡ κατέβη ἡ ‡ βροχὴ, ᾗ ἦλθον οἱ ποταμοὶ, ᾗ ‡ ἔπνευσαν οἱ ‡ ἄνεμοι, ᾗ ‡ προσέκοψαν τῇ ‡ οἰκίᾳ ἐκείνῃ ᾗ ἔπεσε, ᾗ ἦν ἡ ‡ πτῶσις αὐτῆς μεγάλη.

28 Καὶ ἐγένετο ὅτε συνετέλεσεν ὁ Ἰησοῦς τοὺς λόγους τούτους, ἐξεπλήσσοντο οἱ ὄχλοι ἐπὶ τῇ διδαχῇ αὐτοῦ·

29 Ἦν γὰρ διδάσκων αὐτοὺς ὡς ἐξουσίαν ἔχων, ᾗ οὐχ ὡς οἱ γραμματεῖς. 22. † 2.

Κεφ. ή. 8.

1 ΚΑΤΑΒΑΝΤΙ δὲ αὐτῷ ἀπὸ τοῦ ὄρους, ἠκολούθησαν αὐτῷ ὄχλοι πολλοί.

Καὶ περιῆγε τὰς κώμας κύκλῳ, διδάσκων.

28 Δεῦτε πρός με πάντες οἱ κοπιῶντες ᾗ πεφορτισμένοι, κἀγὼ ἀναπαύσω ὑμᾶς.

‡ 29 ‡ Ἄρατε τὸν ‡ ζυγόν με ἐφ' ὑμᾶς, ᾗ ‡ μάθετε ἀπ' ἐμοῦ, ὅτι † πρᾶός ‡ εἰμι, ᾗ ‡ ταπεινὸς τῇ καρδίᾳ ᾗ εὑρήσετε ‡ ἀνάπαυσιν ταῖς ‡ ψυχαῖς ὑμῶν.

30 Ὁ γὰρ ζυγός με χρηςὸς, ᾗ τὸ φορτίον με ἐλαφρόν ἐςιν. 20. † 2.

36 Ἠρώτα δὲ τις αὐτὸν τῶν Φαρισαίων ἵνα φάγῃ μετ' αὐτῷ ᾗ εἰσελθὼν εἰς τὴν οἰκίαν τῷ Φαρισαίῳ, ἀνεκλίθη.

37 Καὶ ἰδὰ, γυνὴ ἐν τῇ πόλει, ἥτις ἦν ἁμαρθωλὸς, ἐπιγνῦσα ὅτι ἀνάκειλαι ἐν τῇ οἰκίᾳ τῷ Φαρισαίῳ, κομίσασα ἀλάβαςρον μύρᾳ,

38 Καὶ ςᾶσα παρὰ τὰς πόδας αὐτῷ ὀπίσω, κλαίῃσα, ἤρξαλο βρέχειν τὰς πόδας αὐτῷ τοῖς δάκρυσι ᾗ ταῖς θριξὶ τῆς κεφαλῆς αὐτῆς ἐξέμασσε, ᾗ κατεφίλει τὰς πόδας αὐτῷ, ᾗ ἤλειφε τῷ μύρᾳ.

---

26 Et omnis audiens mea verba hæc, & non faciens ea, affimilabitur viro ftulto, qui ædificavit domum fuam fuper arenam:

27 Et defcendit pluvia, & venerunt flamina, & flaverunt venti, & proruerant domui illi, & cecidit, & fuit cafus illius magnus.

28 Et factum eft, quum confummaffet Jefus fermones hos, ftupebant illum turbæ fuper doctrina ejus.

29 Erat enim docens eos ut auctoritatem habens, & non ficut Scribæ.

CAPUT VIII.

1 DEfcendente autem eo de monte, fecutæ funt eum turbæ multæ.

& circuibat vicos in orbem, docens.

28 Venite ad me omnes laborantes, & onerati, & ego recreabo vos.

29 Tollite jugum meum fuper vos, & difcite à me, quia mitis fum, & humilis corde: & invenietis requiem animabus veftris.

30 Nam jugum meum blandum, & onus meum leve eft.

36 Rogabat autem quidam illum Pharifæorum, ut manducaret cum illo: Et ingreffus in domum Pharifæi, difcubuit.

37 Et ecce mulier in civitate, quæ erat peccatrix, cognofcens quod accubuit in domo Pharifæi, afferens alabaftrum unguenti:

38 Et ftans fecus pedes ejus retro, flens, cœpit rigare pedes ejus lachrymis, & capillis capitis fui extergebat, & ofculabatur pedes ejus, & ungebat unguento.

26. Mais quiconque entend ces paroles que je dis, et ne les met pas en pratique, sera comparé à un homme insensé, qui a bâti sa maison sur le sable.

27. Et la pluie est tombée, les torrens se sont débordés, et les vents ont soufflé, et sont venus fondre sur cette maison-là; elle *est* tombée, et sa ruine a été grande.

28. Et quand JESUS eut achevé ces discours, le peuple fut étonné de sa doctrine.

29. Car il les enseignoit comme ayant autorité, et non pas comme les Scribes.

QUAND *Jésus* fut descendu de la montagne; une grande multitude de peuple le suivit,

et il parcourut les bourgades des environs, en enseignant.

28. Venez à moi, vous tous qui êtes travaillés et chargés, et je vous soulagerai.

29. Chargez-vous de mon joug, et apprenez de moi, que je suis doux et humble de cœur, et vous trouverez le repos de vos âmes;

30. Car mon joug est aisé, et mon fardeau est léger.

36. Un Pharisien ayant prié *Jésus* de manger chez lui, il entra dans la maison du Pharisien, et il se mit à table.

37. Et une femme de la ville, qui avoit été de mauvaise vie, ayant su qu'il étoit à table dans la maison du Pharisien, elle y apporta un vase d'albâtre plein d'une huile odoriférante.

38. Et se tenant derrière, aux pieds de *Jésus*, elle se mit à pleurer; elle lui arrosoit les pieds de ses larmes, et les essuyoit avec ses cheveux; elle lui baisoit les pieds, et elle les oignoit avec cette huile.

26 And every one that heareth *Mt. 7.* these sayings of mine, and doeth them not, shall be likened unto a foolish man, which built his house upon the sand:

27 And the rain descended, and the floods came, and the winds blew, and beat upon that house; and it fell, and great was the fall of it.

28 And it came to pass when Jesus had ended these sayings, the people were astonished at his doctrine:

29 For he taught them as *one* having authority, and not as the scribes.

WHEN he was come down *Mt. 8.* from the mountain, great multitudes followed him.

6. And he went round *Mk. 6.* about the villages, teaching.

28 Come unto me, all *ye* that la-*Mt. 11.* bour and are heavy laden, and I will give you rest.

29 Take my yoke upon you, and learn of me; for I am meek and lowly in heart: and ye shall find rest unto your souls.

30 For my yoke *is* easy, and my burden is light.

36 And one of the Pharisees de-*L. 7.* sired him that he would eat with him. And he went into the Pharisee's house, and sat down to meat.

37 And, behold, a woman in the city, which was a sinner, when she knew that *Jesus* sat at meat in the Pharisee's house, brought an alabaster box of ointment,

38 And stood at his feet behind *him* weeping, and began to wash his feet with tears, and did wipe *them* with the hairs of her head, and kissed his feet, and anointed *them* with the ointment.

39 Ἰδὼν δὲ ὁ Φαρισαῖος ὁ καλέσας αὐτὸν, εἶπεν ἐν ἑαυτῷ, λέγων· Οὗτος, εἰ ἦν προφήτης, ἐγίνωσκεν ἂν τίς ἡ ποταπὴ ἡ γυνὴ ἥτις ἅπτεται αὐτοῦ ὅτι ἁμαρτωλός ἐςι.

40 Καὶ ἀποκριθεὶς ὁ Ἰησοῦς, εἶπε πρὸς αὐτόν· Σίμων, ἔχω σοι τι εἰπεῖν. Ὁ δὲ φησι· Διδάσκαλε, εἰπέ.

* 41 Δύο ‡ χρεωφειλέται ἦσαν † δανειςῇ τινι· ὁ εἷς ‡ ὤφειλε δηνάρια ‡ πενλακόσια, ὁ δὲ ‡ ἕτερος· ‡ πεντήκονλα.

42 Μὴ ἐχόντων δὲ αὐτῶν ἀποδοῦναι, ἀμφοτέροις ἐχαρίσατο· Τίς οὖν αὐτῶν, εἰπὲ, πλεῖον αὐτὸν ἀγαπήσει;

43 Ἀποκριθεὶς δὲ ὁ Σίμων, εἶπεν· Ὑπολαμβάνω ὅτι ᾧ τὸ πλεῖον ἐχαρίσατο. Ὁ δὲ εἶπεν αὐτῷ· Ὀρθῶς ἔκρινας.

44 Καὶ ςραφεὶς πρὸς τὴν γυναῖκα, τῷ Σίμωνι ἔφη· Βλέπεις ταύτην τὴν γυναῖκα; εἰσῆλθόν σου εἰς τὴν οἰκίαν, ὕδωρ ἐπὶ τὰς πόδας μου οὐκ ἔδωκας· αὕτη δὲ τοῖς δάκρυσιν ἔβρεξέ μου τὰς πόδας, καὶ ταῖς θριξὶ τῆς κεφαλῆς αὐτῆς ἐξέμαξε.

* 45 ‡ Φίλημά μοι οὐκ ἔδωκας· αὕτη δὲ, ἀφ' ἧς εἰσῆλθον, ὐ † διέλιπε ‡ καλαφιλοῦσά μου τὰς ‡ πόδας.

46 Ἐλαίῳ τὴν κεφαλήν μου οὐκ ἤλειψας· αὕτη δὲ μύρῳ ἤλειψέ μου τοὺς πόδας.

31 Ἔρχονλαι οὖν οἱ ἀδελφοὶ καὶ ἡ μήτηρ αὐτοῦ καὶ ἔξω ἑςῶτες ἀπέςειλαν πρὸς αὐτὸν, φωνοῦνλες αὐτόν.

32 Καὶ ἐκάθηλο ὄχλος περὶ αὐτόν· εἶπον δὲ αὐτῷ· Ἰδοὺ, ἡ μήτηρ σου καὶ οἱ ἀδελφοί σου ἔξω ζητοῦσί σε.

33 Καὶ ἀπεκρίθη αὐτοῖς, λέγων· Τίς ἐςιν ἡ μήτηρ μου, ἢ οἱ ἀδελφοί μου;

34 Καὶ περιϐλεψάμενος κύκλῳ τὸς περὶ αὐτὸν καθημένους, λέγει· Ἴδε ἡ μήτηρ μου καὶ οἱ ἀδελφοί μου.

35 Ὃς γὰρ ἂν ποιήσῃ τὸ θέλημα τοῦ Θεοῦ, οὗτος ἀδελφός μου καὶ ἀδελφή μου καὶ μήτηρ ἐςί. 4. †. 1.

---

39 Videns autem Pharisæus vocans eum, ait in seipso, dicens: Hic si esset Propheta, sciret utique quæ & qualis mulier, quæ tangit eum, quia peccatrix est.

40 Et respondens Jesus, dixit ad illum: Simon, habeo tibi aliquid dicere. Is vero ait: Magister, dic.

41 Duo debitores erant fœneratori cuidam: unus debebat denarios quingentos, at alter quinquaginta.

42 Non habentibus autem illis reddere, ambobus donavit: Quis ergo eorum, dic, plus eum diliget?

43 Respondens autem Simon, dixit: subsumo quod cui plus donavit. Ille autem dixit ei: Recte judicasti.

44 Et conversus ad mulierem, Simoni dixit: Vides hanc mulierem? Intravi tuam in domum, aquam ad pedes meos non dedisti: hæc autem lacrymis rigavit meos pedes, & capillis capitis sui extersit.

45 Osculum mihi non dedisti: hæc autem, ex quo intravi, non cessavit osculans meos pedes.

46 Oleo caput meum non unxisti: hæc autem unguento unxit meos pedes.

31 Veniunt igitur fratres & mater ejus: & foris stantes, miserunt ad eum, vocantes eum.

32 Et sedebat turba circum eum: dicebant verò ei: Ecce mater tua, & fratres tui, foris quærunt te.

33 Et respondit eis, dicens: Quæ est mater mea, aut fratres mei?

34 Et circumspiciens circulo circa se sedentes, ait: Ecce mater mea, & fratres mei.

35 Qui enim fecerit voluntatem Dei, hic frater meus, & soror mea, & mater est.

39. Le Pharisien qui l'avoit convié, voyant cela, dit en lui-même : Si cet homme étoit Prophète, il sauroit sans doute qui est cette femme qui le touche, et qu'elle est de mauvaise vie.

40. Alors Jésus prenant la parole, lui dit : Simon, j'ai quelque chose à te dire : et il dit : Maître, dis-la.

41. Un créancier avoit deux débiteurs, *dont* l'un lui devoit cinq cents deniers, et l'autre cinquante.

42. Et comme ils n'avoient pas de quoi payer, il leur quitta à tous deux leur dette. Dis-moi donc lequel des deux l'aimera le plus ?

43. Simon lui répondit : J'estime que c'est celui à qui il a le plus quitté. *Jésus* lui dit : Tu as fort bien jugé.

44. Alors se tournant vers la femme, il dit à Simon : Vois-tu cette femme ? Je suis entré dans ta maison, et tu ne m'as point donné d'eau pour *me laver* les pieds ; mais elle a arrosé mes pieds de larmes, et les a essuyés avec ses cheveux.

45. Tu ne m'as point donné de baiser ; mais elle, depuis qu'elle est entrée, n'a cessé de me baiser les pieds.

46. Tu n'as point oint ma tête d'huile ; mais elle a oint mes pieds d'une huile odoriférante.

31. Ses frères et sa mère arrivèrent donc ; et se tenant dehors, ils l'envoyèrent appeler ; et la multitude étoit assise autour de lui.

32. Et on lui dit : Voilà ta mère et tes frères sont là dehors *qui* te demandent.

33. Mais il répondit : Qui est ma mère, ou qui sont mes frères ?

34. En jetant les yeux sur ceux qui étoient autour de lui, il dit : Voilà ma mère et mes frères.

35. Car, quiconque fera la volonté de Dieu, celui-là est mon frère, et ma sœur, et ma mère.

Κεφ. ιβʹ. ιζ. | CAPUT XII.

1 ἘΝ οἷς ἐπισυναχθεισῶν τῶν μυριάδων τῦ ὄχλυ, ὥϛε καταπατεῖν ἀλλήλυς, ἤρξατο λέγειν πρὸς τὲς μαθητὰς αὐτᾶ· Πρῶτον προσέχετε ἑαυτοῖς ἀπὸ τῆς ζύμης τῶν φαρισαίων, ἥτις ἐϛὶν ὑπόκρισις.

* 2 Οὐδὲν δὲ † συγκεκαλυμμένον ἐϛὶν ὃ οὐκ ἀποκαλυφθήσεται· καὶ κρυπτὸν, ὃ οὐ γνωσθήσεται.

3 Ἀνθʼ ὧν ὅσα ἐν τῇ σκοτίᾳ εἴπατε, ἐν τῷ φωτὶ ἀκυσθήσεται· καὶ ὃ πρὸς τὸ ἒς ἐλαλήσατε ἐν τοῖς ταμείοις, κηρυχθήσεται ἐπὶ τῶν δωμάτων.

4 Λέγω δὲ ὑμῖν τοῖς φίλοις μυ· Μὴ φοβηθῆτε ἀπὸ τῶν ἀποκτεινόντων τὸ σῶμα, καὶ μετὰ ταῦτα μὴ ἐχόντων περισσότερόν τι ποιῆσαι.

* 5 ‡ Ὑποδείξω δὲ ὑμῖν τίνα ‡ φοβηθῆτε· φοβήθητε τὸν μετὰ τὸ ‡ ἀποκτεῖναι, ‡ ἐξυσίαν ἔχοντα † ἐμβαλεῖν εἰς τὴν γέενναν· ναὶ λέγω ὑμῖν, τῦτον φοβήθητε.

6 Οὐχὶ πέντε ϛρυθία πωλεῖται ἀσσαρίων δύο, καὶ ἓν ἐξ αὐτῶν οὐκ ἔϛιν ἐπιλελησμένον ἐνώπιον τῦ Θεῦ;

* 7 Ἀλλὰ καὶ αἱ ‡ τρίχες τῆς κεφαλῆς ὑμῶν πᾶσαι ‡ ἠρίθμηνται· μὴ ἂν φοβεῖσθε· πολλῶν ϛρυθίων † διαφέρετε.

13 Εἶπε δὲ τις αὐτῷ ἐκ τοῦ ὄχλυ· Διδάσκαλε, εἰπὲ τῷ ἀδελφῷ μυ μερίσασθαι μετʼ ἐμῦ τὴν κληρονομίαν.

* 14 Ὁ δὲ εἶπεν αὐτῷ· Ἄνθρωπε, τίς με ‡ κατέϛησε ‡ δικαϛὴν ἢ † μεριϛὴν ἐφʼ ὑμᾶς;

15 Εἶπε δὲ πρὸς αὐτύς· Ὁρᾶτε καὶ φυλάσσεσθε ἀπὸ τῆς πλεονεξίας· ὅτι οὐκ ἐν τῷ περισσεύειν τινὶ ἡ ζωὴ αὐτῦ ἐϛιν ἐκ τῶν ὑπαρχόντων αὐτῦ.

* 16 Εἶπε δὲ παραβολὴν πρὸς αὐτύς, λέγων· Ἀνθρώπυ τινὸς πλυσίυ † εὐφόρησεν ἡ χώρα·

CAPUT XII.

1 IN quibus adcongregatis myriadibus turbæ, ut conculcarent alii alios, cœpit dicere ad discipulos suos primum: Attendite vobis-ipsis à fermento Pharisæorum, quod est hypocrisis.

2 Nihil enim coopertum est, quod non reveletur: & absconditum, quod non sciatur.

3 Propter quæ quæ in tenebris dixistis, in lumine audientur: & quod ad aurem loquuti estis in cubiculis, prædicabitur supra domos.

4 Dico autem vobis amicis meis: Ne timeatis ab occidentibus corpus, & post hæc non habentibus abundantiùs quid facere.

5 Ostendam autem vobis quem timeatis: timete illum post occidere, auctoritatem habentem injicere in gehennam: ita dico vobis, hunc timete.

6 Nonne quinque passeres væneunt assariis duobus, & unus ex illis non est in oblivione coram Deo.

7 Sed & capilli capitis vestri omnes numerati sunt, ne ergo timete: multis passeribus præstatis vos.

13 Ait autem quidam ei de turba: Magister, dic fratri meo partiri cum me hæreditatem.

14 Ille autem dixit ei: Homo, Quis me constituit judicem aut divisorem super vos?

15 Dixit autem ad illos: Videte & cavete ab avaritia: quia non in redundare cuiquam vita ejus est ex substantia ipsius.

16 Dixit autem similitudinem ad illos, dicens: Hominis cujusdam divitis bene tulit regio.

CHAPITRE XII.

Jésus - Christ instruit ses Disciples de se garder d'hypocrisie, de l'avarice; de veiller et d'être prêts à la réconciliation.

CEPENDANT le peuple s'étant assemblé par milliers; en sorte qu'ils se pressoient les uns les autres, il se mit à dire à ses Disciples: Gardez-vous sur toutes choses du levain des Pharisiens, qui est l'hypocrisie.

2. Car il n'y a rien de caché qui ne doive être découvert; ni rien de secret qui ne doive être connu.

3. Les choses donc que vous aurez dites dans les ténèbres, seront entendues dans la lumière; et ce que vous aurez dit à l'oreille dans les chambres, sera prêché sur les maisons.

4. Je vous dis donc, à vous qui êtes mes amis: Ne craignez point ceux qui tuent le corps, et qui après cela ne peuvent rien faire de plus.

5. Mais je vous montrerai qui vous devez craindre; craignez celui qui, après avoir ôté la vie, a le pouvoir d'envoyer dans la géhenne; oui, je vous le dis; c'est celui-là que vous devez craindre!

6. Ne vend-on pas cinq petits passereaux deux pites? Cependant Dieu n'en oublie pas un seul.

7. Et même tous les cheveux de votre tête sont comptés, ne craignez donc point, vous valez plus que beaucoup de passereaux.

13. Alors quelqu'un de la troupe lui dit: Maître, dis à mon frère qu'il partage avec moi notre héritage.

14. Mais *Jésus* lui *répondit:* O homme! qui est-ce qui m'a établi pour être votre Juge, ou pour faire vos partages?

15. Puis il leur dit: Gardez-vous avec soin de l'avarice; car quoique *les biens* abondent à quelqu'un, il n'a pas la vie par ses biens.

16. Il leur proposa *là-dessus* cette parabole: Les terres d'un homme riche avoient rapporté avec abondance;

IN the mean time, when there were gathered together an innumerable multitude of people, insomuch that they trode one upon another, he began to say unto his disciples first of all, Beware ye of the leaven of the Pharisees, which is hypocrisy.

2 For there is nothing covered, that shall not be revealed; neither hid, that shall not be known.

3 Therefore whatsoever ye have spoken in darkness, shall be heard in the light; and that which ye have spoken in the ear in closets, shall be proclaimed upon the house-tops.

4 And I say unto you, my friends, Be not afraid of them that kill the body, and after that have no more that they can do.

5 But I will forewarn you whom ye shall fear: Fear him, which, after he hath killed, hath power to cast into hell; yea, I say unto you, Fear him.

6 Are not five sparrows sold for two farthings? and not one of them is forgotten before God.

7 But even the very hairs of your head are all numbered. Fear not, therefore; ye are of more value than many sparrows.

13 And one of the company said unto him, Master, speak to my brother, that he divide the inheritance with me.

14 And he said unto him, Man, who made me a judge, or a divider over you?

15 And he said unto them, Take heed, and beware of covetousness; for a man's life consisteth not in the abundance of the things which he possesseth.

16 And he spake a parable unto them, saying, The ground of a certain rich man brought forth plentifully.

17 Καὶ διελογίζετο ἐν ἑαυτῷ,
λέγων· Τί ποιήσω; ὅτι οὐκ ἔχω
ποῦ συνάξω τοὺς καρπούς μου.

18 Καὶ εἶπε· Τοῦτο ποιήσω·
καθελῶ μου τὰς ἀποθήκας, καὶ μεί-
ζονας οἰκοδομήσω· καὶ συνάξω ἐκεῖ
πάντα τὰ γεννήματά μου, καὶ τὰ
ἀγαθά μου.

19 Καὶ ἐρῶ τῇ ψυχῇ μου·
Ψυχή, ἔχεις πολλὰ ἀγαθὰ κεί-
μενα εἰς ἔτη πολλά· ἀναπαύου,
φάγε, πίε, εὐφραίνου.

* 20 Εἶπε δὲ αὐτῷ ὁ Θεός·
‡ Ἄφρον, ταύτῃ τῇ νυκτὶ τὴν ψυ-
χήν σου ‡ ἀπαιτοῦσιν ἀπὸ σοῦ· ἃ δὲ
ἡτοίμασας, τίνι ἔσται;

21 Οὕτως ὁ θησαυρίζων ἑαυτῷ,
καὶ μὴ εἰς Θεὸν πλουτῶν.

22 Εἶπε δὲ πρὸς τοὺς μαθητὰς
αὐτοῦ· Διὰ τοῦτο ὑμῖν λέγω, μὴ
μεριμνᾶτε τῇ ψυχῇ ὑμῶν, τί
φάγητε· μηδὲ τῷ σώματι, τί ἐν-
δύσησθε.

23 Ἡ ψυχὴ πλεῖόν ἐστι τῆς
τροφῆς, καὶ τὸ σῶμα, τοῦ ἐνδύμα-
τος.

* 24 ‡ Κατανοήσατε τοὺς † κό-
ρακας, ὅτι οὐ ‡ σπείρουσιν, οὐδὲ
‡ θερίζουσιν· οἷς οὐκ ἔστι ‡ ταμεῖον,
οὐδὲ ἀποθήκη, καὶ ὁ Θεὸς τρέφει αὐ-
τούς· πόσῳ μᾶλλον ὑμεῖς διαφέρετε τῶν πετεινῶν;

25 Τίς δὲ ἐξ ὑμῶν μεριμνῶν
δύναται προσθεῖναι ἐπὶ τὴν ἡλικίαν αὐτοῦ πῆχυν ἕνα;

26 Εἰ οὖν οὔτε ἐλάχιστον δύνασθε, τί περὶ τῶν λοιπῶν μεριμνᾶτε;

27 Κατανοήσατε τὰ κρίνα, πῶς
αὐξάνει· οὐ κοπιᾷ, οὐδὲ νήθει· λέγω δὲ ὑμῖν, οὐδὲ Σολομὼν ἐν
πάσῃ τῇ δόξῃ αὐτοῦ περιεβάλετο
ὡς ἓν τούτων.

28 Εἰ δὲ τὸν χόρτον ἐν τῷ
ἀγρῷ σήμερον ὄντα, καὶ αὔριον εἰς
κλίβανον βαλλόμενον, ὁ Θεὸς οὕτως
ἀμφιέννυσι, πόσῳ μᾶλλον ὑμᾶς,
ὀλιγόπιστοι;

* 29 Καὶ ὑμεῖς μὴ ζητεῖτε τί
φάγητε, ἢ τί πίητε, καὶ μὴ † με-
τεωρίζεσθε.

30 Ταῦτα γὰρ πάντα, τὰ ἔθνη
τοῦ κόσμου ἐπιζητεῖ· ὑμῶν δὲ ὁ
πατήρ οἶδεν ὅτι χρῄζετε τούτων.

---

17 Et ratiocinabatur in seipso, dicens: Quid faciam? quia
non habeo quo congregabo fructus meos?

18 Et dixit: Hoc faciam:
Destruam mea horrea, & majora
ædificabo, & congregabo illuc
omnia nata mea, & bona mea.

19 Et dicam animæ meæ:
Anima, habes multa bona posita in annos plurimos, requiesce,
comede, bibe, oblectare.

20 Dixit autem illi Deus:
Stulte, hac nocte animam tuam
repetunt à te: quæ autem pa-
rasti, cui erunt?

21 Sic thesaurizans sibi ipsi,
& non in Deum ditescens.

22 Dixit autem ad discipulos
suos: Propter hoc vobis dico:
Ne soliciti sitis animæ vestræ,
quid manducetis, neque corpori, quid induamini.

23 Anima plus est alimento,
& corpus, vestimento.

24 Considerate corvos, quia
non seminant, neque metunt,
quibus non est cellarium, neque horreum, & Deus alit illos:
quanto magis vos præstatis vo-
lucribus?

25 Quis autem ex vobis co-
gitans solicitè potest apponere ad
ætatem suam cubitum unum?

26 Si ergo neque minimum
potestis, quid de cæteris soliciti
estis.

27 Considerate lilia, quomodo
crescunt: non laborant, neque
nent: Dico autem vobis, Neque
Solomon in omni gloria sua
circumamiciebatur sicut unum
istorum.

28 Si autem fœnum in agro
hodie existens, & cras in clibanum missum, Deus sic circuma-
micit, quanto magis vos exiguæ
fidei?

29 Et vos ne quærite quid
manducetis, aut quid bibatis,
& ne suspendamini ex sublimi.

30 Hæc enim omnia gentes
mundi quærunt: vester autem
pater scit quoniam indigetis his.

17. Et il disoit en lui-même : Que ferai-je ? Car je n'ai pas assez de place pour serrer toute ma récolte.

18. Voici, dit-il, ce que je ferai ; j'abattrai mes greniers, et j'en bâtirai de plus grands, et j'y amasserai toute ma récolte et tous mes biens.

19. Puis je dirai à mon ame : Mon ame, tu as beaucoup de biens en réserve pour plusieurs années ; repose-toi, mange, bois, et te réjouis.

20. Mais Dieu lui dit : Insensé, cette même nuit ton ame te sera redemandée ; et ce que tu as amasse, pour qui sera-t-il ?

21. Il en est ainsi de celui qui amasse des biens pour soi-même, et qui n'est point riche en Dieu.

22. Alors il dit à ses Disciples : C'est pourquoi je vous dis, ne soyez point en souci pour votre vie, de ce que vous mangerez ; ni pour votre corps, de quoi vous serez vêtus.

23. La vie est plus que la nourriture, et le corps plus que le vêtement.

24. Considérez les corbeaux ; ils ne sèment ni ne moissonnent, et ils n'ont point de cellier ni de grenier, et *toutefois* Dieu les nourrit ; combien ne valez-vous pas plus que des oiseaux ?

25. Et qui de vous peut par ses inquiétudes ajouter une coudée à sa taille ?

26. Si donc vous ne pouvez pas même faire les plus petites choses, pourquoi vous inquiétez-vous du reste ?

27. Considérez comment les lis croissent ; ils ne travaillent ni ne filent ; cependant je vous dis, que Salomon même, dans toute sa gloire, n'a point été vêtu comme l'un d'eux.

28. Que si Dieu revêt ainsi une herbe qui est aujourd'hui dans les champs, et qui sera demain jetée dans le four, combien plus vous *revêtira-t-il*, gens de petite foi ?

29. Ne vous mettez donc point en peine de ce que vous mangerez, ou de ce que vous boirez, et n'ayez point l'esprit inquiet.

30. Car ce sont les nations du monde qui recherchent toutes ces choses ; mais votre Père sait que vous en avez besoin.

17 And he thought within himself, saying, What shall I do, because I have no room where to bestow my fruits?

18 And he said, This will I do: I will pull down my barns, and build greater; and there will I bestow all my fruits and my goods.

19 And I will say to my soul, Soul, thou hast much goods laid up for many years: take thine ease, eat, drink, *and* be merry.

20 But God said unto him, *Thou* fool! this night thy soul shall be required of thee; then whose shall those things be, which thou hast provided?

21 So *is* he that layeth up treasure for himself, and is not rich toward God.

22 And he said unto his disciples, Therefore I say unto you, Take no thought for your life, what ye shall eat; neither for the body, what ye shall put on.

23 The life is more than meat, and the body *is more* than raiment.

24 Consider the ravens: for they neither sow nor reap; which neither have storehouse nor barn; and God feedeth them: How much more are ye better than the fowls?

25 And which of you, with taking thought, can add to his stature one cubit?

26 If ye then be not able to do that thing which is least, why take ye thought for the rest?

27 Consider the lilies how they grow: they toil not, they spin not; and yet I say unto you, That Solomon, in all his glory, was not arrayed like one of these.

28 If then God so clothe the grass, which is to-day in the field, and to-morrow is cast into the oven; how much more *will he clothe* you? O ye of little faith!

29 And seek not ye what ye shall eat, or what ye shall drink; neither be ye of doubtful mind.

30 For all these things do the nations of the world seek after: and your Father knoweth that ye have need of these things.

31 Πλὴν ζητεῖτε τὴν βασιλείαν τοῦ Θεοῦ, κ̀ ταῦτα πάντα προςτεθήσεται ὑμῖν.

31 Verumtamen quærite regnum Dei, & hæc omnia adjicientur vobis.

32 Μὴ φοβοῦ, τὸ μικρὸν ποίμνιον· ὅτι εὐδόκησεν ὁ πατὴρ ὑμῶν δοῦναι ὑμῖν τὴν βασιλείαν.

32 Ne time, pusillus grex, quia bene visum est Patri vestro dare vobis regnum.

* 33 Πωλήσατε τὰ ὑπάρχοντα ὑμῶν, κ̀ δότε ἐλεημοσύνην. Ποιήσατε ἑαυτοῖς ‡ βαλάντια μὴ ‡ παλαιούμενα, θησαυρὸν † ἀνέκλειπτον ἐν τοῖς οὐρανοῖς ὅπου κλέπτης οὐκ ἐγγίζει, οὐδὲ σὴς διαφθείρει.

33 Vendite substantias vestras, & date eleëmosynam, facite vobis crumenas non veterascentes, thesaurum non deficientem in cælis, quo fur non appropriat, neque tinea corrumpit.

34 Ὅπου γάρ ἐστιν ὁ θησαυρὸς ὑμῶν, ἐκεῖ κ̀ ἡ καρδία ὑμῶν ἔσται.

34 Ubi enim est thesaurus vester, ibi & cor vestrum erit.

35 Ἔστωσαν ὑμῶν αἱ ὀσφύες περιεζωσμέναι, κ̀ οἱ λύχνοι καιόμενοι.

35 Sint vestri lumbi præcincti, & lucernæ accensæ:

36 Καὶ ὑμεῖς ὅμοιοι ἀνθρώποις προσδεχομένοις τὸν κύριον ἑαυτῶν, πότε ἀναλύσει ἐκ τῶν γάμων· ἵνα ἐλθόντος κ̀ κρούσαντος, εὐθέως ἀνοίξωσιν αὐτῷ.

36 Et vos similes hominibus expectantibus dominum suum, quando revertatur a nuptiis: ut veniente & pulsante, confestim aperiant ei.

37 Μακάριοι οἱ δοῦλοι ἐκεῖνοι, οὓς ἐλθὼν ὁ κύριος εὑρήσει γρηγοροῦντας. ἀμὴν λέγω ὑμῖν, ὅτι περιζώσεται, κ̀ ἀνακλινεῖ αὐτούς, κ̀ παρελθὼν διακονήσει αὐτοῖς.

37 Beati servi illi, quos veniens dominus invenerit vigilantes. Amen dico vobis, quod succingetur, & faciet discumbere illos, & prodiens ministrabit illis.

38 Καὶ ἐὰν ἔλθῃ ἐν τῇ δευτέρᾳ φυλακῇ, κ̀ ἐν τῇ τρίτῃ φυλακῇ ἔλθῃ, κ̀ εὕρῃ οὕτω, μακάριοί εἰσιν οἱ δοῦλοι ἐκεῖνοι.

38 Et si venerit in secunda vigilia, & in tertia vigilia venerit, & invenerit ita, beati sunt servi illi.

39 Τοῦτο δὲ γινώσκετε, ὅτι εἰ ᾔδει ὁ οἰκοδεσπότης ποίᾳ ὥρᾳ ὁ κλέπτης ἔρχεται, ἐγρηγόρησεν ἂν, κ̀ οὐκ ἂν ἀφῆκε διορυγῆναι τὸν οἶκον αὐτοῦ.

39 Hoc autem scitote, quoniam si sciret paterfamilias qua hora fur veniret, vigilaret utique, & non utique sineret perfodi domum suam.

40 Καὶ ὑμεῖς οὖν γίνεσθε ἕτοιμοι· ὅτι ᾗ ὥρᾳ οὐ δοκεῖτε, ὁ υἱὸς τοῦ ἀνθρώπου ἔρχεται.

40 Et vos igitur estote parati: quia qua hora non putatis, filius hominis venit.

41 Εἶπε δὲ αὐτῷ ὁ Πέτρος· Κύριε, πρὸς ἡμᾶς τὴν παραβολὴν ταύτην λέγεις, ἢ κ̀ πρὸς πάντας;

41 Ait autem ei Petrus: Domine, ad nos parabolam hanc dicis, an & ad omnes?

* 42 Εἶπε δὲ ὁ Κύριος· Τίς ἄρα ἐστὶν ὁ ‡ πιστὸς ‡ οἰκονόμος κ̀ ‡ φρόνιμος, ὃν καταστήσει ὁ κύριος ἐπὶ τῆς ‡ θεραπείας αὐτοῦ, τοῦ διδόναι ἐν ‡ καιρῷ τὸ ‡ σιτομέτριον;

42 Dixit autem Dominus: Quisnam est fidelis dispensator & prudens, quem constituit dominus super famulitio suo, ad dandum in tempore tritici mensuram?

43 Μακάριος ὁ δοῦλος ἐκεῖνος, ὃν ἐλθὼν ὁ κύριος αὐτοῦ εὑρήσει ποιοῦντα οὕτως.

43 Beatus servus ille, quem veniens dominus ejus invenerit facientem ita.

31. Mais cherchez plutôt le royaume de Dieu, et toutes ces choses vous seront données par-dessus.

32. Ne crains point, petit troupeau; car il a plu à votre Père de vous donner le Royaume.

33. Vendez ce que vous avez, et *le* donnez *en* aumônes; faites-vous des bourses qui ne s'usent point, un trésor dans les cieux qui ne manque jamais, d'où les voleurs n'approchent point, *et* où la tigne ne gâte rien.

34. Car où est votre trésor, là aussi sera votre cœur.

35. Que vos reins soient ceints, et vos chandelles allumées;

36. Et *soyez* comme ceux qui attendent que leur maître revienne des nôces; afin que quand il viendra et qu'il heurtera *à la porte*, ils lui ouvrent incontinent.

37. Heureux ces serviteurs, que le maître trouvera veillans quand il arrivera! Je vous dis en vérité, qu'il se ceindra, qu'il les fera mettre à table, et qu'il viendra les servir.

38. Que s'il arrive à la seconde, ou à la troisième veille, et qu'il les trouve dans cet état, heureux ces serviteurs-là!

39. Vous savez, que si un père de famille étoit averti à quelle heure un larron doit venir, il veilleroit, et ne laisseroit pas percer sa maison.

40. Vous donc aussi soyez prêts; car le Fils de l'homme viendra à l'heure que vous ne penserez point.

41. Alors Pierre lui dit : Seigneur, est-ce seulement pour nous que tu dis cette parabole, ou est-ce aussi pour tous?

42. Et le Seigneur lui dit : Mais qui est le dispensateur fidèle et prudent, que le maître a établi sur ses domestiques, pour leur donner dans le tems la mesure ordinaire de bled?

43. Heureux *est* ce serviteur-là que son maître trouvera faisant ainsi *son devoir*, quand il arrivera!

31 But rather seek ye the kingdom of God; and all these things shall be added unto you.

32 Fear not, little flock; for it is your Father's good pleasure to give you the kingdom.

33 Sell that ye have, and give alms; provide yourselves bags which wax not old, a treasure in the heavens that faileth not, where no thief approacheth, neither moth corrupteth.

34 For where your treasure is, there will your heart be also.

35 Let your loins be girded about, and your lights burning:

36 And ye yourselves like unto men that wait for their lord, when he will return from the wedding; that when he cometh and knocketh, they may open unto him immediately.

37 Blessed *are* those servants, whom the lord, when he cometh, shall find watching : verily I say unto you, That he shall gird himself, and make them to sit down to meat, and will come forth and serve them.

38 And if he shall come in the second watch, or come in the third watch, and find *them* so, blessed are those servants.

39 And this know, that if the good man of the house had known what hour the thief would come, he would have watched, and not have suffered his house to be broken through.

40 Be ye, therefore, ready also : for the Son of Man cometh at an hour when ye think not.

41 Then Peter said unto him, Lord, speakest thou this parable unto us, or even to all?

42 And the Lord said, Who then is that faithful and wise steward, whom *his* lord shall make ruler over his household, to give *them their* portion of meat in due season?

43 Blessed *is* that servant, whom his lord, when he cometh, shall find so doing.

44 Ἀληθῶς λέγω ὑμῖν, ὅτι ἐπὶ πᾶσι τοῖς ὑπάρχουσιν αὐτοῦ καταςήσει αὐτόν.

* 45 Ἐὰν δὲ εἴπῃ ὁ δοῦλ⊙ ἐκεῖν⊙ ἐν τῇ καρδίᾳ αὐτοῦ· ‡ Χρονίζει ὁ κύριός μου ἔρχεσθαι· καὶ ἄρξηται τύπτειν τοὺς παῖδας, καὶ τὰς ‡ παιδίσκας, ἐσθίειν τε καὶ πίνειν καὶ ‡ μεθύσκεσθαι·

* 46 Ἥξει ὁ κύρι⊙ τοῦ δούλου ἐκείνου ἐν ἡμέρᾳ ᾗ οὐ προσδοκᾷ, καὶ ἐν ὥρᾳ ᾗ οὐ γινώσκει· καὶ ‡ διχοτομήσει αὐτόν, καὶ τὸ μέρ⊙ αὐτοῦ μετὰ τῶν ἀπίςων θήσει.

47 Ἐκεῖν⊙ δὲ ὁ δοῦλ⊙ ὁ γνοὺς τὸ θέλημα τοῦ κυρίου ἑαυτοῦ, καὶ μὴ ἑτοιμάσας, μηδὲ ποιήσας πρὸς τὸ θέλημα αὐτοῦ, δαρήσεται πολλάς.

48 Ὁ δὲ μὴ γνοὺς, ποιήσας δὲ ἄξια πληγῶν, δαρήσεται ὀλίγας· παντὶ δὲ ᾧ ἐδόθη πολὺ, πολὺ ζητηθήσεται παρ᾽ αὐτοῦ· καὶ ᾧ παρέθεντο πολὺ, περισσότερον αἰτήσουσιν αὐτόν.

* 54 Ἔλεγε δὲ καὶ τοῖς ὄχλοις· Ὅταν ἴδητε τὴν νεφέλην ἀνατέλλουσαν ἀπὸ δυσμῶν, εὐθέως λέγετε· † Ὄμβρⓔ ἔρχεται· καὶ γίνεται οὕτω.

55 Καὶ ὅταν νότον πνέοντα, λέγετε· Ὅτι καύσων ἔςαι· καὶ γίνεται.

56 Ὑποκριταὶ, τὸ πρόσωπον τῆς γῆς καὶ τοῦ οὐρανοῦ οἴδατε δοκιμάζειν· τὸν δὲ καιρὸν τοῦτον πῶς οὐ δοκιμάζετε;

57 Τί δὲ καὶ ἀφ᾽ ἑαυτῶν οὐ κρίνετε τὸ δίκαιον;

* 58 Ὡς γὰρ ὑπάγεις μετὰ τοῦ ἀντιδίκου σου ἐπ᾽ ἄρχοντα, ἐν τῇ ὁδῷ δὸς ἐργασίαν ἀπηλλάχθαι ἀπ᾽ αὐτοῦ· ‡ μήποτε ‡ κατασύρῃ σε πρὸς τὸν κριτὴν, καὶ ὁ κριτής σε παραδῷ τῷ ‡ πράκτορι, καὶ ὁ πράκτωρ σε βάλλῃ εἰς φυλακήν.

59 Λέγω σοι, οὐ μὴ ἐξέλθῃς ἐκεῖθεν, ἕως οὗ καὶ τὸ ἔσχατον λεπτὸν ἀποδῷς. 39. † 12.

---

44 Vere dico vobis, quoniam super omnibus substantiis ipsius constituet illum.

45 Si autem dixerit servus ille in corde suo: Tardat dominus meus venire, & cœperit percutere pueros, & ancillas, edereque & bibere & inebriari:

46 Veniet dominus servi illius in die qua non exspectat, & in hora qua non cognoscit: & dissecabit eum, & partem ejus cum infidelibus ponet.

47 Ille autem servus noscens voluntatem domini sui, & non apparans, neque faciens ad voluntatem ejus, cædetur multis.

48 Qui autem non noscens, faciens autem digna plagis, cædetur paucis: omni autem cui datum est multum, multum quæretur ab eo: & cui deposuerunt multum, abundantius reposcent eum.

54 Dicebat autem & turbis: Quum videritis nubem orientem ab occasibus, statim dicitis: Imber venit, & fit ita.

55 Et quum Austrum flantem, dicitis: quia æstus erit: & fit.

56 Hypocritæ, faciem cæli & terræ nostis probare, at tempus hoc quomodo non probatis?

57 Quid autem & à vobis ipsis non judicatis quod justum?

58 Quum enim vadis cum adversario tuo ad principem, in via da operam liberari ab illo: ne forte trahat te ad judicem, & judex te tradat exactori, & exactor jaciat te in carcerem.

59 Dico tibi: Non egredieris illinc, usquequo etiam novissimum minutum reddas.

44. Je vous dis en vérité, qu'il l'établira sur tout ce qu'il a.

45. Mais si ce serviteur dit en lui-même : Mon maître ne viendra pas sitôt; et qu'il se mette à battre les serviteurs et les servantes, à manger, à boire, et à s'enivrer;

46. Le maître de ce serviteur viendra au jour qu'il ne s'y attend pas, et à l'heure qu'il ne sait pas; et il le séparera, et lui donnera sa portion avec les infidèles.

47. Le serviteur qui a connu la volonté de son maître, et qui ne se sera pas tenu prêt, et n'aura pas fait cette volonté, sera battu de plus de coups.

48. Mais celui qui ne l'a point connue, et qui a fait des choses dignes de châtiment, sera battu de moins de coups. Et il sera beaucoup redemandé à quiconque il aura été beaucoup donné ; et on exigera plus de celui à qui on aura beaucoup confié.

54. Puis il disoit au peuple : Quand vous voyez une nuée qui se lève du côté d'Occident, vous dites d'abord, il va pleuvoir; et cela arrive ainsi.

55. Et quand le vent de Midi souffle, vous dites qu'il fera chaud et cela arrive.

56. Hypocrites, vous savez bien discerner ce qui paroit au ciel et sur la terre; et comment ne discernez-vous pas ce tems-ci?

57. Et pourquoi ne discernez-vous pas aussi vous-mêmes ce qui est juste?

58. Or quand tu vas devant le Magistrat, avec ton adverse partie, tâche en chemin de sortir d'affaire avec elle; de peur qu'elle ne te tire devant le Juge, que le Juge ne te livre au Sergent, et que le Sergent ne te mette en prison.

59. Je te dis que tu ne sortiras point de là, que tu n'aies payé jusqu'à la dernière obole.

44 Of a truth I say unto you, That he will make him ruler over all that he hath.

45 But, and if that servant say in his heart, My lord delayeth his coming; and shall begin to beat the men-servants, and maidens, and to eat and drink, and to be drunken;

46 The lord of that servant will come in a day when he looketh not for *him*, and at an hour when he is not aware, and will cut him in sunder,

47 And that servant, which knew his lord's will, and prepared not *himself*, neither did according to his will, shall be beaten with many *stripes*.

48 But he that knew not, and did commit things worthy of stripes, shall be beaten with few *stripes*. For unto whomsoever much is given, of him shall be much required : and to whom men have committed much, of him they will ask the more.

54 And he said also to the people, When ye see a cloud rise out of the west, straightway ye say, There cometh a shower, and so it is.

55 And when *ye see* the south wind blow, ye say, There will be heat; and it cometh to pass.

56 Ye hypocrites! ye can discern the face of the sky and of the earth ; but how is it, that ye do not discern this time?

57 Yea, and why even of yourselves judge ye not what is right?

58 When thou goest with thine adversary to the magistrate, *as thou art* in the way, give diligence that thou mayest be delivered from him; lest he hale thee to the judge, and the judge deliver thee to the officer, and the officer cast thee into prison.

59 I tell thee, thou shalt not depart thence, till thou hast paid the very last mite.

Κεφ. ιγ. 13.

1 Παρῆσαν δέ τινες ἐν αὐτῷ τῷ καιρῷ ἀπαγγέλλοντες αὐτῷ περὶ τῶν Γαλιλαίων, ὧν τὸ αἷμα Πιλάτ⊙· ἔμιξε μετὰ τῶν θυσιῶν τῶν.

2 Καὶ ἀποκριθεὶς ὁ Ἰησῦς εἶπεν αὐτοῖς· Δοκεῖτε ὅτι οἱ Γαλιλαῖοι οὗτοι ἁμαρτωλοὶ παρὰ πάντας τὲς Γαλιλαίες ἐγένοντο, ὅτι τοιαῦτα πεπόνθασιν;

3 Οὐχὶ, λέγω ὑμῖν· ἀλλ' ἐὰν μὴ μετανοῆτε, πάντες ὡσαύτως ἀπολεῖσθε.

4 Ἢ ἐκεῖνοι οἱ δέκα κὴ ὀκτὼ, ἐφ' ὃς ἔπεσεν ὁ πύργ⊙· ἐν τῷ Σιλωὰμ, κὴ ἀπέκτεινεν αὐτὸς, δοκεῖτε ὅτι οὗτοι ὀφειλέται ἐγένοντο παρὰ πάντας ἀνθρώπες τὸς κατοικοῦντας ἐν Ἱερεσαλήμ;

5 Οὐχὶ, λέγω ὑμῖν· ἀλλ' ἐὰν μὴ μετανοῆτε, πάντες ὁμοίως ἀπολεῖσθε.

6 Ἔλεγε δὲ ταύτην τὴν παραβολήν· Συκῆν εἶχέ τις ἐν τῷ ἀμπελῶνι αὐτοῦ πεφυτευμένην· κὴ ἦλθε καρπὸν ζητῶν ἐν αὐτῇ, κὴ οὐχ εὗρεν.

7 Εἶπε δὲ πρὸς τὸν † ἀμπελεργὸν· Ἰδοὺ, τρία ἔτη ἔρχομαι ζητῶν καρπὸν ἐν τῇ συκῇ ταύτῃ, κὴ οὐχ εὑρίσκω· ‡ ἔκκοψον αὐτὴν· ἱνατί κὴ τὴν γῆν ‡ καταργεῖ;

*, 8 Ὁ δὲ ἀποκριθεὶς λέγει αὐτῷ· Κύριε, ἄφες αὐτὴν κὴ τοῦτο τὸ ἔτ⊙·, ἕως ὅτε σκάψω περὶ αὐτὴν, κὴ βάλω ‡ κοπρίαν·

9 Κἂν μὲν ποιήσῃ καρπόν· εἰ δὲ μήγε, εἰς τὸ μέλλον ἐκκόψεις αὐτήν.

37 Ἐν δὲ τῷ λαλῆσαι, ἠρώτα αὐτὸν Φαρισαῖός τις ὅπως ἀριστήσῃ παρ' αὐτῷ· εἰσελθὼν δὲ ἀνέπεσεν.

38 Ὁ δὲ φαρισαῖ⊙· ἰδὼν ἐθαύμασεν, ὅτι ἐ πρῶτον ἐβαπτίσθη πρὸ τῦ ἀρίσε.

39 Εἶπε δὲ ὁ Κύρι⊙· πρὸς αὐτόν· Νῦν ὑμεῖς οἱ φαρισαῖοι τὸ ἔξωθεν τῦ ποτηρίε κὴ τῦ πίνακ⊙· καθαρίζετε· τὸ δὲ ἔσωθεν ὑμῶν γέμει ἁρπαγῆς κὴ πονηρίας.

40 Ἄφρονες, ἐχ ὁ ποιήσας τὸ ἔξωθεν, κὴ τὸ ἔσωθεν ἐποίησε;

* 41 Πλὴν τὰ † ἐνόντα δότε ‡ ἐλεημοσύνην· κὴ ἰδὲ, πάντα καθαρὰ ὑμῖν ἐστιν.

1 Aderant autem quidam in ipso tempore, nuntiantes illi de Galilæis, quorum sanguinem Pilatus miscuit cum sacrificiis eorum.

2 Et respondens Jesus dixit illis : Putatis quod Galilæi hi peccatores præ omnibus Galilæis fuerint, qui talia passi sunt ?

3 Non, dico vobis, sed si non pœniteamini, omnes similiter peribitis.

4 Vel illi decem & octo, supra quos cecidit turris in Siloam, & occidit eos : putatis qnia ipsi debitores fuerint præter omnes homines habitantes in Hierusalem ?

5 Non dico vobis, sed si non pœnitueritis, omnes similiter peribitis.

6 Dicebat autem hanc similitudinem : Ficum habebat quidam in vinea sua plantatam, & venit fructum quærens : in illa, & non invenit.

7 Dixit autem ad vinitorem : Ecce tres annos venio quærens fructum in ficulnea hac, & non invenio. Exscinde illam : ut quid etiam terram occupat ?

8 Is autem respondens, dicit illi : Domine, relinque eam & hunc annum, usque dum fodiam circa illam, & mittam stercus.

9 Et si quidem fecerit fructum : si vero non, in futurum exscindes eam.

37 In autem loqui, rogavit illum Pharisæus quidam ut pranderet apud se : ingressus autem recubuit.

38 At Pharisæus videns admiratus est, quod non prius ablutus esset ante prandium.

39 Ait autem Dominus ad illum : Nunc vos Pharisæi quod deforis calicis & catini mundatis : quod autem intus vestrum plenum est rapina & malitia.

40 Stulti, nonne faciens quod deforis, & quod deintus fecit ?

41 Veruntamen inexistentia date eleëmosynam, & ecce omnia munda vobis sunt.

CHAPITRE XIII.

Jésus-Christ exhorte à la repentance, et entrer par la porte étroite.

EN ce même tems, quelques personnes, qui se trouvoient là, racontèrent à Jésus ce qui étoit arrivé à des Galiléens, dont Pilate avoit mêlé le sang avec celui de leurs sacrifices.

2. Et Jésus répondant, leur dit : Pensez-vous que ces Galiléens fussent plus grands pécheurs que tous les autres Galiléens, parce qu'ils ont souffert ces choses?

3. Non, vous dis-je; mais si vous ne vous amendez, vous périrez tous aussi bien *qu'eux*.

4. Ou, pensez-vous que ces dix-huit *personnes* sur qui la tour de Siloé est tombée, et qu'elle a tuées, fussent plus coupables que tous les habitans de Jérusalem?

5. Non, vous dis-je; mais si vous ne vous amendez, vous périrez tous aussi bien *qu'eux*.

6. Il leur dit aussi cette similitude : Un homme avoit un figuier planté dans sa vigne, et il y vint chercher du fruit, et n'y en trouva point.

7. Et il dit au vigneron : Voici, il y a déjà trois ans que je viens chercher du fruit à ce figuier, et je n'y en trouve point; coupe-le; pourquoi occupe-t-il la terre inutilement?

8. *Le vigneron* lui répondit : Seigneur, laisse-le encore cette année, jusqu'à-ce que je l'aie déchaussé, et que j'y aie mis du fumier.

9. S'il porte du fruit, *à la bonne heure*; sinon, tu le couperas ci-après.

37. Comme il parloit, un Pharisien le pria à dîner chez lui; et *Jésus* y entra, et se mit à table.

38. Mais le Pharisien s'étonna de ce qu'il vit qu'il ne s'étoit pas lavé avant le dîner.

39. Et le Seigneur lui dit : Vous autres Pharisiens, vous nettoyez le dehors de la coupe et du plat; mais au dedans, vous êtes pleins de rapine et de méchanceté.

40. Insensés! celui qui a fait le dehors n'a-t-il pas aussi fait le dedans?

41. Mais plutôt donnez en aumônes ce que vous avez, et toutes choses vous seront pures.

THERE were present at that season some that told him of the Galileans, whose blood Pilate had mingled with their sacrifices.

2 And Jesus, answering, said unto them, Suppose ye that these Galileans were sinners above all the Galileans, because they suffered such things?

3 I tell you, Nay; but, except ye repent, ye shall all likewise perish.

4 Or those eighteen upon whom the tower in Siloam fell, and slew them, think ye that they were sinners above all men that dwelt in Jerusalem?

5 I tell you, Nay; but except ye repent, ye shall all likewise perish.

6 He spake also this parable: A certain *man* had a fig-tree planted in his vineyard; and he came and sought fruit thereon, and found none.

7 Then said he unto the dresser of his vineyard, Behold, these three years I come seeking fruit on this fig-tree, and find none: cut it down; why cumbereth it the ground?

8 And he, answering, said unto him, Lord, let it alone this year also, till I shall dig about it, and dung *it :*

9 And if it bear fruit, *well :* and if not, *then* after that thou shalt cut it down.

37 And as he spake, a certain Pharisee besought him to dine with him: and he went in, and sat down to meat.

38 And when the Pharisee saw *i*, he marvelled that he had not first washed before dinner.

39 And the Lord said unto him, Now do ye Pharisees make clean the outside of the cup and the platter; but your inward part is full of ravening and wickedness.

40 *Ye* fools! did not he that made that which is without, make that which is within also?

41 But rather give alms of such things as ye have; and, behold, all things are clean unto you.

22

* 42 Ἀλλ' ὑαὶ ὑμῖν τοῖς φαρισαίοις, ὅτι ἀποδεκατᾶτε τὸ ἡ-
δύοσμον κ̀ τὸ † πήγανον κ̀ πᾶν
‡ λάχανον, κ̀ παρέρχεσθε τὴν
κρίσιν κ̀ τὴν ἀγάπην τῦ Θεῦ·
ταῦτα ἔδει ποιῆσαι, κἀκεῖνα μὴ
ἀφιέναι.

43 Οὐαὶ ὑμῖν τοῖς φαρισαίοις,
ὅτι ἀγαπᾶτε τὴν πρωτοκαθεδρίαν
ἐν ταῖς συναγωγαῖς, κ̀ τοὺς ἀ-
σπασμὸς ἐν ταῖς ἀγοραῖς.

44 Οὐαὶ ὑμῖν, γραμμαδεῖς κ̀
φαρισαῖοι ὑποκριταὶ, ὅτι ἐςὲ ὡς
τὰ μνημεῖα τὰ ἄδηλα, κ̀ οἱ ἄνθρωποι οἱ περιπατῦντες ἐπάνω ἐκ
οἴδασιν.

45 Ἀποκριθεὶς δέ τις τῶν νο-
μικῶν λέγει αὐτῷ· Διδάσκαλε,
ταῦτα λέγων κ̀ ἡμᾶς ὑβρίζεις.

* 46 Ὁ δὲ εἶπε· Καὶ ὑμῖν
τοῖς ‡ νομικοῖς οὐαὶ, ὅτι ‡ φορτί-
ζετε τὰς ἀνθρώπυς ‡ φορτία ‡ δυσ-
βάςακτα, κ̀ αὐτοὶ ἑνὶ τῶν δακ-
τύλων ὑμῶν ἠ † προσψαύετε τοῖς
φορτίοις.

52 Οὐαὶ ὑμῖν τοῖς νομικοῖς,
ὅτι ἤρατε τὴν κλεῖδα τῆς γνώσεως·
αὐτοὶ ἐκ εἰσήλθετε, κ̀ τὸς εἰσερ-
χομένυς ἐκωλύσατε.

* 53 Λέγοντ☉ δὲ αὐτῦ ταῦ-
τα πρὸς αὐτὺς, ἤρξαντο οἱ γραμματεῖς κ̀ οἱ φαρισαῖοι ‡ δεινῶς
‡ ἐνέχειν, κ̀ † ἀποςοματίζειν αὐτὸν ‡ περὶ ‡ πλειόνων·

* 54 ‡ Ἐνεδρεύοντες αὐτὸν, κ̀
ζητῦντες ‡ θηρεῦσαί τι ἐκ τῦ
ςόματ☉ αὐτῦ, ἵνα κατηγορήσωσιν αὐτῦ. 45. † 12.

Κεφ. ιγ´. 13.

1 ΕΝ δὲ τῇ ἡμέρα ἐκείνῃ ἐξελθὼν ὁ Ἰησῦς ἀπὸ τῆς οἰκίας,
ἐκάθητο παρὰ τὴν θάλασσαν.

2 Καὶ συνήχθησαν πρὸς αὐτὸν
ὄχλοι πολλοὶ, ὥςε αὐτὸν εἰς τὸ
πλοῖον ἐμβάντα καθῆσθαι· κ̀ πᾶς
ὁ ὄχλ☉ ἐπὶ τὸν αἰγιαλὸν εἱςήκει.

3 Καὶ ἐλάλησεν αὐτοῖς πολλὰ
ἐν παραβολαῖς, λέγων· Ἰδὴ, ἐξῆλθεν ὁ σπείρων τῦ σπείρειν.

4 Καὶ ἐν τῷ σπείρειν αὐτὸν, ἃ
μὲν ἔπεσε παρὰ τὴν ὁδόν· κ̀ ἦλθε
τὰ πετεινὰ, κ̀ κατέφαγεν αὐτά.

---

42 Sed væ vobis Pharisæis,
quia decimatis mentham, & ru-
tam, & omne olus, & præteritis
judicium & charitatem Dei;
hæc oportebat facere, & illa
non omittere.

43 Væ vobis Pharisæis, quia
diligitis primam sessionem in
synagogis, & salutationes in foris.

44 Væ vobis, Scribæ & Pharisæi hypocritæ, quia estis ut
monumenta non apparentia, &
homines deambulantes supra
non sciunt.

45 Respondens autem quidam
Legisperitorum ait illi: Magister, hæc dicens & nos notas.

46 Ille autem ait: Et vobis
Legisperitis væ, quia oneratis
homines oneribus difficulter
portabilibus, & ipsi uno digito-
rum vestrorum non attingitis
onera.

52 Væ vobis Legisperitis,
quia tulistis clavem scientiæ:
ipsi non introistis, & intro-
euntes prohibuistis.

53 Dicente autem illo hæc
ad illos, cœperunt Scribæ &
Pharisæi graviter insistere, &
interrogare ipsum de multis:

54 Insidiantes ei, & quærentes venari aliquid de ore ejus,
ut accusarent eum.

CAPUT XIII.

1 IN verò die illo exiens Jesus de
domo, sedebat secundum mare.

2 Et congregatæ sunt ad eum
turbæ multæ, ita ut ipse in na-
viculam ascendens sederet : &
omnis turba in littore stabat.

3 Et locutus est eis multa in
parabolis, dicens, Ecce exiit se-
minator seminare.

4 Et in seminare ipsum, hæc
quidem ceciderunt secus viam,
& venerunt volucres & come-
derunt ea.

42. Mais malheur à vous, Pharisiens, qui payez la dîme de la menthe, de la rue, et de toutes sortes d'herbes, tandis que vous négligez la justice, et l'amour de Dieu ! Ce sont là les choses qu'il falloit faire sans néanmoins négliger les autres.

43. Malheur à vous, Pharisiens, qui aimez les premiers rangs dans les Synagogues, et à être salués dans les places publiques !

44. Malheur à vous, Scribes et Pharisiens hypocrites ; parce que vous ressemblez aux sépulcres qui ne paroissent point, et les hommes qui marchent dessus n'en savent rien !

45. Alors un des docteurs de la loi prit la parole et lui dit : Maître, en disant ces choses, tu nous outrages aussi.

46. Et *Jésus* dit : Malheur aussi à vous, docteurs de la loi ; parce que vous chargez les hommes de fardeaux qu'ils ne peuvent porter, et vous mêmes n'y touchez pas du bout du doigt !

52. Malheur à vous, docteurs de la loi ; parce qu'ayant pris la clef de la connoissance, vous n'y êtes point entrés vous-mêmes, et vous avez encore empêché d'y entrer ceux qui vouloient le faire !

53. Et comme il leur disoit cela, les Scribes et les Pharisiens se mirent à le presser fortement, en le faisant parler sur plusieurs choses ;

54. Lui tendant des piéges, et tâchant de tirer quelques choses de sa bouche, pour avoir de quoi l'accuser.

CE même jour, Jésus étant sorti de la maison, s'assit au bord de la mer.

2. Et une grande foule de peuple s'assembla vers lui, en sorte qu'il monta dans une barque. Il s'y assit, et toute la multitude se tenoit sur le rivage.

3. Et il leur dit plusieurs choses par des similitudes, et il leur parla ainsi : Un semeur sortit pour semer.

4. Et comme il semoit, une partie *de la semence* tomba le long du chemin, et les oiseaux vinrent, et la mangèrent toute.

---

42 But woe unto you, Pharisees! for ye tithe mint, and rue, and all manner of herbs, and pass over judgment and the love of God : these ought ye to have done, and not to leave the other undone.

43 Woe unto you, Pharisees! for ye love the uppermost seats in the synagogues, and greetings in the markets.

44 Woe unto you, scribes and Pharisees, hypocrites! for ye are as graves which appear not, and the men that walk over *them* are not aware *of them*.

45 Then answered one of the lawyers, and said unto him, Master, thus saying, thou reproachest us also.

46 And he said, Woe unto you also, *ye* lawyers! for ye lade men with burdens grievous to be borne, and ye yourselves touch not the burdens with one of your fingers.

52 Woe unto you, lawyers! for ye have taken away the key of knowledge: ye entered not in yourselves, and them that were entering in ye hindered.

53 And as he said these things unto them, the scribes and the Pharisees began to urge *him* vehemently, and to provoke him to speak of many things ;   I 2

54 Laying wait for him, and seeking to catch something out of his mouth, that they might accuse him.

THE same day went Jesus out of the house, and sat by the sea side.

2 And great multitudes were gathered together unto him, so that he went into a ship and sat; and the whole multitude stood on the shore.

3 And he spake many things unto them in parables, saying, Behold, a sower went forth to sow ;

4 And, when he sowed, some *seeds* fell by the way-side, and the fowls came and devoured them.

23

5 Ἄλλα δὲ ἔπεσεν ἐπὶ τὰ πε-
τρῶδη, ὅπε ἐκ εἶχε γῆν πολλὴν·
κỳ εὐθέως ἐξανέτειλε, διὰ τὸ μὴ
ἔχειν βάθℴ γῆς.

6 Ἡλίε δὲ ἀνατείλαντℴ ἐκαυ-
ματίσθη κỳ διὰ τὸ μὴ ἔχειν ῥίζαν,
ἐξηράνθη.

7 Ἄλλα δὲ ἔπεσεν ἐπὶ τὰς ἀ-
κάνθας, κỳ ἀνέβησαν αἱ ἄκανθαι, κỳ
ἀπέπνιξαν αὐτά.

8 Ἄλλα δὲ ἔπεσεν ἐπὶ τὴν γῆν
τὴν καλὴν, κỳ ἐδίδε καρπὸν, ὃ μὲν
ἑκατὸν, ὃ δὲ ἑξήκοντα, ὃ δὲ τριάκοντα.

9 Ὁ ἔχων ὦτα ἀκέειν, ἀκυέτω.

10 Ὅτε δὲ ἐγένετο καταμόνας,
ἠρώτησαν αὐτὸν οἱ περὶ αὐτὸν σὺν
τοῖς δώδεκα τὴν παραβολήν.

18 Ὑμεῖς οὖν ἀκούσατε τὴν
παραβολὴν τῦ Σπείροντℴ.

19 Παντὸς ἀκούοντℴ τὸν λόγον
τῆς Βασιλείας, κỳ μὴ συνιέντℴ,
ἔρχεται ὁ πονηρὸς, κỳ ἁρπάζει τὸ
ἐσπαρμένον ἐν τῇ καρδίᾳ αὐτῦ· ἄ-
τός ἐςιν ὁ παρὰ τὴν ὁδὸν Σπα-
ρείς.

20 Ὁ δὲ ἐπὶ τὰ πετρώδη Σπαρεὶς, οὗτός ἐςιν ὁ τὸν λόγον ἀκέων,
κỳ εὐθὺς μετὰ χαρᾶς λαμβάνων
αὐτόν·

21 Οὐκ ἔχει δὲ ῥίζαν ἐν ἑαυτῷ,
ἀλλὰ πρόσκαιρός ἐςι· γενομένης
δὲ θλίψεως ἢ διωγμῦ διὰ τὸν λόγον,
εὐθὺς σκανδαλίζεται.

22 Ὁ δὲ εἰς τὰς ἀκάνθας Σπαρεὶς, οὗτός ἐςιν ὁ τὸν λόγον ἀκέ-
ων· κỳ ἡ μέριμνα τῦ αἰῶνℴ τέτυ,
κỳ ἡ ἀπάτη τῦ πλύτυ συμπνίγει
τὸν λόγον, κỳ ἄκαρπℴ γίνεται.

23 Ὁ δὲ ἐπὶ τὴν γῆν τὴν καλὴν
Σπαρεὶς, οὗτός ἐςιν ὁ τὸν λόγον ἀκέων, κỳ συνιῶν· ὃς δὴ καρποφορεῖ, κỳ ποιεῖ, ὁ μὲν ἑκατὸν, ὁ δὲ
ἑξήκοντα, ὁ δὴ τριάκοντα.

---

5 Alia autem ceciderunt in
petrosa, ubi non habebant terram multam : & continuò ex-
orta sunt, propter non habere
altitudinem terræ.

6 Sole autem orto, æstuave-
runt, & propter non habere radicem, exaruerunt.

7 Alia autem ceciderunt in
spinas, & insurrexerunt spinæ,
& suffocaverunt ea.

8 Alia autem ceciderunt in
terram bonam, & dabant fructum, hoc centum, hoc autem
sexaginta, hoc autem triginta.

9 Habens aures audire, audiat.

10 Quum autem factus esset
solus interrogaverunt eum qui
circa eum cum duodecim parabolam.

18 Vos ergo audite parabolam seminantis.

19 Omnis audientis verbum
regni, & non intelligentis, venit
malus, & rapit seminatum in
corde ejus : hic est qui secus
viam seminatus.

20 Qui autem super petrosa
seminatus, hic est qui verbum
audiens, & continuò cum gaudio sumens illud :

21 Non habet autem radicem
in se ipso, sed temporalis est ;
facta autem tribulatione aut
persequutione propter verbum,
statim scandalizatur.

22 Qui autem in spinas seminatus, hic est qui verbum audiens, & anxietas seculi istius, &
deceptio divitiarum suffocat verbum, & infructuosum fit.

23 Qui verò in terram pul-
chram seminatus, hic est qui
verbum audiens & intelligens :
quique fructum fert, & facit, hoc
quidem centum, hoc autem sexaginta, hoc verò triginta.

5. L'autre partie tomba sur des endroits pierreux, où elle n'avoit que peu de terre, et elle leva aussitôt, parce qu'elle n'entroit pas profondément dans la terre;

6. Mais le soleil étant levé, elle fut brûlée; et parce qu'elle n'avoit point de racine, elle sécha.

7. L'autre partie tomba parmi des épines, et les épines crûrent, et l'étouffèrent.

8. Et l'autre partie tomba dans une bonne terre, et rapporta du fruit; un grain en rapporta cent, un autre soixante, et un autre trente.

9. Que celui qui a des oreilles pour ouïr, entende.

10. Et quand il fut en particulier, ceux qui *étoient* autour de lui, avec les douze *Apôtres*, l'interrogèrent touchant le sens de cette parabole.

18. Vous donc, écoutez la similitude du semeur.

19. Lorsqu'un homme entend la parole du Royaume *de Dieu*, et qu'il ne la comprend point, le malin vient, et ravit ce qui est semé dans le cœur; c'est celui qui a reçu la semence le long du chemin.

20. Et celui qui a reçu la semence dans les endroits pierreux, c'est celui qui entend la parole, et qui la reçoit d'abord avec joie;

21. Mais il n'a point de racine en lui-même; c'est pourquoi il n'est que pour un tems; et lorsque l'affliction ou la persécution survient à cause de la parole, il se scandalise aussitôt.

22. Et celui qui a reçu la semence parmi les épines, c'est celui qui entend la parole; mais les soucis de ce monde et la séduction des richesses étouffent la parole, et elle devient infructueuse.

23. Mais celui qui a reçu la semence dans une bonne terre, c'est celui qui entend la parole et qui la comprend, et qui porte du fruit; en sorte qu'un grain en produit cent, un autre soixante, et un autre trente.

Mt. 13.

5 Some fell upon stony places, where they had not much earth: and forthwith they sprung up, because they had no deepness of earth:-

6 And when the sun was up, they were scorched: and, because they had not root, they withered away.

7 And some fell among thorns; and the thorns sprung up and choked them:

8 But other fell into good ground, and brought forth fruit, some an hundred-fold, some sixty-fold, some thirty-fold.

9 Who hath ears to hear, let him hear.

Mt. 4.

10 And when he was alone, they that were about him, with the twelve, asked of him the parable.

Mt. 13.

18 Hear ye, therefore, the parable of the sower.

19 When any one heareth the word of the kingdom, and understandeth *it* not, *then* cometh the wicked *one*, and catcheth away that which was sown in his heart. This is he which received seed by the way *side*.

20 But he that received the seed into stony places, the same is he that heareth the word, and anon with joy receiveth it;

21 Yet hath he not root in himself, but dureth for a while; for when tribulation or persecution ariseth because of the word, by and by he is offended.

22 He also that received seed among the thorns, is he that heareth the word; and the care of this world, and the deceitfulness of riches, choke the word, and he becometh unfruitful.

23 But he that received seed into the good ground, is he that heareth the word and understandeth *it;* which also beareth fruit, and bringeth forth, some an hundred-fold, some sixty, some thirty.

24

21 Καὶ ἔλεγεν αὐτοῖς· Μήτι ὁ λύχνⒺ ἔρχεῖαι, ἵνα ὑπὸ τὸν μόδιον τεθῇ, ἢ ὑπὸ τὴν κλίνην; ἐχ ἵνα ἐπὶ τὴν λυχνίαν ἐπιʼεθῇ;

* 22 Οὐ γάρ ἐςί τι κρυπῖὸν ὃ ἐὰν μὴ φανεξωθῇ· ἐδὲ ἐγένεῖο ‡ ἀπόκρυφον, ἀλλʼ ἵνα εἰς φανεξὸν ἔλθῃ.

23 Εἴ τις ἔχει ὦτα ἀκύειν ἀκυέτω.

24 Ἄλλην ϖαξαβολὴν ϖαξέθηκεν αὐτοῖς, λέγων· Ὡμοιώθη ἡ βασιλεία τῶν οὐρανῶν ἀνθρώπῳ Cϖείξονῖι καλὸν Cϖέξμα ἐν τῷ ἀγξῷ αὐτῦ.

25 Ἐν δὲ τῷ καθεύδειν τὺς ἀνθρώπὺς, ἦλθον αὐτῦ ὁ ἐχθρὸς, κὴ ἔσπειξε ζιζάνια ἀνὰ μέσον τῦ σίτυ κὴ ἀπῆλθεν.

26 Ὅῖε δὲ ἐϐλάςησεν ὁ χόξτυς, κὴ καξπὸν ἐποίησε, τότε ἐφάνη κὴ τὰ ζιζάνια.

27 Πξοσελθόνῖες δὲ οἱ δῦλοι τῦ οἰκοδεσπότυ, εἶπον αὐτῷ· Κύξιε, ἐχὶ καλὸν Cϖέξμα ἔσπειξας ἐν τῷ Cῷ ἀγξῷ; ϖόθεν ὖν ἔχει τὰ ζιζάνια;

28 Ὁ δὲ ἔφη αὐτοῖς· Ἐχθξὸς αἰθξωπⒺ τῦτο ἐποίησεν. Οἱ δὲ δῦλοι εἶπον αὐτῷ· Θέλεις ὖν ἀπελθόνῖες συλλέξωμεν αὐτά;

29 Ὁ δὲ ἔφη· Οὔ· μήποῖε συλλέγονῖες τὰ ζιζάνια, ἐκριζώσηῖε ἅμα αὐτοῖς τὸν σῖτον·

* 30 ‡ Ἄφεʼε † Cυναυξάνεσθαι ἀμφότεξα ‡ μέχξι τῦ ‡ θεξισμῦ, κὴ ἐν τῷ καιξῷ τῦ θεξισμῦ ‡ ἐξῶ τοῖς ‡ θεξιςαῖς· ‡ Συλλέξαῖε ϖξῶτον τὰ ‡ ζιζάνια, κὴ δήσαῖε αὐτὰ ‡ εἰς † δέσμας, ϖξὸς τὸ καῖακαῦσαι αὐτά· τὸν δὲ ‡ σῖτον ‡ συναγάγεῖε εἰς τὴν ‡ ἀποθήκην μυ.

36 Τόῖε ἀφεὶς τὺς ὄχλυς, ἦλθεν εἰς τὴν οἰκίαν ὁ Ἰησῦς· κὴ ϖξοσῆλθον αὐτῷ οἱ μαθηῖαὶ αὐτῦ, λέγονῖες· Φξάσον ἡμῖν τὴν ϖαξαβολὴν τῶν ζιζανίων τῦ ἀγξῦ.

37 Ὁ δὲ ἀποκξιθεὶς, εἶπεν αὐτοῖς· Ὁ Cϖείξων τὸ καλὸν Cϖέξμα, ἐςιν ὁ υἱὸς τῦ ἀνθρώπυ.

38 Ὁ δὲ ἀγξὸς, ἐςιν, ὁ κόσμⒺ· τὸ δὲ καλὸν Cϖέξμα, ὗτοί εἰσιν οἱ υἱοὶ τῆς βασιλείας· τὰ δὲ ζιζάνια, εἰσὶν οἱ υἱοὶ τῦ ϖονηξῦ.

---

21 Et dicebat illis: Nunquid lucerna venit, ut sub modio ponatur, aut sub lecto? nonne ut supra candelabrum imponatur?

22 Non enim est aliquid absconditum, quod non manifestetur: nec factum est occultum, sed ut in palam veniat.

23 Si quis habet aures audire, audiat.

24 Aliam parabolam proposuit illis, dicens: Assimilatum est regnum cælorum homini seminanti pulchrum semen in agro suo.

25 In verò dormire homines, venit ejus inimicus, & seminavit zizania in medio tritici, & abiit.

26 Quum autem crevit herba, & fructum fecit, tunc apparuerunt & zizania?

27 Accedentes autem servi patris familias dixerunt ei: Domine, nonne pulchrum semen seminasti in tuo agro? Unde ergò habet zizania?

28 Ille verò ait illis: Inimicus homo hoc fecit. At servi dixerunt ei: Vis igitur abeuntes colligamus ea?

29 Ille verò ait: Non; ne forte colligentes zizania, eradicetis simul eis triticum.

30 Sinite crescere utraque usque ad messem: & in tempore messis dicam messoribus, Colligite primum zizania & alligate ea in fasciculos, ad comburendum ea: at triticum congregate in horreum meum.

36 Tunc dimittens turbas, venit in domum Jesus: & accesserunt ad eum discipuli ejus, dicentes: Explica nobis parabolam zizaniorum agri.

37 Ille verò respondens ait illis: Seminans pulchrum semen, est Filius hominis.

38 At ager est mundus. Verum pulchrum semen, hi sunt filii regni. At zizania, sunt filii mali.

21 Il leur disoit encore : Apporte-t-on une chandelle pour la mettre sous un boisseau, ou sous un lit ? N'est ce pas pour la mettre sur un chandelier ?

22. Car il n'y a rien de secret qui ne doive être manifesté, et il n'y a rien de caché qui ne doive venir en évidence.

23. Si quelqu'un a des oreilles pour entendre, qu'il entende.

24. Jésus leur proposa une autre similitude, en disant : Le Royaume des cieux est semblable à un homme qui avoit semé de bonne semence en son champ.

25. Mais pendant que les hommes dormoient, son ennemi vint, qui sema de l'yvraie parmi le blé, et s'en alla.

26. Et après que la semence eut poussé, et qu'elle eut produit du fruit, l'yvraie parut aussi.

27. Alors les serviteurs du père de famille lui vinrent dire : Seigneur, n'as-tu pas semé de bonne semence dans ton champ ? D'où vient donc qu'il y a de l'yvraie ?

28. Et il leur dit : C'est un ennemi qui a fait cela. Et les serviteurs lui répondirent : Veux-tu donc que nous allions la cueillir ?

29. Et il leur dit : Non, de peur qu'il n'arrive qu'en cueillant l'yvraie vous n'arrachiez le froment en même tems.

30. Laissez-les croître tous deux ensemble, jusqu'à la moisson ; et au tems de la moisson, je dirai aux moissonneurs : Cueillez premièrement l'yvraie, et liez-la en faisceaux pour la brûler, mais assemblez le froment dans mon grenier.

36. Alors *Jésus* ayant renvoyé le peuple, s'en alla à la maison, et ses Disciples étant venus vers lui, lui dirent : Explique-nous la similitude de l'yvraie du champ.

37. Il leur répondit et leur dit : Celui qui sème la bonne semence, c'est le Fils de l'homme.

38. Le champ, c'est le monde. La bonne semence, ce sont les enfans du Royaume. L'yvraie, ce sont les enfans du malin.

39. L'ennemi qui l'a semée, c'est le Diable. La moisson, c'est la fin du monde ; et les moissonneurs, sont les Anges.

---

21 And he said unto them, Is a candle brought to be put under a bushel, or under a bed, and not to be set on a candlestick?

22 For there is nothing hid which shall not be manifested ; neither was any thing kept secret, but that it should come abroad.

23 If any man have ears to hear, let him hear.

24 Another parable put he forth unto them, saying, The kingdom of heaven is likened unto a man which sowed good seed in his field :

25 But, while men slept, his enemy came and sowed tares among the wheat, and went his way.

26 But when the blade was sprung up, and brought forth fruit, then appeared the tares also.

27 So the servants of the householder came and said unto him, Sir, didst not thou sow good seed in thy field ? from whence then hath it tares ?

28 He said unto them, An enemy hath done this. The servants said unto them, Wilt thou then that we go and gather them up ?

29 But he said, Nay ; lest, while ye gather up the tares, ye root up also the wheat with them.

30 Let both grow together until the harvest ; and in the time of harvest I will say to the reapers, Gather ye together first the tares, and bind them in bundles to burn them : but gather the wheat into my barn.

36 Then Jesus sent the multitude away, and went into the house : and his disciples came unto him, saying, Declare unto us the parable of the tares of the field.

37 H answered and said unto them, He that soweth the good seed is the Son of Man ;

38 The field is the world ; the good seed are the children of the kingdom ; but the tares are the children of the wicked *one* ; .

* 39 Ὁ δὲ ἐχθρὸς ὁ σπείρας αὐτά, ἐςιν ὁ διάβολ@· ὁ δὲ θερισμὸς, † συντέλεια τῦ αἰῶνός ἐςιν· οἱ δὲ θερισταὶ, ἄγγελοί εἰσιν.

40 Ὥσπερ ἔν συλλέγεται τὰ ζιζάνια, καὶ πυρὶ καλακαίεται· ὅτως ἔςαι ἐν τῇ συντελείᾳ τῦ αἰῶν@ τύτυ.

41 Ἀποςελεῖ ὁ υἱὸς τῦ ἀνθρώπυ τὺς ἀγγέλυς αὐτῦ, καὶ συλλέξυσιν ἐκ τῆς βασιλείας αὐτῦ πάντα τὰ σκάνδαλα, καὶ τὺς ποιῦντας τὴν ἀνομίαν.

42 Καὶ βαλῦσιν αὐτὺς εἰς τὴν κάμινον τῦ πυρός· ἐκεῖ ἔςαι ὁ κλαυθμὸς καὶ ὁ βρυγμὸς τῶν ὀδόντων.

* 43 Τότε οἱ ‡ δίκαιοι † ἐκλάμψυσιν ‡ ὡς ὁ ‡ ἥλιος, ἐν τῇ βασιλείᾳ τῦ πατρὸς αὐτῶν. Ὁ ἔχων ὦτα ἀκύειν, ἀκυέτω.

44 Πάλιν ὁμοία ἐςὶν ἡ βασιλεία τῶν ὐρανῶν θησαυρῷ κεκρυμμένῳ ἐν τῷ ἀγρῷ, ὃν εὑρὼν ἄνθρωπ@ ἔκρυψε, καὶ ἀπὸ τῆς χαρᾶς αὐτῦ ὑπάγει, καὶ πάντα ὅσα ἔχει, πωλεῖ, καὶ ἀγοράζει τὸν ἀγρὸν ἐκεῖνον.

45 Πάλιν ὁμοία ἐςὶν ἡ βασιλεία τῶν ὐρανῶν ἀνθρώπῳ ἐμπόρῳ, ζητῦντι καλὺς μαργαρίτας.

46 Ὃς εὑρὼν ἕνα πολύτιμον μαργαρίτην, ἀπελθὼν, πέπρακε πάντα ὅσα εἶχε, καὶ ἠγόρασεν αὐτόν.

* 47 ‡ Πάλιν ‡ ὁμοία ἐςὶν ἡ βασιλεία τῶν ‡ ὐρανῶν † σαγήνῃ βληθείσῃ εἰς τὴν θάλασσαν, καὶ ἐκ παντὸς γένυς συναγαγύσῃ.

* 48 Ἥν, ὅτε ἐπληρώθη, ‡ ἀναβιβάσαντες ‡ ἐπὶ τὸν ‡ αἰγιαλὸν, καὶ καθίσαντες, συνέλεξαν τὰ καλὰ εἰς ‡ ἀγγεῖα, τὰ δὲ ‡ σαπρὰ ἔξω ἔβαλον.

49 Οὕτως ἔςαι ἐν τῇ συντελείᾳ τῦ αἰῶν@ ἐξελεύσονται οἱ ἄγγελοι, καὶ ἀφοριῦσι τὺς πονηρὺς ἐκ μέσυ τῶν δικαίων·

50 Καὶ βαλῦσιν αὐτὺς εἰς τὴν κάμινον τῦ πυρός· ἐκεῖ ἔςαι ὁ κλαυθμὸς καὶ ὁ βρυγμὸς τῶν ὀδόντων.

51 Λέγει αὐτοῖς ὁ Ἰησῦς. Συνήκατε ταῦτα πάντα; Λέγυσιν αὐτῷ· Ναὶ Κύριε.

52 Ὁ δὲ εἶπεν αὐτοῖς· Διὰ τῦτο πᾶς γραμμαλεὺς μαθητευθεὶς εἰς τὴν βασιλείαν τῶν ὐρανῶν, ὅμοιός ἐςιν ἀνθρώπῳ οἰκοδεσπότῃ, ὅςις ἐκβάλλει ἐκ τῦ θησαυρῦ αὐτῦ καινὰ καὶ παλαιά.

---

39 At inimicus seminans ea, est diabolus. At messis, consummatio seculi est. At messores, angeli sunt.

40 Sicut ergo colliguntur zizania, & igni comburuntur: sic erit in consummatione seculi.

41 Mittet Filius hominis angelos suos, & colligent de regno ejus omnia scandala, & facientes iniquitatem:

42 Et mittent eos in caminum ignis, ibi erit fletus & fremitus dentium.

43 Tunc justi fulgebunt sicut Sol in regno Patris eorum. Habens aures audire, audiat.

44 Iterum simile est regnum cælorum thesauro abscondito in agro: quem inveniens homo abscondit, & præ gaudio illius vadit, & universa quæ habet vendit, & emit agrum illum.

45 Iterum simile est regnum cælorum homini negotiatori, quærenti bonas margaritas:

46 Qui inveniens unam pretiosam margaritam, abiens vendidit omnia quæ habuit, et emit eam.

47 Iterum simile est regnum cælorum sagenæ jactæ in mare, & ex omni genere cogenti.

48 Quam, quum impleta esset, producentes super littus, & sedentes, collegerunt pulcra in receptacula, at vitiosa foras ejecerunt.

49 Sic erit in consummatione seculi: exibunt angeli, & segregabunt malos de medio justorum:

50 Et projicient eos in caminum ignis: ibi erit fletus & fremitus dentium.

51 Dicit illis Jesus: Intellexistis hæc omnia? Dicunt ei, utique Domine.

52 Is autem dixit illis: Propter hoc omnis Scriba doctus in regnum cælorum, similis est homini patrisfamilias, qui ejicit de thesauro suo nova & vetera.

39. L'ennemi qui l'a semée, c'est le Diable. La moisson, c'est la fin du monde ; et les moissonneurs, sont les Anges.

40. Comme donc on amasse l'yvraie et qu'on la brûle dans le feu, il en sera de même à la fin du monde.

41. Le Fils de l'homme envoyera ses Anges, qui ôteront de son Royaume tous les scandales, et ceux qui font l'iniquité.

42. Et ils les jeteront dans la fournaise ardente ; c'est là qu'il y aura des pleurs et des grincemens de dents.

43. Alors les justes luiront comme le soleil, dans le Royaume de leur Père. Que celui qui a des oreilles pour ouïr, entende.

44. Le Royaume des cieux est encore semblable à un trésor caché dans un champ, qu'un homme a trouvé, et qu'il cache ; et de la joie qu'il en a, il s'en va, et vend tout ce qu'il a, et achète ce champ-là.

45. Le Royaume des cieux est encore semblable à un marchand qui cherche de belles perles ;

46. Et qui ayant trouvé une perle de grand prix, s'en va, et vend tout ce qu'il a, et l'achète.

47. Le Royaume des cieux est encore semblable à un filet, qui étant jeté dans la mer, ramasse toutes sortes de choses ;

48. Quand il est rempli, les pêcheurs le tirent sur le rivage ; et s'étant assis, ils mettent ce qu'il y a de bon à part dans *leurs* vaisseaux, et ils jettent ce qui ne vaut rien.

49. Il en sera de même à la fin du monde : Les Anges viendront, et sépareront les méchans du milieu des justes.

50. Et ils jeteront *les méchans* dans la fournaise ardente ; c'est là qu'il y aura des pleurs et des grincemens de dents.

51. Et Jésus dit à ses Disciples,

que tout Docteur qui est *bien* instruit dans *ce qui regarde* le Royaume des cieux, est semblable à un père de famille, qui tire de son trésor des choses nouvelles et des choses vieilles.

39 The enemy that sowed them is the devil ; the harvest is the end of the world : and the reapers are the angels.

40 As, therefore, the tares are gathered and burned in the fire ; so shall it be in the end of this world.

41 The Son of Man shall send forth his angels, and they shall gather out of his kingdom all things that offend, and them which do iniquity ;

42 And shall cast them into a furnace of fire : there shall be wailing and gnashing of teeth.

43 Then shall the righteous shine forth as the sun in the kingdom of their Father. Who hath ears to hear, let him hear.

44 Again, the kingdom of heaven is like unto treasure hid in a field ; the which when a man hath found he hideth, and, for joy thereof, goeth and selleth all that he hath, and buyeth that field.

45 Again, the kingdom of heaven is like unto a merchantman, seeking goodly pearls :

46 Who, when he had found one pearl of great price, went and sold all that he had, and bought it.

47 Again, the kingdom of heaven is like unto a net, that was cast into the sea, and gathered of every kind :

48 Which, when it was full, they drew to shore, and sat down, and gathered the good into vessels, but cast the bad away.

49 So shall it be at the end of the world : the angels shall come forth, and sever the wicked from among the just.

50 And, shall cast them into the furnace of fire : there shall be wailing and gnashing of teeth.

51 Jesus saith unto them, Have ye understood all these things ? They say unto him, Yea, Lord.

52 Then said he unto them, Therefore every scribe *which is* instructed unto the kingdom of heaven is like unto a man *that is* an householder, which bringeth forth out of his treasure *things* new and old.

26 Καὶ ἔλεγεν· Οὕτως ἐςὶν ἡ
βασιλεία τῦ Θεῦ, ὡς ἐὰν ἄνθρω-
π⊕· βάλῃ τὸν σπόρον ἐπὶ τῆς γῆς,

* 27 Καὶ καθεύδῃ, κ̄ ἐγείρηlaι
νύκla κ̄ ἡμέραν· κ̄ ὁ ‡ σπόρ⊕·
‡ βλαςάνῃ, κ̄ † μηκύνηlαι, ὡς
ἐκ οἶδεν αὐτός.

* 28 ‡ Αὐτομάτη γὰρ ἡ γῆ ‡
καρποφορεῖ, πρῶτον χόρτον, ‡ εἶτα
‡ ςάχυν, εἶτα πλήρη σῖτον ἐν τῷ
ςάχυϊ.

29 Ὅταν δὲ παραδῷ ὁ καρ-
πὸς, εὐθέως ἀποςέλλει τὸ δρέπα-
νον, ὅτι παρέςηκεν ὁ θερισμός.

30 Καὶ ἔλεγε Τίνι ὁμοιώσω-
μεν τὴν βασιλείαν τῦ Θεῦ; ἢ
ἐν ποίᾳ παραβολῇ παραβάλωμεν
αὐτήν;

31 Ὡς κόκκῳ σινάπεως, ὃς,
ὅταν σπαρῇ ἐπὶ τῆς γῆς, μικρό-
τερ⊕· πάνlων τῶν σπερμάτων
ἐςὶ τῶν ἐπὶ τῆς γῆς.

32 Καὶ ὅταν σπαρῇ, ἀναβαί-
νει, κ̄ γίνεlαι πάνlων τῶν λα-
χάνων μείζων, κ̄ ποιεῖ κλά-
δὺς μεγάλὺς, ὥςε δύναςθαι ὑπὸ
τὴν σκιὰν αὐτῦ τὰ πεlεινὰ τῦ
ὐρανῦ καlασκηνῦν.

33 Καὶ τοιαύταις παραβολαῖς
πολλαῖς ἐλάλει αὐτοῖς τὸν λόγον, καθὼς ἠδύναντο ἀκύειν.

34 Χωρὶς δὲ παραβολῆς ἐκ
ἐλάλει αὐτοῖς· κατ᾽ ἰδίαν δὲ τοῖς
μαθηlαῖς αὐτῦ ἐπέλυε πάνlα.

57 Ἐγένεlο δὲ πορευομένων αὐτῶν ἐν τῇ ὁδῷ, εἶπέ τις πρὸς αὐ-
τόν· Ἀκολυθήσω σοι ὅπυ ἂν ἀ-
πέρχῃ, Κύριε.

* 58 Καὶ εἶπεν αὐτῷ ὁ Ἰησῦς·
Αἱ ἀλώπεκες ‡ φωλεὺς ἔχυ-
σι, κ̄ τὰ ‡ πεlεινὰ τῦ ὐρανῦ
‡ καlασκηνώσεις· ὁ δὲ υἱὸς τῦ
ἀνθρώπυ ἐκ ἔχει πῦ τὴν κεφαλὴν
κλίνῃ.

59 Εἶπε δὲ πρὸς ἕτερον· Ἀκο-
λούθει μοι. Ὁ δὲ εἶπε Κύριε,
ἐπίτρεψόν μοι ἀπελθόνlι πρῶτον
θάψαι τὸν πατέρα μυ.

60 Εἶπε δὲ αὐτῷ ὁ Ἰησῦς·
Ἄφες τὺς νεκρὺς θάψαι τὺς ἑαυτῶν νεκρύς· σὺ δὲ ἀπελθὼν διάγ-
γελλε τὴν βασιλείαν τῦ Θεῦ.

61 Εἶπε δὲ κ̄ ἕτερ⊕· Ἀκο-
λυθήσω σοι, Κύριε· πρῶτον δὲ
ἐπίτρεψόν μοι ἀποτάξασθαι τοῖς
εἰς τὸν οἶκόν μυ.

* 62 Εἶπε δὲ πρὸς αὐτὸν ὁ
Ἰησῦς· Οὐδεὶς ‡ ἐπιβαλὼν τὴν
χεῖρα αὐτῦ ἐπ᾽ ‡ ἄροτρον, κ̄
βλέπων εἰς τὰ ὀπίσω, εὔθετός
ἐςιν εἰς τὴν βασιλείαν τῦ Θεῦ.

---

26 Et dicebat : Sic eſt regnum . Dei, quemadmodum ſi
homo jaciat ſementem in terram :

27 Et dormiat, & excitetur
nocte & die : & ſemen germinet
& augeatur ut neſcit ille.

28 Spontanea enim terra
fructum fert, primùm herbam,
deinde ſpicam, deinde plenum
frumentum in ſpica.

29 Quum verò ediderit fructus, ſtatim mittit falcem, quoniam adeſt meſſis.

30 Et dicebat : Cui aſſimila-
bimus regnum Dei ? aut in qua
parabola comparabimus illud ?

31 Sicut grano ſinapis, quod,
quum ſeminatum fuerit in terra,
minus omnibus ſeminibus eſt
quæ in terra :

32 Et quum ſeminatum fue-
rit, aſcendit, & fit omnibus
oleribus majus, & facit ramos
magnos, ita ut poſſint ſub um-
brâ ejus volatilia cæli nidulari.

33 Et talibus parabolis multis loquebatur eis ſermonem
prout poterant audire.

34 Sine autem parabola non
loquebatur eis : privatim autem
diſcipulis ſuis ſolvebat omnia.

57 Factum eſt autem ambu-
lantibus illis in via, dixit quidam ad illum : Sequar te quo-
cumque abieris, Domine.

58 Et dixit illi Jeſus : Vul-
pes foveas habent, & volucres cæli nidos : verum filius
hominis non habet ubi caput
reclinet.

59 Ait autem ad alterum :
Sequere me. Ille autem dixit :
Domine, permitte mihi ab-
eunti primùm ſepelire patrem
meum.

60 Dixit autem ei Jeſus :
Sine mortuos ſepelire ſuos mortuos : tu autem abiens annuncia
regnum Dei.

61 Ait autem & alter : Sequar te, Domine : primùm autem permitte mihi renuntiare
his qui ad domum meam.

62 Ait autem ad illum Jeſus :
Nemo immittens manum ſuam
ad aratrum, & reſpiciens in quæ
retro, aptus eſt ad regnum
Dei.

26. Il dit encore : Il en est du Royaume de Dieu, comme si un homme avoit jeté de la semence en terre ;

27. Soit qu'il dorme ou qu'il se lève, la nuit ou le jour, la semence germe et croît sans qu'il sache comment.

28. Car la terre produit d'elle-même, premièrement, l'herbe, ensuite l'épi, et puis le grain tout formé dans l'épi.

29. Et quand le fruit est dans sa maturité, on y met aussitôt la faucille, parce que la moisson est prête.

30. Il disoit encore : A quoi comparerons-nous le Royaume de Dieu, ou par quelle similitude le représenterons-nous ?

31. Il en est comme du grain de moutarde, lequel, lorsqu'on le sème, est la plus petite de toutes les semences que l'on jette en terre.

32. Mais après qu'on l'a semé, il monte et devient plus grand que tous les autres légumes, et pousse de grandes branches ; de sorte que les oiseaux du ciel peuvent demeurer sous son ombre.

33. Il leur annonçoit ainsi la parole par plusieurs similitudes de cette sorte, selon qu'ils étoient capables de l'entendre.

34. Et il ne leur parloit point sans similitudes ; mais lorsqu'il étoit en particulier, il expliquoit tout à ses Disciples.

57. Et comme ils étoient en chemin, un homme lui dit : Je te suivrai, Seigneur, par-tout où tu iras.

58. Mais Jésus lui répondit : Les renards ont des tanières, et les oiseaux du ciel ont des nids ; mais le Fils de l'homme n'a pas où reposer sa tête.

59. Il dit à un autre : Suis-moi. Et il lui répondit : Seigneur, permets que j'aille auparavant ensevelir mon père.

60. Jésus lui dit : Laisse les morts ensevelir leurs morts ; mais toi, va et annonce le Règne de Dieu.

61. Un autre lui dit : Je te suivrai, Seigneur ; mais permets-moi de prendre auparavant congé de ceux qui sont dans ma maison.

62. Mais Jésus lui répondit : Celui qui met la main à la charrue, et regarde derrière lui, n'est point propre pour le Royaume de Dieu.

26 And he said, So is the kingdom of God, as if a man should cast seed into the ground ;

27 And should sleep, and rise night and day, and the seed should spring and grow up, he knoweth not how.

28 For the earth bringeth forth fruit of herself ; first the blade, then the ear, after that the full corn in the ear.

29 But when the fruit is brought forth, immediately he putteth in the sickle, because the harvest is come.

30 And he said, Whereunto shall we liken the kingdom of God? or with what comparison shall we compare it?

31 It is like a grain of mustard-seed, which, when it is sown in the earth, is less than all the seeds that be in the earth :

32 But when it is sown, it groweth up, and becometh greater than all herbs, and shooteth out great branches ; so that the fowls of the air may lodge under the shadow of it.

33 And with many such parables spake he the word unto them, as they were able to hear it.

34 But without a parable spake he not unto them : and when they were alone, he expounded all things to his disciples.

57 And it came to pass, that, as they went in the way, a certain man said unto him, Lord, I will follow thee whithersoever thou goest.

58 And Jesus said unto him, Foxes have holes, and birds of the air have nests ; but the Son of Man hath not where to lay his head.

59 And he said unto another, Follow me. But he said, Lord, suffer me first to go and bury my father.

60 Jesus said unto him, Let the dead bury their dead : but go thou and preach the kingdom of God.

61 And another also said, Lord, I will follow thee : but let me first go bid them farewell, which are at home at my house.

62 And Jesus said unto him, No man having put his hand to the plough, and looking back, is fit for the kingdom of God.

27 Καὶ μετὰ ταῦτα ἐξῆλθε, ἢ ἐθεάσαλο τελώνην ὀνόμαλι Λευΐν, καθήμενον ἐπὶ τὸ τελώνιον, ἢ εἶπεν αὐτῷ· Ἀκολύθει μοι.

28 Καὶ καλαλιπὼν ἅπανλα, ἀναςὰς ἠκολύθησεν αὐτῷ.

29 Καὶ ἐποίησε δοχὴν μεγάλην ὁ Λευῒς αὐτῷ ἐν τῇ οἰκίᾳ αὐτῷ· ἢ ϖιλλοὶ τελῶναι ἢ ἁμαρλωλοὶ συνανέκεινλο τῷ Ἰησῦ ἢ τοῖς μαθηλαῖς αὐτῷ· ἦσαν γὰρ ϖολλοὶ, ἢ ἠκολύθησάν αὐτῷ.

16 Καὶ οἱ γραμμαλεῖς ἢ οἱ φαρισαῖοι ἰδόνλες αὐτὸν ἐσθίονλα μετὰ τῶν τελωνῶν ἢ ἁμαρλωλῶν, ἔλεγον τοῖς μαθηλαῖς αὐτῷ· Τί ὅτι μετὰ τῶν τελωνῶν ἢ ἁμαρλωλῶν ἐσθίει ἢ ϖίνει;

17 Καὶ ἀκύσας ὁ Ἰησῦς, λέγει αὐτοῖς· Οὐ χρείαν ἔχυσιν οἱ ἰσχύονλες ἰαlρῦ, ἀλλ᾽ οἱ κακῶς ἔχονλες· ἐκ ἦλθον καλέσαι δικαίυς, ἀλλὰ ἁμαρλωλὺς εἰς μετάνοιαν.

36 Ἔλεγε δὲ ἢ ϖαραβολὴν ϖρὸς αὐτές· Ὅτι ἐδεὶς ἐπίβλημα ἱμαλίυ καινῦ ἐπιβάλλει ἐπὶ ἱμάτιον ϖαλαιόν· εἰ δὲ μήγε, ἢ τὸ καινὸν σχίζει, ἢ τῷ ϖαλαιῷ ἐ συμφωνεῖ ἐπίβλημα τὸ ἀπὸ τῦ καινῦ.

37 Καὶ ἐδεὶς βάλλει οἶνον νέον εἰς ἀσκὺς ϖαλαιύς· εἰ δὲ μήγε, ῥήξει ὁ νέ☉ οἶ☉ τὺς ἀσκὺς, ἢ αὐτὸς ἐκχυθήσεlαι, ἢ οἱ ἀσκοὶ ἀπολῦνlαι.

38 Ἀλλὰ οἶνον νέον εἰς ἀσκὺς καινὺς βλητέον· ἢ ἀμφότεροι συνlηρῦνlαι.

53 Καὶ ἐγένεlο, ὅτε ἐτέλεσεν ὁ Ἰησῦς τὰς ϖαραβολὰς ταύτας, μετῆρεν ἐκεῖθεν.

54 Καὶ ἐλθὼν εἰς τὴν ϖαlρίδα αὐτῦ, ἐδίδασκεν αὐτὺς ἐν τῇ συναγωγῇ αὐτῶν· ὡς ἐκπλήτlεσθαι αὐτὺς, ἢ λέγειν· Πόθεν τύτῳ ἡ σοφία αὕτη, ἢ αἱ δυνάμεις;

55 Οὐχ ὗτός ἐςιν ὁ τῦ τέκτον☉ υἱός; ἐχὶ ἡ μήτηρ αὐτῦ λέγεlαι Μαριὰμ, ἢ οἱ ἀδελφοὶ αὐτῦ Ἰάκωβ☉, ἢ Ἰωσῆς, ἢ Σίμων, ἢ Ἰύδας;

56 Καὶ αἱ ἀδελφαὶ αὐτῦ ἐχὶ ϖᾶσαι ϖρὸς ἡμᾶς εἰσι; ϖόθεν ἐν

---

27 Et post hæc exiit, & conspexit publicanum nomine, Levin, sedentem ad telonium, & ait illi: Sequere me.

28 Et relinquens omnia, surgens sequutus est eum.

29 Et fecit convivium magnum Levis ei in domo sua: & multi publicani & peccatores simul discumbebant Jesu, & discipulis ejus: erant enim multi, & sequebantur eum.

16 Et Scribæ & Pharisæi videntes eum edentem cum publicanis & peccatoribus, dicebant discipulis ejus: Quid, quod cum publicanis & peccatoribus manducat & bibit?

17 Et audiens Jesus, ait illis: Non usum habent valentes medico. sed malè habentes, non veni vocare justos, sed peccatores ad pœnitentiam.

36 Dicebat autem & similitudinem ad illos: Quia nemo adjectionem vestimenti novi adjicit ad vestimentum vetus: si vero non, & novum scindit, & veteri non convenit commissura à novo.

37 Et nemo conjicit vinum novum in utres veteres: si autem non, rumpet novum vinum utres, & ipsum effundetur, & utres peribunt.

38 Sed vinum novum in utres novos injiciendum, & utraque conservantur.

53 Et factum est, quum consummasset Jesus parabolas istas, transiit inde.

54 Et veniens in patriam suam docebat eos in synagoga eorum, ita ut obstupefieri ipsos, & dicere: Unde huic sapientia hæc, & efficacitates?

55 Nonne hic est fabri filius? Nonne mater ejus dicitur Maria, & fratres ejus Jacobus, & Joses, & Simon, & Judas?

56 Et sorores ejus, nonne omnes apud nos sunt? unde ergo

27. Après cela il sortit, et il vit un péager nommé Lévi, assis au bureau des impôts , et il lui dit : Suis-moi.

28. Et lui, quittant tout , se leva et le suivit.

29. Et Lévi lui fit un grand festin dans sa maison , où il se trouva plusieurs péagers et gens de mauvaise vie se mirent aussi à table avec Jésus et ses Disciples ; car il y en avoit beaucoup qui l'avoient suivi.

16. Et les Scribes et les Pharisiens , voyant qu'il mangeoit avec des péagers et des gens de mauvaise vie , disoient à ses Disciples : Pourquoi votre Maître mange-t-il et boit-il avec les péagers, et les gens de mauvaise vie ?

17. Et Jésus ayant ouï *cela*, leur dit : Ce ne sont pas ceux qui sont en santé qui ont besoin de Médecin , mais ce sont ceux qui se portent mal : Je suis venu appeler à la repentance, non les justes , mais les pécheurs.

36. Il leur dit aussi une similitude : Personne ne met une pièce d'un habit neuf à un vieux habit ; autrement ce qui est neuf déchireroit , et la pièce du drap neuf ne convient point au vieux.

37. Personne aussi ne met le vin nouveau dans de vieux vaisseaux ; autrement le vin nouveau romproit les vaisseaux , et se répandroit, et les vaisseaux seroient perdus.

38. Mais le vin nouveau doit être mis dans des vaisseaux neufs , et ainsi tous les deux se conservent.

53. Et il arriva que quand Jésus eut achevé ces similitudes , il se retira de *ce lieu-*là.

54. Et étant venu en sa patrie, il les enseignoit dans leur synagogue ; de sorte qu'ils étoient étonnés , et qu'ils disoient : D'où viennent à cet homme cette sagesse et ces miracles ?

55. N'est-ce pas le fils du charpentier ? sa mère ne s'appelle-t-elle pas Marie , et ses frères , Jaques , Joses , Simon et Jude ?

56. Et ses sœurs ne sont - elles pas toutes parmi nous ? D'où lui

L. 5.

27 And after these things, he went forth, and saw a publican, named Levi, sitting at the receipt of custom: and he said unto him, Follow me.

28 And he left all, rose up, and followed him.

29 And Levi made him a great feast in his own house : and many publicans and sinners sat also together with Jesus and his disciples : for there were many, and they followed him.

15. Mk. 2.

16 And when the scribes and Pharisees saw him eat with publicans and sinners, they said unto his disciples, How is it that he eateth and drinketh with publicans and sinners ?

17 When Jesus heard *it*, he saith unto them, They that are whole have no need of the physician, but they that are sick : I came not to call the righteous, but sinners to repentance.

L. 5.

36 And he spake also a parable unto them ; No man putteth a piece of a new garment upon an old ; if otherwise, then both the new maketh a rent, and the piece that was *taken* out of the new agreeth not with the old.

37 And no man putteth new wine into old bottles ; else the new wine will burst the bottles, and be spilled, and the bottles shall perish.

38 But new wine must be put into new bottles : and both are preserved.

M. 13.

53 And it came to pass, *that* when Jesus had finished these parables, he departed thence.

54 And when he was come into his own country, he taught them in their synagogue, insomuch that they were astonished, and said, Whence hath this *man* this wisdom, and *these* mighty works ?

55 Is not this the carpenter's son ? is not his mother called Mary ? and his brethren, James, and Joses, and Simon, and Judas ?

56 And his sisters, are they not all with us ? Whence then hath

αὐτῷ ταῦτα πάντα;
57 Καὶ ἐσκανδαλίζοντο ἐν αὐτῷ. Ὁ δὲ Ἰησοῦς εἶπεν αὐτοῖς.
Οὐκ ἔςι προφήτης ἄτιμ⊙., εἰ μὴ
ἐν τῇ πατρίδι αὐτῷ, κ, ἐν τῇ οἰκία
αὐτῷ.

36 Ἰδὼν δὲ τοὺς ὄχλους, ἐ-
σπλαγχνίσθη περὶ αὐτῶν, ὅτι ἦσαν
ἐκλελυμένοι κ, ἐρριμμένοι ὡσεὶ πρόβατα μὴ ἔχοντα ποιμένα.

7 Καὶ προσκαλεῖται τοὺς δώδεκα, κ, ἤρξατο αὐτοὺς ἀποςέλ-
λειν δύο δύο· κ,
παραγγείλας αὐτοῖς,
λέγων· Εἰς ὁδὸν ἐθνῶν μὴ ἀπέλθη-
τε, κ, εἰς πόλιν Σαμαρειτῶν μὴ
εἰσέλθητε·

6 Πορεύεσθε δὲ μᾶλλον πρὸς τὰ
πρόβατα τὰ ἀπολωλότα οἴκου
Ἰσραήλ.

9 Μὴ κτήσησθε χρυσὸν, μηδὲ
ἄργυρον, μηδὲ χαλκὸν εἰς τὰς ζώ-
νας ὑμῶν.

* 10 Μὴ ‡ πήραν εἰς ὁδὸν, μηδὲ
δύο χιτῶνας, μηδὲ ὑποδήματα,
μηδὲ ῥάβδον· ἄξι⊙. γὰρ ὁ ἐργάτης τῆς τροφῆς αὐτοῦ ἐςιν.

11 Εἰς ἣν δ᾽ ἂν πόλιν ἢ κώμην
εἰσέλθητε, ἐξετάσατε τίς ἐν αὐτῇ
ἄξιός ἐςι· κἀκεῖ μείνατε ἕως ἂν
ἐξέλθητε.

12 Εἰσερχόμενοι δὲ εἰς τὴν οἰκίαν, ἀσπάσασθε αὐτήν.

13 Καὶ ἐὰν μὲν ᾖ ἡ οἰκία ἀξία,
ἐλθέτω ἡ εἰρήνη ὑμῶν ἐπ᾽ αὐτήν·
ἐὰν δὲ μὴ ᾖ ἀξία, ἡ εἰρήνη ὑμῶν
πρὸς ὑμᾶς ἐπιςραφήτω.

14 Καὶ ὃς ἐὰν μὴ δέξηται ὑμᾶς,
μηδὲ ἀκούσῃ τοὺς λόγους ὑμῶν,
ἐξερχόμενοι τῆς οἰκίας ἢ τῆς πόλεως ἐκείνης, ἐκτινάξατε τὸν κο-
νιορτὸν τῶν ποδῶν ὑμῶν.

15 Ἀμὴν λέγω ὑμῖν, ἀνεκτότε-
ρον ἔςαι γῇ Σοδόμων κ, Γομόρρων
ἐν ἡμέρᾳ κρίσεως, ἢ τῇ πόλει ἐ-
κείνῃ.

16 Ἰδοὺ, ἐγὼ ἀποςέλλω ὑμᾶς
ὡς πρόβατα ἐν μέσῳ λύκων· γίνεσθε οὖν φρόνιμοι ὡς οἱ ὄφεις, κ,
ἀκέραιοι ὡς αἱ περιςεραί.

17 Προσέχετε δὲ ἀπὸ τῶν ἀν-
θρώπων· παραδώσουσι γὰρ ὑμᾶς
εἰς συνέδρια, κ, ἐν ταῖς συναγωγαῖς
αὐτῶν μαςιγώσουσιν ὑμᾶς.

huic illa omnia?
57 Et scandalizabantur in eo.
At Jesus dixit eis: non est Propheta inhonoratus, si non in pa-
tria sua, & in domo sua.

36 Videns autem turbas, misertus est de eis, quia erant vex-
ati, & dispersi sicut oves non
habentes pastorem.

7 Et advocat duodecim: &
cœpit eos mittere duos duos, &
denuncians eis, dicens: In viam
gentium ne abieritis, & in civitatem Samaritanorum ne intraveritis.

6 Ite autem magis ad oves
perditas domus Israël.

9 Ne possideatis aurum, neque argentum, neque æs in zo-
nis vestris:

10 Non peram in viam, neque
duas tunicas, neque calceamenta, neque virgam: dignus enim
operarius alimento suo est.

11 In quamcunque autem civitatem aut castellum intraveritis, interrogate quis in ea dignus
sit: & ibi manete donec exeatis.

12 Intrantes autem in do-
mum, salutate eam.

13 Et si quidem fuerit domus
digna, ingrediatur pax vestra
super eam: si autem non fuerit
digna, pax vestra ad vos conver-
tatur.

14 Et qui non receperit vos
neque audierit sermones vestros,
exeuntes domo vel civitate illâ,
excutite pulverem pedum vestrorum.

15 Amen dico vobis, Tolera-
bilius erit terræ Sodomorum &
Gomorrhæorum in die judicii,
quam civitati illi.

16 Ecce ego mitto vos sicut o-
ves in medio luporum. Estote
ergo prudentes sicut serpentes,
& simplices sicut columbæ.

17 Cavete autem ab hominibus:
Tradent enim vos in confessus, &
in synagogis suis flagellabunt vos.

viennent donc toutes ces choses ? | this *man* all these things ?

57. De sorte qu'ils se scandalisoient de lui. Mais Jésus leur dit: Un Prophète n'est méprisé que dans son pays et dans sa maison.

57 And they were offended in him. But Jesus said unto them, A prophet is not without honour, save in his own country, and in his own house.

58. Et il ne fit là que peu de miracles, à cause de leur incrédulité.

36. Et voyant la multitude de peuple, il fut ému de compassion envers eux, de ce qu'ils étoient dispersés et errans, comme des brebis qui n'ont point de berger.

36 But when he saw the multitudes, he was moved with compassion on them, because they fainted, and were scattered abroad, as sheep having no shepherd.

7. Alors il appela les douze, et il commença à les envoyer deux à deux, il leur donna ses ordres, en disant: N'allez point vers les Gentils; et n'entrez dans aucune ville des Samaritains.

7 And he calleth *unto him* the twelve, and began to send them forth by two and two;

and commanded them, saying, Go not into the way of the Gentiles, and into *any* city of the Samaritans enter ye not:

6. Mais allez plutôt aux brebis de la Maison d'Israël, qui sont perdues.

6 But go rather to the lost sheep of the house of Israel.

9. Ne prenez ni or, ni argent, ni monnoie dans vos ceintures;

9 Provide neither gold, nor silver, nor brass in your purses;

10. Ni sac pour le voyage, ni deux habits, ni souliers, ni bâton; car l'ouvrier est digne de sa nourriture.

10 Nor scrip for your journey, neither two coats, neither shoes, nor yet staves: for the workman is worthy of his meat.

11. Et dans quelque ville ou *dans quelque* bourgade que vous entriez, informez-vous qui est digne *de vous recevoir;* et demeurez-y, jusqu'à-ce que vous partiez *de ce lieu-là.*

11 And into whatsoever city or town ye shall enter, enquire who in it is worthy; and there abide till ye go thence.

12. Et quand vous entrerez dans quelque maison, saluez-la.

12 And when ye come into an house, salute it.

13. Et si la maison en est digne, que votre paix vienne sur elle; mais si elle n'en est pas digne, que votre paix retourne à vous.

13 And if the house be worthy, let your peace come upon it: but if it be not worthy, let your peace return to you.

14. Et par-tout où l'on ne vous recevra pas, et où l'on n'écoutera pas vos paroles, en sortant de cette maison ou de cette ville, secouez la poussière de vos pieds.

14 And whosoever shall not receive you, nor hear your words, when ye depart out of that house, or city, shake off the dust of your feet.

15. Je vous dis en vérité, que Sodome et Gomorrhe seront traitées moins rigoureusement au jour du Jugement, que cette ville-là.

15 Verily I say unto you, It shall be more tolerable for the land of Sodom and Gomorrha, in the day of judgment, than for that city.

16. Voici, je vous envoie comme des brebis au milieu des loups; soyez donc prudens comme des serpens, et simples comme des colombes.

16 Behold, I send you forth as sheep in the midst of wolves: be ye, therefore, wise as serpents, and harmless as doves.

17. Mais donnez-vous garde des hommes; car ils vous livreront aux Tribunaux, et ils vous *feront fouetter* dans les synagogues;

17 But beware of men: for they will deliver you up to the councils, and they will scourge you

29

18 Καὶ ἐπὶ ἡγεμόνας δὲ κ̀ βασιλεῖς ἀχθήσεσθε ἕνεκεν ἐμοῦ, εἰς μαρτύριον αὐτοῖς κ̀ τοῖς ἔθνεσιν.

18 Et ad præſides autem & reges agemini propter me, in teſtimonium illis, & gentibus.

23 Ὅταν δὲ διώκωσιν ὑμᾶς ἐν τῇ πόλει ταύτῃ, φεύγετε εἰς τὴν ἄλλην·

23 Quum autem inſequentur vos in civitate iſtâ, fugite in aliam.

26 Μὴ οὖν φοβηθῆτε αὐτούς· οὐδὲν γάρ ἐςι κεκαλυμμένον, ὃ οὐκ ἀποκαλυφθήσεται, κ̀ κρυπτὸν, ὃ οὐ γνωσθήσεται.

26 Ne ergo timueritis eos. Nihil enim eſt occultum, quod non revelabitur, & abditum, quod non ſcietur.

27 Ὃ λέγω ὑμῖν ἐν τῇ σκοτίᾳ, εἴπατε ἐν τῷ φωτί· κ̀ ὃ εἰς τὸ οὖς ἀκούετε, κηρύξατε ἐπὶ τῶν δωμάτων.

27 Quod dico vobis in tenebris, dicite in lumine: & quod in aurem auditis, prædicate ſuper domos.

28 Καὶ μὴ φοβηθῆτε ἀπὸ τῶν ἀποκτεινόντων τὸ σῶμα, τὴν δὲ ψυχὴν μὴ δυναμένων ἀποκτεῖναι. φοβήθητε δὲ μᾶλλον τὸν δυνάμενον κ̀ ψυχὴν κ̀ σῶμα ἀπολέσαι ἐν γεέννῃ.

28 Et ne timeatis ab occidentibus corpus, at animam non valentibus occidere: timete autem magis potentem & animam & corpus perdere in gehenna.

* 29 Οὐχὶ δύο ‡ ςρουθία ‡ ἀσσαρίου ‡ πωλεῖται, κ̀ ἓν ἐξ αὐτῶν οὐ πεσεῖται ἐπὶ τὴν γῆν, ‡ ἄνευ τοῦ πατρὸς ὑμῶν;

29 Nonne duo paſſeres aſſe væneunt? & unus ex illis non cadet ſuper terram, ſine Patre veſtro.

30 Ὑμῶν δὲ κ̀ αἱ τρίχες τῆς κεφαλῆς πᾶσαι ἐριθμημέναι εἰσί.

30 Veſtri autem & capilli capitis omnes numerati ſunt.

31 Μὴ οὖν φοβηθῆτε· πολλῶν ςρουθίων διαφέρετε ὑμεῖς.

31 Ne ergo timeatis: multis paſſeribus præſtatis vos.

12 Καὶ ἐξελθόντες ἐκήρυσσον, ἵνα μετανοήσωσι·

12 Et exeuntes prædicabant ut pœniterent.

30 Καὶ συνάγονται οἱ ἀπόςολοι πρὸς τὸν Ἰησοῦν, κ̀ ἀπήγγειλαν αὐτῷ πάντα, κ̀ ὅσα ἐποίησαν, κ̀ ὅσα ἐδίδαξαν.

30 Et coguntur Apoſtoli ad Jeſum, & renuntiaverunt ei omnia, & quanta egerant & quanta docuerant.

Κεφ. ζ. 7.

1 ΚΑΙ περιεπάτει ὁ Ἰησοῦς μετὰ ταῦτα ἐν τῇ Γαλιλαίᾳ· οὐ γὰρ ἤθελεν ἐν τῇ Ἰουδαίᾳ περιπατεῖν, ὅτι ἐζήτουν αὐτὸν οἱ Ἰουδαῖοι ἀποκτεῖναι.

CAPUT VII.

1 ET ambulabat Jeſus poſt hæc in Galilæa: non enim volebat in Judæa ambulare, quia quærebant eum Judæi interficere.

Κεφ. ζ'. 7.

1 ΚΑΙ συνάγονται πρὸς αὐτὸν οἱ Φαρισαῖοι, καί τινες τῶν Γραμματέων, ἐλθόντες ἀπὸ Ἱεροσολύμων.

CAPUT VII.

1 ET conveniunt ad eum Phariſæi, & quidam Scribarum venientes ab Hieroſolymis.

* 2 Καὶ ἰδόντες τινὰς τῶν μαθητῶν αὐτοῦ κοιναῖς χερσὶ (τοῦτ' ἔςιν ‡ ἀνίπτοις) ἐσθίοντας ἄρτους, ‡ ἐμέμψαντο.

2 Et videntes quoſdam diſcipulorum ejus communibus manibus (hoc eſt, illotis) edentes panes, incuſarunt.

* 3 (Οἱ γὰρ Φαρισαῖοι κ̀ πάντες οἱ Ἰουδαῖοι, ‡ ἐὰν μὴ ‡ πυγμῇ ‡ νίψωνται τὰς χεῖρας, οὐκ ἐσθίουσι, κρατοῦντες τὴν παράδοσιν τῶν πρεσβυτέρων.

3 Nam Phariſæi & omnes Judæi, ſi non pugillatim laverint manus, non manducant, tenentes traditionem ſeniorum:

in their synagogues:

18. Et vous serez menés devant les Gouverneurs, et devant les Rois, à cause de moi, pour me rendre témoignage devant eux et devant les nations.

18 And ye shall be brought before governors and kings for my sake, for a testimony against them and the Gentiles.

23. Or, quand ils vous persécuteront dans une ville, fuyez dans une autre:

23 But when they persecute you in this city, flee ye into another:

26. Ne les craignez donc point; car il n'y a rien de caché qui ne doive être découvert; ni rien de secret qui ne doive être connu.

26 Fear them not, therefore: for there is nothing covered, that shall not be revealed; and hid, that shall not be known.

27. Ce que je vous dis dans les ténèbres, dites-le dans la lumière; et ce que je vous dis à l'oreille, prêchez-le sur le haut des maisons.

27 What I tell you in darkness, *that* speak ye in light: and what ye hear in the ear, *that* preach ye upon the housetops.

28. Et ne craignez point ceux qui ôtent la vie du corps, et qui ne peuvent faire mourir l'âme; mais craignez plutôt celui qui peut perdre et l'âme et le corps dans la géhenne.

28 And fear not them which kill the body, but are not able to kill the soul: but rather fear him which is able to destroy both soul and body in hell.

29. Deux passereaux ne se vendent-ils pas une pite? Et néanmoins il n'en tombera pas un seul à terre sans *la permission de* votre Père.

29 Are not two sparrows sold for a farthing? and one of them shall not fall on the ground without your Father.

30. Les cheveux même de vôtre tête sont tous comptés.

30 But the very hairs of your head are all numbered.

31. Ne craignez donc rien; vous valez mieux que beaucoup de passereaux.

31 Fear ye not, therefore, ye are of more value than many sparrows.

12. Etant donc partis, ils prêchèrent qu'on s'amendât.

12 And they went out, and preached that men should repent.

30. Et les Apôtres se rassemblèrent auprès de Jésus, et lui racontèrent tout ce qu'ils avoient fait, et tout ce qu'ils avoient enseigné.

30 And the apostles gathered themselves together unto Jesus, and told him all things, both what they had done, and what they had taught.

APRÈS ces choses, Jésus se tenoit en Galilée; car il ne vouloit pas demeurer dans la Judée, parce que les Juifs cherchoient à le faire mourir.

AFTER these things Jesus walked in Galilee: for he would not walk in Jewry, because the Jews sought to kill him.

ALors des Pharisiens et quelques Scribes, qui étoient venus de Jérusalem, s'assemblèrent vers *Jésus*.

THEN came together unto him, the Pharisees, and certain of the scribes, which came from Jerusalem.

2. Et voyant que quelques-uns de ses Disciples prenoient leur repas avec des mains souillées, c'est-à-dire, qui n'avoient pas été lavées, ils les en blâmoient.

2 And when they saw some of his disciples eat bread with defiled (that is to say, with unwashen) hands, they found fault.

3. Car les Pharisiens et tous les Juifs ne mangent point sans se laver les mains jusqu'au coude, gardant en cela la tradition des anciens;

3 For the Pharisees, and all the Jews, except they wash *their* hands oft, eat not, holding the tradition of the elders.

30

* 4 Καὶ ἀπὸ ἀγοϱᾶς, ἐὰν μὴ βαπτίσωνλαι, ἐκ ἐσϑίωσι· κ̄ ἄλλα πολλά ἐςιν, ἃ ‡ παϱέλαϐον κϱατεῖν, ‡ βαπλισμὲς ‡ ποτηϱίων κ̄ ξεςῶν κ̄ ‡ χαλκίων κ̄ κλινῶν.)

5 Ἔπειλα ἐπεϱωτῶσιν αὐτὸν οἱ Φαϱισαῖοι κ̄ οἱ Γϱαμμαλεῖς· Διατί οἱ μαϑηλαί σε ἐ πεϱιπαλῦσι κατὰ τὴν παϱάδοσιν τῶν πϱεσϐυτέϱων, ἀλλὰ ἀνίπλοις χεϱσὶν ἐσϑίεσι τὸν ἄϱλον;

14 Καὶ πϱοσκαλεσάμενος πάντα τὸν ὄχλον, ἔλεγεν αὐτοῖς· Ἀκέετέ με πάνλες, κ̄ συνίελε.

15 Οὐδέν ἐςιν ἔξωϑεν τῦ ἀνϑϱώπε εἰσποϱευόμενον εἰς αὐτὸν, ὃ δύναλαι αὐτὸν κοινῶσαι ἀλλὰ τὰ ἐκποϱευόμενα ἀπ' αὐτῦ, ἐκεῖνά ἐςι τὰ κοινῦνλα τὸν ἄνϑϱωπον.

16 Εἴ τις ἔχει ὦτα ἀκέειν, ἀκέέτω.

17 Καὶ ὅτε εἰσῆλϑεν εἰς οἶκον ἀπὸ τῦ ὄχλε, ἐπηϱώτων αὐτὸν οἱ μαϑηλαὶ αὐτῦ πεϱὶ τῆς παϱαϐολῆς.

18 Καὶ λέγει αὐτοῖς· Οὕτω κ̄ ὑμεῖς ἀσύνελοί ἐςε; ἐ νοεῖτε ὅτι πᾶν τὸ ἔξωϑεν εἰσποϱευόμενον εἰς τὸν ἄνϑϱωπον, ἐ δύναλαι αὐτὸν κοινῶσαι;

19 Ὅτι ἐκ εἰσποϱεύεlαι αὐτῦ εἰς τὴν καϱδίαν, ἀλλ' εἰς τὴν κοιλίαν· κ̄ εἰς τὸν ‡ ἀφεδϱῶνα ‡ ἐκποϱεύεlαι, καϑαϱίζον πάντα τὰ βϱώμαlα.

20 Ἔλεγε δὲ, ὅτι τὸ ἐκ τῦ ἀνϑϱώπε ἐκποϱευόμενον, ἐκεῖνο κοινοῖ τὸν ἄνϑϱωπον.

21 Ἔσωϑεν γὰϱ ἐκ τῆς καϱδίας τῶν ἀνϑϱώπων οἱ διαλογισμοὶ οἱ κακοὶ ἐκποϱεύονlαι, μοιχεῖαι, ποϱεῖαι, φόνοι,

* 22 ‡ Κλοπαὶ, ‡ πλεονεξίαι, ‡ πονηϱίαι, ‡ δόλο⟨ς⟩, ‡ ἀσέλγεια, ὀφϑαλμὸς πονηϱὸς· ‡ βλασφημία, † ὑπεϱηφανία, ‡ ἀφϱοσύνη.

23 Πάνlα ταῦτα τὰ πονηϱὰ ἔσωϑεν ἐκποϱεύεlαι, κ̄ κοινοῖ τὸν ἄνϑϱωπον.

* 24 Καὶ ἐκεῖϑεν ἀναςὰς ἀπῆλϑεν εἰς τὰ † μεϑόϱια Τύϱε κ̄ Σιδῶνο⟨ς⟩· κ̄ εἰσελϑὼν εἰς τὴν οἰκίαν, ἐδένα ἤϑελε γνῶναι· κ̄ ἐκ ἠδυνήϑη ‡ λαϑεῖν.

4 Et à foro, si non baptizentur, non comedunt : & alia multa sunt, quæ assumpserunt tenere, lotiones poculorum & sextariorum, & æramentorum & lectorum.

5 Deinde interrogant eum Pharisæi & Scribæ : Quare discipuli tui non ambulant juxta traditionem seniorum, sed illotis manibus manducant panem ?

14 Et advocans omnem turbam, dicebat illis: Audite me omnes, & intelligite :

15 Nihil est extra hominem introiens in eum, quod potest eum communicare : sed excuntia ab eo, illa sunt communicantia hominem.

16 Si quis habet aures ad audiendum, audiat,

17 Et quum introisset in domum à turba, interrogabant eum discipuli ejus de parabola.

18 Et ait illis: Sic & vos imprudentes estis? Non consideratis, quia omne extrinsecùs introiens in hominem, non potest eum communicare ?

19 Quia non intrat ejus in cor, sed in ventrem, & in secessum exit : purgans omnes escas.

20 Dicebat autem, quod ex homine egressum, illud communicat hominem.

21 Intus enim, de corde hominum ratiocinationes malæ egrediuntur, adultéria, fornicationes, cædes,

22 Furta, avaritiæ, malitiæ, dolus, lascivia, oculus malus, blasphemia, superbia, amentia.

23 Omnia hæc mala ab intus egrediuntur, & communicant hominem.

24 Et inde surgens, abiit in confinia Tyri & Sidonis: & ingressus in domum, neminem voluit scire, & non potuit latere.

4. Et lorsqu'ils reviennent des places publiques, ils ne mangent point non plus sans s'être lavés. Il y a aussi beaucoup d'autres choses qu'ils ont reçues pour les observer, comme de laver les coupes, les pots, les vaisseaux d'airain, et les lits.

5. Là-dessus les Pharisiens et les Scribes lui demandèrent : D'où vient que tes Disciples ne suivent pas la tradition des anciens, et qu'ils prennent leur repas sans se laver les mains ?

14. Alors ayant appelé toute la multitude, il leur dit : Ecoutez-moi tous, et comprenez-ceci :

15. Rien de ce qui est hors de l'homme, et qui entre dans lui, ne le peut souiller ; mais ce qui sort de lui, voilà ce qui souille l'homme.

16. Si quelqu'un a des oreilles pour entendre, qu'il entende.

17. Quand il fut entré dans la maison, après s'être retiré d'avec la multitude, ses Disciples l'interrogèrent sur cette parabole.

18. Et il leur dit : Etes-vous aussi sans intelligence ? Ne comprenez-vous pas, que rien de ce qui entre de dehors dans l'homme ne le peut souiller ?

19. Parce que cela n'entre pas dans son cœur, mais qu'il va au ventre ; et qu'il sort aux lieux secrets, avec tout ce que les alimens ont d'impur ?

20. Il leur disoit donc : Ce qui sort de l'homme, c'est ce qui souille l'homme.

21. Car du dedans du cœur des hommes, sortent les mauvaises pensées, les adultères, les fornications, les meurtres.

22. Les larcins, les mauvais moyens, pour avoir le bien d'autrui, les méchancetés, la fraude, l'impudicité, l'œil envieux, la médisance, la fierté, la folie.

23. Tous ces vices sortent du dedans, et souillent l'homme.

24. Puis étant parti de là, il s'en alla aux frontières de Tyr et de Sidon ; et étant entré dans une maison, il ne vouloit pas que personne le sût ; mais il ne put être caché.

4 And *when they come* from the market, except they wash, they eat not. And many other things there be, which they have received to hold, *as* the washing of cups, and pots, and of brasen vessels, and tables.

5 Then the Pharisees and scribes asked him, Why walk not thy disciples according to the tradition of the elders, but eat bread with unwashen hands?

14 And, when he had called all the people *unto him*, he said unto them, Hearken unto me every one *of you*, and understand :

15 There is nothing from without a man, that entering into him can defile him : but the things which come out of him, those are they that defile the man.

16 If any man have ears to hear, let him hear.

17 And, when he was entered into the house from the people, his disciples asked him concerning the parable.

18 And he saith unto them, Are ye so without understanding also? Do ye not perceive, that whatsoever thing from without entereth into the man, *it* cannot defile him ;

19 Because it entereth not into his heart, but into the belly, and goeth out into the draught, purging all meats?

20 And he said, That which cometh out of the man, that defileth the man.

21 For from within, out of the heart of men, proceed evil thoughts, adulteries, fornications, murders,

22 Thefts, covetousness, wickedness, deceit, lasciviousness, an evil eye, blasphemy, pride, foolishness:

23 All these evil things come from within, and defile the man.

24 And from thence he arose, and went into the borders of Tyre and Sidon, and entered into an house, and would have no man know *it* : but he could not be hid.

Κεφ. ιη΄. 18.　　　CAPUT XVIII.

I Ἐν ἐκείνη τῆ ὥρα προσῆλθον οἱ μαθηταὶ τῷ Ἰησȣ͂, λέγοντες· Τίς ἄρα μείζων ἐςὶν ἐν τῇ βασιλεία τῶν οὐρανῶν;

2 Καὶ προσκαλεσάμεν©. ὁ Ἰησȣ͂ς παιδίον, ἔςησεν αὐτὸ ἐν μέσῳ αὐτῶν,

3 Καὶ εἶπεν· Ἀμὴν λέγω ὑμῖν, ἐὰν μὴ ςραφῆτε, καὶ γένησθε ὡς τὰ παιδία, ȣ͗ μὴ εἰσέλθητε εἰς τὴν βασιλείαν τῶν ȣ͗ρανῶν.

4 Ὅςις ȣ͗ν ταπεινώσῃ ἑαυτὸν ὡς τὸ παιδίον τȣ͂το, ȣτός ἐςιν ὁ μείζων ἐν τῇ βασιλεία τῶν ȣ͗ρανῶν.

7 Οὐαὶ τῷ κόσμῳ ἀπὸ τῶν σκανδάλων· ἀνάγκη γάρ ἐςιν ἐλθεῖν τὰ σκάνδαλα· πλὴν ȣ͗αὶ τῷ ἀνθρώπῳ ἐκείνῳ, δι᾽ ȣ͗ τὸ σκάνδαλον ἔρχεται.

8 Εἰ δὲ ἡ χείρ σȣ, ἢ ὁ πȣ͂ς σȣ σκανδαλίζει σε, ἔκκοψον αὐτὰ, καὶ βάλε ἀπὸ σȣ͂· καλόν σοι ἐςὶν εἰσελθεῖν εἰς τὴν ζωὴν χωλὸν, ἢ κυλλὸν, ἢ δύο χεῖρας ἢ δύο πόδας ἔχοντα, βληθῆναι εἰς τὸ πῦρ τὸ αἰώνιον.

9 Καὶ εἰ ὁ ὀφθαλμός σȣ σκανδαλίζει σε, ἔξελε αὐτὸν, καὶ βάλε ἀπὸ σȣ͂· καλόν σοι ἐςὶ μονόφθαλμον εἰς τὴν ζωὴν εἰσελθεῖν, ἢ δύο ὀφθαλμȣ͗ς ἔχοντα βληθῆναι εἰς τὴν γέενναν τȣ͂ πυρός.

12 Τί ὑμῖν δοκεῖ; ἐὰν γένηται τινι ἀνθρώπῳ ἑκατὸν πρόβατα, καὶ πλανηθῇ ἓν ἐξ αὐτῶν· ȣ͗χὶ ἀφεὶς τὰ ἐννενήκονταεννέα, ἐπὶ τὰ ὄρη πορευθεὶς, ζητεῖ τὸ πλανώμενον;

13 Καὶ ἐὰν γένηται εὑρεῖν αὐτὸ, ἀμὴν λέγω ὑμῖν, ὅτι χαίρει ἐπ᾽ αὐτῷ μᾶλλον, ἢ ἐπὶ τοῖς ἐννενηκονταεννέα, τοῖς μὴ πεπλανημένοις.

14 Οὕτως ȣ͗κ ἔςι θέλημα ἔμπροσθεν τȣ͂ πατρὸς ὑμῶν, τȣ͂ ἐν ȣ͗ρανοῖς, ἵνα ἀπόληται εἷς τῶν μικρῶν τȣ͂των.

15 Ἐὰν δὲ ἁμαρτήσῃ εἰς σὲ ὁ ἀδελφός σȣ, ὕπαγε, καὶ ἔλεγξον αὐτὸν μεταξύ σȣ καὶ αὐτȣ͂ μόνȣ· ἐάν σȣ ἀκȣ͗σῃ, ἐκέρδησας τὸν ἀδελφόν σȣ.

CAPUT XVIII.

1 IN illa hora accesserunt discipuli Jesu; dicentes: Quisnam major est in regno cælorum?

2 Et advocans Jesus puerulum, statuit eum in medio eorum.

3 Et dixit: Amen dico vobis, si non conversi fueritis, & efficiamini sicut pueruli, nequaquam intrabitis in regnum cælorum.

4 Quicumque ergo humiliaverit seipsum ut puerulus iste, hic est major in regno cælorum.

7 Væ mundo à scandalis: Necesse enim est venire scandala: verumtamen væ homini illi, per quem scandalum venit.

8 Si autem manus tua, vel pes tuus scandalizat te, abscinde ea, & jace abs te: pulchrum tibi est ingredi ad vitam claudum vel mancum, quam duas manus vel duos pedes habentem, jaci in ignem æternum.

9 Et si oculus tuus scandalizat te, erue eum, & jace abs te; pulchrum tibi est unoculum in vitam intrare, quam duos oculos habentem jaci in gehennam ignis.

12 Quid vobis videtur? fuerint alicui homini centum oves, & erraverit una ex eis: nonne relinquens nonaginta novem, in montes vadens quærit errantem?

13 Et si fiat invenire eam; amen dico vobis, quia gaudet super ea magis, quam super nonaginta novem non aberrantibus.

14 Sic non est voluntas ante Patrem vestrum qui in cælis, ut pereat unus parvulorum horum.

15 Si autem peccaverit in te frater tuus, vade, & corripe eum inter te & ipsum solum: Si te audierit, lucratus es fratrem tuum.

EN cette même heure-là, les Disciples vinrent à Jésus, et lui dirent : Qui est le plus grand dans le Royaume des cieux?

2. Et Jésus ayant fait venir un enfant, le mit au milieu d'eux,

3. Et dit : Je vous le dis en vérité, que si vous n'êtes changés, et si vous ne devenez comme des enfans, vous n'entrerez point dans le Royaume des cieux.

4. C'est pourquoi, quiconque s'humiliera soi-même, comme cet enfant, celui-là est le plus grand dans le Royaume des cieux.

7. Malheur au monde à cause des scandales ; car il est nécessaire qu'il arrive des scandales ; mais malheur à l'homme par qui le scandale arrive !

8. Que si ta main ou ton pied te fait tomber *dans le péché*, coupe-les, et jette-les loin de toi ; car il vaut mieux que tu entres boiteux ou manchot dans la vie, que d'avoir deux pieds ou deux mains, et d'être jeté dans le feu éternel.

9. Et si ton œil te fait tomber *dans le péché*, arrache-le, et jette-le loin de toi ; car il vaut mieux que tu entres dans la vie n'ayant qu'un œil, que d'avoir deux yeux, et d'être jeté dans la géhenne du feu.

12. Que vous en semble ? Si un homme a cent brebis, et qu'il y en ait une égarée, ne laisse-t-il pas les quatre-vingt-dix-neuf, pour s'en aller par les montagnes chercher celle qui s'est égarée ?

13. Et s'il arrive qu'il la trouve, je vous dis en vérité, qu'il en a plus de joie, que des quatre-vingt-dix-neuf qui ne sont point égarées.

14. Ainsi la volonté de votre Père qui *est* aux cieux, n'est pas qu'aucun de ces petits périsse.

15. Si ton frère a péché contre toi, va, et reprends-le entre toi et lui seul ; s'il t'écoute, tu auras gagné ton frère.

AT the same time came the disciples unto Jesus, saying, Who is the greatest in the kingdom of heaven?

2 And Jesus called a little child unto him, and set him in the midst of them,

3 And said, Verily I say unto you, Except ye be converted, and become as little children, ye shall not enter into the kingdom of heaven.

4 Whosoever, therefore, shall humble himself as this little child, the same is greatest in the kingdom of heaven.

7 Woe unto the world because of offences! for it must needs be that offences come ; but woe to that man by whom the offence cometh!

8 Wherefore, if thy hand or thy foot offend thee, cut them off, and cast *them* from thee : it is better for thee to enter into life halt or maimed, rather than having two hands, or two feet, to be cast into everlasting fire.

9 And if thine eye offend thee, pluck it out, and cast *it* from thee : it is better for thee to enter into life with one eye, rather than having two eyes to be cast into hell-fire.

12 How think ye? if a man have an hundred sheep, and one of them be gone astray, doth he not leave the ninety and nine, and goeth into the mountains, and seeketh that which is gone astray ?

13 And if so be that he find it, verily I say unto you, He rejoiceth more of that *sheep*, than of the ninety and nine which went not astray.

14 Even so it is not the will of your Father which is in heaven, that one of these little ones should perish.

15 Moreover, if thy brother shall trespass against thee, go and tell him his fault between thee and him alone : if he shall hear thee,

32

16 Ἐὰν δὲ μὴ ἀκούσῃ, παράλαβε μετὰ σῦ ἔτι ἕνα ἢ δύο· ἵνα ἐπὶ ϛόμαϊϘ· δύο μαρτύρων ἢ τριῶν ϛαθῇ πᾶν ῥῆμα.

* 17 Ἐὰν δὲ παρακύσῃ αὐτῶν, εἰπὲ τῇ ἐκκλησίᾳ· ἐὰν δὲ κỳ τῆς ‡ ἐκκλησίας ‡ παρακύσῃ, ἔϛω σοι· ὥσπερ ὁ ἐθνικὸς κỳ ὁ τελώνης.

21 Τότε προσελθὼν αὐτῷ ὁ Πέτρϙ·, εἶπε· Κύριε, ποσάκις ἁμαρτήσει εἰς ἐμὲ ὁ ἀδελφός μυ, κỳ ἀφήσω αὐτῷ; ἕως ἑπτάκις;

* 22 Λέγει αὐτῷ ὁ Ἰησῦς· Οὐ λέγω σοι, ἕως ‡ ἑπτάκις, ἀλλ᾽ ἕως † ἑβδομηκοντάκις ‡ ἑπτά.

23 Διὰ τῦτο ὡμοιώθη ἡ βασιλεία τῶν ἐρανῶν ἀνθρώπῳ βασιλεῖ, ὃς ἠθέλησε συνᾶραι λόγον μετὰ τῶν δύλων αὐτῦ.

* 24 ‡ Ἀρξαμένυ δὲ αὐτῦ ‡ συναίρειν, προσηνέχθη αὐτῷ εἷς ‡ ὀφειλέτης ‡ μυρίων ‡ ταλάντων·

25 Μὴ ἔχονΙϘ· δὲ αὐτῦ ἀποδῦναι, ἐκέλευσεν αὐτὸν ὁ κύριϘ· αὐτῦ πραθῆναι, κỳ τὴν γυναῖκα αὐτῦ, κỳ τὰ τέκνα, κỳ πάντα ὅσα εἶχε, κỳ ἀποδοθῆναι.

26 Πεσὼν ὖν ὁ δῦλϘ· προσεκύνει αὐτῷ, λέγων· Κύριε, μακροθύμησον ἐπ᾽ ἐμοὶ, κỳ πάντα σοι ἀποδώσω.

* 27 Σπλαγχνισθεὶς δὲ ὁ κύριϘ· τῦ δύλυ ἐκείνυ, ἀπέλυσεν αὐτὸν, κỳ τὸ † δάνειον ἀφῆκεν αὐτῷ.

28 Ἐξελθὼν δὲ ὁ δῦλϘ· ἐκεῖνϘ·, εὗρεν ἕνα τῶν συνδύλων αὐτῦ, ὃς ὤφειλεν αὐτῷ ἑκατὸν δηνάρια· κỳ κρατήσας αὐτὸν ἔπνιγε, λέγων· ἈπόδϘ· μοι, ὅ,τι ὀφείλεις.

29 Πεσὼν ὖν ὁ σύνδυλϘ· αὐτῦ εἰς τὰς πόδας αὐτῦ, παρεκάλει αὐτὸν, λέγων· Μακροθύμησον ἐπ᾽ ἐμοὶ, κỳ πάντα ἀποδώσω σοι.

30 Ὁ δὲ ἐκ ἤθελεν· ἀλλ᾽ ἀπελθὼν, ἔϐαλεν αὐτὸν εἰς φυλακὴν, ἕως ὖ ἀποδῷ τὸ ὀφειλόμενον.

16 Si autem non audierit, affume cum te adhuc unum vel duos: ut in ore duorum teſtium vel trium ſtet omne verbum.

17 Si autem neglexerit eos, dic eccleſiæ : ſi autem & eccleſiam neglexerit, ſit tibi ſicut ethnicus & publicanus.

21 Tunc accedens ad eum Petrus, dixit : Domine, quoties peccabit in me frater meus, & dimittam ei ? uſque ſepties?

22 Dicit illi Jeſus : Non dico tibi, uſque ſepties, ſed uſque ſeptuagies ſeptem.

23 Propter hoc aſſimilatum eſt regnum cælorum hómini regi, qui voluit conferre rationem cum ſervis ſuis.

24 Incipiente verò ipſo conferre, ob'atus eſt ei unus debitor decies mille talentorum.

25 Non habente autem illo reddere, juſſit eum dominus ejus venundari, & uxorem ejus, & filios, & omnia quæ habebat, & reddi.

26 Procidens autem ſervus adorabat eum, dicens : Domine, longanimis eſto erga me, & omnia tibi reddam.

27 Commotus viſceribus autem dominus ſervi illius, abſolvit eum, & mutuum dimiſit ei.

28 Egreſſus autem ſervus ille, invenit unum conſervorum ſuorum, qui debebat ei centum denarios : & apprehendens eum ſuffocabat, dicens : Redde mihi quod debes.

29 Procidens ergo conſervus ejus ad pedes ejus, rogabat eum, dicens : Longanimis eſto in me, & omnia reddam tibi.

30 Ille autem noluit : ſed abiens conjecit eum in cuſtodiam, donec redderet debitum.

16. Mais s'il ne t'écoute pas, prends avec toi encore une ou deux *personnes*, afin que tout soit confirmé sur la parole de deux ou de trois témoins.

17. Que s'il ne daigne pas les écouter, dis-le à l'Eglise ; et s'il ne daigne pas écouter l'Eglise, regarde-le comme un païen et un péager.

16 But if he will not hear *thee*, *then* take with thee one or two more, that in the mouth of two or three witnesses every word may be established.

17 And if he shall neglect to hear them, tell *it* unto the church: but if he neglect to hear the church, let him be unto thee as an heathen man and a publican.

21. Alors Pierre s'étant approché, lui dit : Seigneur, combien de fois pardonnerai-je à mon frère, lorsqu'il m'aura offensé jusques à sept fois ?

22. Jésus lui *répondit* : Je ne te dis pas jusques à sept fois, mais jusques à septante fois sept fois.

23. C'est pourquoi le Royaume des cieux est comparé à un Roi, qui voulut faire compte avec ses serviteurs :

24. Quand il eut commencé à compter, on lui en présenta un qui devoit dix mille talens ;

25. Et parce qu'il n'avoit pas de quoi payer, son Maître commanda qu'il fût vendu, lui, sa femme et ses enfans, et tout ce qu'il avoit, afin que la dette fût payée.

26. Et ce serviteur se jetant à terre, le supplioit, en lui disant : Seigneur, aie patience envers moi, et je te paierai tout.

27. Alors le Maître de ce serviteur, ému de compassion, le laissa aller, et lui quitta la dette.

28. Mais ce serviteur étant sorti, rencontra un de ses compagnons de service qui lui devoit cent deniers ; et l'ayant saisi, il l'étrangloit, en lui disant : Paie-moi ce que tu me dois.

29. Et son compagnon de service se jetant à ses pieds, le supplioit, en lui disant : Aie patience envers moi, et je te paierai tout.

30. Mais il n'en voulut rien faire, et s'en étant allé, il le fit mettre en prison, jusqu'à ce qu'il eût payé la dette.

21 Then came Peter to him, and said, Lord, how oft shall my brother sin against me, and I forgive him ? till seven times ?

22 Jesus saith unto him, I say not unto thee, Until seven times ; but, Until seventy times seven.

23 Therefore is the kingdom of heaven likened unto a certain king, which would take account of his servants.

24 And when he had begun to reckon, one was brought unto him, which owed him ten thousand talents.

25 But forasmuch as he had not to pay, his lord commanded him to be sold, and his wife, and children, and all that he had, and payment to be made.

26 The servant, therefore fell down, and worshipped him, saying, lord, have patience with me, and I will pay thee all.

27 Then the lord of that servant was moved with compassion, and loosed him, and forgave him the debt.

28 But the same servant went out, and found one of his fellow-servants, which owed him an hundred pence : and he laid hands on him, and took *him* by the throat, saying, Pay me that thou owest.

29 And his fellow-servant fell down at his feet, and besought him, saying, Have patience with me, and I will pay thee all.

30 And he would not : but went and cast him into prison, till he should pay the debt.

* 31 Ἰδόντες δὲ οἱ ‡ σύνδυλοι αὐτῦ τὰ γενόμενα, ἐλυπήθησαν σφόδρα· ἢ ἐλθόντες † διεσάφησαν τῷ ‡ κυρίῳ αὐτῶν πάντα τὰ γενόμενα.

32 Τότε προσκαλεσάμεν۞ αὐτὸν ὁ κύρι۞ αὐτῦ, λέγει αὐτῷ· δῦλε πονηρέ, πᾶσαν τὴν ὀφειλὴν ἐκείνην ἀφῆκά σοι, ἐπεὶ παρεκάλεσάς με·

33 Οὐκ ἔδει καὶ σὲ ἐλεῆσαι τὸν σύνδυλόν σε, ὡς ἢ ἐγώ σε ἠλέησα;

* 34 Καὶ ὀργισθεὶς ὁ κύρι۞ αὐτῦ ‡ παρέδωκεν αὐτὸν τοῖς † βασανιςαῖς, ἕως ὖ ἀποδῷ πᾶν τὸ ὀφειλόμενον αὐτῷ.

35 Οὕτω ἢ ὁ πατήρ μυ ὁ ἐπυράνι۞ ποιήσει ὑμῖν, ἐὰν μὴ ἀφῆτε ἕκας۞ τῷ ἀδελφῷ αὐτῦ ἀπὸ τῶν καρδιῶν ὑμῶν τὰ παραπτώματα αὐτῶν. 19, † 5.

Κεφ. ί. 10.

1 Μετὰ δὲ ταῦτα ἀνέδειξεν ὁ Κύρι۞ ἢ ἑτέρυς, ἑβδομήκοντα, ἢ ἀπέςειλεν αὐτὸς ἀνὰ δύο πρὸ προσώπυ αὐτῦ, εἰς πᾶσαν πόλιν ἢ τόπον ὖ ἔμελλεν αὐτὸς ἔρχεσθαι.

2 Ἔλεγεν ὖν πρὸς αὐτούς· Ὁ μὲν θερισμὸς πολὺς, οἱ δὲ ἐργάται ὀλίγοι· δεήθητε ὖν τῦ Κυρίυ τῦ θερισμῦ, ὅπως ἐκβάλλῃ ἐργάτας εἰς τὸν θερισμὸν αὐτῦ.

* 3 Ὑπάγετε· ἰδὺ, ἐγὼ ἀποςέλλω ὑμᾶς ὡς † ἄρνας ἐν ‡ μέσῳ ‡ λύκων.

4 Μὴ βαςάζετε βαλάντιον, μὴ πήραν, μηδὲ ὑποδήματα· ἢ μηδένα κατὰ τὴν ὁδὸν ἀσπάσησθε.

5 Εἰς ἣν δ' ἂν οἰκίαν εἰσέρχησθε, πρῶτον λέγετε· Εἰρήνη τῷ οἴκῳ τούτῳ.

6 Καὶ ἐὰν μὲν ᾖ ἐκεῖ ὁ υἱὸς εἰρήνης, ἐπαναπαύσεται ἐπ' αὐτὸν ἡ εἰρήνη ὑμῶν· εἰ δὲ μήγε, ἐφ' ὑμᾶς ἀνακάμψει.

7 Ἐν αὐτῇ δὲ τῇ οἰκίᾳ μένετε, ἐσθίοντες ἢ πίνοντες τὰ παρ' αὐτῶν· ἄξι۞ γὰρ ὁ ἐργάτης τῦ μισθῦ αὐτῦ ἐςι. Μὴ μεταβαίνετε ἐξ οἰκίας εἰς οἰκίαν.

8 Καὶ εἰς ἣν δ' ἂν πόλιν εἰσέρχησθε, ἢ δέχωνται ὑμᾶς, ἐσθίετε τὰ παρατιθέμενα ὑμῖν.

---

31 Videntes autem conservi ejus facta, contristati sunt valde: & venientes declaraverunt domino suo omnia facta.

32 Tunc advocans illum dominus suus dicit illi: Serve nequam, omne debitum illud dimisi tibi, quoniam advocasti me.

33 Nonne oportuit & te misereri conservi tui, sicut & ego tui misertus sum?

34 Et iratus dominus ejus tradidit eum tortoribus, quoadusque redderet universum debitum ei.

35 Sic & Pater meus cælestis faciet vobis, si non remiseritis unusquisque fratri suo de cordibus vestris lapsus eorum.

CAPUT X.

1 POST autem hæc designavit Dominus & alios septuaginta, & misit illos per binos ante faciem suam, in omnem civitatem & locum quo futurus erat ipse venire.

2 Dicebat igitur ad illos: Ipsa quidem messis multa, at operarii pauci: rogate ergo dominum messis, ut emittat operarios in messem suam.

3 Ite, ecce ego mitto vos sicut agnos in medio luporum.

4 Ne portate marsupium, non peram, neque calceamenta: & neminem per viam salutaveritis.

5 In quamcunque domum intraveritis, primum dicite: Pax domui huic.

6 Et si quidem fuerit ibi filius pacis, requiescet super illum pax vestra: si vero non, ad vos revertetur.

7 In eadem autem domo manete, edentes & bibentes quæ apud illos: dignus enim operarius mercede sua est, ne transite de domo in domum.

8 Et in quamcumque civitatem intraveritis, & susceperint vos, manducate apposita vobis.

31. Ses autres compagnons de service voyant ce qui s'étoit passé, en furent fort indignés, et ils vinrent rapporter à leur Maître tout ce qui étoit arrivé.

32. Alors son Maître le fit venir, et lui dit : Méchant serviteur, je t'avois quitté toute cette dette, parce que tu m'en avois prié ;

33. Ne te falloit-il pas aussi avoir pitié de ton compagnon de service, comme j'avois eu pitié de toi ?

34. Et son Maître étant irrité, le livra aux sergens, jusqu'à ce qu'il lui eût payé tout ce qu'il lui devoit.

35. C'est ainsi que vous fera mon Père céleste, si vous ne pardonnez pas chacun de vous, de *tout* son cœur, à son frère ses fautes.

Après cela, le Seigneur établit encore soixante et dix autres *Disciples* ; et il les envoya deux à deux devant lui, dans toutes les villes et dans tous les lieux où lui-même devoit aller.

2. Et il leur disoit : La moisson est grande, mais *il y a* peu d'ouvriers ; priez donc le Maître de la moisson d'envoyer des ouvriers dans sa moisson.

3. Allez, je vous envoie comme des agneaux au milieu des loups.

4. Ne portez ni bourse, ni sac, ni souliers ; et ne saluez personne en chemin.

5. Et dans quelque maison que vous entriez, dites en entrant : La paix *soit* sur cette maison.

6. S'il y a là quelque enfant de paix ; votre paix reposera sur lui ; sinon elle retournera à vous.

7. Et demeurez dans cette maison-là, mangeant et buvant de ce qu'on vous donnera, car l'ouvrier est digne de son salaire. Ne passez point d'une maison à une autre.

8. De même, dans quelque ville que vous entriez, si on vous y reçoit, mangez de ce qu'on vous présentera.

31 So when his fellow-servants saw what was done, they were very sorry, and came and told unto their lord all that was done.

32 Then his lord, after that he had called him, said unto him, O thou wicked servant! I forgave thee all that debt, because thou desiredst me :

33 Shouldest not thou also have had compassion on thy fellow-servant, even as I had pity on thee ?

34 And his lord was wroth, and delivered him to the tormentors, till he should pay all that was due unto him.

35 So likewise shall my heavenly Father do also unto you, if ye from your hearts forgive not every one his brother their trespasses.

AFTER these things the Lord appointed other seventy also, and sent them two and two before his face into every city and place, whither he himself would come.

2 Therefore said he unto them, The harvest truly *is* great, but the labourers *are* few : pray ye therefore the lord of the harvest, that he would send forth labourers into his harvest.

3 Go your ways : behold, I send you forth as lambs among wolves.

4 Carry neither purse, nor scrip, nor shoes : and salute no man by the way.

5 And into whatsoever house ye enter, first say, Peace *be* to this house.

6 And if the Son of Peace be there, your peace shall rest upon it : if not, it shall turn to you again.

7 And in the same house remain, eating and drinking such things as they give : for the labourer is worthy of his hire. Go not from house to house.

8 And into whatsoever city ye enter, and they receive you, eat such things as are set before you ;

34

10 Εἰς ἣν δ' ἂν πόλιν εἰσέρχησθε, κ μὴ δέχωνἶαι ὑμᾶς, ἐξελθόντες εἰς τὰς πλαλείας αὐτῆς,
εἴπαἶε·

* 11 Καὶ τὸν ‡ κονιορἶὸν τὸν
‡ κολληθένἶα ἡμῖν ἐκ τῆς πόλεως
ὑμῶν, ‡ ἀπομασσόμεθα ὑμῖν·
πλὴν τῦτο γινώσκεἶε, ὅτι ἤγγικεν
ἐφ' ὑμᾶς ἡ βασιλεία τῦ Θεῦ.

Ἐι Λέγω δὲ ὑμῖν, ὅτι Σοδόμοις
ἐν τῇ ἡμέρᾳ ἐκείνῃ ἀνεκἱότερον
ἔςαι, ἢ τῇ πόλει ἐκείνῃ.

* 2 Ἦν δὲ ἐγγὺς ἡ ἑορἦὴ τῶν
Ἰυδαίων, ἡ † σκηνοπηγία.

3 Εἶπον ἒν πρὸς αὐτὸν οἱ ἀ-
δελφοὶ αὐτῦ· Μεἰάβηθι ἐνἶεῦθεν, κ
ὕπαγε εἰς τὴν Ἰυδαίαν, ἵνα κ οἱ
μαθηἶαί σε θεωρήσωσι τὰ ἔργα
σε ἃ ποιεῖς·

4 Οὐδεὶς γὰρ ἐν κρυπἶῷ τι
ποιεῖ, κ ζηἶεῖ αὐτὸς ἐν παρρησίᾳ
εἶναι. εἰ ταῦτα ποιεῖς, φανέρω-
σόν σεαυτὸν τῷ κόσμῳ.

5 Οὐδὲ γὰρ οἱ ἀδελφοὶ αὐτῦ
ἐπίςευον εἰς αὐτόν.

6 Λέγει ἒν αὐτοῖς ὁ Ἰησῦς·
Ὁ καιρὸς ὁ ἐμὸς ὔπω πάρεςιν·
ὁ δὲ καιρὸς ὁ ὑμέτερ⊙ πάντοἶέ
ἐςιν ἕτοιμ⊙.

7 Οὐ δύναἶαι ὁ κόσμ⊙ μισεῖν
ὑμᾶς· ἐμὲ δὲ μισεῖ, ὅτι ἐγὼ
μαρ]υρῶ περὶ αὐτῦ, ὅτι τὰ ἔργα
αὐτῦ πονηρά ἐςιν.

8 Ὑμεῖς ἀνάβηἶε εἰς τὴν ἑορτὴν ταύτην· ἐγὼ ὔπω ἀναβαίνω
εἰς τὴν ἑορἦὴν ταύτην, ὅτι ὁ καιρὸς
ὁ ἐμὸς ὔπω πεπλήρωἶαι.

9 Ταῦτα δὲ εἰπὼν αὐτοῖς, ἔ-
μεινεν ἐν τῇ Γαλιλαίᾳ.

10 Ὡς δὲ ἀνέβησαν οἱ ἀδελφοὶ
αὐτῦ, τότε κ αὐτὸς ἀνέβη εἰς τὴν
ἑορἦὴν, ὖ φανερῶς, ἀλλ' ὡς ἐν
κρυπἶῷ.

11 Οἱ ἒν Ἰυδαῖοι ἐζήτυν αὐτὸν ἐν τῇ ἑορἦῇ, κ ἔλεγον· Πῦ ἐςιν
ἐκεῖν⊙;

12 Καὶ γογγυσμὸς πολὺς περὶ
αὐτῦ ἦν ἐν τοῖς ὄχλοις. οἱ μὲν
ἔλεγον, ὅτι ἀγαθός ἐςιν. ἄλλοι
δὲ ἔλεγον, Οὔ· ἀλλὰ πλανᾷ τὸν
ὄχλον.

13 Οὐδεὶς μένἶοι παρρησίᾳ ἐ-
λάλει περὶ αὐτῦ, διὰ τὸν φόβον
τῶν Ἰυδαίων.

* [...]Ἤδη δὲ τῆς † ἑορἦῆς † με-
σύσης[...]

* 14 Ἤδη δὲ τῆς † ἑορἦῆς ‡ με-
σύσης, ἀνέβη ὁ Ἰησῦς εἰς τὸ ἱερὸν, κ ἐδίδασκε.

15 Καὶ ἐθαύμαζον οἱ Ἰυδαῖοι,
λέγοντες· Πῶς ὕτ⊙ γράμμαἶα
οἶδε, μὴ μεμαθηκώς;

16 Ἀπεκρίθη αὐτοῖς ὁ Ἰησῦς

---

10 In quamcumque autem
civitatem intraveritis, & non
susceperint vos, exeuntes in
plateas ejus, dicite :

11 Etiam pulverem adhæren-
tem nobis de civitate vestra,
abstergimus vobis : tamen hoc
scitote, quia appropinquavit super vos regnum Dei.

12 Dico autem vobis, quia
Sodomis in die illa remissius
erit, quam civitati illi.

2 Erat autem prope festum
Judæorum, Scenopegia.

3 Dixerunt igitur ad eum
fratres ejus : Transi hinc, &
vade in Judæam, ut & discipuli tui videant opera tua quæ
facis.

4 Nemo quippe in occulto
quid facit, & quærit ipse in manifesto esse. si hæc facis, mani-
festa teipsum mundo.

5 Neque enim fratres ejus
credebant in eum.

6 Dicit ergo eis Jesus : Tempus meum nondum adest : at
tempus vestrum semper est paratum.

7 Non potest mundus odisse
vos, me autem odit, quia ego
testor de illo, quia opera ejus
mala sunt.

8 Vos ascendite ad festum
hoc : ego nondum ascendo ad
festum istud, quia tempus meum nondum impletum est.

9 Hæc autem dicens eis, man-
sit in Galilæa.

10 Ut autem ascenderunt fratres ejus, tunc & ipse ascendit
ad festum, non manifeste, sed
quasi in occulto.

11 Ipsi ergo Judæi quærebant
eum in festo, & dicebant : Ubi
est ille ?

12 Et murmur multum de eo
erat in turbis. hi quidem dicebant, Quia bonus est. alii dicebant, Non : sed seducit turbam.

13 Nemo tamen palam lo-
quebatur de illo, propter metum
Judæorum.

14 Jam autem festo median-
te, ascendit Jesus in templum,
& docebat.

15 Et mirabantur Judæi, dicentes : Quomodo hic literas
scit, non doctus ?

16 Respondit ergo eis Jesus.

10. Mais dans quelque ville que vous entriez, si on ne vous y reçoit pas, sortez dans les rues, et dites :

11. Nous secouons contre vous la poussière qui s'est attachée à nous dans votre ville ; sachez pourtant que le Règne de Dieu s'est approché de vous.

12. Je vous dis qu'en ce jour-là ceux de Sodome seront traités moins rigoureusement que cette ville-là.

2. Or, la fête des Juifs, appellée des Tabernacles, approchoit.

3. Et ses frères lui dirent : Pars d'ici, et t'en va en Judée, afin que tes Disciples voient aussi les œuvres que tu fais.

4. Car personne ne fait rien en cachette, quand il veut agir franchement. Puisque tu fais ces choses, montre-toi toi-même au monde.

5. Car ses frères même ne croyoient pas en lui.

6. Jésus leur dit : Mon tems n'est pas encore venu ; mais le tems est toujours propre pour vous.

7. Le monde ne vous peut haïr ; mais il me hait, parce que je rends ce témoignage contre lui, que ses œuvres sont mauvaises.

8. Pour vous, montez à cette fête : Pour moi, je n'y monte pas encore, parce que mon tems n'est pas encore venu.

9. Et leur ayant dit cela, il demeura en Galilée.

10. Mais lorsque ses frères furent partis, il monta aussi à la fête, non pas publiquement, mais comme en cachette.

11. Les Juifs donc le cherchoient pendant la fête, et disoient : Où est-il ?

12. Et on tenoit plusieurs discours de lui parmi le peuple. Les uns disoient : C'est un homme de bien ; et les autres disoient : Non, mais il séduit le peuple.

13. Toutefois personne ne parloit librement de lui, à cause de la crainte qu'on avoit des Juifs.

14. Comme on étoit déjà au milieu de la fête, Jésus monta au Temple, et il y enseignoit.

15. Et les Juifs étoient étonnés, et disoient : Comment cet homme sait-il les Ecritures, ne les ayant point apprises ?

16. Jésus leur répondit

L. 10.

10 But into whatsoever city ye enter, and they receive you not, go your ways out into the streets of the same, and say,

11 Even the very dust of your city, which cleaveth on us, we do wipe off against you : notwithstanding, be ye sure of this, that the kingdom of God is come nigh unto you.

12 But I say unto you, That it shall be more tolerable in that day for Sodom, than for that city.

J. 7.

2 Now the Jews' feast of tabernacles was at hand.

3 His brethren, therefore, said unto him, Depart hence, and go into Judea, that thy disciples also may see the works that thou doest.

4 For *there is* no man *that* doeth any thing in secret, and he himself seeketh to be known openly. If thou do these things, shew thyself to the world.

5 For neither did his brethren believe in him.

6 Then Jesus said unto them, My time is not yet come : but your time is alway ready.

7 The world cannot hate you : but me it hateth, because I testify of it, that the works thereof are evil.

8 Go ye up unto this feast : I go not up yet unto this feast ; for my time is not yet full come.

9 When he had said these words unto them, he abode *still* in Galilee.

10 But when his brethren were gone up, then went he also up unto the feast, not openly, but as it were in secret.

11 Then the Jews sought him at the feast, and said, Where is he ?

12 And there was much murmuring among the people concerning him : for some said, He is a good man : others said, Nay ; but he deceiveth the people.

13 Howbeit no man spake openly of him for fear of the Jews.

14 Now, about the midst of the feast, Jesus went up into the temple, and taught.

15 And the Jews marvelled, saying, How knoweth this man letters, having never learned ?

16 Jesus answered them, and said,

19 Οὐ Μωσῆς δέδωκεν ὑμῖν τὸν νόμον, κ̀ οὐδεὶς ἐξ ὑμῶν ποιεῖ τὸν νόμον; τί με ζητεῖτε ἀποκτεῖναι;	19 Non Moses dedit vobis legem, & nemo ex vobis facit legem? Quid me quæritis interficere?
20 Ἀπεκρίθη ὁ ὄχλΘ- κ̀ εἶπε· Δαιμόνιον ἔχεις· τίς σε ζητεῖ ἀποκτεῖναι;	20 Respondit turba & dixit: Dæmonium habes: quis te quærit interficere?
21 Ἀπεκρίθη ὁ Ἰησοῦς κ̀ εἶπεν αὐτοῖς· Ἓν ἔργον ἐποίησα, κ̀ πάντες θαυμάζετε.	21 Respondit Jesus, & dixit eis: Unum opus feci, & omnes miramini.
22 Διὰ τοῦτο Μωσῆς δέδωκεν ὑμῖν τὴν περιτομὴν, (οὐχ ὅτι ἐκ τοῦ Μωσέως ἐςὶν ἀλλ᾿ ἐκ τῶν πατέρων) κ̀ ἐν σαββάτῳ περιτέμνετε ἄνθρωπον.	22 Propter hoc Moses dedit vobis circumcisionem, (non quia ex Mose est, sed ex patribus) & in sabbato circumciditis hominem.
* 23 Εἰ περιτομὴν λαμβάνει ἄνθρωπΘ- ἐν σαββάτῳ, ἵνα μὴ λυθῇ ὁ νόμΘ- Μωσέως, ἐμοὶ + χολᾶτε, ὅτι ὅλον ἄνθρωπον ὑγιῆ ἐποίησα ἐν σαββάτῳ;	23 Si circumcisionem accipit homo in sabbato, ut non solvatur lex Mosi, Mihi indignamini quia totum hominem sanum feci in sabbato?
24 Μὴ κρίνετε κατ᾿ ὄψιν, ἀλλὰ τὴν δικαίαν κρίσιν κρίνατε.	24 Ne judicate secundum speciem, sed justum judicium judicate.
25 Ἔλεγον οὖν τινες ἐκ τῶν Ἱεροσολυμιτῶν· Οὐχ οὗτός ἐςιν, ὃν ζητοῦσιν ἀποκτεῖναι;	25 Dicebant ergo quidam ex Hierosolymitanis: Nonne hic est quem quærunt interficere?
26 Καὶ ἴδε, παῤῥησίᾳ λαλεῖ, κ̀ οὐδὲν αὐτῷ λέγουσι· μήποτε ἀληθῶς ἔγνωσαν οἱ ἄρχοντες ὅτι οὗτός ἐςιν ἀληθῶς ὁ Χριςός;	26 Et ecce palam loquitur, & nihil ei dicunt: numquid vere cognoverunt principes, quia hic est vere Christus?
32 Ἤκουσαν οἱ φαρισαῖοι τοῦ ὄχλου γογγύζοντΘ- περὶ αὐτοῦ ταῦτα· κ̀ ἀπέςειλαν οἱ φαρισαῖοι κ̀ οἱ ἀρχιερεῖς ὑπηρέτας, ἵνα πιάσωσιν αὐτόν.	32 Audierunt Pharisæi turbam murmurantem de illo hæc: & miserunt Pharisæi & principes Sacerdotum ministros, ut apprehenderent eum.
43 Σχίσμα οὖν ἐν τῷ ὄχλῳ ἐγένετο δι᾿ αὐτόν.	43 Dissensio itaque in turba facta est propter eum.
44 Τινὲς δὲ ἤθελον ἐξ αὐτῶν πιάσαι αὐτόν· ἀλλ᾿ οὐδεὶς ἐπέβαλεν ἐπ᾿ αὐτὸν τὰς χεῖρας.	44 Quidam autem volebant ex ipsis apprehendere eum: sed nemo immisit super eum manus.
45 Ἦλθον οὖν οἱ ὑπηρέται πρὸς τὺς ἀρχιερεῖς κ̀ φαρισαίους· κ̀ εἶπον αὐτοῖς ἐκεῖνοι· Διὰ τί οὐκ ἠγάγετε αὐτόν;	45 Venerunt ergo ministri ad Pontifices & Pharisæos: & dixerunt eis illi: Quare non adduxistis illum?
46 Ἀπεκρίθησαν οἱ ὑπηρέται· Οὐδέποτε οὕτως ἐλάλησεν ἄνθρωπΘ-, ὡς ὗτΘ- ὁ ἄνθρωπΘ-.	46 Responderunt ministri: Nunquam sic loquutus est homo, sicut hic homo.
47 Ἀπεκρίθησαν οὖν αὐτοῖς οἱ φαρισαίοι· Μὴ κ̀ ὑμεῖς πεπλάνησθε;	47 Respoderunt ergo eis Pharisæi: Numquid & vos seducti estis?
48 Μή τις ἐκ τῶν ἀρχόντων ἐπίςευσεν εἰς αὐτὸν, ἢ ἐκ τῶν φαρισαίων;	48 Numquid aliquis ex principibus credidit in eum, aut ex Pharisæis?
49 Ἀλλ᾿ ὁ ὄχλΘ- ὗτΘ- ὁ μὴ γινώσκων τὸν νόμον, ἐπικατάρατοί εἰσι.	49 Sed turba hæc non noscens legem, maledicti sunt.

19. Moyse ne vous a-t-il pas donné la Loi ? et néanmoins aucun de vous n'observe la Loi. Pourquoi cherchez-vous à me faire mourir ?

19 Did not Moses give you the law, and *yet* none of you keepeth the law? Why go ye about to kill me?

20. Le peuple lui répondit : Tu es possédé du Démon : Qui est-ce qui cherche à te faire mourir ?

20 The people answered, and said, Thou hast a devil: who goeth about to kill thee?

21. Jésus répondit, et leur dit : J'ai fait une œuvre, et vous en êtes tous étonnés.

21 Jesus answered, and said unto them, I have done one work, and ye all marvel.

22. Moyse vous a ordonné la circoncision (non pas qu'elle vienne de Moyse, mais *elle vient* des Pères.), et vous circoncisez un homme au jour du Sabbat.

22 Moses, therefore, gave unto you circumcision, (not because it is of Moses, but of the fathers,) and ye on the sabbath-day circumcise a man.

23. Si donc un homme reçoit la circoncision au jour du Sabbat, afin que la Loi de Moyse ne soit pas violée, pourquoi vous irritez-vous contre moi, parce que j'ai guéri un homme dans tout son corps le jour du Sabbat ?

23 If a man on the sabbath-day receive circumcision, that the law of Moses should not be broken; are ye angry at me, because I have made a man every whit whole on the sabbath-day?

24. Ne jugez point selon l'apparence, mais jugez selon la justice.

24 Judge not according to the appearance, but judge righteous judgment.

25. Et quelques-uns de ceux de Jérusalem disoient : N'est-ce pas celui qu'ils cherchent à faire mourir ?

25 Then said some of them of Jerusalem, Is not this he whom they seek to kill?

26. Et le voilà qui parle librement, et ils ne lui disent rien. Les Chefs auroient-ils en effet reconnu qu'il est véritablement le Christ ?

26 But, lo, he speaketh boldly, and they say nothing unto him; Do the rulers know indeed that this is the very Christ?

32. Les Pharisiens ayant appris ce que le peuple disoit sourdement de lui, ils envoyèrent, de concert avec les principaux Sacrificateurs, des Sergens pour se saisir de lui.

32 The Pharisees heard that the people murmured such things concerning him; and the Pharisees, and the chief priest sent officers to take him.

43. Le peuple étoit donc partagé sur son sujet.

43 So there was a division among the people because of him.

44. Et quelques-uns d'entr'eux vouloient le saisir; mais personne ne mit la main sur lui.

44 And some of them would have taken him: but no man laid hands on him.

45. Les Sergens retournèrent donc vers les principaux Sacrificateurs et les Pharisiens, qui leur dirent : Pourquoi ne l'avez-vous pas amené ?

45 Then came the officers to the chief priests and Pharisees; and they said unto them, Why have ye not brought him? M 2

46. Les Sergens répondirent : Jamais homme n'a parlé comme cet homme.

46 The officers answered, Never man spake like this man.

47. Les Pharisiens leur dirent : Avez-vous aussi été séduits ?

47 Then answered them the Pharisees, Are ye also deceived?

48. Y a-t-il quelques-uns des Chefs ou des Pharisiens qui aient cru en lui ?

48 Have any of the rulers, or of the Pharisees, believed on him?

49. Mais cette populace, qui n'entend point la Loi, est exécrable.

49 But this people who knoweth not the law are cursed.

36

50 Λέγει Νικόδημ@ πρὸς αὐ
τὰς, ὁ ἐλθὼν νυκτὸς πρὸς αὐτὸν,
εἷς ὢν ἐξ αὐτῶν·

51 Μὴ ὁ νόμ@ ἡμῶν κρίνει
τὸν ἄνθρωπον, ἐὰν μὴ ἀκύσῃ παρ᾽
αὐτῷ πρότερον, κỳ γνῷ τί ποιεῖ;

52 Ἀπεκρίθησαν, κỳ εἶπον αὐ
τῷ· Μὴ κỳ σὺ ἐκ τῆς Γαλι
λαίας εἶ; ἐρεύνησον κỳ ἴδε ὅτι
προφήτης ἐκ τῆς Γαλιλαίας ἐκ
ἐγήγερ�αι.

53 Καὶ ἐπορεύθη ἕκασ@ εἰς
τὸν οἶκον αὐτῦ. 9. † 5.

Κεφ. η'. 8.

1 Ἰησῦς δὲ ἐπορεύθη εἰς τὸ ὄρ@
τῶν Ἐλαιῶν.

2 Ὄρθρυ δὲ πάλιν παρεγένε�ο
εἰς τὸ ἱερὸν, κỳ πᾶς ὁ λαὸς ἤρχε�ο
πρὸς αὐτόν· κỳ καθίσας ἐδίδασκεν
αὐτύς.

3 Ἄγυσι δὲ οἱ γραμμα�εῖς κỳ οἱ
φαρισαῖοι πρὸς αὐτὸν γυναῖκα ἐν
μοιχείᾳ κα�ειλημμένην· κỳ ςή
σαν�ες αὐτὴν ἐν μέσῳ,

4 Λέγυσιν αὐτῷ· Διδάσκα
λε, αὕτη ἡ γυνὴ ‡ κα�ειλίφθη † ἐ
παυ�οφώρῳ ¶ μοιχευομένη·

5 Ἐν δὲ τῷ νόμῳ ἡμε�έρῳ Μωσῆς
ἡμῖν ἐνε�είλα�ο τὰς τοιαύτας λι
θοβολεῖσθαι· σὺ ὖν τί λέγεις;

6 Τῦτο δὲ ἔλεγον πειράζον�ες
αὐτὸν, ἵνα ἔχωσι κα�ηγορεῖν αὐ
τῦ. Ὁ δὲ Ἰησῦς κάτω κύψας,
τῷ δακτύλῳ ἔγραφεν εἰς τὴν γῆν.

7 Ὡς δὲ ἐπέμενον ἐρω�ῶν�ες
αὐτὸν, ἀνακύψας εἶπε πρὸς αὐ
τύς· ‡ Ὁ † ἀναμάρτη�@ ὑ
μῶν, πρῶ�@ τὸν λίθον ἐπ᾽ αὐτῇ
βαλέτω.

8 Καὶ πάλιν κάτω κύψας, ἔ
γραφεν εἰς τὴν γῆν.

9 Οἱ δὲ, ἀκύσαν�ες, κỳ ὑπὸ τῆς
συνειδήσεως ἐλεγχόμενοι, ἐξέρ
χον�ο εἷς καθ᾽ εἷς, ἀρξάμενοι ἀπὸ
τῶν πρεσβυ�έρων ἕως τῶν ἐσχά
των· κỳ κα�ελείφθη μόν@ ὁ Ἰη
σῦς, κỳ ἡ γυνὴ ἐν μέσῳ ἑςῶσα.

10 Ἀνακύψας δὲ ὁ Ἰησῦς, κỳ
μηδένα θεασάμεν@ πλὴν τῆς
γυναικὸς, εἶπεν αὐτῇ· Ἡ γυνὴ,
πῦ εἰσιν ἐκεῖνοι οἱ κα�ήγοροί συ;
ὀυδείς σε κα�έκρινεν;

11 Ἡ δὲ εἶπε· Ὀυδείς, Κύ
ριε. Εἶπε δὲ αὐτῇ ὁ Ἰησῦς· Ὀυ
δὲ ἐγώ σε κα�ακρίνω· πορεύυ, κỳ
μηκέτι ἁμάρ�ανε.

---

50 Dicit Nicodemus ad eos,
ille profectus nocte ad eum, unus
existens ex ipsis:

51 Numquid lex nostra judi
cat hominem, si non audierit ab
ipso prius, & cognoverit quid
faciat?

52 Responderunt & dixerunt
ei: Numquid & tu ex Galilæa
es? scrutare, & vide, quia pro
pheta in Galilæa non surrexit.

53 Et perrexit unusquisque
in domum suam.

CAPUT VIII.

1 JEsus autem perrexit in
montem olearum.

2 Diluculo autem iterum ac
cessit in templum, & omnis po
pulus venit ad eum, & sedens
docebat eos.

3 Adducunt autem Scribæ &
Pharisæi ad eum mulierem in
adulterio deprehensam: & sta
tuentes in medio,

4 Dicunt ei: Magister, hanc
invenimus in ipso facto adulte
rantem.

5 In autem Lege nostra Mo
ses mandavit hujusmodi lapida
ri: Tu ergo quid dicis?

6 Hoc autem dicebant ten
tantes eum, ut haberent accusa
tionem adversus eum. At Jesus
deorsum inclinans, digito scri
bebat in terram.

7 Ut autem preseverabant in
terrogantes eum, erectus ait ad
eos: Qui sine peccato est vestrum,
primus lapidem in illam jaciat.

8 Et iterum deorsum incli
nans scribebat in terram.

9 Ii autem audientes, & à
conscientia redarguti, exibant
unus post unum, incipientes à
senioribus usque extremos: &
relictus est solus Jesus, & mu
lier in medio existens.

10 Erectus autem Jesus, &
neminem spectans præter mu
lierem, dixit ei: Mulier, ubi sunt
illi accusatores tui? nemo te
condemnavit?

11 Illa autem dixit: Nemo,
Domine, Dixit autem ei Jesus:
Nec ego te condemno. Vade, &
non amplius pecca.

50. Nicodème (celui qui étoit venu de nuit vers Jésus, et qui étoit l'un d'entr'eux), leur dit :

51. Notre Loi condamne-t-elle un homme sans l'avoir ouï auparavant, et sans s'être informé de ce qu'il a fait ?

52. Ils lui répondirent : Es-tu aussi Galiléen ? Informe-toi, et tu verras qu'aucun Prophète n'a été suscité de la Galilée.

53. Et chacun s'en alla dans sa maison.

Jésus s'en alla ensuite sur la montagne des Oliviers,

2. Et à la pointe du jour, il retourna au Temple, et tout le peuple vint à lui ; et s'étant assis, il les enseignoit.

3. Alors les Scribes et les Pharisiens lui amenèrent une femme qui avoit été surprise en adultère, et l'ayant mise au milieu,

4. Ils lui dirent : Maître, cette femme a été surprise sur le fait, commettant adultère.

5. Or, Moyse nous a ordonné dans la Loi, de lapider ces sortes de personnes ; toi donc, qu'en dis-tu ?

6. Ils disoient cela pour l'éprouver, afin de le pouvoir accuser. Mais Jésus s'étant baissé, écrivoit avec le doigt sur la terre.

7. Et comme ils continuoient à l'interroger, s'étant redressé, il leur dit : Que celui de vous qui est sans péché, jette le premier la pierre contr'elle ;

8. Et s'étant encore baissé, il écrivoit sur la terre.

9. Quand ils entendirent cela, se sentant repris par leur conscience, ils sortirent l'un après l'autre, commençant depuis les plus vieux jusqu'aux derniers ; et Jésus demeura seul avec la femme qui étoit là au milieu.

10. Alors Jésus s'étant redressé, et ne voyant personne que la femme, il lui dit : Femme, où sont ceux qui t'accusoient? Personne ne t'a-t-il condamnée ?

11. Elle dit : Personne, Seigneur. Et Jésus lui dit : Je ne te condamne point non plus ; va-t-en, et ne péche plus à l'avenir.

50 Nicodemus saith unto them, (he that came to Jesus by night, being one of them,)

51 Doth our law judge *any* man, before it hear him, and know what he doeth?

52 They answered, and said unto him, Art thou also of Galilee ? Search, and look : for out of Galilee ariseth no prophet.

53 And every man went unto his own house.

JESUS went unto the mount of Olives,

2 And early in the morning he came again into the temple, and all the people came unto him: and he sat down, and taught them.

3 And the scribes and Pharisees brought unto him a woman taken in adultery ; and, when they had set her in the midst,

4 They say unto him, Master, this woman was taken in adultery, in the very act.

5 Now Moses in the law commanded us, That such should be stoned : but what sayest thou ?

6 This they said, tempting him, that they might have to accuse him. But Jesus stooped down, and with *his* finger wrote on the ground, *as though he heard them not.*

7 So, when they continued asking him, he lifted up himself, and said unto them, He that is without sin among you, let him first cast a stone at her.

8 And again he stooped down, and wrote on the ground.

9 And they which heard *it*, being convicted by *their own* conscience, went out one by one, beginning at the eldest, *even* unto the last ; and Jesus was left alone, and the woman standing in the midst.

10 When Jesus had lifted up himself, and saw none but the woman, he said unto her, Woman, where are those thine accusers ? hath no man condemned thee ?

11 She said, No man, Lord. And Jesus said unto her, Neither do I condemn thee : go, and sin no more.

* 1 ΚΑΙ' παράγων εἶδεν ἄνθρωπον τυφλὸν ἐκ † γενετῆς.

2 Καὶ ἠρώτησαν αὐτὸν οἱ μαθηταὶ αὐτοῦ, λέγοντες· Ῥαββὶ, τίς
ἥμαρτεν, οὗτ۰, ἢ οἱ γονεῖς αὐτοῦ,
ἵνα τυφλὸς γεννηθῇ;

3 Ἀπεκρίθη ὁ Ἰησοῦς· Οὔτε
οὗτ۰ ἥμαρτεν, οὔτε οἱ γονεῖς αὐ-
τοῦ· ἀλλ' ἵνα φανερωθῇ τὰ ἔργα
τοῦ Θεοῦ ἐν αὐτῷ.

1 ET praeteriens vidit hominem caecum ex nativitate.

2 Et interrogaverunt eum
discipuli ejus, dicentes : Rabbi,
quis peccavit, hic aut parentes
ejus, ut caecus nasceretur ?

3 Respondit Jesus: Neque hic
peccavit, neque parentes ejus :
sed ut manifestentur opera Dei
in illo :

* 1 ΑΜὴν, ἀμὴν, λέγω ὑμῖν, ὁ
μὴ εἰσερχόμεν۰ διὰ
τῆς θύρας εἰς τὴν αὐλὴν τῶν προβάτων, ἀλλὰ ἀναβαίνων † ἀλ-
λαχόθεν, ἐκεῖν۰ κλέπτης ἐςὶ ᾗ
ᾗ λῃςής.

2 Ὁ δὲ εἰσερχόμεν۰ διὰ τῆς
θύρας, ποιμήν ἐςι τῶν προβάτων.

3 Τέτῳ ὁ θυρωρὸς ἀνοίγει, ᾗ
τὰ πρόβατα τῆς φωνῆς αὐτῦ ἀ-
κύει· ᾗ τὰ ἴδια πρόβατα καλεῖ
κατ' ὄνομα. ᾗ ἐξάγει αὐτά.

4 Καὶ ὅταν τὰ ἴδια πρόβατα
ἐκβάλῃ, ἔμπροσθεν αὐτῶν πορεύε-
ται· ᾗ τὰ πρόβατα αὐτῷ ἀκολυ-
θεῖ, ὅτι οἴδασι τὴν φωνὴν αὐτῦ.

5 Ἀλλοτρίῳ δὲ ὐ μὴ ἀκολυθή-
σωσιν, ἀλλὰ φεύξονται ἀπ' αὐ-
τῦ· ὅτι ὐκ οἴδασι τῶν ἀλλοτρίων
τὴν φωνήν.

1 AMen, amen, dico vobis,
non intrans per ostium in
ovile ovium, sed ascendens ali-
unde, ille fur est & latro.

2 Intrans verò per ostium,
pastor est ovium.

3 Huic ostiarius aperit, &
oves vocem ejus audiunt, & proprias oves vocat juxta nomen,
& educit eas.

4 Et quum proprias oves e-
miserit, ante eas vadit : & oves
illum sequuntur, quia sciunt
vocem ejus.

5 Alienum autem non se-
quentur, sed fugient ab eo :
quia non noverunt alienorum
vocem.

11 Ἐγώ εἰμι ὁ ποιμὴν ὁ κα-
λός· ὁ ποιμὴν ὁ καλὸς τὴν ψυχὴν αὐτῦ τίθησιν ὑπὲρ τῶν προβάτων.

* 12 Ὁ † μισθωτὸς δὲ, ᾗ ὐκ
ὢν ποιμὴν, ὗ ὐκ εἰσὶ τὰ πρόβατα
ἴδια, θεωρεῖ τὸν λύκον ἐρχόμενον,
ᾗ ἀφίησι τὰ πρόβατα, ᾗ φεύγει·
ᾗ ὁ λύκ۰ ἁρπάζει αὐτὰ, ᾗ σκορ-
πίζει τὰ πρόβατα.

13 Ὁ δὲ μισθωτὸς φεύγει, ὅτι
μισθωτός ἐςι. ᾗ ὐ μέλει αὐτῷ
περὶ τῶν προβάτων.

14 Ἐγώ εἰμι ὁ ποιμὴν ὁ καλὸς,
ᾗ γινώσκω τὰ ἐμὰ, ᾗ γινώσκο-
μαι ὑπὸ τῶν ἐμῶν.

16 Καὶ ἄλλα πρόβατα ἔχω, ἃ
ὐκ ἔςιν ἐκ τῆς αὐλῆς ταύτης· κὰ-
κεῖνά με δεῖ ἀγαγεῖν· ᾗ τῆς φωνῆς μυ ἀκύσυσι· ᾗ γενήσεται μία
ποίμνη, εἷς ποιμήν.

11 Ego sum pastor bonus :
pastor bonus animam suam ponit pro ovibus.

12 Mercenarius autem, & non
existens pastor, cujus non sunt
oves propriae, videt lupum venientem, & dimittit oves, &
fugit : & lupus rapit eas, &
dispergit oves.

13 At mercenarius fugit,
quia mercenarius est, & non cu-
rae est ei de ovibus.

14 Ego sum pastor bonus, &
cognosco meas, & cognoscor à
meis.

16 Et alias oves habeo, quae
non sunt ex caula hac : & illas
me oportet adducere : & vocem
meam audient : & fiet unum
ovile, unus pastor.

Comme *Jésus* passoit, il vit un homme aveugle dès sa naissance.

2. Et ses Disciples lui demandèrent : Maitre, qui est-ce qui a péché ? Est-ce cet homme, ou son père, ou sa mère, qu'il soit ainsi né aveugle ?

3. Jésus répondit : Ce n'est point qu'il ait péché, ni son père, ou sa mère, mais c'est afin que les œuvres de Dieu soient manifestées en lui.

En vérité, en vérité je vous dis, *que* celui qui n'entre pas par la porte dans la bergerie des brebis, mais qui y monte par un autre endroit, est un larron et un voleur.

2. Mais celui qui entre par la porte est le Berger des brebis.

3. Le portier lui ouvre, les brebis entendent sa voix, et il appelle ses propres brebis par *leur* nom, et les mène dehors.

4. Et quand il a mis dehors ses propres brebis, il marche devant elles, et les brebis le suivent, parce qu'elles connoissent sa voix.

5. Mais elles ne suivront point un étranger ; au contraire, elles le fuiront ; parce qu'elles ne connoissent point la voix des étrangers.

11. Je suis le bon Berger : Le bon Berger donne sa vie pour ses brebis.

12. Mais le mercenaire, celui qui n'est point le berger, et à qui les brebis n'appartiennent pas, voit venir le loup, et il abandonne les brebis, et s'enfuit ; et le loup ravit les brebis et les disperse.

13. Le mercenaire s'enfuit, parce qu'il est mercenaire, et qu'il ne se soucie point des brebis.

14. Je suis le bon Berger, et je connois mes brebis, et mes brebis me connoissent,

16. J'ai encore d'autres brebis qui ne sont pas de cette bergerie ; il faut aussi que je les amène, et elles entendront ma voix, et il n'y aura qu'un seul troupeau *et* qu'un seul Berger.

AND as *Jesus* passed by, he saw a man which was blind from *his* birth.

2 And his disciples asked him, saying, Master, who did sin, this man, or his parents, that he was born blind ?

3 Jesus answered, Neither hath this man sinned, nor his parents : but that the works of God should be made manifest in him.

VERILY, verily, I say unto you, He that entereth not by the door into the sheep-fold, but climbeth up some other way, the same is a thief and a robber.

2 But he that entereth in by the door, is the shepherd of the sheep.

3 To him the porter openeth ; and the sheep hear his voice : and he calleth his own sheep by name, and leadeth them out.

4 And when he putteth forth his own sheep, he goeth before them, and the sheep follow him : for they know his voice.

5 And a stranger will they not follow, but will flee from him : for they know not the voice of strangers.

11 I am the good shepherd : the good shepherd giveth his life for the sheep.

12 But he that is an hireling, and not the shepherd, whose own the sheep are not, seeth the wolf coming, and leaveth the sheep, and fleeth : and the wolf catcheth them, and scattereth the sheep.

13 The hireling fleeth, because he is an hireling, and careth not for the sheep.

14 I am the good shepherd, and know my *sheep*, and am known of mine.

16 And other sheep I have, which are not of this fold : them also I must bring, and they shall hear my voice ; and there shall be one fold, *and* one shepherd.

25 Καὶ ἰδὺ, νομικός τις ἀνέςη,
ἐκπειράζων αὐτὸν, κ λέγων· Διδάσκαλε, τί ποιήσας ζωὴν αἰώνιον κληρονομήσω;

26 Ὁ δὲ εἶπε πρὸς αὐτόν· Ἐν
τῷ νόμῳ τί γέγραπλαι; πῶς ἀ-
ναγινώσκεις;

27 Ὁ δὲ ἀποκριθεὶς, εἶπεν·
Ἀγαπήσεις Κύριον τὸν Θεόν σου ἐξ

ὅλης τῆς καρδίας σου, κ ἐξ ὅλης
τῆς ψυχῆς σου, κ ἐξ ὅλης τῆς ἰσ-
χύος σου, κ ἐξ ὅλης τῆς διανοίας
σου· κ τὸν πλησίον σου ὡς σεαυτόν.

* 28 Εἶπε δὲ αὐτῷ· ‡ Ὀρθῶς
ἀπεκρίθης· τοῦτο ποίει, κ ζήσῃ·

29 Ὁ δὲ, θέλων δικαιοῦν ἑαυτὸν,
εἶπε πρὸς τὸν Ἰησοῦν· Καὶ τίς ἐςί
μου πλησίον;

* 30 ‡ Ὑπολαβὼν δὲ ὁ Ἰησοῦς,
εἶπεν· Ἄνθρωπός τις κατέβαινεν
ἀπὸ Ἱερουσαλὴμ εἰς Ἱεριχὼ, κ
‡ λῃςαῖς ‡ περιέπεσεν· οἳ κ ἐκ-
δύσαντες αὐτὸν, κ πληγὰς ἐπι-
θέντες, ἀπῆλθον, ἀφέντες † ἡμι-
θανῆ ‡ τυγχάνονla.

* 31 Καὶ † Cυγκυρίαν δὲ
‡ ἱερεύς τις κατέβαινεν ἐν τῇ ὁδῷ
ἐκείνῃ· κ ἰδὼν αὐτὸν, ‡ ἀνλιπαρῆλθεν.

32 Ὁμοίως δὲ κ Λευίτης, γε-
νόμεν⑨ κατὰ τὸν τόπον, ἐλθὼν κ
ἰδὼν, ἀνλιπαρῆλθεν.

* 33 Σαμαρείτης δέ τις ὁ-
δεύων, ἦλθε κατ᾽ αὐτὸν, κ ἰδὼν
αὐτὸν, ‡ ἐσπλαγχνίσθη.

* 34 Καὶ προσελθὼν † κατέδησε
τὰ ‡ τραύμαla αὐτῦ, † ἐπιχέων
‡ ἔλαιον κ οἶνον· ‡ ἐπιβιβάσας δὲ
αὐτὸν ἐπὶ τὸ ‡ ἴδιον κ1ῆν⑨,
ἤγαγεν αὐτὸν εἰς † πανδ:χεῖον, κ
‡ ἐπεμελήθη αὐτοῦ.

* 35 Καὶ ἐπὶ τὴν αὔριον ἐξελθὼν,
ἐκβαλὼν δύο δηνάρια ἔδωκε τῷ
† πανδοχεῖ, κ εἶπεν αὐτῷ· Ἐ-
πιμελήθηι αὐτῦ· κ ὅ,τι ἂν
† προσδαπανήσῃς, ἐγὼ ἐν τῷ ‡
ἐπανέρχεσθαί με ἀποδώσω σοι.

36 Τίς οὖν τούτων τῶν τριῶν
δοκεῖ Cοι πλησίον γεγονέναι τοῦ
ἐμπεσόν⑨⑨ εἰς τοὺς λῃςάς;

37 Ὁ δὲ εἶπεν· Ὁ ποιήσας τὸ
ἔλε⑨⑨ μετ᾽ αὐτῦ. Εἶπεν οὖν αὐτῷ
ὁ Ἰησῆς· Πορεύυ, κ σὺ ποίει
ὁμοίως.

25 Et ecce Legiſperitus quidam ſurrexit, tentans illum, &
dicens : Magiſter, quid faciens
vitam æternam poſſidebo?

26 Ille autem dixit ad eum :
in Lege quid ſcriptum eſt? quomodo legis?

27 Ille autem reſpondens dixit : Diliges Dominum Deum
tuum ex toto corde tuo, & ex

tota anima tua, & ex tota fortitudine tua, & ex omni cogitatione tua; & proximum tuum
ſicut teipſum.

28 Dixit autem illi : Rectè
reſpondiſti : hoc fac, & vives.

29 Ille autem volens juſtifi-
care ſeipſum, dixit ad Jeſum :
Et quis eſt meus proximus?

30 Suſcipiens autem Jeſus,
dixit : Homo quidam deſcende-
bat ab Hieruſalem in Jericho,
& in latrones incidit : qui etiam
exuentes eum, & plagas impo-
nentes, abierunt, relinquentes
ſemivivum exiſtentem.

31 Secundum ſortem autem
ſacerdos quidam deſcendit in via
illa, & videns illum, præterivit.

32 Similiter autem & Levita,
factus ſecundum locum, veniens
& videns, pertranſiit.

33 Samaritanus autem qui-
dam iter faciens, venit ſecus
eum, & videns eum, viſceribus
commotus eſt.

34 Et accedens alligavit vul-
nera ejus, infundens oleum &
vinum: aſcendere faciens autem illum in proprium jumen-
tum, duxit in diverſorium, &
curam egit ejus.

35 Et in craſtinum exiens,
ejiciens duos denarios dedit ta-
bernario, & ait illi : Curam
habe illius; & quodcumque ad-
inſumpſeris, ego in redire me
reddam tibi.

36 Quis igitur horum trium
videtur tibi proximus fuiſſe in-
cidentis in latrones?

37 Ille autem dixit : Faciens
miſericordiam cum illo, ait ergo
illi Jeſus : Vade, & tu fac ſimi-
liter.

25. Alors un Docteur de la loi se leva, et dit à *Jésus* pour l'éprouver: Maître, que faut-il que je fasse pour hériter la vie éternelle?

26. *Jésus* lui dit: Q'est-ce qui est écrit dans la loi; et qu'y lis-tu?

27. Il répondit: Tu aimeras le Seigneur ton Dieu de tout ton cœur, de toute ton ame, de toute ta force et de toute ta pensée; et ton prochain comme toi-même.

28. Et *Jésus* lui dit: Tu as bien répondu; fais cela, et tu vivras.

29. Mais *cet homme* voulant paroître juste, dit à Jésus: Et qui est mon prochain?

30. Or *Jésus* prenant la parole, lui dit: Un homme descendoit de Jérusalem à Jérico, et tomba entre les mains des voleurs, qui le dépouillèrent; et après l'avoir blessé de plusieurs coups, ils s'en allèrent, le laissant à demi-mort.

31. Or, Il se rencontra qu'un Sacrificateur descendoit par ce chemin-là, et ayant vu *cet homme*, il passa outre.

32. Un Lévite étant aussi venu dans le même endroit, et le voyant, passa outre.

33. Mais un Samaritain passant son chemin, vint vers cet homme, et le voyant; il fut touché de compassion.

34. Et s'approchant, il banda ses plaies, et il y versa de l'huile et du vin; puis il le mit sur sa monture, et le mena à une hôtellerie, et prit soin de lui.

35. Le lendemain, en partant, il tira deux deniers *d'argent*, et les donna à l'hôte, et lui dit: Aie soin de lui; et tout ce que tu dépenseras de plus, je te le rendrai à mon retour.

36. Lequel donc de ces trois te semble avoir été le prochain de celui qui étoit tombé entre les mains des voleurs?

37. *Le Docteur* dit: C'est celui qui a exercé la miséricorde envers lui. Jésus lui dit: Va, et fais la même chose.

38. Comme ils étoient en che-

25 And, behold, a certain lawyer stood up, and tempted him, saying, Master, what shall I do to inherit eternal life?

26 He said unto him, What is written in the law? how readest thou?

27 And he answering, said, Thou shalt love the Lord thy God with all thy heart, and with all thy soul, and with all thy strength, and with all thy mind; and thy neighbour as thyself.

28 And he said unto him, Thou hast answered right: this do, and thou shalt live.

29 But he, willing to justify himself, said unto Jesus, And who is my neighbour?

30 And Jesus, answering, said, A certain *man* went down from Jerusalem to Jericho, and fell among thieves, which stripped him of his raiment, and wounded *him*, and departed, leaving *him* half dead.

31 And, by chance, there came down a certain priest that way; and when he saw him, he passed by on the other side.

32 And likewise a Levite, when he was at the place, came and looked *on him*, and passed by on the other side.

33 But a certain Samaritan, as he journeyed, came where he was: and when he saw him, he had compassion *on him*.

34 And went to *him*, and bound up his wounds, pouring in oil and wine, and set him on his own beast, and brought him to an inn, and took care of him.

35 And on the morrow, when he departed, he took out two pence, and gave *them* to the host, and said unto him, Take care of him: and whatsoever thou spendest more, when I come again, I will repay thee.

36 Which now of these three, thinkest thou was neighbour unto him that fell among the thieves?

37 And he said, He that shewed mercy on him. Then said Jesus unto him, Go, and do thou likewise.

1 ΚΑΙ ἐγένετο ἐν τῷ εἶναι αὐτὸν ἐν τόπῳ τινὶ προσευχόμενον, ὡς ἐπαύσατο, εἶπέ τις τῶν μαθητῶν αὐτῦ πρὸς αὐτόν· Κύριε, δίδαξον ἡμᾶς προσεύχεσθαι, καθὼς κỳ Ἰωάννης ἐδίδαξε τοὺς μαθητὰς αὐτῦ.

2 Εἶπε δὲ αὐτοῖς· Ὅταν προσεύχησθε, λέγετε· ΠΑΤΕΡ ἡμῶν ὁ ἐν τοῖς ὐρανοῖς, ἁγιασθήτω τὸ ὄνομά συ· ἐλθέτω ἡ βασιλεία συ· γενηθήτω τὸ θέλημά συ, ὡς ἐν ὐρανῷ, κỳ ἐπὶ τῆς γῆς·

* 3 Τὸν ἄρτον ἡμῶν τὸν ‡ ἐπιέσιον δίδυ ἡμῖν τὸ καθ' ἡμέραν·

4 Καὶ ἄφες ἡμῖν τὰς ἁμαρτίας ἡμῶν· κỳ γὰρ αὐτοὶ ἀφίεμεν παντὶ ὀφείλοντι ἡμῖν· κỳ μὴ εἰσενέγκῃς ἡμᾶς εἰς πειρασμὸν, ἀλλὰ ῥῦσαι ἡμᾶς ἀπὸ τῦ πονηρῦ.

* 5 Καὶ εἶπε πρὸς αὐτούς· Τίς ἐξ ὑμῶν ἕξει φίλον, κỳ πορεύσεται πρὸς αὐτὸν μεσονυκτίυ, κỳ εἴπη αὐτῷ· Φίλε, † χρῆσόν μοι ‡ τρεῖς ‡ ἄρτυς·

6 Ἐπειδὴ φίλος μυ παρεγένετο ἐξ ὁδῦ πρός με, κỳ ἐκ ἔχω ὃ παραθήσω αὐτῷ·

7 Κἀκεῖνος ἔσωθεν ἀποκριθεὶς εἴπη· Μή μοι κόπυς πάρεχε· ἤδη ἡ θύρα κέκλεισαι, κỳ τὰ παιδία μυ μετ' ἐμῦ εἰς τὴν κοίτην εἰσίν· ὐ δύναμαι ἀναςὰς δῦναί σοι.

* 8 Λέγω ὑμῖν, εἰ κỳ ὐ δώσει αὐτῷ ἀναςὰς, διὰ τὸ εἶναι αὐτῦ φίλον· διά ‡ γε τὴν † ἀναίδειαν αὐτῦ ἐγερθεὶς δώσει αὐτῷ ὅσων χρῆζει.

9 Κἀγὼ ὑμῖν λέγω· Αἰτεῖτε, κỳ δοθήσεται ὑμῖν· ζητεῖτε, κỳ εὑρήσετε· κρύετε, κỳ ἀνοιγήσεται ὑμῖν.

10 Πᾶς γὰρ ὁ αἰτῶν λαμβάνει· κỳ ὁ ζητῶν εὑρίσκει· κỳ τῷ κρύοντι ἀνοιγήσεται.

11 Τίνα δὲ ὑμῶν τὸν πατέρα, αἰτήσει ὁ υἱὸς ἄρτον, μὴ λίθον ἐπιδώσει αὐτῷ; εἰ κỳ ἰχθῦν, μὴ ἀντὶ ἰχθύος ὄφιν ἐπιδώσει αὐτῷ;

* 12 Ἢ κỳ ἐὰν αἰτήσῃ † ᾠὸν, μὴ ἐπιδώσει αὐτῷ σκορπίον;

1 ET factum est in esse ipsum in loco quodâm orantem, ut cessavit, dixit quidam discipulorum ejus ad eum : Domine, doce nos orare, sicut & Joannes docuit discipulos suos.

2 Ait autem illis : Quum oratis, dicite : Pater noster qui in cælis, sanctificetur nomen tuum : adveniat regnum tuum : fiat voluntas tua, sicut in cælo, & in terra.

3 Panem nostrum quotidianum da nobis juxta diem.

4 Et dimitte nobis peccata nostra, & enim ipsi dimittimus omni debenti nobis : & ne inducas nos in tentationem, sed libera nos à malo.

5 Et ait ad illos : Quis ex vobis habebit amicum, & ibit ad illum media nocte, & dicet illi : Amice, commoda mihi tres panes :

6 Quoniam amicus meus venit de via ad me, & non habeo quod apponam ei.

7 Et ille deintus respondens dicat : Ne mihi molestias exhibe : jam ostium clausum est, & pueri mei mecum in cubili sunt : non possum surgens dare tibi.

8 Dico vobis, si & non dederit ei surgens propter esse illius amicum, propter improbitatem ejus excitatus dabit illi quotquot habet opus.

9 Et ego vobis dico : Petite, & dabitur vobis : quærite, & invenietis : pulsate, & aperietur vobis.

10 Omnis enim petens accipit, & quærens invenit, & pulsanti aperietur.

11 Quem autem vestrum patrem petet filius panem, num lapidem dabit illi ? si & piscem, num pro pisce serpentem dabit illi ?

12 Aut & si petierit ovum, num dabit illi scorpionem ?

Un jour que Jésus étoit en prière en un certain lieu, après qu'il eut achevé sa prière, un de ses Disciples lui dit : Seigneur, enseigne-nous à prier, comme Jean l'a aussi enseigné à ses Disciples.

2. Et il leur dit : Quand vous priez, dites : Notre Père qui es aux cieux : Ton nom soit sanctifié. Ton règne vienne. Ta volonté soit faite sur la terre comme au ciel.

3. Donne-nous chaque jour notre pain quotidien.

4. Pardonne-nous nos péchés, car nous pardonnons aussi à tous ceux qui nous ont offensés. Et ne nous abandonne point à la tentation, mais délivre-nous du mal.

5. Puis il leur dit : Si quelqu'un de vous avoit un ami, qui vînt le trouver à minuit, et qui lui dît : Mon ami, prête-moi trois pains.

6. Car un de mes amis est venu me voir en passant, et je n'ai rien à lui présenter.

7. Et que cet homme qui est dans sa maison lui répondit : Ne m'importune pas ; ma porte est fermée, et mes enfans sont avec moi au lit ; je ne saurois me lever pour t'en donner.

8. Je vous dis que quand même il ne se leveroit pas pour lui en donner, parce qu'il est son ami ; il se leveroit à cause de son importunité, et lui en donneroit autant qu'il en auroit besoin.

9. Et moi je vous dis : Demandez, et il vous sera donné ; cherchez, et vous trouverez ; heurtez, et il vous sera ouvert.

10. Car quiconque demande reçoit ; et qui cherche, trouve ; et il sera ouvert à celui qui heurte.

11. Qui est le père d'entre vous, qui donne à son fils une pierre, lorsqu'il lui demande du pain ? Ou s'il lui demande du poisson, lui donnera-t-il un serpent au lieu d'un poisson ?

12. Ou s'il lui demande un œuf, lui donnera-t-il un scorpion ?

AND it came to pass, that, as he was praying in a certain place, when he ceased, one of his disciples said unto him, Lord, teach us to pray, as John also taught his disciples.

2 And he said unto them, When ye pray, say, Our Father, which art in heaven : Hallowed be thy name. Thy kingdom come. Thy will be done, as in heaven, so in earth.

3 Give us day by day our daily bread.

4 And forgive us our sins ; for we also forgive every one that is indebted to us. And lead us not into temptation ; but deliver us from evil.

5 And he said unto them, Which of you shall have a friend, and shall go unto him at midnight, and say unto him, Friend, lend me three loaves ;

6 For a friend of mine in his journey is come to me, and I have nothing to set before him ?

7 And he from within shall answer, and say, Trouble me not : the door is now shut, and my children are with me in bed ; I cannot rise and give thee.

8 I say unto you, Though he will not rise and give him, because he is his friend ; yet because of his importunity he will rise and give him as many as he needeth.

9 And I say unto you, Ask, and it shall be given you ; seek, and ye shall find : knock, and it shall be opened unto you.

10 For every one that asketh, receiveth ; and he that seeketh, findeth ; and to him that knocketh, it shall be opened.

11 If a son shall ask bread of any of you that is a father, will he give him a stone ? or, if he ask a fish, will he for a fish give him a serpent ?

12 Or, if he shall ask an egg, will he offer him a scorpion ?

40

13 Εἰ ἦν ὑμεῖς πονηροὶ ὑπάρχοντες, οἴδατε ἀγαθὰ δόματα διδόναι τοῖς τέκνοις ὑμῶν, πόσῳ μᾶλλον ὁ πατὴρ ὁ ἐξ οὐρανοῦ, δώσει πνεῦμα ἅγιον τοῖς αἰτοῦσιν αὐτόν;

Κεφ. ιδ. 14.

1 ΚΑΙ ἐγένετο ἐν τῷ ἐλθεῖν αὐτὸν εἰς οἶκόν τινῶ· τῶν ἀρχόντων τῶν φαρισαίων σαββάτῳ φαγεῖν ἄρτον, κ̣ αὐτοὶ ἦσαν παρατηρούμενοι αὐτόν.

* 2 Καὶ ἰδὺ, ἄνθρωπός τις ἦν † ὑδρωπικὸς ἔμπροσθεν αὐτοῦ.

3 Καὶ ἀποκριθεὶς ὁ Ἰησοῦς εἶπε πρὸς τοὺς νομικοὺς κ̣ φαρισαίους, λέγων· Εἰ ἔξεςι τῷ σαββάτῳ θεραπεύειν·

* 4 Οἱ δὲ ‡ ἡσύχασαν.

Τίνῶ· ὑμῶν ὄνῶ· ἢ βῶς εἰς φρέαρ ἐμπεσεῖται, κ̣ οὐκ εὐθέως ‡ ἀνασπάσει αὐτὸν ἐν τῇ ἡμέρᾳ τοῦ σαββάτου;

6 Καὶ οὐκ ἴσχυσαν ἀνταποκριθῆναι αὐτῷ πρὸς ταῦτα.

7 Ἔλεγε δὲ πρὸς τοὺς κεκλημένους παραβολὴν, ἐπέχων πῶς τὰς πρωτοκλισίας ἐξελέγοντο, λέγων πρὸς αὐτούς·

8 Ὅταν κληθῇς ὑπό τ.νῶ· εἰς γάμους, μὴ κατακλιθῇς εἰς τὴν πρωτοκλισίαν· μήποτε ἐντιμότερός σε ᾖ κεκλημένῶ· ὑπ᾽ αὐτοῦ.

9 Καὶ ἐλθὼν ὁ σὲ κ̣ αὐτὸν καλέσας, ἐρεῖ σοι· Δὸς τούτῳ τόπον· κ̣ τότε ἄρξῃ μετ᾽ αἰσχύνης τὸν ἔσχατον τόπον κατέχειν.

* 10 Ἀλλ᾽ ὅταν κληθῇς, πορευθεὶς ἀνάπεσον εἰς τὸν ἔσχατον τόπον· ἵνα ὅταν ἔλθῃ ὁ κεκληκώς σε, εἴπῃ σοι· Φίλε, ‡ προσανάβηθι ‡ ἀνώτερον· τότε ἔςαι σοι δόξα ἐνώπιον τῶν ‡ συνανακειμένων σοι.

11 Ὅτι πᾶς ὁ ὑψῶν ἑαυτὸν, ταπεινωθήσεται· κ̣ ὁ ταπεινῶν ἑαυτὸν, ὑψωθήσεται.

* 12 Ἔλεγε δὲ κ̣ τῷ κεκληκότι αὐτόν· Ὅταν ποιῇς ἄριςον ἢ δεῖπνον, μὴ ‡ φώνει τοὺς ‡ φίλους σα, μηδὲ τοὺς ἀδελφούς σα, μηδὲ τοὺς ζυγγενεῖς σα, μηδὲ ‡ γείτονας ‡ πλουσίους· μήποτε κ̣ αὐτοί σε † ἀντικαλέσωσι, κ̣ γένηταί σοι ‡ ἀνταπόδομα.

---

13 Si ergo vos mali subsistentes, nostis bona dona dare filiis vestris, quanto magis Pater de cælo dabit Spiritum sanctum petentibus se?

CAPUT XIV.

1 ET factum est in venire eum in domum cujusdam principum Pharisæorum Sabbato manducare panem, & ipsi erat observantes eum.

2 Et ecce homo quidam erat hydropicus ante illum.

3 Et respondens Jesus dixit ad Legisperitos & Pharisæos, dicens: Si licet Sabbato curare?

4 Illi autem tacuerunt.

Cujus vestrum asinus aut bos in puteum cadet, & non continuo extrahet illum in die Sabbati?

6 Et non poterant respondere illi ad hæc

7 Dicebat autem ad vocatos parabolam, attendens quomodo primos accubitus eligerent, dicens ad illos:

8 Quum vocatus fueris ab aliquo ad nuptias, ne discumbas in primo accubitu, ne quando honoratior te sit vocatus ab illo.

9 Et veniens te & illum vocans, dicat tibi: Da huic locum: & tunc incipias cum pudore ultimum locum obtinere.

10 Sed quum vocatus fueris, vadens recumbe in novissimum locum, ut quum venerit qui te vocavit, dicat tibi: Amice, ascende superius, tunc erit tibi gloria coram simul discumbentibus tibi.

11 Quia omnis extollens seipsum humiliabitur, & humilians seipsum exaltabitur.

12 Dicebat autem & vocanti ipsum: Quum facis prandium aut cœnam, ne voca amicos tuos, neque fratres tuos, neque cognatos tuos, neque vicinos divites, ne quando et ipsi te vicissim vocent, & fiat tibi retributio.

13. Si donc vous , qui êtes mauvais , savez donner de bonnes choses à vos enfans , combien plus votre Père céleste , donnera-t-il le St. Esprit à ceux qui le lui demandent ?

Un jour de Sabbat, *Jésus* étant entré dans la maison d'un des principaux Pharisiens pour y manger , ceux qui étoient là l'observoient,

2. Et un homme hydropique se trouva devant lui.

3. Et Jésus prenant la parole , dit aux Docteurs de la loi et aux Pharisiens : Est-il permis de guérir au jour du Sabbat ?

4. Et ils demeurèrent dans le silence. Alors prenant *le malade* , il le guérit et le renvoia.

5. Puis il leur dit : Qui est celui d'entre vous qui , voyant son âne ou son bœuf tombé dans un puits , ne l'en retire aussitôt le jour du Sabbat ?

6. Et ils ne pouvoient rien répondre à cela.

7. Il proposoit aussi aux conviés une parabole ; remarquant qu'ils choisissoient les premières places ; et il leur disoit :

8. Quand quelqu'un t'invitera à des nôces, ne te mets pas à la première place , de peur qu'il ne se trouve parmi les conviés une personne plus considérable que toi.

9. Et que celui qui vous aura invité, et toi et lui , ne vienne et ne te dise : Cède la place à celui-ci ; et qu'alors tu n'aies la honte d'être mis à la dernière place.

10. Mais quand tu seras invité, va te mettre à la dernière place , afin que quand celui qui t'a invité viendra , il te dise : *Mon ami* , monte plus haut. Alors cela te fera honneur devant ceux qui seront à table avec toi.

11. Car quiconque s'élève sera abaissé ; et quiconque s'abaisse sera élevé.

12. Il disoit aussi à celui qui l'avoit invité : Quand tu fais un dîner ou un souper , n'invite pas tes amis , ni tes frères, ni tes parens , ni tes voisins qui sont riches , de peur qu'ils ne t'invitent à leur tour , et qu'on ne te rende la pareille.

L. 11.

13 If ye then, being evil, know how to give good gifts unto your children ; how much more shall *your* heavenly Father give the Holy Spirit to them that ask him ?

L. 14.

AND it came to pass, as he went into the house of one of the chief Pharisees to eat bread on the sabbath-day, that they watched him.

2 And, behold, there was a certain man before him, which had the dropsy.

3 And Jesus, answering, spake unto the lawyers and Pharisees, saying, Is it lawful to heal on the sabbath-day ?

4 And they held their peace.

5. Which of you shall have an ass or an ox fallen into a pit, and will not straightway pull him out on the sabbath-day ?

6 And they could not answer him again to these things.

7 And he put forth a parable to those which were bidden, when he marked how they chose out the chief rooms ; saying unto them,

8 When thou art bidden of any *man* to a wedding, sit not down in the highest room ; lest a more honourable man than thou be bidden of him ;

9 And he that bade thee and him, come and say to thee, Give this man place ; and thou begin with shame to take the lowest room.

10 But when thou art bidden, go and sit down in the lowest room ; that when he that bade thee cometh, he may say unto thee, Friend, go up higher : then shalt thou have worship in the presence of them that sit at meat with thee.

11 For whosoever exalteth himself shall be abased ; and he that humbleth himself shall be exalted.

12 Then said he also to him that bade him, When thou makest a dinner or a supper, call not thy friends, nor thy brethren, neither thy kinsmen, nor thy rich neighbours ; lest they also bid thee again, and a recompense be made thee.

(And he saith unto them.)

41

* 13 Ἀλλ' ὅταν ποιῇς ‡ δοχὴν, κάλει πλωχοὺς, ‡ ἀναπήρους,
χωλὰς, τυφλὰς·

14 Καὶ μακάρι⊙- ἔσῃ· ὅτι οὐκ
ἔχυσιν ἀνταποδῦναί σοι· ἀντα-
ποδοθήσεται γάρ σοι ἐν τῇ ἀναςάσει τῶν δικαίων.

16 Ὁ δὲ εἶπεν αὐτῷ· Ἄνθρωπός τις ἐποίησε δεῖπνον μέγα, ἢ
ἐκάλεσε πολλούς·

17 Καὶ ἀπέςειλε τὸν δῦλον αὐτῦ τῇ ὥρᾳ τοῦ δείπνυ εἰπεῖν τοῖς
κεκλημένοις· Ἔρχεσθε, ὅτι ἤδη
ἕτοιμά ἐςι πάντα.

18 Καὶ ἤρξαντο ἀπὸ μιᾶς πα-
ραιτεῖσθαι πάντες· Ὁ πρῶτ⊙-
εἶπεν αὐτῷ· Ἀγρὸν ἠγόρασα, ἢ
ἔχω ἀνάγκην ἐξελθεῖν, ἢ ἰδεῖν
αὐτόν· ἐρωτῶ σε, ἔχε με παρῃτημένον.

19 Καὶ ἕτερ⊙- εἶπε. Ζεύγη
βοῶν ἠγόρασα πέντε, ἢ πορεύομαι
δοκιμάσαι αὐτά· ἐρωτῶ σε, ἔχε
με παρῃτημένον.

20 Καὶ ἕτερ⊙- εἶπε· Γυναῖκα
ἔγημα, ἢ διὰ τοῦτο οὐ δύναμαι
ἐλθ-ῖν.

21 Καὶ παραγενόμεν⊙- ὁ δοῦ-
λ⊙- ἐκεῖν⊙- ἀπήγγειλε τῷ κυρίῳ
αὐτῦ ταῦτα. Τότε ὀργισθεὶς ὁ
οἰκοδεσπότης εἶπε τῷ δ-ύλῳ αὐτῦ·
Ἔξελθε ταχέως εἰς τὰς πλατείας
ἢ ῥύμας τῆς πόλεως, ἢ τοὺς πλωχοὺς ἢ ἀναπήρους ἢ χωλοὺς ἢ τυ-
φλοὺς εἰσάγαγε ὧδε.

22 Καὶ εἶπεν ὁ δῦλ⊙-· Κύριε,
γέγονεν ὡς ἐπέταξας, ἢ ἔτι τόπ-
ἐςι.

23 Καὶ εἶπεν ὁ κύρι⊙- πρὸς τὸν
δῦλον· Ἔξελθε εἰς τὰς ὁδοὺς ἢ
φραγμὺς, ἢ ἀνάγκασον εἰσελθεῖν,
ἵνα γεμισθῇ ὁ οἶκός μυ.

24 Λέγω γὰρ ὑμῖν, ὅτι οὐδεὶς
τῶν ἀν- δρῶν ἐκείνων τῶν κεκλημέ-
νων γεύσεταί μυ τοῦ δείπνυ.

* 28 Τίς γὰρ ἐξ ὑμῶν, θέλων
πύργον οἰκοδομῆσαι, οὐχὶ πρῶτον
καθίσας ‡ ψηφίζει τὴν † δαπάνην,
εἰ ἔχει τὰ πρὸς † ἀπαρτισμόν;

29 Ἵνα μήποτε, θέντ⊙- αὐτῦ
θεμέλιον, ἢ μὴ ἰσχύον⊤⊙- ἐκτελέσαι, πάντες οἱ θεωρῦντες· ἄρ-
ξωνται ἐμπαίζειν αὐτῷ,

---

13 Sed quum facis epulum,
voca pauperes, mancos, claudos,
cæcos.

14 Et beatus eris, quia non
habent retribuere tibi : retribue-
tur enim tibi in resurrectione
justorum.

16 Ipse autem dixit ei : Homo quidam fecit cœnam ma-
gnam, & vocavit multos.

17 Et misit servum suum hora cœnæ dicere vocatis : venite,
quia jam parata sunt omnia.

18 Et cœperunt ab una excu-
sare omnes. Primus dixit ei :
Agrum emi, & habeo necesse
exire, & videre illum : rogo te,
habe me excusatum.

19 Et alter dixit : Juga boum
emi quinque, & eo probare illa :
rogo te, habe me excusatum.

20 Et alius dixit : Uxorem
duxi, & propter hoc non possum
venire.

21 Et adveniens servus ille
nuntiavit domino suo hæc.
Tunc iratus paterfamilias dixit
servo suo ; Exi cito in plateas &
vicos civitatis, & pauperes, &
mancos, & claudos, & cæcos in-
troduc huc.

22 Et ait servus : Domine,
factum est ut imperasti, & adhuc locus est.

23 Et ait dominus ad ser-
vum : Exi in vias & sepes, &
coge intrare, ut impleatur domus
mea.

24 Dico enim vobis, quia
nemo virorum illorum vocato-
rum gustabit meam cœnam.

28 Quis enim ex vobis volens
turrim ædificare, nonne prius
sedens computat sumptum, si
habeat ea quæ ad perfectionem ?

29 Ut ne quando ponente ipso
fundamentum, & non potente
perficere, omnes videntes inci-
piant illudere ei,

13. Mais quand tu feras un festin, convie les pauvres, les impotens, les boiteux et les aveugles ;

14. Et tu seras heureux, de ce qu'ils ne peuvent pas te le rendre ;

16. Mais Jésus lui dit : Un homme fit un grand souper, et il y convia beaucoup de gens ;

17. Et il envoya son serviteur, à l'heure du souper, dire aux conviés : Venez, car tout est prêt.

18. Mais ils se mirent tous *comme* de concert, à s'excuser. Le premier lui dit : J'ai acheté une terre, et il me faut nécessairement partir pour aller la voir ; je te prie de m'excuser.

19. Un autre dit : J'ai acheté cinq couples de bœufs, et je m'en vais les éprouver ; je te prie de m'excuser.

20. Un autre dit : J'ai épousé une femme, ainsi je n'y puis aller.

21. Le serviteur étant donc de retour, rapporta cela à son maître. Alors le père de famille, en colère, dit à son serviteur : Va-t-en promptement par les places, et par les rues de la ville, et amène ici les pauvres, les impotens, les boiteux et les aveugles.

22. Ensuite le serviteur dit : Seigneur, on a fait ce que tu as commandé, et il y a encore de la place.

23. Et le maître dit au serviteur : Va dans les chemins et le long des haies, et presse d'entrer ceux que tu trouveras, afin que ma maison soit remplie.

24. Car je vous dis, qu'aucun de ceux qui avoient été conviés, ne goûtera de mon souper.

28. Car qui est celui d'entre vous, qui, voulant bâtir une tour, ne s'asseye premièrement, et ne suppute la dépense, *pour voir* s'il a de quoi l'achever ?

29. De peur qu'après qu'il en aura posé les fondemens, et qu'il n'aura pu achever, tous ceux qui le verront ne viennent à se moquer de lui ;

13 But when thou makest a feast, call the poor, the maimed, the lame, the blind :

14 And thou shalt be blessed ; for they cannot recompense thee : for thou shalt be recompensed at the resurrection of the just.

16 Then said he unto him, A certain man made a great supper, and bade many :

17 And sent his servant at supper-time to say to them that were bidden, Come, for all things are now ready.

18 And they all with one *consent* began to make excuse. The first said unto him, I have bought a piece of ground, and I must needs go and see it : I pray thee have me excused.

19 And another said, I have bought five yoke of oxen, and I go to prove them : I pray thee have me excused.

20 And another said, I have married a wife ; and therefore I cannot come.

21 So that servant came, and shewed his lord these things. Then the master of the house, being angry, said to his servant, Go out quickly into the streets and lanes of the city, and bring in hither the poor, and the maimed, and the halt, and the blind.

22 And the servant said, Lord, it is done as thou hast commanded, and yet there is room.

23 And the lord said unto the servant, Go out into the highways and hedges, and compel *them* to come in, that my house may be filled.

24 For I say unto you, That none of those men which were bidden, shall taste of my supper.

28 For which of you, intending to build a tower, sitteth not down first, and counteth the cost, whether he have *sufficient* to finish *it* ?

29 Lest haply, after he hath laid the foundation, and is not able to finish *it*, all that behold *it* begin to mock him,

42

* 30 Λέγοντες· Ὅτι οὗτ۟ ὁ ἄνθρωπ۟ ἤρξατο οἰκοδομεῖν, ἡ οὐκ ‡ ἴσχυσεν ‡ ἐκτελέσαι.

31 Ἢ τίς βασιλεὺς πορευόμεν۟ συμβαλεῖν ἑτέρῳ βασιλεῖ εἰς πόλεμον, οὐχὶ καθίσας πρῶτον βουλεύεται εἰ δυναῖός ἐςιν ἐν δέκα χιλιάσιν ἀπαντῆσαι τῷ μετὰ εἴκοσι χιλιάδων ἐρχομένῳ ἐπ᾽ αὐτόν;

32 Εἰ δὲ μήγε, ἔτι αὐτοῦ πόρρω ὄντ۟, πρεσβείαν ἀποςείλας, ἐρωῖᾷ τὰ πρὸς εἰρήνην.

Κεφ. ιέ. ιέ.

1 ῍Ησαν δὲ ἐγγίζοντες αὐτῷ πάντες οἱ τελῶναι ἡ οἱ ἁμαρτωλοὶ, ἀκούειν αὐτοῦ

2 Καὶ διεγόγγυζον οἱ φαρισαῖοι ἡ οἱ γραμματεῖς, λέγοντες. Ὅτι οὗτ۟ ἁμαρτωλοὺς προσδέχεται, ἡ συνεσθίει αὐτοῖς.

3 Εἶπε δὲ πρὸς αὐτοὺς τὴν παραβολὴν ταύτην, λέγων.

4 Τίς ἄνθρωπ۟ ἐξ ὑμῶν ἔχων ἑκατὸν πρόβατα, ἡ ἀπολέσας ἓν ἐξ αὐτῶν οὐ καταλείπει τὰ ἐννενηκονταεννέα ἐν τῇ ἐρήμῳ, ἡ πορεύεται ἐπὶ τὸ ἀπολωλὸς, ἕως εὕρῃ αὐτό;

* 5 Καὶ εὑρὼν ἐπιτίθησιν ἐπὶ τοὺς ‡ ὤμως ἑαυτοῦ χαίρων;

6 Καὶ ἐλθὼν εἰς τὸν οἶκον, συγκαλεῖ τοὺς φίλους ἡ τοὺς γείτονας, λέγων αὐτοῖς· Συγχάρητέ μοι, ὅτι εὗρον τὸ πρόβατόν μου τὸ ἀπολωλός.

7 Λέγω ὑμῖν, ὅτι ὕτω χαρὰ ἔςαι ἐν τῷ οὐρανῷ ἐπὶ ἑνὶ ἁμαρτωλῷ μετανοῦντι, ἢ ἐπὶ ἐννενηκονταεννέα δικαίοις, οἵτινες ὒ χρείαν ἔχουσι μετανοίας.

* 8 Ἢ τίς γυνὴ, δραχμὰς ἔχουσα δέκα, ἐὰν ἀπολέσῃ ‡ δραχμὴν μίαν, ‡ ὐχὶ ‡ ἅπτει ‡ λύχνον, ἡ σαροῖ τὴν οἰκίαν, ἡ ζητεῖ † ἐπιμελῶς, ἕως ‡ ὅτε εὕρῃ;

9 Καὶ εὑροῦσα συγκαλεῖται τὰς φίλας ἡ τὰς γείτονας, λέγουσα. Συγχάρητέ μοι, ὅτι εὗρον τὴν δραχμὴν, ἣν ἀπώλεσα.

10 Οὕτω, λέγω ὑμῖν, χαρὰ γίνεται ἐνώπιον τῶν ἀγγέλων τῇ Θεῦ ἐπὶ ἑνὶ ἁμαρτωλῷ μετανοῦντι.

---

30 Dicentes : Quia hic homo cœpit ædificare, & non potuit consummare.

31 Aut quis rex iturus committere alteri regi in bellum, non sedens prius consultat si potens est in decem millibus occurrere cum viginti millibus venienti ad se?

32 Si autem non, adhuc longe illo existente, legationem mittens rogat quæ ad pacem.

CAPUT XV.

1 ERant autem appropinquantes ei omnes publicani & peccatores audire illum.

2 Et murmurabant Pharisæi & Scribæ, dicentes : Quia hic peccatores recipit, & manducat cum illis.

3 Ait autem ad illos parabolam istam, dicens :

4 Quis homo ex vobis habens centum oves, & perdens unam ex illis, nonne dimittit nonaginta novem in deserto, & vadit ad perditam, donec inveniat eam?

5 Et inveniens imponit in humeros suos gaudens?

6 Et veniens in domum, convocat amicos & vicinos, dicens illis : Congratulamini mihi, quia inveni ovem meam perditam.

7 Dico vobis, quod ita gaudium erit in cælo super uno peccatore pœnitente, quam super nonaginta novem justis, qui non opus habent pœnitentia.

8 Aut quæ mulier drachmas habens decem, si perdiderit drachmam unam, nonne accendit lucernam, & everrit domum, & quærit diligenter, usquequo inveniat?

9 Et inveniens convocat amicas & vicinas, dicens : Congratulamini mihi, quia inveni drachmam quam perdideram.

10 Ita, dico vobis gaudium fit coram angelis Dei super uno peccatore pœnitente.

30. Et ne disent : Cet homme a commencé à bâtir, et n'a pu achever.

31. Ou, qui est le Roi, qui, marchant pour livrer bataille à un autre Roi, ne s'asseye premièrement, et ne consulte s'il pourra, avec dix mille *hommes*, aller à la rencontre de celui qui vient contre lui avec vingt mille ?

32. Autrement, pendant que celui-ci est encore loin, il lui envoie une ambassade pour lui demander la paix.

Tous les péagers et les gens de mauvaise vie s'approchoient de *Jésus* pour l'entendre.

2. Et les Pharisiens et les Scribes en murmuroient, et disoient : Cet homme reçoit les gens de mauvaise vie , et mange avec eux.

3. Mais il leur proposa cette parabole :

4. Qui est l'homme d'entre vous, qui , ayant cent brebis , s'il en perd une, ne laisse les quatre-vingt-neuf au désert , et n'aille après celle qui est perdue , jusqu'à ce qu'il l'ait trouvée ;

5. Et qui , l'ayant trouvée , ne la mette sur ses épaules avec joie ;

6. Et étant arrivé dans la maison , n'appelle ses amis et ses voisins , et ne leur dise : Réjouissez-vous avec moi , car j'ai trouvé ma brebis qui étoit perdue ?

7. Je vous dis , qu'il y aura de même plus de joie dans le ciel pour un seul pécheur qui s'amende , que pour quatre-vingt-dix-neuf justes, qui n'ont pas besoin de repentance.

8. Ou , qui est la femme qui , ayant dix drachmes , si elle en perd une , n'allume une chandelle , ne balaie la maison , et ne cherche avec soin , jusqu'à ce qu'elle ait trouvé *sa drachme* ;

9. Et qui , l'ayant trouvée , n'appelle ses amies et ses voisins , et ne leur dise : Réjouissez-vous avec moi , car j'ai trouvé la drachme que j'avois perdue ?

10. Je vous dis , qu'il y a de même de la joie devant les Anges de Dieu , pour un seul pécheur qui s'amende.

---

30 Saying, This man began to build, and was not able to finish.

31 Or what king, going to make war against another king, sitteth not down first, and consulteth whether he be able with ten thousand to meet him that cometh against him with twenty thousand ?

32 Or else, while the other is yet a great way off, he sendeth an ambassage, and desireth conditions of peace.

THEN drew near unto him all the publicans and sinners for to hear him.

2 And the Pharisees and scribes murmured, saying, This man receiveth sinners, and eateth with them.

3 And he spake this parable unto them, saying,

4 What man of you, having an hundred sheep, if he lose one of them, doth not leave the ninety and nine in the wilderness, and go after that which is lost, until he find it ?

5 And when he hath found *it*, he layeth *it* on his shoulders, rejoicing.

6 And when he cometh home, he calleth together *his* friends and neighbours, saying unto them, Rejoice with me ; for I have found my sheep which was lost.

7 I say unto you, That likewise joy shall be in heaven over one sinner that repenteth, more than over ninety and nine just persons, which need no repentance.

8 Either what woman, having ten pieces of silver, if she lose one piece, doth not light a candle, and sweep the house, and seek diligently till she find *it* ?

9 And when she hath found *it*, she calleth *her* friends and *her* neighbours together, saying, Rejoice with me ; for I have found the piece which I had lost.

10 Likewise, I say unto you, There is joy in the presence of the angels of God, over one sinner that repenteth.

43

11 Εἶπε δέ· Ἄνθρωπός τις εἶχε δύο υἱὲς.

12 Καὶ εἶπεν ὁ νεώτερ@ αὐτῶν τῶ πατρὶ Πάτερ, δός μοι
τὸ ἐπιβάλλον μέρ@ τῆς ὀσίας.
Καὶ διεῖλεν αὐτοῖς τὸν βίον.

* 13 Καὶ μετ᾽ ἐ πολλὰς ἡμέρας συναγαγὼν ἅπαντα ὁ νεώτε-
ρ@ υἱὸς, ‡ ἀπεδήμησεν εἰς χώραν
‡ μακρὰν· κ᾽ ἐκεῖ ‡ διεσκόρπισε
τὸν ‡ ὐσίαν αὐτῦ, ‡ ζῶν † ἀ-
σώτως.

14 ΔαπανήσανΙ@ δὲ αὐτοῦ
πάντα, ἐγένετο λιμὸς ἰσχυρὸς κατὰ τὴν χώραν ἐκείνην· κ᾽ αὐτὸς
ἤρξατο ὑστερεῖσθαι.

15 Καὶ πορευθεὶς ἐκολλήθη ἑνὶ
τῶν πολιτῶν τῆς χώρας ἐκείνης· κ᾽
ἔπεμψεν αὐτὸν εἰς τοὺς ἀγροὺς αὐτοῦ βόσκειν χοίρους.

* 16 Καὶ ἐπεθύμει ‡ γεμίσαι
τὸν κοιλίαν αὐτῦ ἀπὸ τῶν † κε-
ρατίων, ὧν ἤσθιον οἱ ‡ χοῖροι· κ᾽
ὐδεὶς ἐδίδυ αὐτῷ.

17 Εἰς ἑαυτὸν δὲ ἐλθὼν, εἶπε·
Πόσοι μίσθιοι τοῦ πατρός μυ
περισσεύυσιν ἄρτων, ἐγὼ δὲ λιμῷ
ἀπόλλυμαι;

18 Ἀναςὰς πορεύσομαι πρὸς
τὸν πατέρα μυ, κ᾽ ἐρῶ αὐτῷ·
Πάτερ, ἥμαρτον εἰς τὸν ὐρανὸν, κ᾽
ἐνώπιόν σε.

* 19 Καὶ ὐκέτι εἰμὶ ‡ ἄξι@
κληθῆναι υἱός σε· ποίησόν με ὡς
ἕνα τῶν ‡ μισθίων σε.

20 Καὶ ἀναςὰς ἦλθε πρὸς τὸν
πατέρα ἑαυτῦ. Ἔτι δὲ αὐτῦ
μακρὰν ἀπέχονΙ@, εἶδεν αὐτὸν ὁ
πατὴρ αὐτῦ, κ᾽ ἐσπλαγχνίσθη·
κ᾽ δραμὼν ἐπέπεσεν ἐπὶ τὸν τράχηλον αὐτοῦ, κ᾽ κατεφίλησεν αὐτόν.

21 Εἶπε δὲ αὐτῷ ὁ υἱός· Πάτερ, ἥμαρτον εἰς τὸν ὐρανὸν κ᾽ ἐ-
νώπιόν σε, κ᾽ ὐκέτι εἰμὶ ἄξι@
κληθῆναι υἱός σε.

* 22 Εἶπε δὲ ὁ πατὴρ πρὸς
τοὺς δούλυς αὐτῦ· ‡ Ἐξενέγκατε
τὴν ‡ σολὴν τὴν πρώτην, κ᾽ ἐνδύ-
σατε αὐτόν, κ᾽ δότε † δακτύλιον εἰς
τὴν χεῖρα αὐτῦ, κ᾽ ὑποδήματα εἰς
τοὺς πόδας·

* 23 Καὶ ἐνέγκαντες τὸν ‡ μόσχον τὸν ‡ σιτευτὸν θύσατε· κ᾽
φαγόντες εὐφρανθῶμεν·

---

peccatore pœnitente.

11 Ait autem: Homo qui-
dam habuit duos filios

12 Et dixit junior eorum patri: Pater, da mihi competen-
tem partem substantiæ, & di-
visit illis vitam.

13 Et post non multos dies
congregans omnia junior filius
peregre profectus est in regionem longinquam, & ibi dissipa-
vit substantiam suam vivens pro-
fusè.

14 Consumente autem ipso
omnia, facta est fames valida
per regionem illam, & ipse cœpit deficti.

15 Et abiens adhæsit uni ci-
vium regionis illius: & misit
illum in agros suos pascere porcos

16 Et desiderabat implere
ventrem suum de siliquis quas
manducabant porci: & nemo
dabat illi.

17 In se autem veniens, dixit; Quot mercenarii patris mei
abundant panibus, ego autem
fame pereo?

18 Surgens ibo ad patrem
meum, & dicam ei: Pater, peccavi in cælum, & coram te:

19 Et non amplius sum di-
gnus vocari filius tuus, fac me
sicut unum mercenariorum tuorum.

20 Et surgens venit ad patrem suum. Adhuc autem eo
longè absente, vidit illum pater
ipsius, & misericordia motus est,
& currens cecidit super collum
ejus, & osculatus est eum.

21 Dixit autem ei filius: Pater peccavi in cælum & coram
te, & non amplius sum dignus
vocari filius tuus.

22 Dixit autem pater ad servos suos: Afferte stolam primam, & induite illum, & date
annulum in manum ejus, &
calceamenta in pedes.

23 Et afferentes vitulum saginatum occidite, & comedentes
oblectemur.

11. Il leur dit encore : Un homme avoit deux fils ;

12. Dont le plus jeune dit à son père : Mon père, donne-moi la part du bien qui me doit échoir. Ainsi le père leur partagea son bien.

13. Et peu de jours après, ce plus jeune fils ayant amassé, s'en alla dehors dans un pays éloigné, et il y dissipa son bien en vivant dans la débauche.

14. Après qu'il eut tout dépensé, il survint une grande famine en ce pays-là ; et il commença à être dans l'indigence.

15. Alors il s'en alla, et se mit au service d'un des habitans de ce pays-là, qui l'envoya dans ses possessions, pour paître les pourceaux.

16. Et il eût bien voulu se rassasier des carrouges que les pourceaux mangeoient ; mais personne ne lui en donnoit.

17. Etant donc rentré en lui-même, il dit : Combien y a-t-il de gens aux gages de mon père, qui ont du pain en abondance, et moi je meurs de faim ?

18. Je me leverai, et m'en irai vers mon père, et je lui dirai : Mon père, j'ai péché contre le ciel, et contre toi ;

19. Et je ne suis plus digne d'être appelé ton fils : Traite-moi comme l'un de tes domestiques.

20. Il partit donc, et vint vers son père. Et comme il étoit encore loin, son père le vit, et fut touché de compassion ; et courant à lui, il se jeta à son cou et le baisa.

21. Et son fils lui dit : Mon père, j'ai péché contre le ciel et contre toi ; et je ne suis plus digne d'être appelé ton fils.

22. Mais le père dit à ses serviteurs : Apportez la plus belle robe, et l'en revêtez, et mettez-lui un anneau au doigt, et des souliers aux pieds ;

23. Et amenez un veau gras, et le tuez ; mangeons, et réjouissons-nous ;

11 And he said, A certain man had two sons :

12 And the younger of them said to his father, Father, give me the portion of goods that falleth to me. And he divided unto them his living.

13 And not many days after the younger son gathered all together, and took his journey into a far country, and there wasted his substance with riotous living.

14 And when he had spent all, there arose a mighty famine in that land ; and he began to be in want.

15 And he went and joined himself to a citizen of that country ; and he sent him into his fields to feed swine.

16 And he would fain have filled his belly with the husks that the swine did eat : and no man gave unto him.

17 And when he came to himself, he said, How many hired servants of my father's have bread enough, and to spare, and I perish with hunger !

18 I will arise, and go to my father, and will say unto him, Father, I have sinned against heaven, and before thee,

19 And am no more worthy to be called thy son : make me as one of thy hired servants.

20 And he arose, and came to his father. But, when he was yet a great way off, his father saw him, and had compassion, and ran, and fell on his neck, and kissed him.

21 And the son said unto him, Father, I have sinned against heaven, and in thy sight, and am no more worthy to be called thy son.

22 But the father said to his servants, Bring forth the best robe, and put it on him ; and put a ring on his hand, and shoes on his feet :

23 And bring hither the fatted calf, and kill it ; and let us eat, and be merry :

44

24 Ὅτι ὗτ۞ ὁ υἱός μου νεκρὸς ἦν, ἢ ἀνέζησε· ἢ ἀπολωλὼς ἦν, ἢ εὑρέθη. Καὶ ἤρξαντο εὐφραίνεσθαι.

* 25 Ἦν δὲ ὁ υἱὸς αὐτοῦ ὁ πρεσβύτερ۞ ἐν ἀγρῷ· ἢ ὡς ἐρχόμεν۞ ἤγγισε τῇ οἰκίᾳ, ἤκουσε † συμφωνίας ἢ † χορῶν.

26 Καὶ προσκαλεσάμεν۞ ἕνα τῶν παίδων ἐπυνθάνετο τί εἴη ταῦτα.

27 Ὁ δὲ εἶπεν αὐτῷ Ὅτι ὁ ἀδελφός σου ἥκει· ἢ ἔθυσεν ὁ πατήρ σου τὸν μόσχον τὸν σιτευτὸν, ὅτι ὑγιαίνοντα αὐτὸν ἀπέλαβεν.

28 Ὠργίσθη δὲ, ἢ οὐκ ἤθελεν εἰσελθεῖν. Ὁ οὖν πατὴρ αὐτοῦ ἐξελθὼν παρεκάλει αὐτόν·

* 29 Ὁ δὲ ἀποκριθεὶς εἶπε τῷ πατρί. Ἰδοὺ, τοσαῦτα ἔτη δουλεύω σοι, ἢ οὐδέποτε ἐντολήν σου παρῆλθον, ἢ ἐμοὶ οὐδέποτε ἔδωκας ‡ ἔριφον, ἵνα μετὰ τῶν φίλων μου εὐφρανθῶ·

30 Ὅτε δὲ ὁ υἱός σου οὗτ۞, ὁ καταφαγών σου τὸν βίον μετὰ πορνῶν, ἦλθεν, ἔθυσας αὐτῷ τὸν μόσχον τὸν σιτευτόν.

31 Ὁ δὲ εἶπεν αὐτῷ Τέκνον, σὺ πάντοτε μετ' ἐμοῦ εἶ, ἢ πάντα τὰ ἐμὰ, σά ἐστιν.

32 Εὐφρανθῆναι δὲ ἢ χαρῆναι ἔδει, ὅτι ὁ ἀδελφός σου ὗτ۞ νεκρὸς ἦν, ἢ ἀνέζησε· ἢ ἀπολωλὼς ἦν, ἢ εὑρέθη. 27. † 6.

Κεφ. ιϚ'. 16.

* 1 Ἔλεγε δὲ ἢ πρὸς τοὺς μαθητὰς αὐτοῦ. Ἄνθρωπός τις ἦν πλούσι۞, ὃς εἶχεν οἰκονόμον· ἢ οὗτ۞ † διεβλήθη αὐτῷ ὡς διασκορπίζων τὰ ὑπάρχοντα αὐτοῦ.

* 2 Καὶ φωνήσας αὐτὸν, εἶπεν αὐτῷ. Τί τοῦτο ἀκούω περὶ σοῦ; ‡ ἀπόδο۞ τὸν λόγον τῆς ‡ οἰκονομίας σου· οὐ γὰρ δυνήσῃ ἔτι † οἰκονομεῖν.

* 3 Εἶπε δὲ ἐν ἑαυτῷ ὁ οἰκονόμ۞. Τί ποιήσω, ὅτι ὁ κύριός μου ἀφαιρεῖται τὴν οἰκονομίαν ἀπ' ἐμοῦ; ʒκάπτειν οὐκ ἰσχύω, † ἐπαιτεῖν † αἰσχύνομαι.

---

24 Quia hic filius meus mortuus erat, & revixit: & perditus fuerat, & inventus est: & cœperunt oblectari.

25 Erat autem filius ejus senior in agro: & ut veniens appropinquavit domui, audivit symphoniam & choros.

26 Et advocans unum puerorum, interrogavit quid essent hæc.

27 Is autem dixit illi: Quia frater tuus venit: & occidit pater tuus vitulum saginatum: quia valentem illum recepit.

28 Indignatus est autem. & non volebat introire, ergo pater illius egressus advocabat illum.

29 Is autem respondens dixit patri: Ecce tot annos servio tibi, & nunquam mandatum tuum præterivi, & mihi nunquam dedisti hœdum, ut cum amicis meis oblectarer.

30 Quum autem filius tuus hic, devorans tuam vitam cum meretricibus, venit, occidisti illi vitulum saginatum.

31 Is autem dixit illi: Fili, tu semper cum me es, & omnia mea tua sunt.

32 Oblectari autem & gaudere oportebat, quia frater tuus hic mortuus erat, & revixit: & perditus erat, & inventus est.

CAPUT XVI.

1 DIcebat autem & ad discipulos suos: Homo quidam erat dives, qui habebat dispensatorem, & hic delatus est ei, ut dissipans substantias illius.

2 Et vocans illum, ait illi: Quid hoc audio de te? Redde rationem dispensationis tuæ, non enim poteris adhuc dispensare.

3 Ait autem in seipso dispensator: Quid faciam, quia dominus meus aufert dispensationem à me? fodere non valeo, mendicare erubesco.

24. Parce que mon fils, que voici étoit mort, et il est revenu à la vie; il étoit perdu, mais il est retrouvé. Et ils commencèrent à se réjouir.

25. Cependant son fils aîné, qui étoit à la campagne, revint; et comme il approchait de la maison, il entendit les chants et les danses.

26. Et il appela un des serviteurs, à qui il demanda ce que c'étoit.

27. Et *le serviteur* lui dit: Ton frère est de retour, et ton père a tué un veau gras, parce qu'il l'a recouvré en *bonne* santé.

28. Mais il se mit en colère, et ne voulut point entrer. Son père donc sortit, et le pria *d'entrer.*

29. Mais il répondit à son père: Voici, il y a tant d'années que je te sers, sans avoir jamais contrevenu à ton commandement, et tu ne m'as jamais donné un chevreau pour me réjouir avec mes amis.

30. Mais quand ton fils que voilà, qui a mangé tout son bien avec des femmes débauchées, est revenu, tu as fait tuer un veau gras pour lui.

31. Et *son père* lui dit: *Mon* fils, tu es toujours avec moi, et tout ce que j'ai est à toi.

32. Mais il falloit bien faire un festin et se réjouir, parce que ton frère que voilà est mort, et il est revenu à la vie; il étoit perdu, et il est retrouvé.

CHAPITRE XVI.

Les paraboles de l'Econome injuste, du Riche et de Lazare.

Jésus disoit aussi à ses Disciples: Un homme riche avoit un économe qui fut accusé devant lui de dissiper son bien.

2. Et l'ayant fait venir, il lui dit: Qu'est-ce que j'entends dire de toi? Rends compte de ton administration; car tu ne pourras plus désormais administrer *mon bien.*

3. Alors cet économe dit en lui-même: Que ferai-je, puisque mon maître m'ôte l'administration *de son bien?* Je ne saurois travailler à la terre, et j'aurois honte de mendier.

24 For this my son was dead, and is alive again; he was lost, and is found. And they began to be merry.

25 Now, his elder son was in the field: and as he came and drew nigh to the house, he heard musick and dancing.

26 And he called one of the servants, and asked what these things meant.

27 And he said unto him, Thy brother is come; and thy father hath killed the fatted calf, because he hath received him safe and sound.

28 And he was angry, and would not go in: therefore came his father out, and entreated him.

29 And he, answering, said to *his* father, Lo, these many years do I serve thee, neither transgressed I at any time thy commandment; and yet thou never gavest me a kid, that I might make merry with my friends:

30 But as soon as this thy son was come, which hath devoured thy living with harlots, thou hast killed for him the fatted calf.

31 And he said unto him, Son, thou art ever with me, and all that I have is thine.

32 It was meet that we should make merry, and be glad: for this thy brother was dead, and is alive again; and was lost, and is found.

CHAP. XVI.

Of the unjust steward.

AND he said also unto his disciples, There was a certain rich man, which had a steward; and the same was accused unto him that he had wasted his goods.

2 And he called him, and said unto him, How is it that I hear this of thee? give an account of thy stewardship; for thou mayest be no longer steward.

3 Then the steward said within himself, What shall I do, for my lord taketh away from me the stewardship? I cannot dig; to beg I am ashamed.

45

4 Ἔγνων τί ποιήσω, ἵνα ὅταν μετασταθῶ τῆς οἰκονομίας, δέξωνταί με εἰς τοὺς οἴκους αὐτῶν.

5 Καὶ προσκαλεσάμενος ἕνα ἕκαστον τῶν χρεωφειλετῶν τῷ κυρίῳ ἑαυτοῦ, ἔλεγε τῷ πρώτῳ· Πόσον ὀφείλεις τῷ κυρίῳ μου;

6 Ὁ δὲ εἶπεν· Ἑκατὸν βάτους ἐλαίου. Καὶ εἶπεν αὐτῷ· Δέξαι σου τὸ γράμμα, καὶ καθίσας ταχέως γράψον πεντήκοντα.

7 Ἔπειτα ἑτέρῳ εἶπε· Σὺ δὲ πόσον ὀφείλεις; Ὁ δὲ εἶπεν· Ἑκατὸν κόρους σίτου. Καὶ λέγει αὐτῷ· Δέξαι σου τὸ γράμμα, καὶ γράψον ὀγδοήκοντα.

8 Καὶ ἐπῄνεσεν ὁ κύριος τὸν οἰκονόμον τῆς ἀδικίας, ὅτι φρονίμως ἐποίησεν· ὅτι οἱ υἱοὶ τοῦ αἰῶνος τούτου φρονιμώτεροι ὑπὲρ τοὺς υἱοὺς τοῦ φωτὸς εἰς τὴν γενεὰν τὴν ἑαυτῶν εἰσι.

9 Κἀγὼ ὑμῖν λέγω· Ποιήσατε ἑαυτοῖς φίλους ἐκ τοῦ μαμωνᾶ τῆς ἀδικίας, ἵνα ὅταν ἐκλίπητε, δέξωνται ὑμᾶς εἰς τὰς αἰωνίους σκηνάς.

10 Ὁ πιστὸς ἐν ἐλαχίστῳ, καὶ ἐν πολλῷ πιστός ἐστι· καὶ ὁ ἐν ἐλαχίστῳ ἄδικος, καὶ ἐν πολλῷ ἄδικός ἐστιν.

11 Εἰ οὖν ἐν τῷ ἀδίκῳ μαμωνᾷ πιστοὶ οὐκ ἐγένεσθε, τὸ ἀληθινὸν τίς ὑμῖν πιστεύσει;

12 Καὶ εἰ ἐν τῷ ἀλλοτρίῳ πιστοὶ οὐκ ἐγένεσθε, τὸ ὑμέτερον τίς ὑμῖν δώσει;

13 Οὐδεὶς οἰκέτης δύναται δυσὶ κυρίοις δουλεύειν· ἢ γὰρ τὸν ἕνα μισήσει, καὶ τὸν ἕτερον ἀγαπήσει· ἢ ἑνὸς ἀνθέξεται, καὶ τοῦ ἑτέρου καταφρονήσει· οὐ δύνασθε Θεῷ δουλεύειν καὶ μαμωνᾷ.

14 Ἤκουον δὲ ταῦτα πάντα καὶ οἱ Φαρισαῖοι, φιλάργυροι ὑπάρχοντες· καὶ ἐξεμυκτήριζον αὐτόν.

15 Καὶ εἶπεν αὐτοῖς· Ὑμεῖς ἐστε οἱ δικαιοῦντες ἑαυτοὺς ἐνώπιον τῶν ἀνθρώπων· ὁ δὲ Θεὸς γινώσκει τὰς καρδίας ὑμῶν· ὅτι τὸ ἐν ἀνθρώποις ὑψηλὸν, βδέλυγμα ἐνώπιον τοῦ Θεοῦ ἐστιν.

---

4 Scio quid faciam, ut quum amotus fuero dispensatione, recipiant me in domos suas.

5 Et convocans unumquemque debitorum Domini sui, dicebat primo: Quantum debes domino meo?

6 Is autem dixit: Centum batos olei, & dixit illi: Accipe tuum scriptum, & sedens citò scribe quinquaginta.

7 Deinde alii dixit: Tu verò quantum debes? is autem ait: Centum coros tritici, & ait illi: Accipe tuas literas, & scribe octoginta.

8 Et laudavit dominus dispensatorem injustitiae, quia prudenter fecisset: quia filii seculi hujus prudentiores super filios lucis in generationem suam sunt.

9 Et ego vobis dico: Facite vobis ipsis amicos de mamona injustitiae, ut quum defeceritis, recipiant vos in aeterna tabernacula.

10 Fidelis in minimo, & in multo fidelis est: & in modico injustus, etiam in multo injustus est.

11 Si ergo in injusto mamona fideles non fuistis, verum quis vobis credet?

12 Et si in alieno fideles non fuistis, vestrum quis vobis dabit?

13 Nemo servus potest duobus dominis servire aut enim unum odiet, & alterum diliget: aut uni adhaerebit, & alterum contemnet; non potestis Deo servire & mamonae

14 Audiebant autem haec omnia & Pharisaei avari subsistentes, & deridebant illum.

15 Et ait illis: Vos estis justificantes vos ipsos coram hominibus: at Deus novit corda vestra, quia quod in hominibus altum, abominatio ante Deum est.

4. Je sais ce que je ferai, afin que quand on m'aura ôté mon administration, il y ait des gens qui me reçoivent dans leurs maisons.

5. Alors il fit venir séparément chacun des débiteurs de son maître; et il dit au premier : Combien dois-tu à mon maître ?

6. Il répondit : Cent mesures d'huile. Et l'*économe* lui dit : Reprends ton billet; assieds-toi là, et écris-en promptement *un autre* de cinquante.

7. Il dit ensuite à un autre : Et toi, Combien dois-tu ? Il dit : Cent mesures de froment. Et l'*économe* lui dit : Reprends ton billet, et écris-en un *autre* de quatre-vingts.

8. Et le maître loua cet économe infidèle de ce qu'il avoit agi avec habileté ; car les enfans de ce siècle sont plus prudens dans leur génération, que les enfans de lumière.

9. Et moi, je vous dis aussi : Faites-vous des amis avec les richesses injustes, afin que quand vous viendrez à manquer, ils vous reçoivent dans les tabernacles éternels.

10. Celui qui est fidèle dans les petites choses, sera aussi fidèle dans les grandes ; et celui qui est injuste dans les petites choses, sera aussi injuste dans les grandes.

11. Si donc vous n'avez pas été fidèle dans les richesses injustes, qui vous confiera les véritables *richesses?*

12. Et si vous n'avez pas été fidèles dans ce qui est à autrui : qui vous donnera ce qui est à vous ?

13. Nul serviteur ne peut servir deux maîtres ; car ou il haïra l'un, et aimera l'autre ; ou il s'attachera à l'un, et méprisera l'autre. Vous ne pouvez servir Dieu et Mammon.

14. Les Pharisiens, qui étoient avares, écoutoient tout cela, et se moquoient de lui.

15. Et il leur dit : Pour vous, ous voulez passer pour justes devant les hommes, mais Dieu connoît vos cœurs ; car ce qui est élevé devant les hommes est une abomination devant Dieu.

---

4 I am resolved what to do, that when I am put out of the stewardship, they may receive me into their houses.

5 So he called every one of his lord's debtors *unto him*, and said unto the first, How much owest thou unto my lord ?

6 And he said, An hundred measures of oil. And he said unto him, Take thy bill, and sit down quickly, and write fifty.

7 Then said he to another, And how much owest thou ? And he said, An hundred measures of wheat. And he said unto him, Take thy bill, and write fourscore.

8 And the lord commended the unjust steward, because he had done wisely : for the children of this world are in their generation wiser than the children of light.

9 And I say unto you, Make to yourselves friends of the mammon of unrighteousness ; that, when ye fail, they may receive you into everlasting habitations.

10 He that is faithful in that which is least, is faithful also in much ; and he that is unjust in the least, is unjust also in much.

11 If, therefore, ye have not been faithful in the unrighteous mammon, who will commit to your trust the true *riches?*

12 And if ye have not been faithful in that which is another man's, who shall give you that which is your own ?

13 No servant can serve two masters : for either he will hate the one, and love the other ; or else he will hold to the one, and despise the other. Ye cannot serve God and mammon.

14 And the Pharisees also, who were covetous, heard all these things : and they derided him.

15 And he said unto them, Ye are they which justify yourselves before men ; but God knoweth your hearts : for that which is highly esteemed among men is abomination in the sight of God.

46

18 Πᾶς ὁ ἀπολύων τὴν γυναῖκα

18 Omnis repudians uxorem

αὐτῦ, κỳ γαμῶν ἑτέραν, μοιχεύει·
κỳ πᾶς ὁ ἀπολελυμένην ἀπὸ ἀνδρὸς
γαμῶν, μοιχεύει.

* 19 Ἄνθρωπ@- δέ τις ἦν πλύσι@-, κỳ ‡ ἐνεδιδύσκείο ‡ πορφύραν κỳ ‡ βύσσον, ‡ εὐφραινόμεν@- καθ' ἡμέραν † λαμπρῶς.

* 20 Πτωχὸς δέ τις ἦν ὀνόμαλι Λάζαρ@-, ὃς ἐβέβληίο πρὸς τὸν πυλῶνα αὐτῦ ἡλκωμέν@-.

* 21 Καὶ ‡ ἐπιθυμῶν χορτασθῆναι ἀπὸ τῶν ‡ ψιχίων τῶν πιπτόντων ἀπὸ τῆς τραπέζης τῦ πλυσίυ· ἀλλὰ κỳ οἱ ‡ κύνες ἐρχόμενοι † ἀπέλειχον τὰ ‡ ἕλκη αὐτῦ.

* 22 Ἐγένείο δὲ ἀποθανεῖν τὸν πτωχὸν, κỳ ‡ ἀπενεχθῆναι αὐτὸν ὑπὸ τῶν ἀγγέλων εἰς τὸν κόλπον τῦ Ἀβραάμ· ἀπέθανε δὲ κỳ ὁ πλύσι@-, κỳ ‡ ἐτάφη.

23 Καὶ ἐν τῇ ᾅδη ἐπάρας τοὺς ὀφθαλμὺς αὐτῦ, ὑπάρχων ἐν βασάνοις, ὁρᾷ τὸν Ἀβραὰμ ἀπὸ μακρόθεν, κỳ Λάζαρον ἐν τοῖς κόλποις αὐτῦ.

* 24 Καὶ αὐτὸς φωνήσας εἶπε· Πάτερ Ἀβραάμ ἐλέησόν με, κỳ πέμψον Λάζαρον, ἵνα ‡ βάψῃ τὸ ‡ ἄκρον τῦ ‡ δακτύλυ αὐτῦ ‡ ὕδαί@-, κỳ † καταψύξῃ τὴν γλῶσσάν μυ· ὅτι ‡ ὀδυνῶμαι ἐν τῇ ‡ φλογὶ ταύτῃ.

25 Εἶπε δὲ Ἀβραάμ· Τέκνον, μνήσθηίι ὅτι ἀπέλαβες σὺ τὰ ἀγαθά συ ἐν τῇ ζωῇ συ, κỳ Λάζαρ@- ὁμοίως τὰ κακά· νῦν δὲ ὅδε παρακαλεῖται, σὺ δὲ ὀδυνᾶσαι.

* 26 Καὶ ἐπὶ πᾶσι τούτοις, μεταξὺ ἡμῶν κỳ ὑμῶν † χάσμα μέγα ‡ ἐςήρικίαι, ὅπως οἱ θέλοντες ‡ διαβῆναι ‡ ἐντεῦθεν πρὸς ὑμᾶς, μὴ δύνωνίαι, μηδὲ οἱ ἐκεῖθεν πρὸς ἡμᾶς διαπερῶσιν.

27 Εἶπε δέ· Ἐρωίῶ οὖν σε πάτερ, ἵνα πέμψῃς αὐτὸν εἰς τὸν οἶκον τῦ πατρός μυ·

28 Ἔχω γὰρ πένίε ἀδελφὺς,

ὅπως διαμαρτύρηίαι αὐτοῖς, ἵνα μὴ κỳ αὐτὶ ἔλθωσιν εἰς τὶν τόπον τούτον τῆς βασάνυ.

29 Λέγει αὐτῷ Ἀβραάμ· Ἔχυσι Μωσέα κỳ τοὺς προφήτας· ἀκυσάτωσαν αὐτῶν.

---

suam, & ducens alteram, mœchatur : & omnis repudiatam à viro ducens, mœchatur.

19 Homo autem quidem erat dives, & induebatur purpuram & byssum, oblectatus quotidie splendide.

20 Pauper autem qui am erat nomine Lazarus, qui ejectus erat ad januam ejus ulcerosus.

21 Et cupiens saturari de micis cadentibus de mensa divitis : sed & canes venientes lingebant ulcera ejus.

22 Factum est autem mori pauperem, & asportari eum ab angelis in sinum Abrahæ : Mortuus est autem & dives, & sepultus est.

23 Et in inferno elevans oculos suos, existens in tormentis, vidit Abraham à longè, & Lazarum in gremiis ejus.

24 Et ipse clamans dixit : Pater Abraham miserere mei, & mitte Lazarum, ut intingat extremum digiti sui aqua, & refrigeret linguam meam : quia crucior in flamma hac.

25 Dixit autem Abraham : Fili, recordare quia recepisti tu bona tua in vita tua, & Lazarus similiter mala : nunc autem hic consolatur, tu verò cruciaris.

26 Et omnibus his, inter nos & vos hiatus magnus firmatus est, ut volentes transire hinc ad vos, non possint : neque qui inde ad nos transmeent.

27 Ait autem : Rogo ergo te, pater, ut mittas eum in domum patris mei.

28 Habeo enim quinque fratres, ut testetur illis, ut non & ipsi veniant in locum hunc tormenti.

29 Ait illi Abraham : Habent Mosen, & Prophetas : audiant illos.

18. Quiconque répudie sa femme et en épouse une autre , commet adultère ; et quiconque épouse celle que son mari a répudiée , commet adultère.

19. Il y avoit un homme riche qui se vêtoit de pourpre et de fin lin , et qui se traitoit bien et magnifiquement tous les jours.

20. Il y avoit aussi un pauvre , nommé Lazare , qui étoit couché à la porte *de ce riche* , et qui étoit couvert d'ulcères.

21. Il désiroit de se rassasier des miettes qui tomboient de la table du riche ; et même les chiens venoient lécher ses ulcères.

22. Or , il arriva que le pauvre mourut , et il fut porté par les Anges dans le sein d'Abraham ; le riche mourut aussi , et fut enseveli.

23. Et étant en enfer et dans les tourmens, il leva les yeux , et vit de loin Abraham , et Lazare dans son sein.

24. Et s'écriant , il dit : Père Abraham , aie pitié de moi , et envoie Lazare , afin qu'il trempe dans l'eau le bout de son doigt , pour me rafraîchir la langue ; car je suis extrêmement tourmenté dans cette flamme.

25. Mais Abraham lui répondit : Mon fils , souviens-toi que tu as eu tes biens pendant ta vie , et Lazare y a eu des maux ; et maintenant il est consolé , et tu es dans les tourmens.

26. Outre cela , il y a un grand abyme entre vous et nous ; de sorte que ceux qui voudront passer d'ici vers vous ne le peuvent ; non plus que ceux qui *voudroient* passer de là ici.

27. Et *le riche* dit : Je te prie donc , Père *Abraham*, d'envoyer *Lazare* dans la maison de mon Père ;

28. Car j'ai cinq frères , afin qu'il les avertisse , de peur qu'ils ne viennent aussi eux-mêmes dans ce lieu de tourmens.

29. Abraham lui répondit : Ils ont Moyse et les Prophètes; qu'ils les écoutent.

18 Whosoever putteth away his wife, and marrieth another, committeth adultery: and whosoever marrieth her that is put away from *her* husband, committeth adultery.

19 There was a certain rich man, which was clothed in purple and fine linen, and fared sumptuously every day :

20 And there was a certain beggar, named Lazarus, which was laid at his gate full of sores,

21 And desiring to be fed with the crumbs which fell from the rich man's table : moreover, the dogs came and licked his sores.

22 And it came to pass, that the beggar died, and was carried by the angels into Abraham's bosom: the rich man also died, and was buried ;

23 And in hell he lifted up his eyes, being in torments, and seeth Abraham afar off, and Lazarus in his bosom.

24 And he cried, and said, Father Abraham, have mercy on me : and send Lazarus, that he may dip the tip of his finger in water, and cool my tongue ; for I am tormented in this flame.

25 But Abraham said, Son, remember that thou in thy life time receivedst thy good things, and likewise Lazarus evil things : but now he is comforted, and thou art tormented.

26 And, besides all this, between us and you there is a great gulf fixed : so that they which would pass from hence to you cannot ; neither can they pass to us, that *would come* from thence.

27 Then he said, I pray thee, therefore, father, that thou wouldest send him to my father's house:

28 For I have five brethren ; that he may testify unto them, lest they also come into this place of torment.

29 Abraham saith unto him, They have Moses and the prophets ; let them hear them.

47

30 Ὁ δὲ εἶπεν· Οὐχὶ, πάτερ Ἀβραάμ· ἀλλ' ἐάν τις ἀπὸ νεκρῶν πορευθῇ πρὸς αὐτὸς, μετανοήσουσιν.

31 Εἶπε δὲ αὐτῷ. Εἰ Μωσέως ἢ τῶν προφητῶν οὐκ ἀκούουσιν, οὐδὲ ἐάν τις ἐκ νεκρῶν ἀναςῇ, πεισθήσονται. 39. † 11.

Κεφ. ιζ'. 17.

* 1 Εἶπε δὲ πρὸς τοὺς μαθητάς· † Ἀνένδεκτόν ἐςι μὴ ἐλθεῖν τὰ ζκάνδαλα· οὐαὶ δὲ δι' οὗ ἔρχεται.

* 2 † Λυσιτελεῖ αὐτῷ, εἰ † μύλ☉. ‡ ὀνικὸς περίκειται περὶ τὸν τράχηλον αὐτοῦ, ἢ ἔῤῥιπται εἰς τὴν θάλασσαν, ἢ ἵνα ζκανδαλίσῃ ἕνα τῶν μικρῶν τούτων.

3 Προσέχιλε ἑαυτοῖς. Ἐὰν δὲ ἁμάρτῃ εἰς σὲ ὁ ἀδελφός σου, ἐπιτίμησον αὐτῷ· ἢ ἐὰν μετανοήσῃ, ἄφες αὐτῷ.

4 Καὶ ἐὰν ἑπτάκις τῆς ἡμέρας ἁμάρτῃ εἰς σὲ, ἢ ἑπτάκις τῆς ἡμέρας ἐπιςρέψῃ ἐπί σε, λέγων· Μετανοῶ· ἀφήσεις αὐτῷ.

7 Τίς δὲ ἐξ ἡμῶν δοῦλον ἔχων ἀροτριῶντα, ἢ ποιμαίνοντα, ὃς εἰσελθόντι ἐκ τοῦ ἀγροῦ ἐρεῖ εὐθέως· Παρελθὼν ἀνάπεσαι;

8 Ἀλλ' οὐχὶ ἐρεῖ αὐτῷ. Ἑτοίμασον τί δειπνήσω, ἢ περιζωσάμενΘ. διακόνει μοι, ἕως φάγω ἢ πίω· ἢ μετὰ ταῦτα φάγεσαι ἢ πίεσαι σύ;

9 Μὴ χάριν ἔχει τῷ δούλῳ ἐκείνῳ ὅτι ἐποίησε τὰ διαταχθέντα αὐτῷ; οὐ δοκῶ.

* 10 Οὕτω ἢ ὑμεῖς, ὅταν ποιήσητε πάντα τὰ διαταχθέντα ὑμῖν, λέγετε· Ὅτι δοῦλοι ‡ ἀχρεῖοί ἐσμεν· ὅτι ὃ ὠφείλομεν ποιῆσαι, πεποιήκαμεν.

* 20 Ἐπερωτηθεὶς δὲ ὑπὸ τῶν Φαρισαίων πότε ἔρχεται ἡ βασιλεία τοῦ Θεοῦ, ἀπεκρίθη αὐτοῖς, ἢ εἶπεν· Οὐκ ἔρχεται ἡ βασιλεία τοῦ Θεοῦ μετὰ † παρατηρήσεως·

30 Is autem dixit: Non pater Abraham: sed si quis ex mortuis ierit ad eos, pœnitebunt.

31 Ait autem illi: Si Mosen & Prophetas non audiunt, neque si quis ex mortuis resurrexerit, credent.

CAPUT XVII.

1 AIT autem ad discipulos: Impossibile est non venire scandala: væ autem per quem veniunt.

2 Expedit illi, si mola asinaria circumponatur circa collum ejus, & projiciatur in mare, quam ut scandalizet unum parvorum istorum.

3 Attendite vobis ipsis: si verò peccaverit in te frater tuus, increpa illum. Et si pœnituerit, dimitte illi:

4 Et si septies die peccaverit in te, & septies die conversus fuerit ad te, dicens: Pœniteo, dimittes illi.

7 Quis autem ex vobis servum habens arantem aut pascentem, qui regresso de agro dicat statim: Adveniens recumbe.

8 Imo nonne dicet ei: Para quod cœnem, & circumcinctus ministra mihi, donec manducem & bibam, & post hæc manducabis & bibes tu?

9 Num gratiam habet servo illi, quia fecit præcepta ei? non puto.

10 Sic & vos quum feceritis omnia præcepta vobis, dicite, quod servi inutiles sumus, quia quod debuimus facere, fecimus.

20 Interrogatus autem à Pharisæis, quando venit regnum Dei, respondit eis & dixit: Non venit regnum Dei cum observatione:

30. *Le riche* dit : Non , Père Abraham ; mais si quelqu'un des morts va vers eux, ils s'amenderont.

31. Et *Abraham* lui dit : S'ils n'écoutent pas Moyse et les Prophètes, ils ne seroient pas non plus persuadés, quand même quelqu'un des morts ressusciteroit.

CHAPITRE XVII.

Jésus-Christ entretient du scandale , du pardon, des serviteurs inutiles ; guérit dix lépreux , et parle du jour du fils de l'homme.

JÉSUS dit *aussi* à ses Disciples : Il ne se peut faire qu'il n'arrive des scandales ; toutefois malheur à celui par qui ils arrivent !

2. Il vaudroit mieux pour lui qu'on lui mît au cou une meule de moulin , et qu'on le jetât dans la mer , que de scandaliser un de ces petits.

3. Prenez *donc* garde à vous. Si ton frère t'a offensé , reprends-le ; et s'il se répent , pardonne-lui.

4. Et s'il t'a offensé sept fois le jour , et que sept fois le jour il revienne vers toi , et te dise : Je me repens ; pardonne-lui.

7. Qui de vous ayant un serviteur qui laboure ou qui paisse *les* troupeaux , et le *voyant* revenir des champs , lui dise aussitôt : Avance-toi , et te mets à table ?

8. Ne lui dira-t-il pas plutôt : Prépare-moi à souper . et ceins-toi et me sers, jusqu'à ce que j'aie mangé et bu ; et après cela tu mangeras et tu boiras.

9. Sera-t-il redevable à ce serviteur , parce qu'il aura fait ce qui lui avoit été commandé ? Je ne le pense pas.

10. Vous aussi de même , quand vous aurez fait tout ce qui vous est commandé , dites : Nous sommes des serviteurs inutiles ; parce que nous n'avons fait que ce que nous étions obligés de faire.

20. Les Pharisiens lui ayant demandé quand le Règne de Dieu viendroit ; il leur répondit : Le Règne de Dieu ne viendra point avec éclat.

30 And he said, Nay, father Abraham : but if one went unto them from the dead, they will repent.

31 And he said unto him, If they hear not Moses and the prophets, neither will they be persuaded though one rose from the dead.

CHAP. XVII.
To avoid giving offence.

THEN said he unto the disciples, It is impossible but that offences will come : but woe *unto him* through whom they come ?

2 It were better for him that a mill-stone were hanged about his neck, and he cast into the sea, than that he should offend one of these little ones.

3 Take heed to yourselves : If thy brother trespass against thee, rebuke him ; and if he repent, forgive him.

4 And if he trespass against thee seven times in a day, and seven times in a day turn again to thee, saying, I repent ; thou shalt forgive him.

7 But which of you having a servant plowing, or feeding cattle, will say unto him by and by, when he is come from the field, Go and sit down to meat ?

8 And will not rather say unto him, Make ready wherewith I may sup, and gird thyself, and serve me, till I have eaten and drunken ; and afterward thou shalt eat and drink ?

9 Doth he thank that servant because he did the things that were commanded him ? I trow not.

10 So likewise ye, when ye shall have done all those things which are commanded you, say, We are unprofitable servants: we have done that which was our duty to do.

20 And when he was demanded of the Pharisees, when the kingdom of God should come, he answered them, and said, The kingdom of God cometh not with observation.

48

20 Καὶ καθὼς ἐγένετο ἐν ταῖς ἡμέραις τοῦ Νῶε, ὕτως ἔςαι κ ἐν ταῖς ἡμέραις τοῦ υἱοῦ τοῦ ἀνθρώπω.

27 Ἤσθιον, ἔπινον, ἐγάμεν, ἐξεγαμίζοντο, ἄχρι ἧς ἡμέρας εἰσῆλθε Νῶε εἰς τὴν κιβωτόν· κ ἦλθεν ὁ κατακλυσμὸς, κ ἀπώλεσεν ἅπαντας.

28 Ὁμοίως κ ὡς ἐγένετο ἐν ταῖς ἡμέραις Λώτ· ἤσθιον, ἔπινον, ἠγόραζον, ἐπώλυν, ἐφύτευον, ᾠκοδόμυν.

29 Ἧι δὲ ἡμέρᾳ ἐξῆλθε Λώτ ἀπὸ Συδόμων, ἔβρεξε πῦρ κ θεῖον ἀπ᾽ ὑρανῦ, κ ἀπώλεσεν ἅπαντας.

30 Κατὰ ταῦτα ἔςαι ᾗ ἡμέρᾳ ὁ υἱὸς τοῦ ἀνθρώπω ἀποκαλύπτεται.

31 Ἐν ἐκείνῃ τῇ ἡμέρᾳ, ὃς ἔςαι ἐπὶ τῦ δώματ(ος), κ τὰ σκεύη αὐτῦ ἐν τῇ οἰκίᾳ, μὴ καταβάτω ἆραι αὐτά· κ ὁ ἐν τῷ ἀγρῷ, ὁμοίως μὴ ἐπιςρεψάτω εἰς τὰ ὀπίσω.

32 Μνημονεύετε τῆς γυναικὸς Λώτ.

33 Ὃς ἐὰν ζητήσῃ τὴν ψυχὴν αὐτῦ σῶσαι, ἀπολέσει αὐτήν· ὃς ἐὰν ἀπ᾽ λέσῃ αἰτήν, ζωογονήσει αὐτήν.

34 Λέγω ὑμῖν, ταύτῃ τῇ νυκτὶ ἔσονται δύο ἐπὶ κλίνης μιᾶς· ὁ εἷς παραληφθήσεται, κ ὁ ἕτερ(ος) ἀφεθήσεται.

35 Δύο ἔσονται ἀλήθυσαι ἐπὶ τὸ αὐτό· ἡ μία παραληφθήσεται, κ ἡ ἑτέρα ἀφεθήσεται.

36 Δύο ἔσονται ἐν τῷ ἀγρῷ· ὁ εἷς παραληφθήσεται, κ ὁ ἕτερ(ος) ἀφεθήσεται.

Κεφ ιή 18.

1 Ἔλεγε δὲ κ παραβολὴν αὐτοῖς πρὸς τὸ δεῖν πάντοτε προσεύχεσθαι, κ μὴ ἐκκακεῖν.

2 Λέγων Κριτής τις ἦν ἔν τινι πόλει τὸν Θεὸν μὴ φοβύμεν(ος), κ ἄνθρωπον μὴ ἐντρεπόμεν(ος).

3 Χήρα δὲ τις ἦν ἐν τῇ πόλει ἐκείνῃ κ ἤρχετο πρὸς αὐτὸν, λέγουσα· Ἐκδίκησόν με ἀπὸ τῦ ἀντιδίκυ μυ.

---

26 Et sicut factum est in diebus Noë, ita & erit in diebus filii hominis.

27 Edebant, bibebant, uxores ducebant, nubebant, usque quâ die intravit Noë in arcam, & venit diluvium, & perdidit omnes.

28 Similiter & sicut factum est in diebus Lot : edebant, bibebant, emebant, vendebant, plantabant, ædificabant.

29 Quâ autem die exiit Lot à Sodomis, pluit ignem & sulphur de cælo, & perdidit omnes.

30 Secundum hæc erit quâ die filius hominis revelatur.

31 In illa die, qui fuerit super domum, & vasa ejus in domo, ne descendat tollere illa : & qui in agro, similiter non redeat in quæ retrò :

32 Memores estote uxoris Lot.

33 Quicumque quæsierit animam suam servare, perdet illam : & quicumque perdiderit illam, vivificabit eam.

34 Dico vobis, illâ nocte erunt duo in lecto uno : unus assumetur, & alter relinquetur.

35 Duæ erunt molentes in idem : una assumetur, & altera relinquetur.

36 Duo erunt in agro, unus assumetur, & alter relinquetur.

1 Dicebat autem & parabolam illis, oportere semper orare, & non segnescere :

2 Dicens : Judex quidam erat in quadam civitate, Deum non timens, & hominem non reveritus.

3 Vidua autem erat in civitate illa, & veniebat ad eum, dicens : Vindica me de adversario meo.

26. Et ce qui arriva du tems de Noé, arrivera de même au tems du Fils de l'homme :

27. On mangeoit, on buvoit, on prenoit et on donnoit en mariage, jusqu'au jour que Noé entra dans l'arche ; et le Déluge vint qui les fit tous périr.

28. De même aussi, comme du tems de Lot, on mangeoit, on buvoit, on achetoit, on vendoit, on plantoit et on bâtissoit ;

29. Mais le jour que Lot sortit de Sodome, il plut du ciel du feu et du soufre, qui les fit tous périr.

30. Il en sera de même au jour que le Fils de l'homme paroîtra.

31. En ce jour-là, que celui qui sera au haut de la maison, et qui aura ses meubles dans la maison, ne descende pas pour les emporter ; et que celui qui sera aux champs ne revienne pas sur ses pas.

32. Souvenez-vous de la femme de Lot.

33. Quiconque cherchera à sauver sa vie la perdra ; et quiconque l'aura perdue la retrouvera.

34. Je vous dis qu'en cette nuit-là, de deux *hommes* qui seront dans un même lit, l'un sera pris, et l'autre laissé.

35. De deux *femmes* qui moudront ensemble, l'une sera prise, et l'autre laissée.

36. De deux *hommes* qui seront aux champs, l'un sera pris, et l'autre laissé.

CHAPITRE XVIII.

Notre Seigneur propose la parabole du Juge inique ; celle du Pharisien et du Péager ; et il impose les mains à de petits enfans qu'on lui présente.

Jésus leur dit aussi cette parabole, *pour montrer* qu'il faut toujours prier, et ne se relâcher point :

2. Il y avoit dans une ville un Juge qui ne craignoit point Dieu, et qui n'avoit aucun égard pour personne.

3. Il y avoit aussi dans cette ville-là une veuve qui venoit *souvent* à lui, et qui lui disoit : Faismoi justice de ma partie adverse.

26 And as it was in the days of Noe, so shall it be also in the days of the Son of Man:

27 They did eat, they drank, they married wives, they were given in marriage, until the day that Noe entered into the ark; and the flood came, and destroyed them all.

28 Likewise also, as it was in the days of Lot, they did eat, they drank, they bought, they sold, they planted, they builded:

29 But the same day that Lot went out of Sodom, it rained fire and brimstone from heaven, and destroyed *them* all.

30 Even thus shall it be in the day when the Son of Man is revealed.

31 In that day, he which shall be upon the house-top, and his stuff in the house, let him not come down to take it away: and he that is in the field, let him likewise not return back.

32 Remember Lot's wife.

33 Whosoever shall seek to save his life shall lose it; and whosoever shall lose his life shall preserve it.

34 I tell you, in that night there shall be two *men* in one bed; the one shall be taken, and the other shall be left.

35 Two *women* shall be grinding together; the one shall be taken, and the other left.

36 Two *men* shall be in the field; the one shall be taken, and the other left.

CHAP. XVIII.

The importunate widow.

AND he spake a parable unto them, *to this end*, that men ought always *to* pray, and not to faint;

2 Saying, There was in a city a judge, which feared not God, neither regarded man:

3 And there was a widow in that city; and she came unto him, saying, Avenge me of mine adversary.

49

4 Καὶ οὐκ ἠθέλησεν ἐπὶ χρόνον· μετὰ δὲ ταῦτα εἶπεν ἐν ἑαυτῷ· Εἰ καὶ τὸν Θεὸν οὐ φοβοῦμαι, καὶ ἄνθρωπον οὐκ ἐντρέπομαι,

5 Διά γε τὸ παρέχειν μοι κόπον τὴν χήραν ταύτην, ἐκδικήσω αὐτήν· ἵνα μὴ εἰς τέλος ἐρχομένη ὑπωπιάζῃ με.

6 Εἶπε δὲ ὁ Κύριος· Ἀκούσατε τί ὁ κριτὴς τῆς ἀδικίας λέγει·

7 Ὁ δὲ Θεὸς οὐ μὴ ποιήσει τὴν ἐκδίκησιν τῶν ἐκλεκτῶν αὐτοῦ τῶν βοώντων πρὸς αὐτὸν ἡμέρας καὶ νυκτός, καὶ μακροθυμῶν ἐπ' αὐτοῖς;

8 Λέγω ὑμῖν, ὅτι ποιήσει τὴν ἐκδίκησιν αὐτῶν ἐν τάχει· πλὴν ὁ υἱὸς τοῦ ἀνθρώπου ἐλθὼν ἆρα εὑρήσει τὴν πίστιν ἐπὶ τῆς γῆς;

9 Εἶπε δὲ πρὸς τινας τοὺς πεποιθότας ἐφ' ἑαυτοῖς ὅτι εἰσὶ δίκαιοι, καὶ ἐξουθενοῦντας τοὺς λοιπούς, τὴν παραβολὴν ταύτην·

10 Ἄνθρωποι δύο ἀνέβησαν εἰς τὸ ἱερὸν προσεύξασθαι· ὁ εἷς Φαρισαῖος, καὶ ὁ ἕτερος τελώνης·

11 Ὁ Φαρισαῖος σταθεὶς πρὸς ἑαυτὸν ταῦτα προσηύχετο· Ὁ Θεός, εὐχαριστῶ σοι, ὅτι οὐκ εἰμὶ ὥσπερ οἱ λοιποὶ τῶν ἀνθρώπων, ἅρπαγες, ἄδικοι, μοιχοί, ἢ καὶ ὡς οὗτος ὁ τελώνης·

12 Νηστεύω δὶς τοῦ σαββάτου, ἀποδεκατῶ πάντα ὅσα κτῶμαι.

13 Καὶ ὁ τελώνης μακρόθεν ἑστὼς οὐκ ἤθελεν οὐδὲ τοὺς ὀφθαλμοὺς εἰς τὸν οὐρανὸν ἐπᾶραι· ἀλλ' ἔτυπτεν εἰς τὸ στῆθος αὐτοῦ, λέγων· Ὁ Θεὸς ἱλάσθητί μοι τῷ ἁμαρτωλῷ.

14 Λέγω ὑμῖν, κατέβη οὗτος δεδικαιωμένος εἰς τὸν οἶκον αὐτοῦ, ἢ ἐκεῖνος· ὅτι πᾶς ὁ ὑψῶν ἑαυτὸν, ταπεινωθήσεται· ὁ δὲ ταπεινῶν ἑαυτὸν, ὑψωθήσεται.

38 Ἐγένετο δὲ ἐν τῷ πορεύεσθαι αὐτούς, καὶ αὐτὸς εἰσῆλθεν εἰς κώμην τινά· γυνὴ δέ τις ὀνόματι Μάρθα ὑπεδέξατο αὐτὸν εἰς τὸν οἶκον αὐτῆς.

* 39 Καὶ τῇδε ἦν ἀδελφὴ καλουμένη Μαρία, ἣ καὶ παρακαθίσασα παρὰ τοὺς πόδας τοῦ Ἰησοῦ, ἤκουε τὸν λόγον αὐτοῦ.

* 40 Ἡ δὲ Μάρθα † περιεσπᾶ-

---

4 Et non volebat ad tempus: post autem hæc dixit in seipso: Si & Deum non timeo, & hominem non revereor:

5 Propter præbere mihi molestiam viduam hanc, vindicabo istam, ne in finem veniens sugillet me.

6 Ait autem Dominus: Audite quid judex iniquus dicit:

7 At Deus non faciet vindictam electorum suorum clamantium ad se die & nocte, & longanimis super illos?

8 Etiam dico vobis, quia faciet vindictam illorum in celeritate, veruntamen filius hominis veniens num inveniet fidem in terra?

9 Dixit autem ad quosdam persuasos in seipsis, quod essent justi, & nihilifacientes cæteros, parabolam istam:

10 Homines duo ascendebant in templum orare, unus Pharisæus, & alter publicanus.

11 Pharisæus stans apud se hæc orabat: Deus gratias ago tibi: quia non sum sicut cæteri hominum, raptores, injusti, adulteri, aut & ut hic publicanus.

12 Jejuno bis sabbato, decimo omnia quæ possideo.

13 Et publicanus à longe stans non volebat nec oculos ad cælum levare, sed percutiebat in pectus suum, dicens: Deus propitius esto mihi peccatori.

14 Dico vobis, descendit hic justificatus in domum suam, quam ille: quia omnis exaltans seipsum humiliabitur: at humilians seipsum, exaltabitur.

38 Factum est autem in ire eos, & ipse intravit in vicum quendam: mulier autem quædam nomine Martha excepit illum in domum suam.

39 Et huic erat soror vocata Maria, quæ etiam sedens secus pedes Jesu, audiebat verbum illius.

40 At Martha distrahebatur

4. Pendant long-tems il n'en voulut rien faire. Cependant il dit enfin en lui-même : Quoique je ne craigne point Dieu, et que je n'aie nul égard pour aucun homme,

5. Néanmoins, parce que cette veuve m'importune, je lui ferai justice, afin qu'elle ne vienne pas toujours me rompre la tête.

6. Et le Seigneur dit : Ecoutez ce que dit ce Juge injuste.

7. Et Dieu ne vengera-t-il point ses élus, qui crient à lui jour et nuit, quoiqu'il diffère sa vengeance ?

8. Je vous dis qu'il les vengera bientôt. Mais quand le Fils de l'homme viendra, pensez-vous qu'il trouve de la foi sur la terre?

9. Il dit aussi cette parabole, au sujet de quelques-uns, qui présumoient d'eux-mêmes, comme s'ils étoient justes, et méprisoient les autres.

10. Deux hommes montèrent au Temple pour prier ; l'un étoit Pharisien, et l'autre Péager.

11. Le Pharisien se tenant debout, prioit ainsi en lui-même : O Dieu ! je te rends graces de ce que je ne suis pas comme le reste des hommes, *qui sont* ravisseurs, injustes, adultères ; ni même aussi comme ce péager.

12. Je jeûne deux fois la semaine, je donne la dîme de tout ce que je possède.

13. Mais le péager se tenant éloigné, n'osoit pas même lever les yeux au ciel ; mais il se frappoit la poitrine, en disant : O Dieu ! sois appaisé envers moi qui suis pécheur.

14. Je vous déclare que celui-ci s'en retournera justifié dans sa maison, préférablement à l'autre; car quiconque s'élève sera abaissé; et quiconque s'abaisse sera élevé.

min, il entra dans un bourg, et une femme nommée Marthe le reçut dans sa maison.

39. Elle avoit une sœur nommée Marie, qui se tenant assise aux pieds de Jésus, écoutoit sa parole.

40. Mais comme Marthe étoit

4 And he would not for a while: but afterward he said within himself, Though I fear not God, nor regard man ;

5 Yet, because this widow troubleth me, I will avenge her, lest by her continual coming she weary me.

6 And the Lord said, Hear what the unjust judge saith.

7 And shall not God avenge his own elect, which cry day and night unto him, though he bear long with them ?

8 I tell you, that he will avenge them speedily. Nevertheless, when the Son of Man cometh, shall he find faith on the earth ?

9 And he spake this parable unto certain which trusted in themselves, that they were righteous, and despised others :

10 Two men went up into the temple to pray; the one a Pharisee, and the other a publican.

11 The Pharisee stood and prayed thus with himself, God, I thank thee, that I am not as other men *are*, extortioners, unjust, adulterers, or even as this publican.

12 I fast twice in the week, I give tithes of all that I possess.

13 And the publican, standing afar off, would not lift up so much as *his* eyes unto heaven, but smote upon his breast, saying, God be merciful to me a sinner.

14 I tell you, this man went down to his house justified *rather* than the other: for every one that exalteth himself shall be abased; and he that humbleth himself shall be exalted.

38 Now it came to pass, as they went, that he entered into a certain village: and a certain woman, named Martha, received him into her house.

39 And she had a sister called Mary, which also sat at Jesus' feet, and heard his word.

40 But Martha was cumbered

το περὶ πολλὴν ‡ διακονίαν· ‡ ἐπι-
ςᾶσα δὲ εἶπε· Κύριε, ἐ̓ ‡ μέλει
σοι ὅτι ἡ ‡ ἀδελφή μ8 ‡ μό ην
με ‡ κατέλιπε ‡ διακονεῖν; εἰπὲ
ἔν αὐτῇ ἵνα μοι ‡ συναντιλάβηται.

* 41 Ἀποκριθεὶς δὲ εἶπεν αὐτῇ ὁ Ἰησᾶς Μάρθα, Μάρθα,
‡ μεριμνᾶς κ̔ ‡ τυρβάζη περὶ
πολλά.

42 Ἑνὸς δέ ἐςι χρεία. Μαρία
δὲ τὴν ἀγαθὴν μερίδα ἐξελέξαλο,
ἥτις ἐκ ἀφαιρεθήσεῖαι ἀπ᾽ αὐτῆς.
45. † 14.

ΚΕΦ. ιθ´. 19.

* 1 ΚΑὶ ἐγένετο, ὅτε ἐτέλεσεν
ὁ Ἰησῦς τὲς λόγες τύ-
τες, ‡ μετῆρεν ἀπὸ τῆς Γαλιλαίας,
κ̔ ἦλθεν εἰς τὰ ὅρια τῆς Ἰεδαίας,
πέραν τῦ Ἰορδάνε.

2 Καὶ ἠκολέθησαν αὐτῷ ὄχλοι
πολλοί·

3 Καὶ προσῆλθον αὐτῷ οἱ Φαρισαῖοι, πειράζοντες αὐτὸν, κ̔ λέγοντες αὐτῷ· Εἰ ἔξεςιν ἀνθρώπῳ
ἀπολῦσαι τὴν γυναῖκα αὐτῦ κατὰ
πᾶσαν αἰτίαν;

* 4 Ὁ δὲ ἀποκριθεὶς, εἶπεν αὐ-
τοῖς· Οὐκ ἀνέγνωτε, ὅτι ὁ ποιήσας ἀπ᾽ ἀρχῆς, ‡ ἄρσεν κ̔ ‡ θῆλυ
ἐποίησεν αὐτὲς;

5 Καὶ εἶπεν· Ἕνεκεν τύτε κα-
ταλείψει ἄνθρωπ☉ τὸν πατέρα κ̔
τὴν μητέρα, κ̔ προσκολληθήσεται
τῇ γυναικὶ αὐτῦ· κ̔ ἔσονται οἱ δύο
εἰς σάρκα μίαν.

6 Ὥςε ἐκ ἔτι εἰσὶ δύο, ἀλλὰ
σὰρξ μία, ὃ ἒν ὁ Θεὸς συνέζευξεν,
ἄνθρωπ☉ μὴ χωριζέτω.

7 Λέγεσιν αὐτῷ· Τί ἒν Μωσῆς
ἐνετείλατο δῦναι βιβλίον ἀποςα-
σίε, κ̔ ἀπολῦσαι αὐτήν;

* 8 Λέγει αὐτοῖς· Ὅτι Μωσῆς
πρὸς τὴν ‡ σκληροκαρδίαν ὑμῶν
‡ ἐπέτρεψεν ὑμῖν ἀπολῦσαι τὰς
γυναῖκας ὑμῶν· ἀπ᾽ ἀρχῆς δὲ ἐ
γέγονεν ὕτω.

9 Λέγω δὲ ὑμῖν, ὅτι ὃς ἂν ἀ-
πολύσῃ τὴν γυναῖκα αὐτῦ, εἰ μὴ
ἐπὶ πορνείᾳ, κ̔ γαμήσῃ ἄλλην,
μοιχᾶται· κ̔ ὁ ἀπολελυμένην γαμήσας, μοιχᾶται.

10 Λέγεσιν αὐτῷ οἱ μαθηταὶ
αὐτῷ· Εἰ ὕτως ἐςὶν ἡ αἰτία τῦ
ἀνθρώπε μετὰ τῆς γυναικὸς, ὀ
συμφέρει γαμῆσαι.

circa multum ministerium :
stans autem ait : Domine, non
curæ est tibi quod soror mea so-
lam me reliquit ministrare ? dic
ergo illi mihi ut simul suscipiat.

41 Respondens autem dixit
illi Jesus : Martha, Martha, so-
licita es, & turbaris circa multa.

42 Unius vero est usus. Maria autem bonam partem elegit,
quæ non auferetur ab ea.

CAPUT XIX.

1 ET factum est quum con-
summasset Jesus sermones
istos, transtulit se à Galilæâ, &
venit in fines Judææ trans Jordanem.

2 Et sequutæ sunt eum turbæ
multæ :

3 Et accesserunt ad eum Pharisæi tentantes eum, & dicentes
ei : Si licet homini absolvere
uxorem suam juxta omnem
causam ?

4 Qui verò respondens ait
eis : Non legistis, quia faciens
ab initio, masculum & fœmi-
nam fecit eos ?

5 Et dixit : Propter hoc dimittet homo patrem, & ma-
trem, & adhærebit uxori suæ :
& erunt duo in carnem unam.

6 Itaque non amplius sunt duo,
sed caro una. Quod ergo Deus
conjunxit, homo non separet.

7 Dicunt illi : Quid ergo Moses mandavit dare libellum dis-
cessionis, & absolvere eam ?

8 Ait illis : Quòd Moses ad
duritiem cordis vestri permisit
vobis absolvere uxores vestras :
ab initio autem non factum est
itâ.

9 Dico autem vobis, Quia
quicumque absolverit uxorem
suam, nisi super fornicatione, &
duxerit aliam, mœchatur : &
dimissam ducens, mœchatur.

10 Dicunt ei discipuli ejus :
Si ita est causa hominis cum
uxore, non confert nubere.

distraite par divers soins, elle vint et dit à *Jésus* : Seigneur, ne considères-tu point que ma sœur me laisse servir toute seule? Dis-lui donc qu'elle m'aide aussi.

41. Et Jésus lui répondit : Marthe, Marthe, tu te mets en peine et tu t'embarrasses de plusieurs choses;

42. Mais une seule chose est nécessaire ; or, Marie à choisi la bonne part qui ne lui sera point ôtée.

about much serving, and came to him, and said, Lord, dost thou not care that my sister hath left me to serve alone? bid her, therefore, that she help me.

41 And Jesus, answered, and said unto her, Martha, Martha, thou art careful, and troubled about many things :

42 But one thing is needful: and Mary hath chosen that good part, which shall not be taken away from her.

CHAPITRE XIX.
Doctrine de Jésus-Christ. Du Divorce et des Richesses.

QUAND Jésus eut achevé ces discours, il partit de Galilée, et s'en alla dans les quartiers de la Judée, au-delà du Jourdain.

2. Et beaucoup de peuple l'y suivit,

3. Des Pharisiens y vinrent aussi pour le tenter, et ils lui dirent : Est-il permis à un homme de répudier sa femme, pour quelque sujet que ce soit ?

4. Et il leur répondit : N'avez-vous pas lu que celui qui créa *l'homme*, au commencement, fit un homme et une femme;

5. Et qu'il est dit : C'est à cause de cela que l'homme quittera *son* père et *sa* mère, et qu'il s'attachera à sa femme, et les deux ne seront qu'une seule chair ?

6. Ainsi ils ne sont plus deux, mais *ils sont* une seule chair. Que l'homme ne sépare donc point ce que Dieu a uni.

7. Ils lui dirent : Pourquoi donc Moyse a-t-il commandé de donner la lettre de divorce, quand on veut répudier sa femme ?

8. Il leur dit : C'est à cause de la dureté de votre cœur, que Moyse vous a permis de répudier vos femmes ; mais il n'en étoit pas ainsi au commencement.

9. Mais moi je vous dis, que quiconque répudiera sa femme, si ce n'est pour cause d'adultère, et en épousera une autre, commet un adultère ; et celui qui épousera celle qui a été répudiée, commet aussi un adultère.

10. Ses Disciples lui dirent : Si telle est la condition de l'homme avec la femme, il ne convient pas de se marier.

AND it came to pass, *that*, when Jesus had finished these sayings, he departed from Galilee, and came into the coasts of Judea beyond Jordan :

2 And great multitudes followed him,

3 The Pharisees also came unto him, tempting him, and saying unto him, Is it lawful for a man to put away his wife for every cause?

4 And he answered and said unto them, Have ye not read, that he which made *them* at the beginning, made them male and female?

5 And said, For this cause shall a man leave father and mother, and shall cleave to his wife ; and they twain shall be one flesh.

6 Wherefore they are no more twain, but one flesh. What, therefore, God hath joined together, let no man put asunder.

7 They say unto him, Why did Moses then command to give a writing of divorcement, and to put her away ?

8 He saith unto them, Moses, because of the hardness of your hearts, suffered you to put away your wives : but from the beginning it was not so.

9 And I say unto you, Whosoever shall put away his wife, except *it be* for fornication, and shall marry another, committeth adultery : and whoso marrieth her which is put away doth commit adultery.

10 His disciples say unto him, If the case of the man be so with *his* wife, it is not good to marry.

51

11 Ὁ δὲ εἶπεν αὐτοῖς· Οὐ πάντες χωρῦσι τὸν λόγον τῦτον, ἀλλ᾽ οἷς δέδοται.

* 12 Εἰσὶ γὰρ εὐνῦχοι, οἵτινες ἐκ κοιλίας μητρὸς ἐγεννήθησαν ὕτω· καί εἰσιν εὐνῦχοι, οἵτινες † εὐνυχίσθησαν ὑπὸ τῶν ἀνθρώπων· κ᾽ εἰσιν εὐνῦχοι, οἵτινες εὐνέχισαν ἑαυτὸς διὰ τὴν βασιλείαν τῶν ὐρανῶν. Ὁ δυνάμεν⊙ χωρεῖν, χωρείτω.

13 Τότε προσηνέχθη αὐτῷ παιδία, ἵνα τὰς χεῖρας ἐπιθῇ αὐτοῖς, κ᾽ προσεύξηται· οἱ δὲ μαθηταὶ ἐπετίμησαν αὐτοῖς.

14 Ὁ δὲ Ἰησῦς εἶπεν· Ἄφετε τὰ παιδία, κ᾽ μὴ κωλύετε αὐτὰ ἐλθεῖν πρός με· τῶν γὰρ τοιῦτων ἐςὶν ἡ βασιλεία τῶν ὐρανῶν.

15 Καὶ ἐπιθεὶς αὐτοῖς τὰς χεῖρας, ἐπορεύθη ἐκεῖθεν.

16 Καὶ ἰδὺ, εἷς προσελθὼν, εἶπεν αὐτῷ. Διδάσκαλε ἀγαθὲ, τί ἀγαθὸν ποιήσω, ἵνα ἔχω ζωὴν αἰώνιον;

17 Ὁ δὲ εἶπεν αὐτῷ· Τί με λέγεις ἀγαθόν· ὐδεὶς ἀγαθὸς, εἰ μὴ εἷς, ὁ Θεός· εἰ δὲ θέλεις εἰσελθεῖν εἰς τὴν ζωὴν, τήρησον τὰς ἐντολάς.

18 Λέγει αὐτῷ· Ποίας; Ὁ δὲ Ἰησῦς εἶπε· Τὸ Οὐ φονεύσεις· Οὐ μοιχεύσεις· Οὐ κλέψεις· Οὐ ψευδομαρτυρήσεις·

19 Τίμα τὸν πατέρα σῦ, κ᾽ τὴν μητέρα· καὶ Ἀγαπήσεις τὸν πλησίον σῦ ὡς σεαυτόν.

20 Λέγει αὐτῷ ὁ νεανίσκ⊙· Πάντα ταῦτα ἐφυλαξάμην ἐκ νεότητός μῦ· τί ἔτι ὑςερῶ;

21 Ἔφη αὐτῷ ὁ Ἰησῦς· Εἰ θέλεις τέλει⊙ εἶναι, ὕπαγε, πώλησόν σῦ τὰ ὑπάρχοντα, κ᾽ δὸς πτωχοῖς· κ᾽ ἕξεις θησαυρὸν ἐν ὐρανῷ· κ᾽ δεῦρο, ἀκολύθει μοι.

22 Ἀκύσας δὲ ὁ νεανίσκ⊙ τὸν λόγον, ἀπῆλθε λυπύμεν⊙· ἦν γὰρ ἔχων κτήματα πολλά.

23 Ὁ δὲ Ἰησῦς εἶπε τοῖς μαθηταῖς αὐτῦ· Ἀμὴν λέγω ὑμῖν, ὅτι δυσκόλως πλύσι⊙ εἰσελεύσεται εἰς τὴν βασιλείαν τῶν ὐρανῶν.

* 24 Πάλιν δὲ λέγω ὑμῖν, † εὐκοπώτερόν ἐςι ‡ κάμηλον † διὰ † τρυπήμ[l.]⊙ ‡ ῥαφίδ⊙ ‡ διελθεῖν, ἢ πλύσιον εἰς τὴν βασιλείαν τῦ Θεῦ εἰσελθεῖν.

25 Ἀκύσαντες δὲ οἱ μαθηταὶ

---

11 Ille verò dixit illis : Non omnes capiunt verbum istud, sed quibus datum est.

12 Sunt enim eunuchi, qui de utero matris nati sunt sic : & sunt eunuchi, qui castrati sunt ab hominibus : & sunt eunuchi, qui castraverunt seipsos propter regnum cælorum, potens capere, capiat.

13 Tunc oblati sunt ei pueruli, ut manus imponeret eis, & oraret : At Discipuli increpabant eos.

14 At Jesus ait : Sinite puerulos, & ne prohibete eos venire ad me : nam talium est regnum cælorum.

15 Et imponens eis manus, abiit inde.

16 Et ecce unus accedens, ait illi : Magister bone, quid boni faciam, ut habeam vitam æternam?

17 Ipse verò dixit ei : Quid me dicis bonum? nemo bonus si non unus, Deus. Si autem vis ingredi ad vitam, serva mandata.

18 Dicit illi : Quæ? At Jesus dixit : hoc, Non occides : Non adulterabis : Non furaberis : Non falsò testaberis :

19 Honora patrem tuum & matrem : & : Diliges proximum tuum sicut teipsum.

20 Dicit illi adolescens : Omnia hæc custodivi à juventute mea : quid adhuc deficio?

21 Ait illi Jesus : Si vis perfectus esse, vade, vende tuam substantiam, & da pauperibus : & habebis thesaurum in cælo : & veni, sequere me.

22 Audiens autem adolescens verbum, abiit tristis : erat enim habens possessiones multas.

23 At Jesus dixit discipulis suis : Amen dico vobis, quia difficile dives intrabit in regnum cælorum.

24 Iterum autem dico vobis, facilius est camelum per foramen acus transire, quam divitem in regnum Dei intrare.

25 Audientes autem discipuli

11. Mais il leur dit : Tous ne sont pas capables de cela, mais ceux-là seulement à qui il a été donné.

12. Car il y a des eunuques, qui sont nés tels dès le ventre de *leur* mère ; il y en a qui ont été faits eunuques par les hommes ; et il y en a qui se sont faits eunuques eux-mêmes pour le Royaume des cieux. Que celui qui peut comprendre *ceci, le* comprenne.

13. Alors on lui présenta de petits enfans, afin qu'il leur imposât les mains, et qu'il priât *pour eux ;* mais les Disciples reprenoient *ceux qui les présentoient.*

14. Mais Jésus *leur* dit : Laissez ces petits enfans, et ne les empêchez point de venir à moi ; car le Royaume des cieux est pour ceux qui leur ressemblent.

15. Et leur ayant imposé les mains, il partit de là.

16. Et voici, quelqu'un s'approchant, lui dit : Mon bon Maître, que dois-je faire pour avoir la Vie éternelle ?

17. Il lui *répondit :* Pourquoi m'appelles-tu bon ? Il n'y a qu'un seul bon ; *c'est* Dieu. Que si tu veux entrer dans la vie, garde les commandemens.

18. Il leur dit : Quels *commandemens ?* Et Jésus lui *répondit :* Tu ne tueras point ; Tu ne commettras point adultère : Tu ne déroberas point : Tu ne diras point de faux témoignage :

19. Honore ton père et ta mère : Et tu aimeras ton prochain comme toi-même.

20. Le jeune homme lui dit : J'ai observé toutes ces choses-là dès ma jeunesse ; que me manque-t-il encore ?

21. Jésus lui dit : Si tu veux être parfait, vends ce que tu as, et le donne aux pauvres ; et tu auras un trésor dans le ciel ; après cela, viens, et suis-moi.

22. Mais quand le jeune homme eut entendu cette parole, il s'en alla tout triste, car il possédoit de grands biens.

23. Alors Jésus dit à ses Disciples : Je vous dis en vérité, qu'un riche entrera difficilement dans le Royaume des cieux.

24. Et je vous dis encore : Il est plus aisé qu'un chameau passe par le trou d'une aiguille, qu'il ne l'est qu'un riche entre dans le Royaume de Dieu.

25. Ses Disciples ayant entendu

11 But he said unto them, All *men* cannot receive this saying, save *they* to whom it is given.

12 For there are some eunuchs, which were so born from *their* of heaven's sake. He that is able to receive *it,* let him receive *it.*

13 Then were there brought unto him little children, that he should put *his* hands on them and pray : and the disciples rebuked them.

14 But Jesus said, Suffer little children, and forbid them not, to come unto me : for of such is the kingdom of heaven.

15 And he laid *his* hands on them, and departed thence.

16 And, behold, one came and said unto him, Good Master, what good thing shall I do, that I may have eternal life ?

17 And he said unto him, Why callest thou me good ? *there is* none good but one, *that is,* God : but if thou wilt enter into life, keep the commandments.

18 He saith unto him, Which ? Jesus said, Thou shalt do no murder, Thou shalt not commit adultery, Thou shalt not steal, Thou shalt not bear false witness,

19 Honour thy father and *thy* mother : and, Thou shalt love thy neighbour as thyself.

20 The young man saith unto him, All these things have I kept from my youth up : what lack I yet ?

21 Jesus said unto him, If thou wilt be perfect, go *and* sell that thou hast, and give to the poor, and thou shalt have treasure in heaven ; and come *and* follow me.

22 But when the young man heard that saying, he went away sorrowful : for he had great possessions.

23 Then said Jesus unto his disciples, Verily I say unto you, That a rich man shall hardly enter into the kingdom of heaven.

24 And again I say unto you, It is easier for a camel to go through the eye of a needle, than for a rich man to enter into the kingdom of God.

25 When his disciples heard *it,*

αὐτῷ, ἐξεπλήσσοντο σφόδρα, λέ-
γοντες· Τίς ἄρα δύναται σωθῆναι;

26 Ἐμβλέψας δὲ ὁ Ἰησοῦς, εἶπεν αὐτοῖς· Παρὰ ἀνθρώποις τοῦτο
ἀδύνατόν ἐστι, παρὰ δὲ Θεῷ πάντα
δυνατά ἐστι.

Κεφ. κ'. 20.

16 Ὁμοία γάρ ἐστιν ἡ βασιλεία
τῶν οὐρανῶν ἀνθρώπῳ οἰ-
κοδεσπότῃ, ὅστις ἐξῆλθεν ἅμα
πρωῒ μισθώσασθαι ἐργάτας
εἰς τὸν ἀμπελῶνα αὐτοῦ.

2 Συμφωνήσας δὲ μετὰ τῶν ἐρ-
γατῶν ἐκ δηναρίου τὴν ἡμέραν,
ἀπέστειλεν αὐτοὺς εἰς τὸν ἀμπελῶνα αὐτοῦ.

3 Καὶ ἐξελθὼν περὶ τὴν τρίτην
ὥραν, εἶδεν ἄλλους ἑστῶτας ἐν τῇ
ἀγορᾷ ἀργούς·

4 Κἀκείνοις εἶπεν· Ὑπάγετε καὶ
ὑμεῖς εἰς τὸν ἀμπελῶνα· ὃ ὃ ἐὰν
ᾖ δίκαιον, δώσω ὑμῖν.

5 Οἱ δὲ ἀπῆλθον. Πάλιν ἐξελθὼν περὶ ἕκτην καὶ ἐνάτην ὥραν,
ἐποίησεν ὡσαύτως.

6 Περὶ δὲ τὴν ἑνδεκάτην ὥραν
ἐξελθών, εὗρεν ἄλλους ἑστῶτας ἀρ-
γούς, καὶ λέγει αὐτοῖς· Τί ὧδε ἑστή-
κατε ὅλην τὴν ἡμέραν ἀργοί;

7 Λέγουσιν αὐτῷ· Ὅτι οὐδεὶς ἡ-
μᾶς ἐμισθώσατο. Λέγει αὐτοῖς·
Ὑπάγετε καὶ ὑμεῖς εἰς τὸν ἀμπελῶνα, καὶ ὃ ἐὰν ᾖ δίκαιον, λήψεσθε.

8 Ὀψίας δὲ γενομένης, λέγει ὁ
κύριος τοῦ ἀμπελῶνος τῷ ἐπιτρό-
πῳ αὐτοῦ· Κάλεσον τοὺς ἐργάτας,
καὶ ἀπόδος αὐτοῖς τὸν μισθόν, ἀρξά-
μενος ἀπὸ τῶν ἐσχάτων, ἕως
τῶν πρώτων.

9 Καὶ ἐλθόντες οἱ περὶ τὴν ἑνδεκάτην ὥραν, ἔλαβον ἀνὰ δηνάριον.

10 Ἐλθόντες δὲ οἱ πρῶτοι, ἐ-
νόμισαν ὅτι πλείονα λήψονται·
καὶ ἔλαβον καὶ αὐτοὶ ἀνὰ δηνάριον.

11 Λαβόντες δὲ ἐγόγγυζον κατὰ
τοῦ οἰκοδεσπότου,

12 Λέγοντες· Ὅτι οὗτοι οἱ ἔ-
σχατοι μίαν ὥραν ἐποίησαν, καὶ
ἴσους ἡμῖν αὐτοὺς ἐποίησας, τοῖς
βαστάσασι τὸ βάρος τῆς ἡμέρας,
καὶ τὸν καύσωνα.

ejus, mirabantur valde, dicentes:
Quis ergo potest servari?

26 Aspiciens autem Jesus,
dixit illis: Apud homines hoc
impossibile est, apud autem Deum omnia possibilia sunt.

CAPUT. XX.

1 Simile enim est regnum cælorum homini patrifami-
lias, qui exiit cum diluculo con-
ducere operarios in vineam
suam.

2 Conveniens autem cum o-
perariis ex denario diem, misit
eos in vineam suam.

3 Et egressus circa tertiam horam, vidit alios stantes in foro
otiosos:

4 Et illis dixit: Abite & vos
in vineam: & quod fuerit
justum dabo vobis.

5 Illi autem abierunt. Iterum
exiens circa sextam & nonam
horam, fecit similiter.

6 Circa vero undecimam horam exiens, invenit alios stantes
otiosos, & dicit illis: Quid hic
statis totam diem otiosi?

7 Dicunt ei: Quia nemo nos
mercede conduxit. Dicit eis:
Ite & vos in vineam, & quod
fuerit justum, sumetis.

8 Vespere autem facto, dicit
dominus vineæ procuratori suo:
Voca operarios & redde illis
mercedem, incipiens à novissi-
mis usque ad primos.

9 Et venientes qui circa undecimam horam, acceperunt singuli denarium.

10 Venientes autem primi,
arbitrati sunt quòd plus essent
accepturi: & acceperunt & ipsi
singuli denarium.

11 Accipientes autem mur-
murabant adversus patrem-fa-
milias,

12 Dicentes: Quòd hi novissi-
mi unam horam fecerunt, &
pares nobis illos fecisti, portan-
tibus pondus diei, & æstum.

cela, furent fort étonnés, et ils disoient : Qui peut donc être sauvé ?

26. Et Jésus les regardant, leur dit : Quant aux hommes, cela est impossible ; mais quant à Dieu, toutes choses sont possibles.

CAR le Royaume des cieux est semblable à un père de famille, qui sortit dès la pointe du jour, afin de louer des ouvriers pour *travailler à* sa vigne.

2. Et ayant accordé avec les ouvriers à un denier par jour, il les envoya à sa vigne.

3. Il sortit encore environ la troisième heure *du jour*, et il en vit d'autres qui étoient dans la place sans rien faire ;

4. Auxquels il dit : Allez-vous-en aussi à ma vigne, et je vous donnerai ce qui sera raisonnable.

5. Et ils y allèrent. Il sortit encore environ la sixième et la neuvième heure, et il fit la même chose.

6. Et vers l'onzième heure, il sortit, et il en trouva d'autres qui étoient sans rien faire, auxquels il dit : Pourquoi vous tenez-vous ici tout le jour sans rien faire ?

7. Et ils lui répondirent : Parce que personne ne nous a loués. Et il leur dit : Allez-vous-en aussi à ma vigne, vous recevrez ce qui sera raisonnable.

8. Quand le soir fut venu, le Maître de la vigne dit à celui qui avoit le soin de ses affaires : Appelle les ouvriers, et leur paie *leur* salaire, en commençant depuis les derniers jusqu'aux premiers.

9. Et ceux *qui avoient été loués* sur l'onzième heure, étant venus, ils reçurent chacun un denier.

10. Or, quand les premiers furent venus, ils s'attendoient à recevoir davantage ; mais ils reçurent aussi chacun un denier.

11. Et l'ayant reçu, ils murmuroient contre le père de famille,

12. Disant : Ces derniers n'ont travaillé qu'une heure, et tu les égales à nous, qui avons supporté la fatigue de *tout le* jour et la chaleur.

they were exceedingly amazed, saying, Who then can be saved ?

26 But Jesus beheld *them*, and said unto them, With men this is impossible ; but with God all things are possible.

CHAP. XX.

The labourers in the vineyard.

FOR the kingdom of heaven is like unto a man *that is* an householder, which went out early in the morning to hire labourers into his vineyard.

2 And when he had agreed with the labourers for a penny a day, he sent them into his vineyard.

3 And he went out about the third hour, and saw others standing idle in the market-place,

4 And said unto them, Go ye also into the vineyard ; and whatsoever is right I will give you. And they went their way.

5 Again he went out about the sixth and ninth hour, and did likewise.

6 And about the eleventh hour he went out, and found others standing idle, and saith unto them, Why stand ye here all the day idle ?

7 They say unto him, Because no man hath hired us. He saith unto them, Go ye also into the vineyard ; and whatsoever is right, *that* shall ye receive.

8 So when even was come, the lord of the vineyard saith unto his steward, Call the labourers, and give them *their* hire, beginning from the last unto the first.

9 And when they came that *were hired* about the eleventh hour, they received every man a penny.

10 But when the first came, they supposed that they should have received more ; and they likewise received every man a penny.

11 And when they had received *it*, they murmured against the good man of the house,

12 Saying, These last have wrought *but* one hour, and thou hast made them equal unto us, which have borne the burden and heat of the day.

53

13 Ὁ δὲ ἀποκριθεὶς, εἶπεν ἑνὶ αὐτῶν· ‡ Ἑταῖρε, ἔκ ‡ ἀδικῶ σε· ἔχὶ ‡ δηναρίε ‡ συνεφώνησάς μοι;

14 Ἆρον τὸ σὸν, κ̧ Ὕπαγε· θέλω δὲ τύτῳ τῷ ἐσχάτῳ δῶναι ὡς κ̧ σοι.

15 Ἢ ἔκ ἔξεςί μοι ποιῆσαι ὃ θέλω ἐν τοῖς ἐμοῖς; ἢ ὁ ὀφθαλμός σε πονηρός ἐςιν, ὅτι ἐγὼ ἀγαθός εἰμι;

16 Οὕτως ἔσονται οἱ ἔσχατοι, πρῶτοι. κ̧ οἱ πρῶτοι, ἔσχατοι. πολλοὶ γάρ εἰσι ‡ κλητοί, ὀλίγοι δὲ ἐκλεκτοί.

Κεφ. ιθ´. 19.

1 ΚΑΙ εἰσελθὼν διήρχετο τὴν Ἰεριχώ.

2 Καὶ ἰδὺ ἀνὴρ ὀνόματι καλύμεν⊙ Ζακχαῖος· κ̧ αὐτὸς ἦν † ἀρχιτελώνης, κ̧ ἅτος ἦν πλούσιος.

3 Καὶ ἐζήτει ἰδεῖν τὸν Ἰησῦν τίς ἐςι· κ̧ οὐκ ἠδύνατο ἀπὸ τοῦ ὄχλυ, ὅτι τῇ ἡλικίᾳ μικρὸς ἦν.

4 Καὶ ‡ προσδραμὼν ἔμπροσθεν, ἀνέβη ἐπὶ † συκομορέαν, ἵνα ἴδῃ αὐτὸν· ὅτι δι᾽ ἐκείνης ἤμελλε διέρχεσθαι.

5 Καὶ ὡς ἦλθεν ἐπὶ τὸν τόπον, ἀναβλέψας ὁ Ἰησῦς εἶδεν αὐτὸν, κ̧ εἶπε πρὸς αὐτὸν Ζακχαῖε, (πεύσας κατάβηθι· σήμερον γὰρ ἐν τῷ οἴκῳ σε δεῖ με μεῖναι.

6 Καὶ (πεύσας κατέβη, κ̧ ὑπεδέξατο αὐτὸν χαίρων.

7 Καὶ ἰδόντες ἅπαντες ‡ διεγόγγυζον, λέγοντες· Ὅτι παρὰ ἁμαρτωλῷ ἀνδρὶ εἰσῆλθε καταλῦσαι.

8 Σταθεὶς δὲ Ζακχαῖος εἶπε πρὸς τὸν Κύριον· Ἰδὺ, τὰ ‡ ἡμίση τῶν ‡ ὑπαρχόντων μυ, Κύριε, δίδωμι τοῖς πτωχοῖς· κ̧ εἴ τινός τι ἐσυκοφάντησα, ἀποδίδωμι † τετραπλῦν.

9 Εἶπε δὲ πρὸς αὐτὸν ὁ Ἰησῦς· Ὅτι σήμερον σωτηρία τῷ οἴκῳ τούτῳ ἐγένετο, καθ᾽ τι κ̧ αὐτὸς υἱὸς Ἀβραάμ ἐςιν.

10 Ἦλθε γὰρ ὁ υἱὸς τῦ ἀνθρώπυ ζητῆσαι κ̧ σῶσαι τὸ ἀπολωλός.

11 Ἀκυόντων δὲ αὐτῶν ταῦτα, προσθεὶς εἶπε παραβολὴν, διὰ τὸ ἐγγὺς αὐτὸν εἶναι Ἰερυσαλήμ, κ̧

---

13 Ille verò respondens dixit uni eorum: Amice, non facio injuriam tibi: nonne denario conve nisti mecum?

14 Tolle quod tuum, & abi, volo autem huic noviſſimo dare ſicut & tibi.

15 Aut non licet mihi facere quod volo in meis? an oculus tuus malus eſt, quia ego bonus ſum?

16 Sic erunt noviſſimi, primi: & primi, noviſſimi. Multi enim ſunt vocati, pauci verò electi.

CAPUT XIX.

1 ET ingreſſus pertranſibat Jericho.

2 Et ecce vir nomine vocatus Zachæus, & hic erat princeps publicanorum: & ipſe erat dives.

3 Et quærebat videre Jeſum quis eſſet, & non poterat præ turba: quia ſtatura puſillus erat.

4 Et præcur ens coram, aſcendit in ſycomorum, ut videret eum: quia illàc erat tranſiturus.

5 Et ut venit ad locum, ſuſpiciens Jeſus vidit illum, & dixit ad eum: Zachæe, feſtinans deſcende: hodie enim in domo tua oportet me mane re.

6 Et feſtinans deſcendit, & excepit illum gaudens.

7 Et videntes omnes murmurabant, dicentes: quod ad peccatorem hominem introivit diverſari.

8 Stans autem Zachæus dixit ad Dominum: Ecce dimidia ſubſtantiarum mearum, Domine, do pauperibus, & ſi aliquid defraudavi, reddo quadruplum.

9 Ait autem ad eum Jeſus: Quia hodie ſalus domui huic facta eſt, eo quod & ipſe filius Abrahæ ſit.

10 Venit enim filius hominis quærere & ſervare perditum.

11 Audientibus autem illis hæc, adjiciens dixit parabolam, propter prope eum eſſe Hieru-

13. Mais il répondit à l'un d'eux, et lui dit : Mon ami , je ne te fais point de tort ; n'as-tu pas accordé avec moi à un denier *par jour* ?

14. Prends ce qui est à toi , et t'en va ; mais je veux donner à ce dernier autant qu'à toi.

15. Ne m'est-il pas permis de faire ce que je veux de ce qui est à moi ? Ton œil est-il malin de ce que je suis bon ?

16. Ainsi les derniers seront les premiers , et les premiers seront les derniers ; car il y en a beaucoup d'appelés , mais peu d'élus.

13 But he answered one of them, and said, Friend, I do thee no wrong : didst not thou agree with me for a penny ?

14 Take *that* thine *is*, and go thy way : I will give unto this last, even as unto thee.

15 Is it not lawful for me to do what I will with mine own ? is thine eye evil because I am good ?

16 So the last shall be first, and the first last : for many be called, but few chosen.

CHAPITRE XIX.

La conversion de Zachée ; la parabole des dix marcs. Jésus fait son entrée à Jérusalem ; il répand des larmes sur elle , et purge le Temple.

J É S U S étant entré dans Jérico , passoit par la ville.

2. Et un homme appelé Zachée, chef des péagers , qui étoit riche ,

3. Cherchoit à voir qui étoit Jésus ; mais il ne le pouvoit pas à cause de la foule, parce qu'il étoit de petite taille.

4. C'est pourquoi il courut devant , et monta sur un sycomore, pour le voir ; parce qu'il devoit passer par-là.

5. Jésus étant venu en cet endroit , et regardant en haut , le vit , et lui dit : Zachée , hâte-toi de descendre ; car il faut que je loge aujourd'hui dans ta maison.

6. Et il descendit promptement , et le reçut avec joie.

7. Et tous ceux qui virent cela , murmuroient , disant qu'il étoit entré chez un homme de mauvaise vie pour y loger.

8. Et Zachée se présentant devant le Seigneur , lui dit : Seigneur , je donne la moitié de mes biens aux pauvres , et si j'ai fait tort à quelqu'un en quelque chose, je lui en rends quatre fois autant.

9. Sur quoi Jésus lui dit : Le salut est entré aujourd'hui dans cette maison, parce que celui-ci est aussi enfant d'Abraham.

10. Car le Fils de l'homme est venu chercher et sauver ce qui étoit perdu.

11. Comme ils écoutoient ce discours , Jésus continuant, proposa une parabole , sur ce qu'il étoit près de Jérusalem , et qu'ils

CHAP. XIX.

The publican Zaccheus.

A ND *Jesus* entered and passed through Jericho.

2 And, behold, *there was* a man named Zaccheus, which was the chief among the publicans, and he was rich.

3 And he sought to see Jesus who he was ; and could not for the press, because he was little of stature.

4 And he ran before, and climbed up into a sycamore-tree to see him ; for he was to pass that *way*.

5 And, when Jesus came to the place, he looked up, and saw him, and said unto him, Zaccheus, make haste, and come down ; for to-day I must abide at thy house.

6 And he made haste, and came down, and received him joyfully.

7 And when they saw *it*, they all murmured, saying, That he was gone to be guest with a man that is a sinner.

8 And Zaccheus stood, and said unto the Lord, Behold, Lord, the half of my goods I give to the poor ; and if I have taken any thing from any man by false accusation, I restore him fourfold.

9 And Jesus said unto him, This day is salvation come to this house, forasmuch as he also is a son of Abraham.

10 For the Son of Man is come to seek and to save that which was lost.

11 And, as they heard these things, he added, and spake a parable, because he was nigh to Je-

L.

δοκεῖν αὐτοῖς ὅτι παραχϱῆμα μέλλει ἡ βασιλεία τοῦ Θεῦ ἀναφαίνεσθαι.

12 Εἶπεν ἦν· Ἄνϑρωπός τις εὐγενὴς ἐπορεύθη εἰς χώραν μακράν, λαβεῖν ἑαυτῷ βασιλείαν, κ̀ ὑποςρέψαι.

* 13 Καλέσας δὲ δέκα δάλυς ἑαυτῦ, ἔδωκεν αὐτοῖς δέκα μνᾶς, κ̀ εἶπε πϱὸς αὐτούς· † Πϱαγματεύσασθε ἕως ἔρχομαι.

* 14 Οἱ δὲ πολῖται αὐτῦ ‡ ἐμίσην αὐτὸν, κ̀ ἀπέςειλαν ‡ πϱεςβείαν ‡ ὀπίσω αὐτῆ, λέγοντες. Οὐ θέλομεν τῆτον βασιλεῦσαι ἐφ᾽ ἡμᾶς.

* 15 Καὶ ἐγένετο ἐν τῷ ἐπανελθεῖν αὐτὸν λαβόντα τὴν βασιλείαν, κ̀ εἶπε φωνηθῆναι αὐτῷ τὺς δούλυς τύτυς, οἷς ἔδωκε τὸ ἀργύϱιον ἵνα γνῷ τίς τί † διεπϱαγματεύσατο.

* 16 Παϱεγένετο δὲ ὁ πρῶτ⊙, λέγων Κύϱιε, ἡ ‡ μνᾶ συ † προσειργάσατο δέκα μνᾶς.

17 Καὶ εἶπεν αὐτῷ· Εὖ ἀγαθὲ δῦλε· ὅτι ἐν ἐλαχίςῳ πιςὸς ἐγένυ, ἴσθι ἐξυσίαν ἔχων ἐπάνω δέκα πόλεων.

18 Καὶ ἦλθεν ὁ δεύτεϱ⊙, λέγων· Κύϱιε, ἡ μνᾶ συ ἐποίησε πέντε μνᾶς.

19 Εἶπε δὲ κ̀ τέτῳ· Καὶ σὺ γίνυ ἐπάνω πέντε πόλεων.

20 Καὶ ἕτεϱ⊙ ἦλθε, λέγων· Κύϱιε, ἰδὲ, ἡ μνᾶ συ, ἣν εἶχον ἀποκειμένην ἐν συδαϱίῳ.

21 Ἐφοβύμην γάϱ σε, ὅτι ἄνθϱωπ⊙ αὐςηϱὸς εἶ· αἴϱεις ὃ ὐκ ἔθηκας, κ̀ θεϱίζεις ὃ ὐκ ἔσπειρας.

* 22 Λέγει δὲ αὐτῷ. Ἐκ τῦ ςόμαλός συ κϱινῶ σε, πονηϱὲ δῦλε· ᾔδεις ὅτι ἐγὼ † ἄνθϱωπ⊙ ‡ αὐςηϱός εἰμι αἴϱων ὃ ὐκ ἔθηκα, κ̀ θεϱίζων ὃ ὐκ ἔσπειρα.

23 Καὶ διατί ὐκ ἔδωκας τὸ ἀργύϱιόν μυ ἐπὶ τὴν τράπεζαν, κ̀ ἐγὼ ἐλθὼν σὺν τόκῳ ἂν ἔπραξα αὐτό;

---

salem, & videri eis quod confestim esset regnum Dei appariturum.

12 Dixit ergo: Homo quidam nobilis abiit in regionem longinquam accipere sibi ipsi regnum, & reverti.

13 Vocans autem decem servos suos, dedit eis decem minas, & ait ad illos: Negotiamini dum venio.

14 At cives ejus oderant eum, & miserunt legationem post illum, dicentes: Non volumus hunc regnare super nos.

15 Et factum est in redire ipsum accipientem regnum, ait vocari sibi servos hos, quibus dedit argentum, ut sciret quis quid negotiatus esset,

16 Adfuit autem primus, dicens: Domine, mina tua acquisivit decem minas.

17 Et ait illi: Euge bone serve: quia in modico fidelis fuisti, esto potestatem habens super decem civitates.

18 Et venit secundus, dicens: Domine, mina tua fecit quinque minas.

19 Ait autem & huic: Et tu esto super quinque civitates.

20 Et alter venit, dicens: Domine, ecce mina tua, quam habui repositam in sudario.

21 Timui enim te, quia homo austerus es: tollis quod non posuisti, & metis quod non seminasti.

22 Dicit autem ei: Ex ore tuo judico te, scelerate serve: sciebas quod ego homo austerus sum, tollens quod non posui, & metens quod non seminavi.

23 Et quare non dedisti argentum meum mensariis, & veniens ego cum usura utique exegissem illud?

croyoient que le règne de Dieu alloit paroitre bientôt.

12. Il dit donc : Un homme de grande naissance s'en alla dans un pays éloigné , pour prendre possession d'un royaume , et s'en revenir ensuite.

13. Et ayant appelé dix de ses serviteurs, il leur donna dix marcs d'argent , et leur dit : Faites-les valoir jusqu'à-ce que je revienne.

14. Mais les gens de son pays le haïssoient ; et ils envoyèrent une ambassade après lui , pour dire :

Nous ne voulons point que celui-ci règne sur nous.

15. Il arriva donc , lorsqu'il fut de retour , après avoir pris possession du royaume , qu'il commanda qu'on fît venir ces serviteurs auxquels il avoit donné l'argent , pour savoir combien chacun l'avoit fait valoir.

16. Et le premier se présenta , et dit : Seigneur , ton marc a produit dix autres marcs.

17. Et il lui dit : Cela est bien , bon serviteur ; parce que tu as été fidèle dans peu de chose , tu auras le gouvernement de dix villes.

18. Et le second vint , et dit : Seigneur , ton marc a produit cinq autres marcs.

19. Et il dit aussi à celui-ci : Et toi , commande à cinq villes.

20. Et un autre vint , et dit : Seigneur , voici ton marc que j'ai gardé enveloppé dans un linge;

21. Car je te craignois, parce que tu es un homme sévère; tu prends où tu n'as rien mis , et tu moissonnes où tu n'as point semé.

22. Et son maître lui dit : Méchant serviteur , je te jugerai par tes propres paroles : Tu savois que je suis un homme sévère, qui prends où je n'ai rien mis , et qui moissonne où je n'ai point semé ;

23. Et pourquoi n'as-tu pas mis mon argent à la banque ; et à mon retour je l'eusse retiré avec les intérêts ?

rusalem, and because they thought that the kingdom of God should immediately appear.

12 He said, therefore, A certain nobleman went into a far country to receive for himself a kingdom, and to return.

13 And he called his ten servants, and delivered them ten pounds, and said unto them, Occupy till I come.

14 But his citizens hated him, and sent a message after him, saying, We will not have this *man* to reign over us.

15 And it came to pass, that when he was returned, having received the kingdom, then he commanded these servants to be called unto him, to whom he had given the money, that he might know how much every man had gained by trading.

16 Then came the first, saying, Lord, thy pound hath gained ten pounds.

17 And he said unto him, Well, thou good servant; because thou hast been faithful in a very little, have thou authority over ten cities.

18 And the second came, saying, Lord, thy pound hath gained five pounds.

19 And he said likewise to him, Be thou also over five cities.

20 And another came, saying, Lord, behold, *here is* thy pound, which I have kept laid up in a napkin :

21 For I feared thee, because thou art an austere man ; thou takest up that thou layedst not down, and reapest that thou didst not sow.

22 And he saith unto him, Out of thine own mouth will I judge thee, *thou* wicked servant. Thou knewest that I was an austere man, taking up that I laid not down, and reaping that I did not sow: K2

23 Wherefore then gavest not thou my money into the bank, that at my coming I might have required mine own with usury ?

55

24 Καὶ τοῖς παρεςῶσιν εἶπεν·
Ἄρατε ἀπ᾽ αὐτῦ τὴν μνᾶν, ἡ δότε
τῷ τὰς δέκα μνᾶς ἔχοντι.

25 Καὶ εἶπον αὐτῷ· Κύριε,
ἔχει δέκα μνᾶς·

26 Λέγω γὰρ ὑμῖν, ὅτι παντὶ
τῷ ἔχοντι δοθήσεται· ἀπὸ δὲ τῦ
μὴ ἔχοντ⸌, ἡ ὃ ἔχει, ἀρθήσεται
ἀπ᾽ αὐτῦ.

* 27 Πλὴν τὺς ἐχθρύς μυ
ἐκείνυς, τὺς μὴ θελήσαντάς με
βασιλεῦσαι ἐπ᾽ αὐτὺς, ἀγάγετε
ὧδε, ἡ † κατασφάξατε ἔμπροσθέν μυ.

28 Καὶ εἰπὼν ταῦτα, ἐπορεύε-
το ἔμπροσθεν, ἀναβαίνων εἰς Ἱεροσόλυμα.

Κεφ. κα'. 21.

1 ΚΑὶ ὅτε ἤγγισαν εἰς Ἱεροσόλυμα, ἡ ἦλθον εἰς Βηθφαγῆ
πρὸς τὸ ὄρος τῶν ἐλαιῶν, τότε ὁ
Ἰησῦς ἀπέστειλε δύο μαθητὰς, λέγων αὐτοῖς·

2 Πορεύθητε εἰς τὴν κώμην, τὴν
ἀπέναντι ὑμῶν· ἡ εὐθέως εὑρήσετε
ὄνον δεδεμένην, ἡ πῶλον μετ᾽ αὐ-
τῆς· λύσαντες ἀγάγετέ μοι.

3 Καὶ ἐάν τις ὑμῖν εἴπῃ τι,
ἐρεῖτε ὅτι ὁ Κύρι⸌ αὐτῶν χρείαν
ἔχει. εὐθέως δὲ ἀποςελεῖ αὐτύς.

6 Πορευθέντες δὲ οἱ μαθηταὶ, ἡ
ποιήσαντες καθὼς προσέταξεν αὐτοῖς ὁ Ἰησῦς,

* 7 Ἤγαγον τὴν ὄνον ἡ τὸν πῶλον, ἡ ἐπέθηκαν ἐπάνω αὐτῶν τὰ
ἱμάτια αὐτῶν, ἡ † ἐπεκάθισαν
‡ ἐπάνω αὐτῶν.

8 Ὁ δὲ πλεῖςος ὄχλος ἔςρωσαν
ἑαυτῶν τὰ ἱμάτια ἐν τῇ ὁδῷ· ἄλλοι δὲ ἔκοπτον κλάδυς ἀπὸ τῶν
δένδρων, ἡ ἐςρώννυον ἐν τῇ ὁδῷ.

10 Καὶ εἰσελθόντ⸌ αὐτῦ εἰς
Ἱεροσόλυμα, ἐσείσθη πᾶσα ἡ πό-
λις· λέγυσα· Τίς ἐςιν ὗτ⸌;

19 Οἱ ἦν Φαρισαῖοι εἶπον πρὸς
ἑαυτύς· Θεωρεῖτε ὅτι ὐκ ὠφελεῖτε
ὐδέν; ἴδε, ὁ κόσμ⸌ ὀπίσω αὐτῦ ἀπῆλθεν.

20 Ἦσαν δέ τινες Ἕλληνες ἐκ
τῶν ἀναβαινόντων ἵνα προσκυνήσω-
σιν ἐν τῇ ἑορτῇ.

---

24 Et astantibus dixit : Auferte ab illo minam : & date
decem minas habenti.

25 Et dixerunt ei : Domine,
habet decem minas.

26 Dico enim vobis, quia o-
mni habenti dabitur : ab autem
non habente, & quod habet,
auferetur ab eo.

27 Verumtamen inimicos meos illos, non volentes me regnare super se, adducite huc, &
jugulate ante me.

28 Et dicens hæc, ibat ante
ascendens in Hierosolyma.

---

1 ET quum appropinquassent
in Hierosolyma, & venis-
sent in Bethphage ad montem
Olivarum, tunc Jesus misit duos
discipulos, dicens eis :

2 Ite in vicum qui adversum
vos : & statim invenietis asinam
alligatam, & pullum cum ea :
solventes adducite mihi.

3 Et si quis vobis dixerit aliquid, dicite, quia Dominus eorum usum habet : statim autem
dimittet eos.

6 Euntes autem discipuli, &
facientes sicut mandavit illis
Jesus,

7 Adduxerunt asinam, & pullum, & imposuerunt super eos
vestimenta sua, & collocarunt
eum desuper eos.

8 At plurima turba strave-
runt sua vestimenta in via : alii
autem cædebant ramos de arbo-
ribus, & sternebant in via.

10 Et intrante eo in Hierosolyma, commota est universa
civitas, dicens : Quis est hic ?

19 Ergo Pharisæi dixerunt
ad semetipsos : Videtis quia non
proficitis quicquam ? ecce mundus post eum abiit.

20 Erant autem quidam Græ-
ci ex ascendentibus, ut adora-
rent in die festo.

24. Et il dit à ceux qui étoient présens : Otez-lui le marc, et le donnez à celui qui a les dix marcs.

24 And he said unto them that stood by, Take from him the pound, and give *it* to him that hath ten pounds.

25. Et ils lui dirent : Seigneur, il a déjà dix marcs.

25 (And they said unto him, Lord, he hath ten pounds.)

26. Aussi vous dis-je, qu'on donnera à quiconque a déjà ; et que pour celui qui n'a pas, cela même qu'il a lui sera ôté.

26 For I say unto you, That unto every one which hath, shall be given ; and from him that hath not, even that he hath, shall be taken away from him.

27. Quant à mes ennemis, qui n'ont pas voulu que je regnasse sur eux, amenez-les ici, et faites-les mourir en ma présence.

27 But those mine enemies, which would not that I should reign over them, bring hither, and slay *them* before me.

28. Et après avoir dit cela, il marchoit devant eux, montant à Jérusalem.

28 And when he had thus spoken, he went before, ascending up to Jerusalem.

CHAPITRE XXI.

Jésus-Christ entre dans Jérusalem, chasse les marchands du Temple, et répond aux Pharisiens.

COMME ils approchoient de Jérusalem, et qu'ils étoient déjà à Bethphagé, près du mont des Oliviers, Jésus envoya deux Disciples ;

AND when they drew nigh unto Jerusalem, and were come to Bethpage, unto the mount of Olives, then sent Jesus two disciples,

2. Leur disant : Allez à la bourgade qui est devant vous ; vous y trouverez d'abord une ânesse attachée, et *son* ânon avec elle ; détachez-les et amenez-les-moi.

2 Saying unto them, Go into the village over against you, and straightway ye shall find an ass tied, and a colt with her : loose *them*, and bring *them* unto me.

3. Et si quelqu'un vous dit quelque chose, vous direz que le Seigneur en a besoin ; et aussitôt il les envoiera.

3 And if any *man* say aught unto you, ye shall say, The Lord hath need of them ; and straightway he will send them.

6. Les Disciples s'en allèrent donc, et firent comme Jésus leur avoit ordonné.

6 And the disciples went, and did as Jesus commanded them,

7. Et ils amenèrent l'ânesse et l'ânon, et ayant mis leurs vêtemens dessus, ils l'y firent asseoir.

7 And brought the ass, and the colt, and put on them their clothes, and they set *him* thereon.

8. Alors des gens en grand nombre étendoient leurs vêtemens par le chemin ; et d'autres coupoient des branches d'arbres, et les étendoient par le chemin.

8 And a very great multitude spread their garments in the way ; others cut down branches from the trees, and strawed them in the way.

10. Et quand il fut entré dans Jérusalem, toute la ville fut émue, et on disoit : Qui est celui-ci ?

10 And when he was come into Jerusalem, all the city was moved, saying, Who is this ?

19. De sorte que les Pharisiens disoient entr'eux : Vous voyez que vous ne gagnez rien ; voilà que tout le monde va après lui.

19 The Pharisees, therefore, said among themselves, Perceive ye how ye prevail nothing? behold, the world is gone after him.

20. Or quelques Grecs, de ceux qui étoient montés pour adorer pendant la fête,

20 And there were certain Greeks among them, that came up to worship at the feast :

21 Οὗτοι ἔν προσῆλθον Φιλίππῳ τῷ ἀπὸ Βηθσαϊδὰ τῆς Γαλιλαίας, ἢ ἠρώτων αὐτὸν, λέγοντες· Κύριε, θέλομεν τὸν Ἰησῦν ἰδεῖν.

22 Ἔρχεται Φίλιππος ἢ λέγει τῷ Ἀνδρέᾳ ἢ πάλιν Ἀνδρέας ἢ Φίλιππος λέγουσι τῷ Ἰησῦ.

23 Ὁ δὲ Ἰησῦς, ἀπεκρίνατο αὐτοῖς, λέγων· Ἐλήλυθεν ἡ ὥρα ἵνα δοξασθῇ ὁ υἱὸς τῦ ἀνθρώπε.

24 Ἀμὴν, ἀμὴν, λέγω ὑμῖν, ἐὰν μὴ ὁ κόκκος τῦ σίτε πεσὼν εἰς τὴν γῆν ἀποθάνῃ, αὐτὸς μόνος μένει· ἐὰν δὲ ἀποθάνῃ, πολὺν καρπὸν φέρει.

17 Καὶ καταλιπὼν αὐτοὺς, ἐξῆλθεν ἔξω τῆς πόλεως εἰς Βηθανίαν· ἢ ηὐλίσθη ἐκεῖ.

12 Καὶ τῇ ἐπαύριον ἐξελθόντων αὐτῶν ἀπὸ Βηθανίας,

εἰσελθὼν ὁ Ἰησῦς εἰς τὸ ἱερὸν, ἤρξατο ἐκβάλλειν τὲς πωλῦντας ἢ ἀγοράζοντας ἐν τῷ ἱερῷ ἢ τὰς τραπέζας τῶν κολλυβιστῶν, ἢ τὰς καθέδρας τῶν πωλῶντων τὰς περιστερὰς κατέστρεψε.

16 Καὶ ἐκ ἤφιεν ἵνα τις διενέγκῃ σκεῦος διὰ τῦ ἱερῦ.

17 Καὶ ἐδίδασκε, λέγων αὐτοῖς· Οὐ γέγραπται· Ὅτι ὁ οἶκός μυ, οἶκος προσευχῆς κληθήσεται πᾶσι τοῖς ἔθνεσιν; ὑμεῖς δὲ ἐποιήσατε αὐτὸν σπήλαιον λῃστῶν.

18 Καὶ ἤκυσαν οἱ γραμματεῖς ἢ οἱ ἀρχιερεῖς, ἢ ἐζήτυν πῶς αὐτὸν ἀπολέσυσιν· ἐφοβῦντο γὰρ αὐτὸν, ὅτι πᾶς ὁ ὄχλος ἐξεπλήσσετο ἐπὶ τῇ διδαχῇ αὐτῦ.

19 Καὶ ὅτε ὀψὲ ἐγένετο, ἐξεπορεύετο ἔξω τῆς πόλεως.

27 Καὶ ἔρχονται πάλιν εἰς Ἱεροσόλυμα· ἢ ἐν τῷ ἱερῷ περιπατῦντι αὐτῦ, ἔρχονται πρὸς αὐτὸν οἱ ἀρχιερεῖς ἢ οἱ γραμματεῖς ἢ οἱ πρεσβύτεροι.

Καὶ λέγει αὐτοῖς·

28 Τί δὲ ὑμῖν δοκεῖ; Ἄνθρωπος εἶχε τέκνα δύο, ἢ προσελθὼν τῷ πρώτῳ, εἶπε· Τέκνον ὕπαγε, σήμερον ἐργάζυ ἐν τῷ ἀμπελῶνί μυ.

29 Ὁ δὲ ἀποκριθεὶς, εἶπεν. Οὐ θέλω. ὕστερον δὲ μεταμεληθεὶς, ἀπῆλθε.

30 Καὶ προσελθὼν τῷ δευτέρῳ, εἶπεν ὡσαύτως. Ὁ δὲ ἀποκριθεὶς, εἶπεν· Ἐγὼ κύριε· ἢ ἐκ ἀπῆλθε.

31 Τίς ἐκ τῶν δύο ἐποίησε τὸ θέλημα τῦ πατρός; Λέγυσιν αὐτῷ· Ὁ πρῶτος. Λέγει αὐτοῖς ὁ Ἰησῦς· Ἀμὴν λέγω ὑμῖν, ὅτι οἱ τελῶναι ἢ αἱ πόρναι προάγυσιν ὑμᾶς εἰς τὴν βασιλείαν τῦ Θεῦ.

---

21 Hi ergo accesserunt Philippo illi à Bethsaida Galilææ : & rogabant eum, dicentes : Domine, volumus Jesum videre.

22 Venit Philippus, & dicit Andreæ : & rursum Andreas & Philippus dicunt Jesu.

23 At Jesus respondit eis, dicens : Venit hora ut glorificetur filius hominis.

24 Amen, amen, dico vobis, si non granum frumenti cadens in terram mortuum fuerit, ipsum solum manet : si autem mortuum fuerit, multum fructum affert.

17 Et relinquens ipsos, abiit extra civitatem in Bethaniam, & diversatus est ibi.

12 Et posterâ die exeuntibus illis de Bethania,

ingressus Jesus in templum, cœpit ejicere vendentes & ementes in templo : & mensas nummulariorum, & cathedras vendentium columbas evertit.

16 Et non sinebat ut quisquam transferret vas per templum.

17 Et docebat, dicens eis : Nonne scriptum est, Quia domus mea, domus orationis vocatur omnibus gentibus ? vos autem fecistis eam speluncam latronum.

18 Et audierunt Scribæ, & principes Sacerdotum, & quærebant quomodo eum perderent : timebant enim eum, quia omnis turba admirabatur super doctrina ejus.

19 Et quum vespera facta esset, egrediebatur ex civitate.

27 Et veniunt rursus in Hierosolymam : Et in templo deambulante ipso, accedunt ad eum summi sacerdotes, & Scribæ, & seniores.

Et dicit eis :

28 Quid autem vobis videtur ? Homo quidam habebat natos duos : & accedens primo, dixit : Fili, vade, hodie operare in vinea mea.

29 Ille autem respondens, ait : Nolo. Postea autem pœnitentiâ affectus, abiit.

30 Et accedens alteri, dixit similiter. Ille verò respondens, ait : Ego Domine, & non abiit.

31 Quis ex duobus fecit voluntatem patris ? Dicunt ei : Primus. Dicit illis Jesus : Amen dico vobis, quod publicani & meretrices præeunt vobis in regnum Dei.

24. Et il dit à ceux qui étoient présens : Otez-lui le marc, et le donnez à celui qui a les dix marcs.

25. Et ils lui dirent : Seigneur, il a déjà dix marcs.

26. Aussi vous dis-je, qu'on donnera à quiconque a déjà ; et que pour celui qui n'a pas, cela même qu'il a lui sera ôté.

27. Quant à mes ennemis, qui n'ont pas voulu que je regnasse sur eux, amenez-les ici, et faites-les mourir en ma présence.

28. Et après avoir dit cela, il marchoit devant eux, montant à Jérusalem.

---

24 And he said unto them that stood by, Take from him the pound, and give *it* to him that hath ten pounds.

25 (And they said unto him, Lord, he hath ten pounds.)

26 For I say unto you, That unto every one which hath, shall be given ; and from him that hath not, even that he hath, shall be taken away from him.

27 But those mine enemies, which would not that I should reign over them, bring hither, and slay *them* before me.

28 And when he had thus spoken, he went before, ascending up to Jerusalem.

CHAPITRE XXI.

Jésus-Christ entre dans Jérusalem, chasse les marchands du Temple, et répond aux Pharisiens.

COMME ils approchoient de Jérusalem, et qu'ils étoient déjà à Bethphagé, près du mont des Oliviers, Jésus envoya deux Disciples ;

2. Leur disant : Allez à la bourgade qui est devant vous ; vous y trouverez d'abord une ânesse attachée, et *son* ânon avec elle ; détachez-les et amenez-les-moi.

3. Et si quelqu'un vous dit quelque chose, vous direz que le Seigneur en a besoin ; et aussitôt il les envoiera.

6. Les Disciples s'en allèrent donc, et firent comme Jésus leur avoit ordonné.

7. Et ils amenèrent l'ânesse et l'ânon, et ayant mis leurs vêtemens dessus, ils l'y firent asseoir.

8. Alors des gens en grand nombre étendoient leurs vêtemens par le chemin ; et d'autres coupoient des branches d'arbres, et les étendoient par le chemin.

10. Et quand il fut entré dans Jérusalem, toute la ville fut émue, et on disoit : Qui est celui-ci ?

19. De sorte que les Pharisiens disoient entr'eux : Vous voyez que vous ne gagnez rien ; voilà que tout le monde va après lui.

20. Or quelques Grecs, de ceux qui étoient montés pour adorer pendant la fête,

---

AND when they drew nigh unto Jerusalem, and were come to Bethphage, unto the mount of Olives, then sent Jesus two disciples,

2 Saying unto them, Go into the village over against you, and straightway ye shall find an ass tied, and a colt with her : loose *them*, and bring *them* unto me.

3 And if any *man* say aught unto you, ye shall say, The Lord hath need of them ; and straightway he will send them.

6 And the disciples went, and did as Jesus commanded them,

7 And brought the ass, and the colt, and put on them their clothes, and they set *him* thereon.

8 And a very great multitude spread their garments in the way ; others cut down branches from the trees, and strawed them in the way.

10 And when he was come into Jerusalem, all the city was moved, saying, Who is this ?

19 The Pharisees, therefore, said among themselves, Perceive ye how ye prevail nothing ? behold, the world is gone after him.

20 And there were certain Greeks among them, that came up to worship at the feast :

56

21 Οὗτοι ἦν προσῆλθον Φιλίππῳ τῷ ἀπὸ Βηθσαϊδὰ τῆς Γαλιλαίας, κỳ ἠρώτων αὐτὸν, λέγοντες· Κύριε, θέλομεν τὸν Ἰησῦν ἰδεῖν.

22 Ἔρχεται Φίλιππ⸱ κỳ λέγει τῷ Ἀνδρέᾳ· κỳ πάλιν Ἀνδρέας κỳ Φίλιππ⸱ λέγεσι τῷ Ἰησῦ.

23 Ὁ δὲ Ἰησῦς, ἀπεκρίνατο αὐτοῖς, λέγων· Ἐλήλυθεν ἡ ὥρα ἵνα δοξασθῇ ὁ υἱὸς τῦ ἀνθρώπε.

24 Ἀμὴν, ἀμὴν, λέγω ὑμῖν, ἐὰν μὴ ὁ κόκκ⸱ τῦ σίτε πεσὼν εἰς τὴν γῆν ἀποθάνῃ, αὐτὸς μόν⸱ μένει· ἐὰν δὲ ἀποθάνῃ, πολὺν καρπὸν φέρει.

17 Καὶ καταλιπὼν αὐτὸς, ἐξῆλθεν ἔξω τῆς πόλεως εἰς Βηθανίαν· κỳ ηὐλίσθη ἐκεῖ.

12 Καὶ τῇ ἐπαύριον ἐξελθόντων αὐτῶν ἀπὸ Βηθανίας,

εἰσελθὼν ὁ Ἰησῦς εἰς τὸ ἱερὸν, ἤρξατο ἐκβάλλειν τὰς πωλῦντας κỳ ἀγοράζοντας ἐν τῷ ἱερῷ· κỳ τὰς τραπέζας τῶν κολλυβιστῶν, κỳ τὰς καθέδρας τῶν πωλύντων τὰς περιστερὰς κατέστρεψε.

16 Καὶ ἐκ ἤφιεν ἵνα τις διενέγκῃ σκεῦ⸱ διὰ τῦ ἱερῦ.

17 Καὶ ἐδίδασκε, λέγων αὐτοῖς· Οὐ γέγραπται· Ὅτι ὁ οἶκός μυ, οἶκ⸱ προσευχῆς κληθήσεται πᾶσι τοῖς ἔθνεσιν; ὑμεῖς δὲ ἐποιήσατε αὐτὸν σπήλαιον λῃστῶν.

18 Καὶ ἤκυσαν οἱ γραμματεῖς κỳ οἱ ἀρχιερεῖς, κỳ ἐζήτυν πῶς αὐτὸν ἀπολέσυσιν· ἐφοβῦντο γὰρ αὐτὸν, ὅτι πᾶς ὁ ὄχλ⸱ ἐξεπλήσσετο ἐπὶ τῇ διδαχῇ αὐτῦ.

19 Καὶ ὅτε ὀψὲ ἐγένετο, ἐξεπορεύετο ἔξω τῆς πόλεως.

27 Καὶ ἔρχονται πάλιν εἰς Ἱεροσόλυμα· κỳ ἐν τῷ ἱερῷ περιπατῦντ⸱ αὐτῦ, ἔρχονται πρὸς αὐτὸν οἱ ἀρχιερεῖς κỳ οἱ γραμματεῖς κỳ οἱ πρεσβύτεροι.

Καὶ λέγει αὐτοῖς·

28 Τί δὲ ὑμῖν δοκεῖ; Ἄνθρωπ⸱ εἶχε τέκνα δύο, κỳ προσελθὼν τῷ πρώτῳ, εἶπε· Τέκνον ὕπαγε, σήμερον ἐργάζυ ἐν τῷ ἀμπελῶνί μυ.

29 Ὁ δὲ ἀποκριθεὶς, εἶπεν· Οὐ θέλω. ὕστερον δὲ μεταμεληθεὶς, ἀπῆλθε.

30 Καὶ προσελθὼν τῷ δευτέρῳ, εἶπεν ὡσαύτως. Ὁ δὲ ἀποκριθεὶς, εἶπεν· Ἐγὼ κύριε· κỳ ἐκ ἀπῆλθε.

31 Τίς ἐκ τῶν δύο ἐποίησε τὸ θέλημα τῦ πατρός; Λέγυσιν αὐτῷ· Ὁ πρῶτ⸱. Λέγει αὐτοῖς ὁ Ἰησῦς· Ἀμὴν λέγω ὑμῖν, ὅτι οἱ τελῶναι κỳ αἱ πόρναι προάγυσιν ὑμᾶς εἰς τὴν βασιλείαν τῦ Θεῦ.

21 Hi ergo accesserunt Philippo illi à Bethsaidà Galilææ : & rogabant eum, dicentes : Domine, volumus Jesum videre.

22 Venit Philippus, & dicit Andreæ : & rursum Andreas & Philippus dicunt Jesu.

23 At Jesus respondit eis, dicens : Venit hora ut glorificetur filius hominis.

24 Amen, amen, dico vobis, si non granum frumenti cadens in terram mortuum fuerit, ipsum solum manet : si autem mortuum fuerit, multum fructum affert.

17 Et relinquens ipsos, abiit extra civitatem in Bethaniam, & diversatus est ibi.

12 Et posterà die exeuntibus illis de Bethania,

ingressus Jesus in templum, cœpit ejicere vendentes & ementes in templo : & mensas nummulariorum, & cathedras vendentium columbas evertit.

16 Et non sinebat ut quisquam transferret vas per templum.

17 Et docebat, dicens eis : Nonne scriptum est, Quia domus mea, domus orationis vocatur omnibus gentibus ? vos autem fecistis eam speluncam latronum.

18 Et audierunt Scribæ, & principes Sacerdotum, & quærebant quomodo eum perderent : timebant enim eum, quia omnis turba admirabatur super doctrina ejus.

19 Et quum vespera facta esset, egrediebatur ex civitate.

27 Et veniunt rursus in Hierosolymam : Et in templo deambulante ipso, accedunt ad eum summi sacerdotes, & Scribæ, & seniores.

Et dicit eis :

28 Quid autem vobis videtur ? Homo quidam habebat natos duos : & accedens primo, dixit : Fili, vade, hodie operare in vinea mea.

29 Ille autem respondens, ait : Nolo. Postea autem pœnitentiâ affectus, abiit.

30 Et accedens alteri, dixit similiter. Ille verò respondens, ait : Ego Domine, & non abiit.

31 Quis ex duobus fecit voluntatem patris ? Dicunt ei : Primus. Dicit illis Jesus : Amen dico vobis, quod publicani & meretrices præeunt vobis in regnum Dei.

21. Vinrent vers Philippe, qui étoit de Bethsaïde en Galilée, et ils lui dirent en le priant : Seigneur, nous voudrions bien voir Jésus.

22. Philippe vint et le dit à André, et André et Philippe le dirent à Jésus.

23. Et Jésus leur répondit : L'heure est venue que le Fils de l'homme doit être glorifié.

24. En vérité, en vérité je vous le dis : Si le grain de froment ne meurt après qu'on l'a jeté dans la terre, il demeure seul ; mais s'il meurt, il porte beaucoup de fruit.

17. Et les ayant laissés, il sortit de la ville, et s'en alla à Béthanie, où il passa la nuit.

12. Le lendemain, comme ils sortoient de Béthanie.

Jésus étant entré dans le Temple, se mit à chasser ceux qui vendoient et qui achetoient dans le Temple, et il renversa les tables des changeurs, et les siéges de ceux qui vendoient des pigeons.

16. Et il ne permettoit pas que personne portât *aucun* vaisseau par le Temple.

17. Et il les instruisoit, en leur disant : N'est-il pas écrit : Ma maison sera appelée, par toutes les nations, une maison de prière ; mais vous en avez fait une caverne de voleurs ?

18. Ce que les Scribes et les principaux Sacrificateurs ayant entendu, ils cherchoient les moyens de le faire périr ; car ils le craignoient, parce que tout le peuple étoit ravi de sa doctrine.

19. Le soir étant venu, Jésus sortit de la ville.

27. Puis ils revinrent à Jérusalem ; et comme il alloit par le Temple, les principaux Sacrificateurs, les Scribes, et les Sénateurs, s'approchèrent de lui ;

Et il leur dit

28. Mais que vous semble-t-il de ceci ? Un homme avoit deux fils ; et s'adressant au premier, il *lui* dit : *Mon* fils, va, et travaille aujourd'hui dans ma vigne.

29. Mais il répondit : Je n'y veux point *aller* ; cependant s'étant repenti ensuite, il y alla.

30. Puis il vint à l'autre, et lui dit la même chose. Celui-ci répondit : J'y *vais*, Seigneur ; mais il n'y alla pas.

31. Lequel des deux fit la volonté de *son* père ? Ils lui dirent : C'est le premier. Jésus leur dit : Je vous dis en vérité, que les péagers et les femmes de mauvaise vie, vous dévancent au Royaume de Dieu.

---

21 The same came, therefore, to Philip, which was of Bethsaida of Galilee, and desired him, saying, Sir, we would see Jesus.

22 Philip cometh and telleth Andrew ; and again, Andrew and Philip tell Jesus.

23 And Jesus answered them, saying,

24 Verily, verily, I say unto you, Except a corn of wheat fall into the ground and die, it abideth alone : but if it die, it bringeth forth much fruit.

17 And he left them, and went out of the city into Bethany ; and he lodged there.

12 And on the morrow, when they were come from Bethany,

15. Jesus went into the temple, and began to cast out them that sold and bought in the temple, and overthrew the tables of the money-changers, and the seats of them that sold doves ;

16 And would not suffer any man should carry *any* v through the temple.

17 And he taught, saying them, Is it not written, My l shall be called of all nation house of prayer ? but ye made it a den of thieves.

18 And the scribes and priests heard *it*, and sough they might destroy him : fo feared him, because all the p was astonished at his doctri

19 And when even was he went out of the city. +27.

28 But what think ye ? A *certain* man had two sons ; and he came to the first, and said, Son, go work to-day in my vineyard.

29 He answered and said, I will not : but afterward he repented, and went.

30 And he came to the second, and said likewise. And he answered and said, I *go*, sir : and went not.

31 Whether of them twain did the will of *his* father ? They say unto him, The first. Jesus saith unto them, Verily I say unto you, That the publicans and the harlots go into the kingdom of God before you.

57

* 4 Πάλιν ἀπέϛειλεν ἄλλυς δύλυς, λέγων· Εἴπαle τοῖς κεκλημένοις· Ἰδοὺ, τὸ ‡ ἄριϛόν μυ ‡ ἡτοίμασα, οἱ ‡ ταῦροί μυ ἢ τὰ ‡ σιτιϛὰ ‡ τεθυμένα, ἢ πάνla ‡ ἕτοιμα· ‡ δεῦτε εἰς τοὺς ‡ γάμυς.

* 5 Οἱ δὲ ‡ ἀμελήσανles, ἀπῆλθον ὁ μὲν εἰς τὸν ἴδιον ἀγρὸν, ὁ δὲ εἰς τὴν †ἐμποςίαν αὐτῦ.

6 Οἱ δὲ λοιποὶ, κρατήσανles τοὺς δύλυς αὐτῦ, ὕβρισαν ἢ ἀπέκτειναν.

* 7 Ἀκύσας δὲ ὁ βασιλεὺς ὠργίϛθη· ἢ πέμψας τὰ ϛραleύμαla αὐτῦ, ἀπώλεσε τοὺς φονεῖς ἐκείνυς, ἢ τὴν ‡ πόλιν αὐτῶν † ἐνέπρησε.

8 Τότε λέγει τοῖς δύλοις αὐτῦ· Ὁ μὲν γάμ☉ ἕτοιμός ἐϛιν, οἱ δὲ κεκλημένοι ὐκ ἦσαν ἄξιοι.

* 9 ‡ Πορεύεϛθε ‡ ὖν ἐπὶ τὰς † διεξόδυς τῶν ὁδῶν, ἢ ὅσυς ἂν εὕρηle, καλέσαle εἰς τοὺς γάμυς.

10 Καὶ ἐξελθόνles οἱ δῦλοι ἐκεῖνοι εἰς τὰς ὁδοὺς, συνήγαγον πάνlας ὅσυς εὗρον, πονηρύς τε ἢ ἀγαθύς· ἢ ἐπλήσθη ὁ γάμ☉ ἀνακειμένων.

11 Εἰσελθὼν δὲ ὁ βασιλεὺς θεάσασθαι τοὺς ἀνακειμένυς εἶδεν ἐκεῖ ἄνθρωπον ὀυκ ἐνδεδυμένον ἔνδυμα γάμυ.

12 Καὶ λέγει αὐτῷ· Ἑταῖρε, πῶς εἰσῆλθες ὧδε μὴ ἔχων ἔνδυμα γάμυ; Ὁ δὲ ἐφιμώθη.

13 Τότε εἶπεν ὁ βασιλεὺς τοῖς διακόνοις· Δήσανles αὐτῦ πόδας ἢ χεῖρας, ἄραle αὐτὸν, ἢ ἐκβάλεle εἰς τὸ σκότ☉ τὸ ἐξώτερον· ἐκεῖ ἔϛαι ὁ κλαυθμὸς ἢ ὁ βρυγμὸς τῶν ὀδόντων.

14 Πολλοὶ γάρ εἰσι κλητοὶ, ὀλίγοι δὲ ἐκλεκτοί.

* 15 Τότε πορευθένles οἱ Φαρισαῖοι, ‡ συμβύλιον ἔλαβον ὅπως αὐτὸν † παγιδεύσωσιν ἐν λόγῳ.

16 Καὶ ἀποϛέλλυσιν αὐτῷ τοὺς μαθητὰς αὐτῶν μεlὰ τῶν Ἡρωδιανῶν, λέγονles· Διδάσκαλε, οἴδαμεν ὅτι ἀληθὴς εἶ, ἢ τὴν ὁδὸν τῦ Θεῦ ἐν ἀληθείᾳ διδάσκεις, ἢ ὐ μέλει σοι περὶ ὐδενὸς· ὐ γὰρ βλέπεις εἰς πρόσωπον ἀνθρώπων.

17 Εἰπὲ ὖν ἡμῖν, τί σοι δοκεῖ; ἔξεϛι δῦναι κῆνσον Καίσαρι, ἢ ὔ;

18 Γνοὺς δὲ ὁ Ἰησῦς τὴν πονη-

---

4 Iterum mifit alios fervos, dicens: Dicite vocatis: Ecce prandium meum paravi, tauri mei & altilia occifa, & omnia expedita: venite ad nuptias.

5 Illi autem negligentes abierunt: ille quidem in proprium agrum, ille verò ad mercaturam fuam.

6 At reliqui prehendentes fervos ejus, contumeliis affecerunt, & occiderunt.

7 Audiens autem rex ille, iratus eft: & mittens exercitus fuos, perdidit homicidas illos, & civitatem illorum incendit.

8 Tunc ait fervis fuis: Quidem nuptiæ expeditæ funt: qui autem vocati non fuerunt digni.

9 Iter ergo ad compita viarum, & quæcumque inveneritis, vocate ad nuptias.

10 Et egreffi fervi illi in vias congregaverunt omnes quos invenerunt, malofque & bonos: & impletæ funt nuptiæ difcumbentium.

11 Ingreffus autem rex fpectare difcumbentes, vidit ibi hominem non veftitum indumentum nuptiarum.

12 Et ait illi: Amice, quomodo intrafti huc, non habens veftem nuptialem? Ille verò ore occlufus eft.

13 Tunc dixit rex miniftris: Ligantes ejus pedes & manus, tollite eum, & ejicite in tenebras exteriores: ibi erit fletus & fremitus dentium.

14 Multi enim funt vocati, pauci verò electi.

15 Tunc abeuntes Pharifæi, confilium fumpferunt ut eum illaquearent in fermone.

16 Et mittunt ei difcipulos fuos cum Herodianis, dicentes: Magifter, fcimus quia verax es, & viam Dei in veritate doces: & non eft cura tibi de aliquo: non enim refpicis in faciem hominum.

17 Dic ergo nobis, quid tibi videtur? Licet dare cenfum Cæfari, an non?

18 Cognofcens autem Jefus

for the Fr. and Eng. text see pa. 58. c. d.

Un homme, *dit-il*, planta une vigne, il l'environna d'une haie, il y fit un creux pour un pressoir, il y bâtit une tour, et il la loua à des vignerons, et s'en alla.

2. Et dans la saison, il envoya un de ses serviteurs vers les vignerons, afin de recevoir d'eux du fruit de la vigne.

3. Mais l'ayant pris, ils le battirent, et le renvoyèrent à vuide.

4. Il leur envoya encore un autre serviteur; mais ils lui jetèrent des pierres, et lui meurtrirent toute la tête, et le renvoyèrent, après l'avoir traité outrageusement.

5. Et il en envoya encore un autre qu'ils tuèrent; et plusieurs autres, dont ils battirent les uns, et tuèrent les autres.

6. Enfin, ayant un fils qu'il chérissoit, il le leur envoya encore le dernier, disant, ils auront du respect pour mon fils.

7. Mais ces vignerons dirent entr'eux: C'est ici l'héritier; venez, tuons-le, et l'héritage sera à nous.

8. Et *le* prenant, ils le tuèrent, et le jetèrent hors de la vigne.

9. Que fera donc le maître de la vigne? Il viendra, et fera périr ces vignerons, et il donnera la vigne à d'autres.

10. Et quand les principaux Sacrificateurs et les Pharisiens eurent entendu ces similitudes, ils reconnurent qu'il parloit d'eux.

46. Et ils cherchoient à se saisir de lui; mais ils craignirent le peuple, parce qu'il regardoit *Jésus* comme un Prophète.

Jésus, prenant la parole, continua à leur parler en paraboles, et leur dit:

2. Le Royaume des cieux est semblable à un Roi, qui fit les noces de son Fils.

3. Et il envoya ses serviteurs pour appeler ceux qui avoient été invités aux noces; mais ils n'y voulurent point venir.

A *certain* M̃. 21 M̃. 12

man planted a vineyard, and set an hedge about *it*, and digged *a place for* the wine-fat, and built a tower, and let it out to husbandmen, and went into a far country.

2 And at the season he sent to the husbandmen a servant, that he might receive from the husbandmen of the fruit of the vineyard.

3 And they caught *him*, and beat him, and sent *him* away empty.

4 And again he sent unto them another servant; and at him they cast stones, and wounded *him* in the head, and sent *him* away shamefully handled.

5 And again he sent another; and him they killed, and many others; beating some, and killing some.

6 Having yet, therefore, one son, his well-beloved, he sent him also last unto them, saying, They will reverence my son.

7 But those husbandmen said among themselves, This is the heir; come, let us kill him, and the inheritance shall be ours.

8 And they took him, and killed *him*, and cast *him* out of the vineyard.

9 What shall, therefore, the lord of the vineyard do? he will come and destroy the husbandmen, and will give the vineyard unto others.

45 And when the chief priests and Pharisees had heard his parables, they perceived that he spake of them. M̃. 21

46 But when they sought to lay hands on him, they feared the multitude, because they took him for a prophet.

AND Jesus answered, and spake unto them again by parables, and said, M̃. 22

2 The kingdom of heaven is like unto a certain king, which made a marriage for his son,

3 And sent forth his servants to call them that were bidden to the wedding; and they would not come

for the Gr. & Lat. text see next page. col. a. b.

33 Ἄλλην παραβολὴν ἀκούσα΄ε.

Ἄμπε-
λῶνα ἐφύτευσεν ἄνθρωπ۟۟, ὶ πε-
ειέθηκε ‡ φραγμὸν, ὶ ὤρυξεν
† ὑπολήνιον, ὶ ‡ ᾠκοδόμησε
‡ πύργον, ὶ ‡ ἐξέδοτο αὐτὸν ‡
γεωργοῖς· ὶ ἀπεδήμησε.

2 Καὶ ἀπέςειλε πρὸς τὰς
γεωργὰς τῷ καιρῷ δῦλον, ἵνα
παρὰ τῶν γεωργῶν λάβη ἀπὸ τῦ
καρπῦ τῦ ἀμπελῶν۟.

3 Οἱ δὲ, λαβόντες αὐτὸν, ἔ-
δειραν, ὶ ἀπέςειλαν κενόν.

4 Καὶ πάλιν ἀπέςειλε πρὸς
αὐτὰς ἄλλον δῦλον· ‡ κἀκεῖνον
λιθοβολήσαντες † ἐκεφαλαίωσαν,
ὶ ἀπέςειλαν † ἠτιμωμένον.

5 Καὶ πάλιν ἄλλον ἀπέςειλε·
κἀκεῖνον ἀπέκλειναν· ὶ πολλὰς
ἄλλας, τὰς μὲν δέροντες, τὰς δὲ
ἀποκλείνοντες.

6 Ἔτι ἓν ἕνα υἱὸν ἔχων ἀγα-
πητὸν αὐτῦ, ἀπέςειλε ὶ αὐτὸν
πρὸς αὐτὰς ἔσχαιον, λέγων· Ὅτι
ἐνξέαπήσονται τὸν υἱόν μα.

7 Ἐκεῖνοι δὲ οἱ γεωργοὶ εἶπον
πρὸς ἑαυτάς· Ὅτι ἕτός ἐςιν ὁ
κληρονόμ۟· δεῦτε, ἀποκλείνω-
μεν αὐτὸν, ὶ ἡμῶν ἔςαι ἡ κλη-
ρονομία.

8 Καὶ λαβόντες αὐτὸν, ἀπ-
έκλειναν, ὶ ἐξέβαλον ἔξω τῦ ἀμ-
πελῶν۟.

9 Τί ἂν ποιήσει ὁ κύρι۟ τῦ
ἀμπελῶν۟; Ἐλεύσεται ὶ ἀπολέσει τὰς γεωργὰς, ὶ δώσει τὸν
ἀμπελῶνα ἄλλοις.

45 Καὶ ἀκούσαντες οἱ ἀρχιερεῖς
ὶ οἱ Φαρισαῖοι τὰς παραβολὰς
αὐτῦ, ἔγνωσαν ὅτι περὶ αὐτῶν
λέγει.

46 Καὶ ζητῦντες αὐτὸν κρατῆ-
σαι, ἐφοβήθησαν τὰς ὄχλας, ἐ-
πειδὴ ὡς προφήτην αὐτὸν εἶχον.
24. † 2.

Κεφ. κβ΄ 22.

1 Καὶ ἀποκριθεὶς ὁ Ἰησῦς, πάλιν εἶπεν αὐτοῖς ἐν παραβολαῖς, λέγων·

2 Ὡμοιώθη ἡ βασιλεία τῶν ὀ-
ρανῶν ἀνθρώπῳ βασιλεῖ, ὅςις ἐ-
ποίησε γάμας τῷ υἱῷ αὐτῦ·

3 Καὶ ἀπέςειλε τὰς δύλας αὐτῦ καλέσαι τὰς κεκλημένας εἰς
τὰς γάμας· ὶ οὐκ ἤθελον ἐλθεῖν.

---

33 Aliam parabolam audite.
Vineam plan-
tavit homo, & circumposuit
sepem, & fodit lacum, & ædificavit turrim, & elocavit eam
agricolis, & peregre profectus
est.

2 Et misit ad agricolas tempore servum, ut ab agricolis
acciperet de fructu vineæ.

3 Illi autem sumentes eum
ceciderunt, & dimiserunt va-
cuum.

4 Et iterum misit ad illos
alium servum : & illum lapi-
dantes in capite vulneraverunt,
& ablegaverunt inhonoratum.

5 Et rursum alium misit : &
illum occiderunt, & plures alios,
hos quidem cædentes, hos verò
occidentes.

6 Adhuc ergo unum filium
habens dilectum suum, misit
& illum ad eos novissimum, dicens : Quia reverebuntur filium
meum.

7 Illi verò agricolæ dixerunt
apud seipsos : Quod hic est hæ-
res : venite occidamus eum, &
nostra erit hæreditas.

8 Et apprehendentes eum,
occiderunt, & ejecerunt extra
vineam.

9 Quid ergo faciet dominus
vineæ? Veniet, & perdet co-
lonos, & dabit vineam aliis.

45 Et audientes principes Sacerdotum & Pharisæi parabolas
ejus, cognoverunt quod de ipsis
diceret.

46 Et quærentes eum pre-
hendere, timuerunt turbas quoniam sicut Prophetam eum habebant.

CAPUT XXII.

1 ET respondens Jesus, iterum dixit eis in parabo-
lis, dicens :

2 Simile factum est regnum
cælorum homini regi, qui fecit
nuptias filio suo :

3 Et misit servos suos vocare
vocatos ad nuptias : & nolebant
venire.

for the Fr. & Eng. text see preceding pag. c.d.

4. Il envoya encore d'autres serviteurs, avec cet ordre : Dites à
ceux qui ont été invités : J'ai *fait*
préparer mon dîner ; mes taureaux
et mes bêtes grasses sont tuées, et
tout est prêt ; venez aux noces.

5. Mais eux n'en tenant compte,
s'en allèrent, l'un à sa métairie,
et l'autre à son trafic.

6. Et les autres prirent ses serviteurs, et les outragèrent, et les
tuèrent.

7. Le Roi l'ayant appris, se mit
en colère, et y ayant envoyé ses
troupes, il fit périr ces meurtriers,
et brûla leur ville.

8. Alors il dit à ses serviteurs :
Le festin des noces est prêt, mais
ceux qui étoient invités n'en étoient
pas dignes.

9. Allez donc dans les carrefours
des chemins, et invitez aux noces
tous ceux que vous trouverez.

10. Et ses serviteurs étant allés
dans les chemins, assemblèrent
tous ceux qu'ils trouvèrent, tant
mauvais que bons, en sorte que la
salle des noces fut remplie de gens
qui étoient à table.

11. Et le Roi étant entré pour
voir ceux qui étoient à table,
aperçut un homme qui n'avoit pas
un habit de noces.

12. Et il lui dit : Mon ami,
comment es-tu entré ici sans avoir
un habit de noces ? Et il eut la
bouche fermée.

13. Alors le Roi dit aux serviteurs : Liez-le pieds et mains, em-
portez-le, et le jetez dans les ténèbres de dehors ; c'est là qu'il y
aura des pleurs et des grincemens
de dents.

14. Car il y en a beaucoup d'appelés, mais peu d'élus.

15. Alors les Pharisiens s'étant
retirés, consultèrent pour le sur-
prendre dans ses discours.

16. Et ils lui envoyèrent de leurs
disciples, avec des Hérodiens, qui
lui dirent : Maître, nous savons
que tu es sincère, et que tu en-
seignes la voie de Dieu selon la
vérité, sans avoir égard à qui que
ce soit ; car tu ne regardes point
l'apparence des hommes.

17. Dis-nous donc ce qui te
semble *de ceci :* Est-il permis de
payer le tribut à César, ou non ?

18. Mais Jésus connoissant leur

4 Again, he sent forth other servants, saying, Tell them which are
bidden, Behold, I have prepared
my dinner: my oxen and *my* fat-
lings *are* killed, and all things *are*
ready: come unto the marriage.

5 But they made light of *it*, and
went their ways, one to his farm,
another to his merchandise:

6 And the remnant took his servants, and intreated *them* spiteful-
ly, and slew *them*.

7 But when the king heard *thereof*, he was wroth: and he sent forth
his armies, and destroyed those
murderers, and burnt up their
city.

8 Then saith he to his servants,
The wedding is ready, but they
which were bidden were not worthy.

9 Go ye therefore into the highways, and, as many as ye shall
find, bid to the marriage.

10 So those servants went out
into the highways, and gathered
together all as many as they found,
both bad and good: and the wedding was furnished with guests.

11 And when the king came in
to see the guests, he saw there a
man which had not on a wedding
garment:

12 And he saith unto him,
Friend, how camest thou in hither, not having a wedding garment? And he was speechless.

13 Then saith the king to the
servants, Bind him hand and foot,
and take him away; and cast *him*
into outer darkness; there shall
be weeping and gnashing of teeth.

14 For many are called, but few
are chosen.

15 Then went the Pharisees, and
took counsel how they might en-
tangle him in *his* talk.

16 And they sent out unto him
their disciples, with the Hero-
dians, saying, Master, we know
that thou art true, and teachest
the way of God in truth, neither
carest thou for any *man*: for thou
regardest not the person of men.

17 Tell us, therefore, What thinkest thou? Is it lawful to give tri-
bute unto Cesar, or not?

18 But Jesus perceived their

*for the Gr. & Lat. text see
pa. 57. col. a. b.*

ξίαν αὐτῶν, εἶπε· Τί με πειράζετε ὑποκριταί;

nequitiam eorum, ait: Quid me tentatis hypocritæ?

* 19 ‡ Ἐπιδείξετέ μοι τὸ † νόμισμα τῦ ‡ κήνσυ· Οἱ δὲ προσήνεγκαν αὐτῷ δηνάριον.

19 Ostendite mihi numisma census. Illi verò obtulerunt ei denarium.

* 20 Καὶ λέγει αὐτοῖς· Τίνος ἡ εἰκὼν αὕτη καὶ ἡ ‡ ἐπιγραφή;

20 Et ait illis: Cujus imago hæc, & superscriptio?

21 Λέγυσιν αὐτῷ· Καίσαρος. Τότε λέγει αὐτοῖς· Ἀπόδοτε ὖν τὰ Καίσαρος, Καίσαρι· καὶ τὰ τῦ Θεῦ, τῷ Θεῷ.

21 Dicunt ei: Cæsaris. Tunc ait illis: Reddite ergò quæ Cæsaris, Cæsari: & quæ Dei, Deo.

22 Καὶ ἀκύσαντες ἐθαύμασαν· καὶ ἀφέντες αὐτὸν ἀπῆλθον.

22 Et audientes mirati sunt: & relinquentes eum abierunt.

23 Ἐν ἐκείνῃ τῇ ἡμέρα προσῆλθον αὐτῷ Σαδδυκαῖοι, οἱ λέγοντες μὴ εἶναι ἀνάςασιν· καὶ ἐπηρώτησαν αὐτὸν,

23 In illo die accesserunt ad eum Sadducæi, dicentes non esse resurrectionem: & interrogaverunt eum,

* 24 Λέγοντες· Διδάσκαλε, Μωσῆς εἶπεν· Ἐάν τις ἀποθάνῃ μὴ ἔχων τέκνα, † ἐπιγαμβρεύσει ὁ ‡ ἀδελφὸς αὐτῦ τὴν γυναῖκα αὐτῦ, καὶ ἀναςήσει σπέρμα τῷ ἀδελφῷ αὐτῦ.

24 Dicentes: Magister, Moses dixit: Si quis mortuus fuerit non habens genitos, ob affinitatem ducet frater ejus uxorem illius, & suscitabit semen fratri suo.

25 Ἦσαν δὲ παρ' ἡμῖν ἑπτὰ ἀδελφοί· καὶ ὁ πρῶτος, γαμήσας, ἐτελεύτησε· καὶ μὴ ἔχων σπέρμα, ἀφῆκε τὴν γυναῖκα αὐτῦ τῷ ἀδελφῷ αὐτῦ.

25 Erant autem apud nos septem fratres: & primus uxore ductâ, obiit: & non habens semen, reliquit uxorem suam fratri suo.

26 Ὁμοίως καὶ ὁ δεύτερος, καὶ ὁ τρίτος, ἕως τῶν ἑπτά.

26 Similiter & secundus, & tertius usque ad septem.

27 Ὕςερον δὲ πάντων ἀπέθανε καὶ ἡ γυνή.

27 Postremum autem omnium defuncta est & mulier.

28 Ἐν τῇ ὖν ἀναςάσει, τίνος τῶν ἑπτὰ ἔςαι γυνή; πάντες γὰρ ἔσχον αὐτήν.

28 In ergò resurrectione, cujus septem erit uxor? omnes enim habuerunt eam.

29 Ἀποκριθεὶς δὲ ὁ Ἰησῦς εἶπεν αὐτοῖς· Πλανᾶσθε, μὴ εἰδότες τὰς γραφάς, μηδὲ τὴν δύναμιν τῦ Θεῦ.

29 Respondens autem Jesus, ait illis: Erratis, nescientes Scripturas, neque efficaciam Dei.

30 Ἐν γὰρ τῇ ἀναςάσει ὔτε γαμῦσιν, ὔτε ἐκγαμίζονται, ἀλλ' ὡς ἄγγελοι τῦ Θεῦ ἐν ὀρανῷ εἰσι.

30 In enim resurrectione neque nubent, neque dantur nuptui, sed sicut angeli Dei in cælo sunt.

31 Περὶ δὲ τῆς ἀναςάσεως τῶν νεκρῶν ὀκ ἀνέγνωτε τὸ ῥηθὲν ὑμῖν ὑπὸ τῦ Θεῦ, λέγοντος·

31 De autem resurrectione mortuorum, non legistis effatum vobis à Deo, dicente:

32 Ἐγώ εἰμι ὁ Θεὸς Ἀβραάμ, καὶ ὁ Θεὸς Ἰσαάκ, καὶ ὁ Θεὸς Ἰακώβ; ὀκ ἔςιν ὁ Θεὸς, Θεὸς νεκρῶν, ἀλλὰ ζώντων.

32 Ego sum Deus Abraham, & Deus Isaac, & Deus Jacob. Non est Deus, Deus mortuorum, sed viventium.

33 Καὶ ἀκύσαντες οἱ ὄχλοι, ἐξεπλήσσοντο ἐπὶ τῇ διδαχῇ αὐτῦ.

33 Et audientes turbæ, percellebantur in doctrina ejus.

malice, leur dit : Hypocrites, pourquoi me tentez-vous ?

19. Montrez-moi la monnoie *dont on paie* le tribut. Et ils lui présentèrent un denier.

20. Et il leur dit : De qui est cette image et cette inscription ?

21. Ils lui dirent : De César. Alors il leur dit : Rendez donc à César ce qui appartient à César, et à Dieu ce qui appartient à Dieu.

22. Et ayant entendu *cette réponse*, ils l'admirèrent ; et le laissant, ils s'en allèrent.

23. Ce jour-là, les Sadducéens, qui disent qu'il n'y a point de résurrection, vinrent à *Jésus*, et lui firent cette question :

24. Maître, Moyse a dit : Si quelqu'un meurt sans enfans, son frère épousera sa veuve, et suscitera lignée à son frère.

25. Or, il y avoit parmi nous sept frères, dont le premier s'étant marié mourut ; et n'ayant point eu d'enfans, il laissa sa femme à son frère.

26. De même aussi le second, puis le troisième, jusqu'au septième.

27. Or, après eux tous, la femme mourut aussi.

28. Duquel donc des sept sera-t-elle femme dans la résurrection; car tous *les sept* l'ont eue ?

29. Mais Jésus répondant, leur dit : Vous êtes dans l'erreur, parce que vous n'entendez pas les Ecritures, ni quelle est la puissance de Dieu.

30. Car après la résurrection, les hommes ne prendront point de femmes, ni les femmes de maris ; mais ils seront comme les Anges de Dieu, qui sont dans le ciel.

31. Et quant à la résurrection des morts, n'avez-vous point lu ce que Dieu vous a dit :

32. Je suis le Dieu d'Abraham, le Dieu d'Isaac, et le Dieu de Jacob. Dieu n'est pas le Dieu des morts, mais *il est le Dieu* des vivans.

33. Et le peuple entendant *cela*, admiroit à doctrine.

wickedness, and said, Why tempt ye me, *ye* hypocrites?

19 Shew me the tribute-money. And they brought unto him a penny.

20 And he saith unto them, Whose *is* this image and superscription?

21 They say unto him, Cesar's. Then saith he unto them, Render, therefore, unto Cesar the things which are Cesar's; and unto God the things that are God's.

22 When they had heard *these words*, they marvelled, and left him, and went their way.

23 The same day came to him the Sadducees, which say that there is no resurrection, and asked him,

24 Saying, Master, Moses said, If a man die, having no children, his brother shall marry his wife, and raise up seed unto his brother.

25 Now, there were with us seven brethren: and the first, when he had married a wife, deceased; and having no issue, left his wife unto his brother:

26 Likewise the second also, and the third, unto the seventh.

27 And last of all the woman died also.

28 Therefore, in the resurrection, whose wife shall she be of the seven? for they all had her.

29 Jesus answered, and said unto them, Ye do err, not knowing the scriptures, nor the power of God.

30 For in the resurrection they neither marry, nor are given in marriage; but are as the angels of God in heaven.

31 But as touching the resurrection of the dead, have ye not read that which was spoken unto you by God, saying,

32 I am the God of Abraham, and the God of Isaac, and the God of Jacob? God is not the God of the dead, but of the living.

33 And when the multitude heard *this*, they were astonished at his doctrine.

60

28 Καὶ προσελθὼν εἷς τῶν γραμματέων, ἀκούσας αὐτῶν συζητούντων, εἰδὼς ὅτι καλῶς αὐτοῖς ἀπεκρίθη, ἐπηρώτησεν αὐτόν· Ποία ἐςὶ πρώτη πασῶν ἐντολή;

29 Ὁ δὲ Ἰησοῦς ἀπεκρίθη αὐτῷ· Ὅτι πρώτη πασῶν τῶν ἐντολῶν· Ἄκυε Ἰσραὴλ, Κύρι⍟, ὁ Θεὸς ἡμῶν, Κύρι⍟ εἷς ἐςι.

30 Καὶ ἀγαπήσεις Κύριον τὸν Θεόν σε ἐξ ὅλης τῆς καρδίας σε, ἐξ ὅλης τῆς ψυχῆς σε, ἐξ ὅλης τῆς διανοίας σε, ἐξ ὅλης τῆς ἰσχύ⍟ σε· αὕτη πρώτη ἐντολή.

31 Καὶ δευτέρα ὁμοία αὕτη· Ἀγαπήσεις τὸν πλησίον σε ὡς σεαυτόν· μείζων τέτων ἄλλη ἐντολὴ ἐκ ἔςι.

40 Ἐν ταύταις ταῖς δυσὶν ἐντολαῖς ὅλ⍟ ὁ νόμ⍟ ἐ οἱ προφῆται κρέμανλαι.

32 Καὶ εἶπεν αὐτῷ ὁ γραμμαλεύς· Καλῶς, διδάσκαλε, ἐπ᾽ ἀληθείας εἶπας, ὅτι εἷς ἐςι Θεὸς, ἐ ἐκ ἔςιν ἄλλ⍟ πλὴν αὐτοῦ.

33 Καὶ τὸ ἀγαπᾷν αὐτὸν ἐξ ὅλης τῆς καρδίας, ἐ ἐξ ὅλης τῆς συνέσεως, ἐ ἐξ ὅλης τῆς ψυχῆς, ἐ ἐξ ὅλης τῆς ἰσχύ⍟, ἐ τὸ ἀγαπᾷν τὸν πλησίον ὡς ἑαυτὸν, πλεῖόν ἐςι πάνλων τῶν ὁλοκαυσωμάτων ἐ τῶν θυσιῶν.

Κεφ. κγ´. 23.

1 ΤΟτε ὁ Ἰησᾶς ἐλάλησε τοῖς ὄχλοις ἐ τοῖς μαθηλαῖς

2 Λέγων· Ἐπὶ τῆς Μωσέως καθέδρας ἐκάθισαν οἱ Γραμμαλεῖς ἐ οἱ Φαρισαῖοι·

3 Πάνλα ἐν ὅσα ἂν εἴπωσιν ὑμῖν τηρεῖν, τηρεῖτε ἐ ποιεῖτε· καλὰ δὲ τὰ ἔργα αὐτῶν μὴ ποιεῖτε· λέγυσι γὰρ, ἐ ὐ ποιᾶσι.

4 Δεσμεύυσι γὰρ φορλία βαρέα ἐ δυςβάςακλα, ἐ ἐπιλιθέασιν ἐπὶ τὰς ὤμες τῶν ἀνθρώπων· τῷ δὲ δακτύλῳ αὐτῶν ὐ θέλυσι κινῆσαι αὐτά·

* 5 Πάνλα δὲ τὰ ἔργα αὐτῶν ποιᾶσι πρὸς τὸ ‡ θεαθῆναι τοῖς ἀνθρώποις· ‡ πλατύνυσι δὲ τὰ † φυλακλήρια αὐτῶν, ἐ ‡ μεγαλύνυσι τὰ κράσπεδα τῶν ἱμαλίων αὐτῶν.

* 6 ‡ Φιλᾶσί τε τὴν ‡ πρωτοκλισίαν ἐν τοῖς ‡ δείπνοις, ἐ τὰς ‡ πρωλοκαθεδρίας ἐν ταῖς συναγωγαῖς,

---

28 Et accedens unus Scribarum, audiens illos conquirentes, videns quod pulchre illis responderit, interrogavit eum: quod esset primum omnium mandatum?

29 At Jesus respondit ei, quia primum omnium mandatorum: Audi Israël, Dominus Deus noster, Dominus unus est.

30 Et diliges Dominum Deum tuum ex toto corde tuo, & ex tota anima tua, & ex tota cogitatione tua, & ex tota virtute tua. Hoc primum mandatum.

31 Et secundum simile huic: Diliges proximum tuum ut teipsum. Majus horum aliud mandatum non est.

40 In his du bus mandatis universa Lex & Prophetæ pendent.

32 Et ait illi Scriba: Pulchre Magister in veritate dixisti, quia unus est Deus, & non est alius præter eum.

33 Et diligere eum ex toto corde, & ex toto intellectu, & ex tota anima, & ex tota fortitudine: & diligere proximum ut seipsum, plus est omnibus holocautomatibus, & sacrificiis.

CAPUT XXIII.

1 TUnc Jesus loquutus est turbis, & discipulis

2 Dicens: Super Mosi cathedram sederunt Scribæ & Pharisæi:

3 Omnia ergo quæcumque dixerint vobis servare, servate & facite: secundùm verò opera eorum ne facite: dicunt enim, & non faciunt.

4 Alligant enim onera gravia & importabilia, & imponunt in humeros hominum: ea digito suo non volunt movere ea.

5 Omnia verò opera sua faciunt adspectari hominibus, dilatant verò phylacteria sua, & magnificant fimbrias vestimentorum suorum.

6 Amantque primos recubitus in cœnis, & primas cathedras in synagogis.

28. Alors un des Scribes, qui les avoit ouï disputer ensemble, voyant qu'il leur avoit bien répondu, s'approcha, et lui demanda : Quel est le premier de tous les commandemens?

29. Jésus lui répondit : Le premier de tous les commandemens *est celui-ci :* Ecoute Israël, le Seigneur notre Dieu est le seul Seigneur.

30. Tu aimeras le Seigneur ton Dieu, de tout ton cœur, de toute ton ame, de toute ta pensée, et de toute ta force. C'est là le premier commandement.

31. Et voici le second, *qui lui est* semblable : Tu aimeras ton prochain comme toi-même. Il n'y a point d'autre commandement, plus grand que ceux-ci.

40. Toute la loi et les Prophètes se rapportent à ces deux commandemens.

32. Et le Scribe lui répondit : Maître, tu as bien dit, et selon la vérité, qu'il n'y a qu'un seul Dieu, et qu'il n'y en a point d'autre que lui ;

33. Et que l'aimer de tout son cœur, de toute *son* intelligence, de toute *son* ame, et de toute sa force, et aimer *son* prochain comme soi-même, c'est plus que tous les holocaustes et que tous les sacrifices.

ALORS Jésus parla au peuple, et à ses Disciples,

2. Et leur dit : Les Scribes et les Pharisiens sont assis sur la chaire de Moyse.

3. Observez donc, et faites tout ce qu'ils vous diront d'observer ; mais ne faites pas comme ils font ; parce qu'ils disent et ne font pas.

4. Car ils lient des fardeaux pesans et insupportables, et les mettent sur les épaules des hommes ; mais ils ne voudroient pas les remuer du doigt.

5. Et ils font toutes leurs actions, afin que les hommes les voient ; car ils portent de larges phylactères, et ils ont de plus longues franges à leurs habits ;

6. Ils aiment à avoir les premières places dans les festins, et les premiers siéges dans les Synagogues ;

28 And one of the scribes came, and having heard them reasoning together, and perceiving that he had answered them well, asked him, Which is the first commandment of all?

29 And Jesus answered him, The first of all the commandments *is,* Hear, O Israel; The Lord our God is one Lord:

30 And thou shalt love the Lord thy God with all thy heart, and with all thy soul, and with all thy mind, and with all thy strength. This *is* the first commandment.

31 And the second *is* like, *namely* this, Thou shalt love thy neighbour as thyself. There is none other commandment greater than these.

40 On these two commandments hang all the law and the prophets.

32 And the scribe said unto him, Well, Master, thou hast said the truth: for there is one God; and there is none other but he:

33 And to love him with all the heart, and with all the understanding, and with all the soul, and with all the strength, and to love *his* neighbour as himself, is more than all whole burnt-offerings and sacrifices.

CHAP. XXIII.

The Pharisees exposed, &c.

THEN spake Jesus to the multitude, and to his disciples,

2 Saying, The scribes and the Pharisees sit in Moses' seat:

3 All therefore whatsoever they bid you observe, *that* observe and do; but do not ye after their works: for they say and do not.

4 For they bind heavy burdens and grievous to be borne, and lay *them* on mens' shoulders; but they *themselves* will not move them with one of their fingers.

5 But all their works they do for to be seen of men: they make broad their phylacteries, and enlarge the borders of their garments.

6 And love the uppermost rooms at feasts, and the chief seats in the synagogues.

61

7 Καὶ τοὺς ἀσπασμοὺς ἐν ταῖς ἀγοραῖς, κ καλεῖσθαι ὑπὸ τῶν ἀνθρώπων, ῥαββί, ῥαββί.

8 Ὑμεῖς δὲ μὴ κληθῆτε ῥαββί· εἷς γάρ ἐςιν ὑμῶν ὁ καθηγητὴς, ὁ Χριςός· πάντες δὲ ὑμεῖς, ἀδελφοί ἐςε.

9 Καὶ πατέρα μὴ καλέσητε ὑμῶν ἐπὶ τῆς γῆς· εἷς γάρ ἐςιν ὁ πατὴρ ὑμῶν, ὁ ἐν τοῖς οὐρανοῖς.

* 10 Μηδὲ ‡ κληθῆτε ‡ καθηγηταί· εἷς γάρ ὑμῶν ἐςιν ὁ καθηγητὴς, ὁ Χριςός.

11 Ὁ δὲ μείζων ὑμῶν, ἔςαι ὑμῶν διάκονⓈ.

12 Ὅςις δὲ ὑψώσει ἑαυτὸν, ταπεινωθήσεται· κ ὅςις ταπεινώσει ἑαυτὸν, ὑψωθήσεται.

13 Οὐαὶ δὲ ὑμῖν Γραμματεῖς κ Φαρισαῖοι ὑποκριταὶ, ὅτι κλείετε τὴν βασιλείαν τῶν οὐρανῶν ἔμπροσθεν τῶν ἀνθρώπων· ὑμεῖς γὰρ οὐκ εἰσέρχεσθε, οὐδὲ τοὺς εἰσερχομένους ἀφίετε εἰσελθεῖν.

14 Οὐαὶ ὑμῖν Γραμματεῖς κ Φαρισαῖοι ὑποκριταὶ, ὅτι κατεσθίετε τὰς οἰκίας τῶν χηρῶν, κ προφάσει μακρὰ προσευχόμενοι· διὰ τοῦτο λήψεσθε περισσότερον κρίμα.

* 15 Οὐαὶ ὑμῖν Γραμματεῖς κ Φαρισαῖοι ὑποκριταὶ, ὅτι ‡ περιάγετε τὴν θάλασσαν κ τὴν ξηρὰν, ποιῆσαι ἕνα ‡ προσήλυτον· κ ὅταν γένηται, ποιεῖτε αὐτὸν υἱὸν γεέννης διπλότερον ὑμῶν.

16 Οὐαὶ ὑμῖν ὁδηγοὶ τυφλοὶ, οἱ λέγοντες· Ὃς ἂν ὀμόσῃ ἐν τῷ ναῷ, οὐδέν ἐςιν· ὃς δ᾽ ἂν ὀμόσῃ ἐν τῷ χρυσῷ τοῦ ναοῦ, ὀφείλει.

17 Μωροὶ κ τυφλοὶ· τίς γὰρ μείζων ἐςίν, ὁ χρυσὸς, ἢ ὁ ναὸς ὁ ἁγιάζων τὸν χρυσόν;

18 Καί· Ὃς ἐὰν ὀμόσῃ ἐν τῷ θυσιαςηρίῳ, οὐδέν ἐςιν· ὃς δ᾽ ἂν ὀμόσῃ ἐν τῷ δώρῳ τῷ ἐπάνω αὐτοῦ, ὀφείλει.

19 Μωροὶ κ τυφλοὶ· τί γὰρ μεῖζον; τὸ δῶρον, ἢ τὸ θυσιαςήριον τὸ ἁγιάζον τὸ δῶρον;

---

7 Et salutationes in foris, & vocari ab hominibus, Rabbi, Rabbi.

8 Vos autem ne vocemini Rabbi : unus enim est vester doctor Christus : omnes autem vos fratres estis.

9 Et patrem ne vocetis vestrûm super terram : unus enim, est Pater vester qui in cælis.

10 Nec vocemini doctores : unus enim vester est doctor, Christus.

11 Qui verò major vestrûm, erit vester minister.

12 Qui autem exaltaverit seipsum, humiliabitur : & qui humiliaverit seipsum, exaltabitur.

13 Væ autem vobis Scribæ & Pharisæi hypocritæ, quia clauditis regnum cælorum ante homines : vos enim non intratis, nec introëuntes sinitis intrare.

14 Væ vobis Scribæ & Pharisæi hypocritæ, quia comeditis domos viduarum, & prætextu prolixa orantes : propter hoc accipietis abundantius judicium.

15 Væ vobis Scribæ & Pharisæi hypocritæ, quia circuitis mare & aridam, facere unum proselytum : & quum fuerit factus, facitis eum filium gehennæ, dupliciorem vobis.

16 Væ vobis duces cæci, dicentes : Quicumque juraverit in templo, nihil est : qui autem juraverit in auro templi, debet.

17 Stulti & cæci : quid enim majus est, aurum, aut templum sanctificans aurum ?

18 Et quicumque juraverit in altari, nihil est : quicumque autem juraverit in dono quod super illud, debet.

19 Stulti & cæci : quid enim majus, donum, an altare sanctificans donum ?

7. Et à être salués dans les places publiques, et à être appelés par les hommes, Maître, Maître.

8. Mais vous, ne vous faites point appeler Maître ; car vous n'avez qu'un Maître, qui est le Christ ; et pour vous, vous êtes tous frères.

9. Et n'appelez personne sur la terre *votre* Père ; car vous n'avez qu'un seul Père, *savoir,* celui qui *est* dans les cieux.

10. Et ne vous faites point appeler Docteur ; car vous n'avez qu'un seul Docteur, qui est le Christ.

11. Mais que le plus grand d'entre vous soit votre serviteur.

12. Car quiconque s'élevera sera abaissé, et quiconque s'abaissera sera élevé.

13. Mais malheur à vous, Scribes et Pharisiens hypocrites ; parce que vous fermez aux hommes le Royaume des cieux ; vous n'y entrez point, et vous n'y laissez pas entrer ceux qui voudroient y entrer.

14. Malheur à vous, Scribes et Pharisiens hypocrites ; car vous dévorez les maisons des veuves, en affectant de faire de longues prières ; à cause de cela vous serez punis d'autant plus sévèrement.

15. Malheur à vous, Scribes et Pharisiens hypocrites ; car vous courez la mer et la terre, pour faire un prosélyte ; et quand il l'est devenu, vous le rendez digne de la géhenne deux fois plus que vous !

16. Malheur à vous, Conducteurs aveugles, qui dites : Si quelqu'un jure par le temple, cela n'est rien ; mais celui qui aura juré par l'or du temple, est obligé *de tenir son serment !*

17. Insensés et aveugles ! Car lequel est le plus considérable, ou l'or, ou le temple qui rend cet or sacré ?

18. Et si quelqu'un, *dites-vous,* jure par l'autel, cela n'est rien ; mais celui qui aura juré par le don qui est sur *l'autel,* est obligé *de tenir son serment.*

19. Insensés et aveugles ! Car lequel est le plus grand, le don, ou l'autel qui rend ce don sacré ?

7 And greetings in the markets, and to be called of men, Rabbi, Rabbi.

8 But be not ye called Rabbi ; for one is your Master, *even* Christ ; and all ye are brethren.

9 And call no *man* your Father upon the earth : for one is your Father, which is in heaven.

10 Neither be ye called masters : for one is your master, *even* Christ.

11 But he that is greatest among you shall be your servant.

12 And whosoever shall exalt himself shall be abased ; and he that shall humble himself shall be exalted.

13 But woe unto you, scribes and Pharisees, hypocrites ! for ye shut up the kingdom of heaven against men : for ye neither go in *your selves,* neither suffer ye them that are entering, to go in.

14 Woe unto you, scribes and Pharisees, hypocrites ! for ye devour widows' houses, and for a pretence make long prayer : therefore ye shall receive the greater damnation.

15 Woe unto you, scribes and Pharisees, hypocrites ! for ye compass sea and land to make one proselyte ; and when he is made, ye make him two-fold more the child of hell than yourselves.

16 Woe unto you, *ye* blind guides ! which say, Whosoever shall swear by the temple, it is nothing ; but whosoever shall swear by the gold of the temple, he is a debtor.

17 *Ye* fools and blind ! for whether *is* greater, the gold, or the temple that sanctifieth the gold ?

18 And, whosoever shall swear by the altar, it is nothing ; but whosoever sweareth by the gift that is upon it, he is guilty.

19 *Ye* fools, and blind ! for whether *is* greater, the gift, or the altar that sanctifieth the gift ?

62

20 Ὁ ἂν ὁμόσας ἐν τῷ θυ-
σιαςηρίῳ, ὀμνύει ἐν αὐτῷ κỳ ἐν
πᾶσι τοῖς ἐπάνω αὐτῦ·

21 Καὶ ὁ ὁμόσας ἐν τῷ ναῷ,
ὀμνύει ἐν αὐτῷ κỳ ἐν τῷ καὶοικῦνὶι
αὐτόν.

22 Καὶ ὁ ὁμόσας ἐν τῷ ἐρανῷ,
ὀμνύει ἐν τῷ θρόνῳ τῦ Θεῦ κỳ ἐν
τῷ καθημένῳ ἐπάνω αὐτῦ.

* 23 Οὐαὶ ὑμῖν Γραμμαῖεῖς κỳ
Φαρισαῖοι ὑποκριταί, ὅτι ‡ ἀπο-
δεκατῦτε τὸ ‡ ἡδύοσμον κỳ τὸ † ἄ-
νηθον κỳ τὸ † κύμινον, κỳ ἀφήκαῖε
τὰ βαρύτερα τῦ νόμᾳ, τὴν κρίσιν, κỳ τὸν ἔλεον κỳ τὴν πίςιν·
Ταῦτα ἔδει ποιῆσαι, κἀκεῖνα μὴ
ἀφιέναι.

* 24 ‡ Ὁδηγοὶ τυφλοὶ, οἱ
† διϋλίζονῖες τὸν † κώνωπα, τὴν
δὲ κάμηλον ‡ καῖαπίνοῖες·

* 25 Οὐαὶ ὑμῖν Γραμμαῖεῖς
κỳ Φαρισαῖοι ὑποκρῖαὶ, ὅτι καθα-
ρίζεῖε τὸ ‡ ἔξωθεν τῦ ποῖηρίᾳ κỳ

τῆς ‡ παροψίδ☉·, ἔσωθεν δὲ
‡ γέμᾳσιν ἐξ ‡ ἀρπαγῆς κỳ ἀ-
κρασίας.

26 Φαρισαῖε τυφλὲ, καθάρι-
σον πρῶτον τὸ ἐντὸς τῦ ποῖηρίᾳ
κỳ τῆς παροψίδ☉·, ἵνα γένηὶαι κỳ
τὸ ἐκὶὸς αὐτῶν καθαρόν.

* 27 Οὐαὶ ὑμῖν Γραμμαῖεῖς κỳ
Φαρισαῖοι ὑποκρῖαὶ, ὅτι † παρο-
μοιάζεῖε ‡ τάφοις ‡ κεκονιαμένοις,
οἵτινες ἔξωθεν μὲν φαίνονῖαι ‡ ὡ-
ραῖοι, ‡ ἔξωθεν δὲ γέμᾳσιν ¾ ὀ-
ςέων νεκρῶν κỳ πάσης ἀκαθαρσίας.

28 Οὕτω κỳ ὑμεῖς ἔξωθεν μὲν
φαίνεσθε τοῖς ἀνθρώποις δίκαιοι,
ἔσωθεν δὲ μεςοὶ ἐςε ὑποκρίσεως
κỳ ἀνομίας.

29 Οὐαὶ ὑμῖν Γραμμαῖεῖς κỳ
Φαρισαῖοι ὑποκρῖαὶ, ὅτι οἰκοδο-
μεῖτε τὰς τάφᾳς τῶν προφηῶν, κỳ
κοσμεῖτε τὰ μνημεῖα τῶν δι-
καίων·

30 Καὶ λέγεῖε· Εἰ ἦμεν ἐν ταῖς
ἡμέραις τῶν παῖέρων ἡμῶν, ἐκ
ἂν ἦμεν κοινωνοὶ αὐτῶν ἐν τῷ αἵ-
μαῖι τῶν προφηῶν.

31 Ὥςε μαρῖυρεῖτε ἑαυῖοῖς,
ὅτι υἱοί ἐςε τῶν φονευσάνῖων τὰς
προφήτας.

32 Καὶ ὑμεῖς πληρώσαῖε τὸ
μέτρον τῶν παῖέρων ὑμῶν.

* 33 Ὄφεις, ‡ γεννήμαῖα ‡ ἐ-
χιδνῶν, πῶς ‡ φύγηῖε ἀπὸ τῆς
κρίσεως τῆς γεέννης ;

20 Ergo jurans in altari, jurat
in eo, & in omnibus quæ fuper
illud.

21 Et jurans in templo, jurat
in illo, & in habitante illud.

22 Et jurans in cælo, jurat in
throno Dei, & in fedente fuper
eum.

23 Væ vobis Scribæ, & Pharifæi hypocritæ, quia decimatis
mentham, & anethum, & cy-
minum, & reliquiftis graviora
Legis, judicium, & mifericor-
diam, & fidem, hæc oportuit
faeere, & illa non omittere.

24 Duces cæci, excolantes cu-
licem, at camelum glutientes.

25 Væ vobis Scribæ & Pha-
rifæi hypocritæ, quia mundatis
quod deforis poculi & patinæ,
intus autem plena funt ex rapina & intemperantia.

26 Pharifæe cæce, munda
prius quod intus poculi, & patinæ, ut fiat & quod deforis
ipforum mundum.

27 Væ vobis Scribæ & Pha-
rifæi hyporitæ, quia adfimila-
mini fepulchris dealbatis, quæ à
foris quidem apparent fpeciofa,
intus verò plena funt offibus
mortuorum, & omni immundi-
tia.

28 Sic & vos à foris quidem
paretis hominibus jufti : intus
autem pleni eftis hypocrifi &
iniquitate.

29 Væ vobis Scribæ & Pha-
rifæi hypocritæ, quia ædificatis
fepulchra Prophetarum, & or-
natis monumenta juftorum :

30 Et dicitis : quod fi fuiffe-
mus in diebus patrum noftro-
rum, non effemus communica-
tores eorum in fanguine Prophetarum.

31 Itaque teftamini vobifmet-
ipfis, quia filii eftis occiden-
tium Prophetas.

32 Et vos implete menfuram
patrum veftrorum.

33 Serpentes, geminina vipe-
rarum, quomodo fugietis à judicio gehennæ ?

20. Celui donc qui jure par l'autel, jure par l'autel, et par ce qui est dessus.

21. Et celui qui jure par le temple, jure par le temple et par celui qui y habite.

22. Et celui qui jure par le ciel, jure par le trône de Dieu et par celui qui est assis dessus.

23. Malheur à vous, Scribes et Pharisiens hypocrites; car vous payez la dîme de la mente, de l'anet, et du cumin, et vous négligez les choses les plus importantes de la loi, la justice, la miséricorde, et la fidélité. Ce sont là les choses qu'il falloit faire, sans néanmoins omettre les autres.

24. Conducteurs aveugles, qui coulez un moucheron, et qui avalez un chameau.

25. Malheur à vous, Scribes et Pharisiens hypocrites; car vous nettoyez le dehors de la coupe et du plat, pendant qu'au-dedans vous êtes pleins de rapines et d'intempérance.

26. Pharisien aveugle, nettoie premièrement le dedans de la coupe et du plat, afin que ce qui est dehors devienne aussi net.

27. Malheur à vous, Scribes et Pharisiens hypocrites; car vous ressemblez à des sépulcres blanchis, qui paroissent beaux par dehors; mais qui, au-dedans, sont pleins d'ossemens de morts, et de toute sorte de pourriture.

28. De même aussi au-dehors, vous paroissez justes aux hommes, mais au-dedans, vous êtes remplis d'hypocrisie et d'injustice.

29. Malheur à vous, Scribes et Pharisiens hypocrites; car vous bâtissez les tombeaux des Prophètes, et vous ornez les sépulcres des justes;

30. Et vous dites : Si nous eussions été du temps de nos pères, nous ne nous serions pas joints à eux pour répandre le sang des Prophètes.

31. Ainsi vous êtes témoins contre vous-mêmes, que vous êtes les enfans de ceux qui ont tué les Prophètes.

32. Vous *donc* aussi, vous achevez de combler la mesure de vos pères.

33. Serpens, race de vipères, comment éviterez-vous le jugement de la géhenne?

---

20 Whoso, therefore, shall swear by the altar, sweareth by it, and by all things thereon.

21 And whoso shall swear by the temple, sweareth by it, and by him that dwelleth therein.

22 And he that shall swear by heaven, sweareth by the throne of God, and by him that sitteth thereon.

23 Woe unto you, scribes and Pharisees, hypocrites! for ye pay tithe of mint, and anise, and cummin, and have omitted the weightier *matters* of the law, judgment, mercy, and faith : these ought ye to have done, and not to leave the other undone.

24 *Ye* blind guides! which strain at a gnat, and swallow a camel.

25 Woe unto you, scribes and Pharisees, hypocrites! for ye make clean the outside of the cup and of the platter, but within they are full of extortion and excess.

26 *Thou* blind Pharisee! cleanse first that *which* is within the cup and platter, that the outside of them may be clean also.

27 Woe unto you, scribes and Pharisees, hypocrites! for ye are like unto whited sepulchres, which indeed appear beautiful outward, but are within full of dead *mens'* bones, and of all uncleanness.

28 Even so ye also outwardly appear righteous unto men, but within ye are full of hypocrisy and iniquity.

29 Woe unto you, scribes and Pharisees, hypocrites! because ye build the tombs of the prophets, and garnish the sepulchres of the righteous,

30 And say, If we had been in the days of our fathers, we would not have been partakers with them in the blood of the prophets.

31 Wherefore ye be witnesses unto yourselves, that ye are the children of them which killed the prophets.

32 Fill ye up then the measure of your fathers.

33 *Ye* serpents, *ye* generation of vipers! how can ye escape the damnation of hell?

* 41 Καὶ καθίσας ὁ Ἰησοῦς ‡ κατέναντι τῦ ‡ γαζοφυλακίυ, ἐθεώρει πῶς ὁ ὄχλῷ‑ βάλλει χαλκὸν εἰς τὸ γαζοφυλάκιον· καὶ πολλοὶ πλύσιοι ἔβαλλον πολλά.	41 Et fedens Jefus contra gazophylacium, afpiciebat quomodo turba jactaret æs in gazophylacium : & multi divites jactabant multa.
* 42 Καὶ ἐλθῦσα μία ‡ χήρα πτωχὴ ἔβαλε ‡ λεπτὰ δύο, ὅ ἐσι ‡ κοδράντης.	42 Et veniens una vidua pauper, injecit minuta duo, quod eſt quadrans.
43 Καὶ προσκαλεσάμενῷ‑ τὺς μαθητὰς αὐτοῦ, λέγει αὐτοῖς· Ἀμὴν λέγω ὑμῖν, ὅτι ἡ χήρα αὕτη ἡ πτωχὴ πλεῖον πάντων βέβληκε τῶν βαλόντων εἰς τὸ γαζοφυλάκιον.	43 Et advocans difcipulos fuos, ait illis : Amen dico vobis, quoniam vidua hæc pauper plus omnibus injecit injicientibus in gazophylacium.
44 Πάντες γὰρ ἐκ τῦ περισσεύοντῷ‑ αὐτοῖς ἔβαλον· αὕτη δὲ ἐκ τῆς ὑςερήσεως αὐτῆς πάντα ὅσα εἶχεν ἔβαλεν, ὅλον τὸν βίον αὐτῆς. 25. † 6.	44 Omnes enim ex redundante fibi injecerunt : hæc verò ex penuria fua omnia quæ habuit jecit, totum victum fuum.

Κεφ. κδ´ 24.

1 Καὶ ἐξελθὼν ὁ Ἰησῦς ἐπορεύετο ἀπὸ τῦ ἱερῦ· καὶ προσῆλθον οἱ μαθηταὶ αὐτῦ ἐπιδεῖξαι αὐτῷ τὰς οἰκοδομάς· τῦ ἱερῦ.	1 ET egreſſus Jeſus ibat de templo : & acceſſerunt difcipuli ejus oſtendere ei ædificationes templi.
2 Ὁ δὲ Ἰησῦς εἶπεν αὐτοῖς· Οὐ βλέπετε πάντα ταῦτα; ἀμὴν λέγω ὑμῖν, ἢ μὴ ἀφεθῇ ὧδε λίθῷ ἐπὶ λίθον, ὃς ἢ μὴ καταλυθήσεται.	2 At Jeſus dixit illis : Non intuemini hæc omnia? Amen dico vobis, non relinquetur hic lapis super lapidem, qui non diſſolvetur.
16 Τότε οἱ ἐν τῇ Ἰυδαίᾳ φευγέτωσαν ἐπὶ τὰ ὄρη.	16 Tunc qui in Judæa fugiant ad montes.
17 Ὁ ἐπὶ τῦ δώματῷ, μὴ καταβαινέτω ἆραί τι ἐκ τῆς οἰκίας αὐτῦ·	17 Qui super domum, non deſcendat tollere quid de æde fua.
18 Καὶ ὁ ἐν τῷ ἀγρῷ, μὴ ἐπιστρεψάτω ὀπίσω ἆραι τὰ ἱμάτια αὐτῦ·	18 Et qui in agro, non revertatur retrò tollere veſtem fuam.
19 Οὐαὶ δὲ ταῖς ἐν γαςρὶ ἐχύσαις καὶ ταῖς θηλαζύσαις ἐν ἐκείναις ταῖς ἡμέραις.	19 Væ autem in utero habentibus, & lactantibus in illis diebus.
20 Προσεύχεσθε δὲ ἵνα μὴ γένηται ἡ φυγὴ ὑμῶν χειμῶνῷ, μηδὲ ἐν σαββάτῳ.	20 Orate autem ut non fiat, fuga veſtra hyeme, neque in Sabbato.
21 Ἔσαι γὰρ τότε θλίψις μεγάλη, οἵα ἢ γέγονεν ἀπ᾽ ἀρχῆς κόσμου ἕως τῦ νῦν, ἠδ᾽ ἢ μὴ γένηται.	21 Erit enim tunc tribulatio magna, qualis non fuit ab initio mundi, ufque modo, neque non fiet.
29 Εὐθέως δὲ μετὰ τὴν θλίψιν τῶν ἡμερῶν ἐκείνων ὁ ἥλιῷ σκοτισθήσεται, καὶ ἡ σελήνη ἢ δώσει τὸ φέγγῷ αὐτῆς, καὶ οἱ ἀςέρες πεσῦνται ἀπὸ τῦ ἐρανῦ, καὶ αἱ δυνάμεις τῶν ἐρανῶν σαλευθήσονται.	29 Statim autem poſt tribulationem dierum illorum Sol obfcurabitur, & Luna non dabit lumen fuum, & ſtellæ cadent de cælo, & efficaciæ cælorum concutientur.

41. Et Jésus étant assis vis-à-vis du tronc, regardoit comment le peuple mettoit de l'argent dans le tronc.

42. Et plusieurs *personnes* riches y mettoient beaucoup; et une pauvre veuve vint, qui y mit deux petites pièces, qui font un quadrin.

43. Alors ayant appelé ses Disciples, il leur dit : Je vous dis en vérité, que cette pauvre veuve a plus mis au tronc, que tous ceux qui y ont mis.

44. Car tous *les autres* y ont mis de leur superflu ; mais celle-ci y a mis de son indigence, tout ce qu'elle avoit, tout ce qui lui restoit pour vivre.

Comme Jésus sortoit du Temple et qu'il s'en alloit, ses Disciples vinrent pour lui en faire considérer les édifices.

2. Et Jésus leur dit : Voyez-vous tous ces bâtimens ? Je vous dis en vérité, qu'il ne restera ici pierre sur pierre qui ne soit renversée.

16. Alors, que ceux qui seront dans la Judée, s'enfuient aux montagnes ;

17. Que celui qui sera au haut de la maison, ne descende point pour s'arrêter à emporter quoi que ce soit de sa maison ;

18. Et que celui qui est aux champs, ne retourne point en arrière, pour emporter ses habits.

19. Malheur aux femmes qui seront enceintes, et à celles qui allaiteront en ces jours-là.

20. Priez que votre fuite n'arrive pas en hiver, ni en un jour de Sabbat.

21. Car il y aura une grande affliction, telle que, depuis le commencement du monde jusqu'à présent, il n'y en a point eu, et qu'il n'y en aura jamais de semblable.

29. Et aussitôt après l'affliction de ces jours-là, le soleil s'obscurcira, la lune ne donnera point sa lumière, les étoiles tomberont du ciel, et les puissances des cieux seront ébranlées.

41 And Jesus sat over against the treasury, and beheld how the people cast money into the treasury : and many that were rich cast in much.

42 And there came a certain poor widow, and she threw in two mites, which make a farthing.

43 And he called *unto him* his disciples, and saith unto them, Verily I say unto you, That this poor widow hath cast more in than all they which have cast into the treasury :

44 For all *they* did cast in of their abundance ; but she of her want did cast in all that she had, *even* all her living.

CHAP. XXIV.
Jerusalem's destruction foretold.

AND Jesus went out, and departed from the temple ; and his disciples came to him, for to shew him the buildings of the temple.

2 And Jesus said unto them, See ye not all these things ? Verily I say unto you, There shall not be left here one stone upon another, that shall not be thrown down.

16 Then let them which be in Judea flee into the mountains :

17 Let him which is on the house-top not come down to take any thing out of his house :

18 Neither let him which is in the field return back to take his clothes.

19 And woe unto them that are with child, and to them that give suck in those days !

20 But pray ye that your flight be not in the winter, neither on the sabbath-day :

21 For then shall be great tribulation, such as was not since the beginning of the world to this time, no, nor ever shall be.

29 Immediately after the tribulation of those days shall the sun be darkened, and the moon shall not give her light, and the stars shall fall from heaven, and the powers of the heavens shall be shaken:

64.

32 Ἀπὸ δὲ τῆς συκῆς μάθετε τὴν παραβολήν· ὅταν ἤδη ὁ κλάδος αὐτῆς γένηται ἁπαλὸς, ᾧ τὰ φύλλα ἐκφύῃ, γινώσκετε ὅτι ἐγγὺς τὸ θέρος.

33 Οὕτω ᾧ ὑμεῖς, ὅταν ἴδητε πάντα ταῦτα, γινώσκετε ὅτι ἐγγύς ἐςιν ἐπὶ θύραις.

36 Περὶ δὲ τῆς ἡμέρας ἐκείνης ᾧ τῆς ὥρας ἐδεὶς οἶδεν, ἐδὲ οἱ ἄγγελοι τῶν ἐρανῶν, εἰ μὴ ὁ πατήρ μου μόνος.

37 Ὥσπερ δὲ αἱ ἡμέραι τῶ Νῶε, ἕτως ἔςαι ᾧ ἡ παρυσία τῶ υἱῶ τῶ ἀνθρώπου.

38 Ὥσπερ γὰρ ἦσαν ἐν ταῖς ἡμέραις ταῖς πρὸ τῶ κατακλυσμῶ τρώγοντες ᾧ πίνοντες, γαμῶντες ᾧ ἐκγαμίζοντες, ἄχρι ἧς ἡμέρας εἰσῆλθε Νῶε εἰς τὴν κιβωτόν·

39 Καὶ ἐκ ἔγνωσαν, ἕως ἦλθεν ὁ κατακλυσμός, ᾧ ἦρεν ἅπαντας· ἕτως ἔςαι ᾧ ἡ παρυσία τῶ υἱῶ τῶ ἀνθρώπου.

40 Τότε δύο ἔσονται ἐν τῷ ἀγρῷ· ὁ εἷς παραλαμβάνεται ᾧ ὁ εἷς ἀφίεται.

* 41 Δύο ‡ ἀλήθωσαι ἐν τῷ † μύλωνι· μία παραλαμβάνεται, ᾧ μία ἀφίεται.

42 Γρηγορεῖτε ἐν, ὅτι ἐκ οἴδατε ποίᾳ ὥρᾳ ὁ κύριος ὑμῶν ἔρχεται.

43 Ἐκεῖνο δὲ γινώσκετε, ὅτι εἰ ᾔδει ὁ οἰκοδεσπότης ποίᾳ φυλακῇ ὁ κλέπτης ἔρχεται, ἐγρηγόρησεν ἂν, ᾧ ἐκ ἂν εἴασε διορυγῆναι τὴν οἰκίαν αὐτῶ.

44 Διὰ τῶτο ᾧ ὑμεῖς γίνεσθε ἕτοιμοι·

45 Τίς ἄρα ἐςὶν ὁ πιςὸς δῦλος ᾧ φρόνιμος, ὃν κατέςησεν ὁ κύριος αὐτῶ ἐπὶ τῆς θεραπείας αὐτῶ, τῶ διδόναι αὐτοῖς τὴν τροφὴν ἐν καιρῷ;

46 Μακάριος ὁ δῦλος ἐκεῖνος, ὃν ἐλθὼν ὁ κύριος αὐτῶ εὑρήσει ποιῶντα ἕτως.

47 Ἀμὴν λέγω ὑμῖν, ὅτι ἐπὶ πᾶσι τοῖς ὑπάρχουσιν αὐτῶ καταςήσει αὐτόν.

48 Ἐὰν δὲ εἴπῃ ὁ κακὸς δῦλος ἐκεῖνος ἐν τῇ καρδίᾳ αὐτῶ· Χρονίζει ὁ κύριός μου ἐλθεῖν·

49 Καὶ ἄρξηται τύπτειν τοὺς συνδούλους, ἐσθίειν δὲ ᾧ πίνειν μετὰ τῶν μεθυόντων·

32 A verò ficu difcite parabolam: quum jam ramus ejus fuerit tener, & folia germinaverint, fcitis quia prope æftas.

33 Ita & vos, quum videritis hæc omnia, fcitote quia propè eft in januis.

36 De autem die illa & horâ nemo fcit, neque angeli cælorum, fi non Pater meus folus.

37 Sicut autem dies Noë ita erit & adventus Filii hominis.

38 Sicut enim erant in diebu ante diluvium, comedentes & bibentes, nubentes & nuptui tra dentes, ufque quo die intravi Noë in arcam:

39 Et non cognoverunt done venit diluvium, & tulit omnes ita erit & præfentia Filii hominis.

40 Tunc duo erunt in agro unus affumitur, & unus relinquitur.

41 Duæ molentes in mola una affumetur, & una relinquetur.

42 Vigilate ergo, quia nefcitis quâ horâ Dominus vefter venit.

43 Illud autem fcitote, quoniam fi fciret paterfamilias quâ cuftodiâ fur venit, vigilaret utique, & non fineret perfodi domum fuam.

44 Propter hoc & vos eftote parati,

45 Quis putas eft fidelis fervus & prudens, quem conftituit dominus fuus fuper familiam fuam, ad dandum illis cibum in tempore?

46 Beatus fervus ille, quem veniens dominus ejus, invenerit facientem fic.

47 Amen dico vobis, quoniam fuper omnibus fubftantiis fuis conftituet eum.

48 Si autem dixerit malus fervus ille in corde fuo: Tardat dominus meus venire.

49 Et cœperit percutere confervos, edere autem & bibere cum ebriofis:

32. Apprenez ceci par la similitude du figuier : Quand ses branches commencent à être tendres, et qu'il poussent des feuilles, vous connoissez que l'été est proche.

33. Vous aussi de même, quand vous verrez toutes ces choses, sachez que *le Fils de l'homme* est proche, et à la porte.

36. Pour ce qui est du jour et de l'heure, personne ne le sait, non pas même les Anges du ciel, mais mon Père seul.

37. Mais comme il en étoit dans les jours de Noé, il en sera de même à l'avénement du Fils de l'homme ;

38. Car comme, dans les jours avant le Déluge, *les hommes* mangeoient et buvoient, se marioient et donnoient en mariage, jusqu'au jour que Noé entra dans l'arche :

39. Et qu'ils ne pensèrent au Déluge, que lorsqu'il vint et qu'il les emporta tous ; il en sera aussi de même à l'avénement du Fils de l'homme.

40. Alors de deux *hommes* qui seront dans un champ, l'un sera pris, et l'autre laissé.

41. De deux femmes qui moudront au moulin, l'une sera prise, et l'autre laissée.

42. Veillez donc ; car vous ne savez pas à quelle heure votre Seigneur doit venir.

43. Vous savez que si un père de famille étoit averti à quelle veille *de la nuit* un larron doit venir, il veilleroit, et ne laisseroit pas percer sa maison.

44. C'est pourquoi, vous aussi tenez-vous prêts ;

45. Qui est donc le serviteur fidèle et prudent que son Maître a établi sur ses domestiques, pour leur donner la nourriture dans le tems *qu'il faut ?*

46. Heureux ce serviteur que son Maître trouvera faisant ainsi quand il arrivera !

47. Je vous dis en vérité, qu'il l'établira sur tous ses biens.

48. Mais si c'est un méchant serviteur, qui dise en lui-même, Mon Maître tarde à venir ;

49. Et qu'il se mette à battre ses compagnons de service, et à manger et à boire avec des ivrognes ;

32 Now learn a parable of the fig-tree; When his branch is yet tender, and putteth forth leaves, ye know that summer *is* nigh:

33 So likewise ye, when ye shall see all these things, know that it is near, *even* at the doors.

36 But of that day and hour knoweth no *man;* no, not the angels of heaven, but my Father only.

37 But as the days of Noe *were,* so shall also the coming of the Son of Man be.

38 For in the days that were before the flood they were eating and drinking, marrying and giving in marriage, until the day that Noe entered into the ark,

39 And knew not until the flood came, and took them all away;

40 Then shall two be in the field; the one shall be taken, and the other left.

41 Two *women shall be* grinding at the mill; the one shall be taken, and the other left.

42 Watch, therefore; for ye know not what hour your Lord doth come.

43 But know this, that if the good man of the house had known in what watch the thief would come, he would have watched, and would not have suffered his house to be broken up.

44 Therefore be ye also ready:

45 Who then is a faithful and wise servant, whom his lord hath made ruler over his household, to give them meat in due season?

46 Blessed *is* that servant, whom his lord, when he cometh, shall find so doing.

47 Verily I say unto you, That he shall make him ruler over all his goods.

48 But and if that evil servant shall say in his heart, My lord delayeth his coming;

49 And shall begin to smite *his* fellow-servants, and to eat and drink with the drunken;

65

50 Ἥξει ὁ κύριος τοῦ δούλου ἐκείνου ἐν ἡμέρᾳ ᾗ οὐ προσδοκᾷ, καὶ ἐν ὥρᾳ ᾗ οὐ γινώσκει.

51 Καὶ διχοτομήσει αὐτὸν, καὶ τὸ μέρος αὐτοῦ μετὰ τῶν ὑποκριτῶν θήσει· ἐκεῖ ἔσται ὁ κλαυθμὸς καὶ ὁ βρυγμὸς τῶν ὀδόντων. 14. † 2.

Κεφ. κε'. 25.

1 Τότε ὁμοιωθήσεται ἡ βασιλεία τῶν οὐρανῶν δέκα παρθένοις, αἵτινες λαβοῦσαι τὰς λαμπάδας αὐτῶν, ἐξῆλθον εἰς ἀπάντησιν τοῦ νυμφίου.

2 Πέντε δὲ ἦσαν ἐξ αὐτῶν φρόνιμοι, καὶ πέντε μωραί.

3 Αἵτινες μωραὶ, λαβοῦσαι τὰς λαμπάδας ἑαυτῶν, οὐκ ἔλαβον μεθ' ἑαυτῶν ἔλαιον.

4 Αἱ δὲ φρόνιμοι ἔλαβον ἔλαιον ἐν τοῖς ἀγγείοις αὐτῶν μετὰ τῶν λαμπάδων αὐτῶν.

5 Χρονίζοντος δὲ τοῦ νυμφίου, ἐνύσταξαν πᾶσαι, καὶ ἐκάθευδον.

6 Μέσης δὲ νυκτὸς κραυγὴ γέγονεν· Ἰδοὺ, ὁ νυμφίος ἔρχεται, ἐξέρχεσθε εἰς ἀπάντησιν αὐτοῦ.

7 Τότε ἠγέρθησαν πᾶσαι αἱ παρθένοι ἐκεῖναι, καὶ ἐκόσμησαν τὰς λαμπάδας αὐτῶν.

8 Αἱ δὲ μωραὶ ταῖς φρονίμοις εἶπον· Δότε ἡμῖν ἐκ τοῦ ἐλαίου ὑμῶν ὅτι αἱ λαμπάδες ἡμῶν σβέννυνται.

9 Ἀπεκρίθησαν δὲ αἱ φρόνιμοι, λέγουσαι· Μήποτε οὐκ ἀρκέσῃ ἡμῖν καὶ ‡ ὑμῖν· πορεύεσθε δὲ μᾶλλον πρὸς τοὺς πωλοῦντας, καὶ ἀγοράσατε ἑαυταῖς.

10 Ἀπερχομένων δὲ αὐτῶν ἀγοράσαι, ἦλθεν ὁ νυμφίος· καὶ αἱ ἕτοιμοι εἰσῆλθον μετ' αὐτῶ εἰς τοὺς γάμους, καὶ ἐκλείσθη ἡ θύρα.

11 Ὕστερον δὲ ἔρχονται καὶ αἱ λοιπαὶ παρθένοι, λέγουσαι· Κύριε, κύριε, ἄνοιξον ἡμῖν.

12 Ὁ δὲ ἀποκριθεὶς, εἶπεν· Ἀμὴν λέγω ὑμῖν, οὐκ οἶδα ὑμᾶς.

13 Γρηγορεῖτε οὖν,

14 Ὥσπερ γὰρ ἄνθρωπος ἀποδημῶν ἐκάλεσε τοὺς ἰδίους δούλους, καὶ παρέδωκεν αὐτοῖς τὰ ὑπάρχοντα αὐτοῦ.

15 Καὶ ᾧ μὲν ἔδωκε πέντε τάλαντα, ᾧ δὲ δύο, ᾧ δὲ ἕν· ἑκάστῳ

---

50 Veniet dominus servi illius in die quâ non expectat, & in horâ quâ non scit.

51 Et dividet eum, & partem ejus cum hypocritis ponet : illic erit fletus, & stridor dentium.

CAPUT XXV.

1 TUnc similabitur regnum cælorum decem virginibus, quæ accipientes lampadas suas, exierunt in occursum sponsi.

2 Quinque autem erant ex eis prudentes, & quinque fatuæ.

3 Quæ fatuæ sumentes lampadas suas, non sumpserunt secum oleum.

4 Verùm prudentes accepêrunt oleum in vasis suis cum lampadibus suis.

5 Tardante autem sponso dormitaverunt omnes, & dormierunt.

6 Mediâ autem nocte clamor factus est : Ecce sponsus venit : exite in occursum ejus.

7 Tunc surrexerunt omnes virgines illæ : & ornaverunt lampadas suas.

8 At fatuæ sapientibus dixerunt : Date nobis de oleo vestro, quia lampades nostræ extinguuntur.

9 Responderunt autem prudentes, dicentes : Ne forte non sufficiat nobis, & vobis : ite autem potiùs ad vendentes, & emite vobis ipsis.

10 Abeuntibus autem illis mercari, venit sponsus : & expeditæ intraverunt cum eo ad nuptias, & clausa est janua.

11 Posteriùs verò veniunt & reliquæ virgines, dicentes : Domine, Domine, aperi nobis.

12 Ille verò respondens, ait : Amen dico vobis, non novi vos.

13 Vigilate itaque,

14 Sicut enim homo peregrè proficiscens, vocavit proprios servos, & tradidit illis substantias suas :

15 Et huic quidem dedit quinque talenta, illi autem duo, illi

50. Le Maître de ce serviteur-là viendra le jour qu'il ne l'attend pas, et à l'heure qu'il ne sait pas;

51. Et il le séparera, et il lui donnera sa portion avec les hypocrites; c'est là qu'il y aura des pleurs et des grincemens de dents.

CHAPITRE XXV.

La Parabole des Vierges et des Talens. La description du Jugement dernier.

ALORS le Royaume des cieux sera semblable à dix vierges, qui ayant pris leurs lampes, allèrent au-devant de l'Epoux.

2. Or, il y en avoit cinq d'entre elles *qui étoient* sages, et cinq *qui étoient* folles.

3. Celles qui *étoient* folles, en prenant leurs lampes, n'avoient point pris d'huile avec elles.

4. Mais les sages avoient pris de l'huile dans leurs vaisseaux avec leurs lampes.

5. Et comme l'époux tardoit à venir, elles s'assoupirent toutes et s'endormirent.

6. Et sur le minuit, on entendit crier : Voici l'époux qui vient, sortez au-devant de lui.

7. Alors ces vierges se levèrent toutes, et préparèrent leurs lampes.

8. Et les folles dirent aux sages : Donnez-nous de votre huile ; car nos lampes s'éteignent.

9. Mais les sages répondirent : *Nous ne le pouvons*, de peur que nous n'en ayons pas assez pour nous et pour vous; allez plutôt vers ceux qui en vendent, et en achetez pour vous.

10. Mais pendant qu'elles en alloient acheter, l'Epoux vint; et celles qui étoient prêtes entrèrent avec lui aux noces, et la porte fut fermée.

11. Après cela les autres vierges vinrent aussi, et dirent : Seigneur, Seigneur, ouvre-nous.

12. Mais il leur répondit : Je vous dis en vérité, que je ne vous connois point.

13. Veillez donc;

14. Car il en *est* comme d'un homme, qui, s'en allant en voyage, appela ses serviteurs et leur remit ses biens.

15. Et il donna cinq talens à l'un, à l'autre deux, et à l'autre

---

50 The lord of that servant shall come in a day when he looketh not for *him*, and in an hour that he is not aware of.

51 And shall cut him asunder and appoint *him* his portion with the hypocrites: there shall be weeping and gnashing of teeth.

CHAP. XXV.

Parable of the ten virgins.

THEN shall the kingdom of heaven be likened unto ten virgins, which took their lamps, and went forth to meet the bridegroom.

2 And five of them were wise, and five *were* foolish.

3 They that *were* foolish took their lamps, and took no oil with them:

4 But the wise took oil in their vessels with their lamps.

5 While the bridegroom tarried, they all slumbered and slept.

6 And at midnight there was a cry made, Behold, the bridegroom cometh; go ye out to meet him.

7 Then all those virgins arose, and trimmed their lamps.

8 And the foolish said unto the wise, Give us of your oil; for our lamps are gone out.

9 But the wise answered, saying, *Not so:* lest there be not enough for us and you: but go ye rather to them that sell, and buy for yourselves.

10 And while they went to buy, the bridegroom came; and they that were ready went in with him to the marriage: and the door was shut.

11 Afterward came also the other virgins, saying, Lord, Lord, open to us.

12 But he answered and said, Verily I say unto you, I know you not.

13 Watch, therefore,

14 For *the kingdom of heaven is* as a man travelling into a far country, *who* called his own servants, and delivered unto them his goods.

15 And unto one he gave five talents, to another two, and to

καλὰ τὴν ἰδίαν δύναμιν· καὶ ἀπεδήμησεν εὐθέως.

16 Πορευθεὶς δὲ ὁ τὰ πέντε
τάλαντα λαβὼν, εἰργάσατο ἐν
αὐτοῖς, καὶ ἐποίησεν ἄλλα πέντε
τάλαντα.

17 Ὡσαύτως καὶ ὁ τὰ δύο,
ἐκέρδησε καὶ αὐτὸς ἄλλα δύο.

18 Ὁ δὲ τὸ ἓν λαβὼν, ἀπελθὼν ὤρυξεν ἐν τῇ γῇ, καὶ ἀπέ-
κρυψε τὸ ἀργύριον τοῦ κυρίου αὐτοῦ.

19 Μετὰ δὲ χρόνον πολὺν ἔρχεται ὁ κύριος τῶν δούλων ἐκείνων, καὶ συναίρει μετ' αὐτῶν λόγον.

20 Καὶ προσελθὼν ὁ τὰ πέντε
τάλαντα λαβὼν, προσήνεγκεν ἄλλα πέντε τάλαντα, λέγων· Κύριε,
πέντε τάλαντά μοι παρέδωκας·
ἴδε, ἄλλα πέντε τάλαντα ἐκέρδησα ἐπ' αὐτοῖς.

21 Ἔφη δὲ αὐτῷ ὁ κύριος αὐ-
τοῦ· Εὖ, δοῦλε ἀγαθὲ καὶ πιστέ·
ἐπὶ ὀλίγα ἧς πιστός, ἐπὶ πολλῶν
σε καταστήσω· εἴσελθε εἰς τὴν
χαρὰν τοῦ κυρίου σου.

22 Προσελθὼν δὲ καὶ ὁ τὰ δύο
τάλαντα λαβὼν, εἶπε· Κύριε, δύο
τάλαντά μοι παρέδωκας· ἴδε, ἄλλα δύο τάλαντα ἐκέρδησα ἐπ' αὐτοῖς.

23 Ἔφη αὐτῷ ὁ κύριος αὐτοῦ·
Εὖ, δοῦλε ἀγαθὲ καὶ πιστέ· ἐπὶ
ὀλίγα ἧς πιστός, ἐπὶ πολλῶν σε
καταστήσω· εἴσελθε εἰς τὴν χαρὰν τοῦ κυρίου σου.

24 Προσελθὼν δὲ καὶ ὁ τὸ ἓν τάλαντον εἰληφώς, εἶπε· Κύριε, ἔγνων σε ὅτι σκληρὸς εἶ ἄνθρωπος,
θερίζων ὅπου οὐκ ἔσπειρας, καὶ συ-
νάγων ὅθεν οὐ διεσκόρπισας·

25 Καὶ φοβηθεὶς, ἀπελθὼν ἔκ-
ρυψα τὸ τάλαντόν σου ἐν τῇ γῇ·
ἴδε ἔχεις τὸ σόν.

26 Ἀποκριθεὶς δὲ ὁ κύριος αὐτοῦ, εἶπεν αὐτῷ· Πονηρὲ δοῦλε
καὶ ὀκνηρέ, ᾔδεις ὅτι θερίζω ὅπου
οὐκ ἔσπειρα, καὶ συνάγω ὅθεν οὐ
διεσκόρπισα·

---

verò unum : unicuique secundùm propriam facultatem : &
peregrè profectus est statim.

16 Profectus autem quinque
talenta accipiens, operatus est in
eis, & fecit alia quinque talenta.

17 Similiter & qui duo, lucratus est & ipse alia duo.

18 Verùm unum accipiens,
abiens fodit in terra, & abscondit pecuniam domini sui.

19 Post verò tempus multum
venit dominus servorum illorum, & confert rationem cum
eis.

20 Et accedens quinque talenta accipiens, attulit alia quinque talenta, dicens: Domine,
quinque talenta mihi tradidisti:
ecce alia quinque talenta lucratus sum super illis.

21 Ait verò illi dominus
ejus: Benè, serve bone & fidelis, super pauca fuisti fidelis:
super multa te constituam: ingredere in gaudium domini tui.

22 Accedens autem & qui duo
talenta accipiens, dixit: Domine, duo talenta mihi tradidisti: ecce alia duo talenta lucratus sum super illis.

23 Ait illi dominus ejus:
Benè, serve bone & fidelis: super pauca fuisti fidelis, super
multa te constituam: ingredere
in gaudium domini tui.

24 Accedens autem & unum
talentum sumens, ait: Domine,
scio te quia durus es homo, metens ubi non seminasti, & congregans unde non sparsisti:

25 Et timore perculsus, abiens abscondi talentum tuum in
terra: ecce habes tuum.

26 Respondens autem domi-
nus ejus, dixit ei: Malè serve
& piger, sciebas quia meto ubi
non seminavi, & congrego unde
non sparsi.

un ; à chacun selon ses forces ; et il partit aussitôt.

16. Or celui qui avoit reçu cinq talens s'en alla et en trafiqua ; et il gagna cinq autres talens.

17. De même celui qui en *avoit* reçu deux, en gagna aussi deux autres.

18. Mais celui qui n'en avoit reçu qu'un, s'en alla et creusa dans la terre , et y cacha l'argent de son Maître.

19. Long-tems après , le Maître de ces serviteurs revint , et il leur fit rendre compte.

20. Alors celui qui avoit reçu cinq talens vint , et présenta cinq autres talens , et dit : Seigneur , tu m'avois remis cinq talens ; en voici cinq autres que j'ai gagnés de plus.

21. Et son Maître lui dit : Cela va bien , bon et fidèle serviteur ; tu as été fidèle en peu de chose ; je t'établirai sur beaucoup ; entre dans la joie de ton Seigneur.

22. Et celui qui avoit reçu deux talens , vint et dit : Seigneur , tu m'avois remis deux talens ; en voici deux autres que j'ai gagnés de plus.

23. Et son Maître lui dit : Cela va bien , bon et fidèle serviteur ; tu as été fidèle en peu de chose ; je t'établirai sur beaucoup ; entre dans la joie de ton Seigneur.

24. Mais celui qui n'avoit reçu qu'un talent,vint et dit : Seigneur , je savois que tu étois un homme dur qui moissonnes où tu n'as pas semé , et qui recueilles où tu n'as pas répandu ;

25. C'est pourquoi *te* craignant, je suis allé , et j'ai caché ton talent dans la terre ; voici , tu as ce qui est à toi.

26. Et son Maître lui répondit : Méchant et paresseux serviteur , tu savois que je moissonnois où je n'ai pas semé , et que je recueillois où je n'ai pas répandu ;

16 Then he that had received the five talents went and traded with the same, and made *them* other five talents.

17 And likewise he that *had received* two, he also gained other two.

18 But he that had received one, went and digged in the earth, and hid his lord's money.

19 After a long time the lord of those servants cometh, and reckoneth with them.

20 And so he that had received five talents came, and brought other five talents, saying, Lord, thou deliveredst unto me five talents: behold, I have gained beside them five talents more.

21 His lord said unto him, Well done, *thou* good and faithful servant: thou hast been faithful over a few things, I will make thee ruler over many things : enter thou into the joy of thy lord.

22 He also that had received two talents came, and said, Lord, thou deliveredst unto me two talents: behold, I have gained two other talents beside them.

23 His lord said unto him, Well done, good and faithful servant: thou hast been faithful over a few things, I will make thee ruler over many things : enter thou into the joy of thy lord.

24 Then he which had received the one talent came, and said, Lord, I knew thee, that thou art an hard man, reaping where thou hast not sown, and gathering where thou hast not strawed :

25 And I was afraid, and went and hid thy talent in the earth : lo, *there* thou hast *that is* thine.

26 His lord answered, and said unto him, *Thou* wicked and slothful servant, thou knewest that I reap where I sowed not, and gather where I have not strawed :

67

27 Ἔδει οὖν σε βαλεῖν τὸ ἀργύριόν μου τοῖς τραπεζίταις· καὶ ἐλθὼν ἐγὼ ἐκομισάμην ἂν τὸ ἐμὸν σὺν τόκῳ.

28 Ἄρατε οὖν ἀπ' αὐτοῦ τὸ τάλαντον, καὶ δότε τῷ ἔχοντι τὰ δέκα τάλαντα.

29 (Τῷ γὰρ ἔχοντι παντὶ δοθήσεται, καὶ περισσευθήσεται· ἀπὸ δὲ τοῦ μὴ ἔχοντος, καὶ ὃ ἔχει, ἀρθήσεται ἀπ' αὐτοῦ.)

30 Καὶ τὸν ἀχρεῖον δοῦλον ἐκβάλλετε εἰς τὸ σκότος τὸ ἐξώτερον· ἐκεῖ ἔσται ὁ κλαυθμὸς καὶ ὁ βρυγμὸς τῶν ὀδόντων.

34 Προσέχετε δὲ ἑαυτοῖς, μήποτε βαρυνθῶσιν ὑμῶν αἱ καρδίαι ἐν κραιπάλῃ, καὶ μέθῃ, καὶ μερίμναις βιωτικαῖς, καὶ αἰφνίδιος ἐφ' ὑμᾶς ἐπιστῇ ἡ ἡμέρα ἐκείνη.

35 Ὡς παγὶς γὰρ ἐπελεύσεται ἐπὶ πάντας τοὺς καθημένους ἐπὶ πρόσωπον πάσης τῆς γῆς.

36 Ἀγρυπνεῖτε οὖν, ἐν παντὶ καιρῷ δεόμενοι, ἵνα καταξιωθῆτε ἐκφυγεῖν ταῦτα πάντα τὰ μέλ-

31 Ὅταν δὲ ἔλθῃ ὁ υἱὸς τοῦ ἀνθρώπου ἐν τῇ δόξῃ αὐτοῦ, καὶ πάντες οἱ ἅγιοι ἄγγελοι μετ' αὐτοῦ, τότε καθίσει ἐπὶ θρόνου δόξης αὐτοῦ.

32 Καὶ συναχθήσεται ἔμπροσθεν αὐτοῦ πάντα τὰ ἔθνη· καὶ ἀφοριεῖ αὐτοὺς ἀπ' ἀλλήλων, ὥσπερ ὁ ποιμὴν ἀφορίζει τὰ πρόβατα ἀπὸ τῶν ἐρίφων.

33 Καὶ στήσει τὰ μὲν πρόβατα ἐκ δεξιῶν αὐτοῦ, τὰ δὲ ἐρίφια ἐξ εὐωνύμων.

34 Τότε ἐρεῖ ὁ βασιλεὺς τοῖς ἐκ δεξιῶν αὐτοῦ· Δεῦτε οἱ εὐλογημένοι τοῦ πατρός μου, κληρονομήσατε τὴν ἡτοιμασμένην ὑμῖν βασιλείαν ἀπὸ καταβολῆς κόσμου.

35 Ἐπείνασα γάρ, καὶ ἐδώκατέ μοι φαγεῖν· ἐδίψησα, καὶ ἐποτίσατέ με· ξένος ἤμην, καὶ συνηγάγετέ με·

36 Γυμνός, καὶ περιεβάλετέ με· ἠσθένησα, καὶ ἐπεσκέψασθέ με· ἐν φυλακῇ ἤμην, καὶ ἤλθετε πρός με.

---

27 Oportuit ergo te jacere argentum meum mensariis: & veniens ego recepissem utique meum cum usura.

28 Tollite itaque ab eo talentum, & date habenti decem talenta.

29 (Nam habenti omni dabitur, & augebitur: à verò non habente, & quod videtur habere, auferetur ab eo.)

30 Et inutilem servum ejicite in tenebras exteriores: illic erit fletus & fremitus dentium.

34 Attendite autem vobis ipsis, ne forte graventur vestra corda in crapula, & ebrietate, & curis vitalibus, & repentina in vos superveniat dies illa.

35 Tanquam laqueus enim superveniet in omnes sedentes super faciem omnis terræ.

36 Vigilate itaque in omni tempore rogantes, ut digni habeamini effugere ista omnia fu-

31 Quum autem venerit Filius hominis in gloriâ suâ, & omnes sancti angeli cum eo, tunc sedebit super throno gloriæ suæ:

32 Et cogentur ante eum omnes gentes, & separabit eos ab invicem, sicut pastor segregat oves ab hœdis.

33 Et statuet quidem oves à dexteris suis, at hœdos a sinistris.

34 Tunc dicet rex his qui à dextris ejus: Venite benedicti Patris mei, possidete paratum vobis regnum à fundamento mundi.

35 Esurivi enim, & dedistis mihi manducare: sitivi, & potastis me: hospes eram, & collegistis me:

36 Nudus, & amicivistis me: ægrotavi, & visitastis me: in carcere eram, & venistis ad me.

27. Il te falloit donc donner mon argent aux banquiers; et à mon retour, j'aurois retiré ce qui est à moi avec l'intérêt.

28. Otez-lui donc le talent, et le donnez à celui qui a dix talens.

29. Car on donnera à celui qui a, et il aura encore davantage ; mais à celui qui n'a pas, on lui ôtera même ce qu'il a.

30. Jetez donc le serviteur inutile dans les ténèbres de déhors ; c'est là qu'il y aura des pleurs et des grincemens de dents.

34. Prenez donc garde à vous-mêmes, de peur que vos cœurs ne soient appesantis par la gourmandise, par les excès du vin, et par les inquiétudes de cette vie ; et que ce jour-là ne vous surprenne subitement.

35. Car il surprendra comme un filet tous ceux qui habitent sur la face de la terre.

36. Veillez donc, et priez en tout tems, afin que vous soyez trouvés dignes d'éviter toutes ces choses qui doivent arriver, et de subsister devant le Fils de l'homme.

31. Or, quand le Fils de l'homme viendra dans sa gloire, avec tous les saints Anges, alors il s'asseiera sur le trône de sa gloire.

32. Et toutes les nations seront assemblées devant lui ; et il séparera les uns d'avec les autres, comme un berger sépare les brebis d'avec les boucs.

33. Et il mettra les brebis à sa droite, et les boucs à sa gauche.

34. Alors le Roi dira à ceux qui seront à sa droite : Venez, vous qui êtes bénis de mon Père, possédez en héritage le Royaume qui vous a été préparé dès la création du monde.

35. Car j'ai eu faim, et vous m'avez donné à manger ; j'ai eu soif, et vous m'avez donné à boire ; j'étois étranger, et vous m'avez recueilli ;

36. J'étois nud, et vous m'avez vêtu ; j'étois malade, et vous m'avez visité ; j'étois en prison, et vous m'êtes venu voir.

---

27 Thou oughtest, therefore, to have put my money to the exchangers, and *then* at my coming I should have received mine own with usury.

28 Take, therefore, the talent from him, and give it unto him which hath ten talents.

29 For unto every one that hath shall be given, and he shall have abundance: but from him that hath not, shall be taken away even that which he hath.

30 And cast ye the unprofitable servant into outer darkness: there shall be weeping and gnashing of teeth.

34 And take heed to yourselves, lest at any time your hearts be overcharged with surfeiting, and drunkenness, and cares of this life, and *so* that day come upon you unawares.

35 For as a snare shall it come on all them that dwell on the face of the whole earth.

36 Watch ye, therefore, and pray always, that ye may be accounted worthy to escape all these things that shall come to pass, and to stand before the Son of Man.

31 When the Son of Man shall come in his glory, and all the holy angels with him, then shall he sit upon the throne of his glory:

32 And before him shall be gathered all nations: and he shall separate them one from another, as a shepherd divideth his sheep from the goats:

33 And he shall set the sheep on his right hand, but the goats on the left.

34 Then shall the King say unto them on his right hand, Come, ye blessed of my Father, inherit the kingdom prepared for you from the foundation of the world:

35 For I was an hungered, and ye gave me meat: I was thirsty, and ye gave me drink: I was a stranger, and ye took me in:

36 Naked, and ye clothed me: I was sick, and ye visited me: I was in prison, and ye came unto me.

68

37 Τότε ἀποκριθήσονlαι αὐτῷ
οἱ δίκαιοι, λέγονlες· Κύριε, πότε
σε εἴδομεν πεινῶνlα, ἢ ἐθρέψα-
μεν; ἢ διψῶνlα, ἢ ἐποτίσαμεν;

38 Πότε δέ σε εἴδομεν ξένον,
ἢ συνηγάγομεν; ἢ γυμνὸν, ἢ πε-
ριεβάλομεν;

39 Πότε δέ σε εἴδομεν ἀσθενῆ,
ἢ ἐν φυλακῇ, ἢ ἤλθομεν πρός σε;

40 Καὶ ἀποκριθεὶς ὁ βασιλεὺς,
ἐρεῖ αὐτοῖς· Ἀμὴν λέγω ὑμῖν,
ἐφ' ὅσον ἐποιήσαlε ἑνὶ τούτων τῶν
ἀδελφῶν μου τῶν ἐλαχίςων, ἐμοὶ
ἐποιήσαlε.

41 Τότε ἐρεῖ ἢ τοῖς ἐξ εὐωνύ-
μων· Πορεύεσθε ἀπ' ἐμοῦ οἱ κα-
τηραμένοι εἰς τὸ πῦρ τὸ αἰώνιον,
τὸ ἡτοιμασμένον τῷ διαβόλῳ ἢ
τοῖς ἀγγέλοις αὐτοῦ·

42 Ἐπείνασα γὰρ, ἢ οὐκ ἐδώ-
καlέ μοι φαγεῖν· ἐδίψησα, ἢ οὐκ
ἐποτίσαlέ με·

43 ξένος ἤμην, ἢ οὐ συνηγά-
γεlέ με· γυμνὸς, ἢ οὐ περιεβά-
λεlέ με· ἀσθενὴς ἢ ἐν φυλακῇ, ἢ
οὐκ ἐπεσκέψασθέ με.

44 Τότε ἀποκριθήσονlαι αὐτῷ
ἢ αὐτοὶ, λέγονlες· Κύριε, πότε
σε εἴδομεν πεινῶνlα, ἢ διψῶνlα,
ἢ ξένον, ἢ γυμνὸν, ἢ ἀσθενῆ, ἢ ἐν
φυλακῇ, ἢ οὐ διηκονήσαμέν σοι;

45 Τότε ἀποκριθήσεlαι αὐτοῖς,
λέγων· Ἀμὴν λέγω ὑμῖν, ἐφ'
ὅσον οὐκ ἐποιήσαlε ἑνὶ τούτων τῶν
ἐλαχίςων, οὐδὲ ἐμοὶ ἐποιήσαlε.

46 Καὶ ἀπελεύσονlαι οὗτοι εἰς
κόλασιν αἰώνιον· οἱ δὲ δίκαιοι εἰς
ζωὴν αἰώνιον. 24 † 2.

Κεφ. ιδ. 14.

1 Ἦν δὲ τὸ πάσχα ἢ τὰ
ἄζυμα μετὰ δύο ἡμέρας·
ἢ ἐζήτουν οἱ ἀρχιερεῖς ἢ οἱ γραμ-
μαlεῖς πῶς αὐτὸν ἐν δόλῳ κρα-
τήσανlες ἀποκlείνωσιν.

2 Ἔλεγον δέ· Μὴ ἐν τῇ ἑορτῇ,
μήποτε θόρυβος ἔςαι τῷ λαῷ.

* 3 Καὶ ὄνlος αὐτῷ ἐν Βη-
θανίᾳ ἐν τῇ οἰκίᾳ Σίμωνος τῷ
‡ λεπρῷ, καlακειμένου αὐτῷ, ἦλθε

---

37 Tunc respondebunt ei justi, dicentes: Domine, quando
te vidimus esurientem, & alui-
mus? vel sitientem, & potavi-
mus?

38 Quando autem te vidimus
hospitem, & collegimus? aut
nudum, & amicivimus?

39 Quando verò te vidimus
infirmum, aut in carcere, &
venimus ad te?

40 Et respondens rex dicet illis: Amen dico vobis, quatenus
fecistis uni horum fratrum meo-
rum minimorum, mihi fecistis.

41 Tunc dicet & his qui à
sinistris: Ite à me maledicti in
ignem æternum, præparatum
diabolo & angelis ejus.

42 Esurivi enim, & non dedistis mihi manducare: sitivi,
& non potastis me:

43 Hospes eram, & non collegistis me: nudus, & non a-
micivistis me: infirmus, & in
carcere, & non visitastis me.

44 Tunc respondebunt ei &
ipsi, dicentes: Domine, quando
te vidimus esurientem, aut sitientem, aut hospitem, aut nudum, aut infirmum, aut in carcere, & non ministravimus tibi?

45 Tunc respondebit illis,
dicens: Amen dico vobis, quatenus non fecistis uni horum
minimorum, nec mihi fecistis.

46 Et ibunt hi in supplicium
æternum: at justi in vitam æ-
ternam.

CAPUT XIV.

1 ERat autem Pascha, & A-
zyma post duos dies:
& quærebant summi Sacerdotes
& Scribæ quomodo eum dolo
prehendentes occiderent.

2 Dicebant autem: non in
festo, ne quando tumultus sit
populi.

3 Et existente eo in Bethania, in domo Simonis leprosi,
accumbente eo, venit mulier

37. Alors les justes lui répondront : Seigneur, quand est-ce que nous t'avons vu avoir faim, et que nous t'avons donné à manger ; ou avoir soif, et que nous t'avons donné à boire ?

38. Et quand est-ce que nous t'avons vu étranger, et que nous t'avons recueilli ; ou nud, et que nous t'avons vêtu.

39. Ou quand est-ce que nous t'avons vu malade, ou en prison, et que nous sommes venus te voir ?

40. Et le Roi répondant, leur dira : Je vous dis en vérité, qu'en tant que vous avez fait ces choses à l'un de ces plus petits de mes frères, vous me les avez faites.

41. Ensuite il dira à ceux qui seront à sa gauche : Retirez-vous de moi, maudits, et allez dans le feu éternel, qui est préparé au Diable et à ses Anges.

42. Car j'ai eu faim, et vous ne m'avez pas donné à manger ; j'ai eu soif, et vous ne m'avez pas donné à boire.

43. J'étois étranger, et vous ne m'avez pas recueilli ; j'étois nud, et vous ne m'avez pas vêtu ; j'étois malade et en prison, et vous ne m'avez pas visité.

44. Alors ceux-là lui répondront aussi : Seigneur, quand est-ce que nous t'avons vu avoir faim, ou soif, ou être étranger, ou nud, ou malade, ou en prison, et que nous ne t'avons point assisté ?

45. Et il leur répondra : Je vous dis en vérité, qu'en ce que vous ne l'avez pas fait à l'un de ces plus petits, vous ne me l'avez pas fait non plus.

46. Et ceux-ci s'en iront aux peines éternelles ; mais les justes s'en iront à la vie éternelle.

CHAPITRE XIV.

Jésus-Christ oint d'une femme ; trahi par Judas ; institue la Sainte Cène ; se prépare à la mort par de très-ardentes prières. Il est saisi dans le jardin, amené au procès et renié de Pierre.

LA fête de Pâque et des pains sans levain étoit deux jours après ; et les Scribes cherchoient comment ils pourroient se saisir de Jésus par finesse, et le faire mourir.

2. Mais ils disoient : Il ne faut pas que ce soit durant la fête, de peur qu'il ne se fasse du tumulte parmi le peuple.

3. Et Jésus étant à Béthanie, dans la maison de Simon le lépreux,

37 Then shall the righteous answer him, saying, Lord, when saw we thee an hungered, and fed *thee?* or thirsty, and gave *thee* drink ?

38 When saw we thee a stranger, and took *thee* in ? or naked, and clothed *thee ?*

39 Or when saw we thee sick, or in prison, and came unto *thee?*

40 And the King shall answer, and say unto them, Verily I say unto you, Inasmuch as ye have done *it* unto one of the least of these my brethren, ye have done *it* unto me.

41 Then shall he say also unto them on the left hand, Depart from me, ye cursed, into everlasting fire, prepared for the devil and his angels ;

42 For I was an hungered, and ye gave me no meat : I was thirsty, and ye gave me no drink :

43 I was a stranger, and ye took me not in : naked, and ye clothed me not : sick, and in prison, and ye visited me not.

44 Then shall they also answer him, saying, Lord, when saw we *thee* an hungered, or athirst, or a stranger, or naked, or sick, or in prison, and did not minister unto thee ?

45 Then shall he answer them, saying, Verily I say unto you, Inasmuch as ye did *it* not to one of the least of these, ye did *it* not to me.

46 And these shall go away into everlasting punishment : but the righteous into life eternal.

CHAP. XIV.
Conspiracy against Christ.

AFTER two days was *the feast* of the passover, and of unleavened bread : and the chief priests and the scribes sought how they might take him by craft, and put *him* to death.

2 But they said, Not on the feast-day, lest there be an uproar of the people.

3 And being in Bethany, in the house of Simon the leper, as he sat at meat, there came a woman,

γυνὴ ἔχυσα ἀλάβαςρον μύρυ,
‡ νάρδυ ‡ πιςικῆς ‡ πολυτελῆς·
ἢ συντρίψασα τὸ ἀλάβαςρον,
κατέχεεν αὐτῦ κατὰ τῆς κεφαλῆς.

4 Ἦσαν δέ τινες ἀγανακτῦν-
τες πρὸς ἑαυτὺς, ἢ λέγοντες;
Εἰς τί ἡ ἀπώλεια αὐτη τῦ μύρυ
γέγονεν;

5 Ἠδύναλο γὰρ τῦτο πραθῆ-
ναι ἐπάνω τριακοσίων δηναρίων,
ἢ δοθῆναι τοῖς πτωχοῖς. Καὶ
ἐνεβριμῶντο αὐτῇ.

6 Ὁ δὲ Ἰησῦς εἶπεν· Ἄφετε
αὐτήν· τί αὐτῇ κόπυς παρέχετε;
καλὸν ἔργον εἰργάσαλο εἰς ἐμέ.

7 Πάντοτε γὰρ τὺς πτωχὺς
ἔχετε μεθ' ἑαυτῶν, ἢ ὅταν θέλητε, δύνασθε αὐτὺς εὖ ποιῆσαι·
ἐμὲ δὲ ὐ πάντοτε ἔχετε.

* 8 Ὁ εἶχεν αὐτη, ἐποίησε·
‡ προέλαβε † μυρίσαι μυ τὸ
σῶμα εἰς τὸν ‡ ἐνταφιασμόν.

14 Τότε πορευθεὶς εἷς τῶν δώδεκα, ὁ λεγόμενος Ἰύδας Ἰσκα-
ριώτης, πρὸς τὺς ἀρχιερεῖς,

15 Εἶπε· Τί θέλετέ μοι δῦναι,
κἀγὼ ὑμῖν παραδώσω αὐτόν;
Οἱ δὲ ἔςησαν αὐτῷ τριάκοντα ἀργύρια.

16 Καὶ ἀπὸ τότε ἐζήτει εὐ-
καιρίαν ἵνα αὐτὸν παραδῷ.

17 Τῇ δὲ πρώτῃ τῶν ἀζύμων
προσῆλθον οἱ μαθηταὶ τῷ Ἰησῦ,
λέγοντες αὐτῷ· Πῦ θέλεις ἑτοι-
μάσωμέν σοι φαγεῖν τὸ πάσχα;

18 Ὁ δὲ εἶπεν· Ὑπάγετε
εἰς τὴν πόλιν ‡ πρὸς τὸν † δεῖνα,
ἢ εἴπατε αὐτῷ· Ὁ διδάσκαλος
λέγει· Ὁ καιρός μυ ἐγγύς ἐςιν,
πρὸς σὲ ποιῶ τὸ πάσχα μετὰ
τῶν μαθητῶν μυ.

19 Καὶ ἐποίησαν οἱ μαθηταὶ
ὡς συνέταξεν αὐτοῖς ὁ Ἰησῦς· ἢ
ἡτοίμασαν τὸ πάσχα.

20 Ὀψίας δὲ γενομένης ἀνέ-
κειλο μετὰ τῶν δώδεκα.

24 Ἐγένετο δὲ ἢ † φιλονει-
κία ἐν αὐτοῖς, τὸ τίς αὐτῶν δοκεῖ εἶναι ‡ μείζων.

* 25 Ὁ δὲ εἶπεν αὐτοῖς· Οἱ
βασιλεῖς τῶν ἐθνῶν † κυριεύυσιν
αὐτῶν· ἢ οἱ ‡ ἐξυσιάζοντες αὐτῶν,
† εὐεργέται καλῦνται.

---

habens alabaſtrum unguenti,
nardi probati multi pretii : &
confringens alabaſtrum, effudit
ei juxta caput.

4 Erant autem quidam in-
dignati apud ſemetipſos, & dicentes? Ad quid perditio iſta
unguenti facta eſt?

5 Poterat enim iſtud venundari ſuper trecentis denariis, &
dari pauperibus. Et fremebant
ei.

6 At Jeſus dixit : Sinite eam :
Quid illi moleſtias exhibetis?
Pulchrum opus operata eſt in me.

7 Semper enim pauperes habetis cum vobis, & quum vo-
lueritis poteſtis illis benefacere :
me autem non ſemper habetis.

8 Quod habuit hæc, fecit :
præoccupavit ungere meum
corpus in ſepulturam.

14 Tunc vadens unus duodecim, dictus Judas Iſcariotes, ad
principes Sacerdotum,

15 Ait : Quid vultis mihi
dare, & ego vobis tradam eum?
Illi verò conſtituerunt ei triginta argentos.

16 Et exinde quærebat oppor-
tunitatem ut eum traderet.

17 At primâ Azymorum ac-
ceſſerunt diſcipuli Jeſu, dicentes
ei : Ubi vis paremus tibi come-
dere Paſcha?

18 Ille autem dixit : Ite in
civitatem ad quendam, & dicite
ei : Magiſter dicit : Tempus
meum prope eſt, apud te facio
Paſcha cum diſcipulis meis.

19 Et fecerunt diſcipuli ſicut
ordinaverat illis Jeſus, & para-
verunt Paſcha.

20 Veſpere autem facto, diſ-
cumbebat cum duodecim.

24 Facta eſt autem & con-
tentio in eis, hoc, quis eorum
videretur eſſe major.

25 Is autem dixit eis ; Reges
gentium dominantur in eos : &
poteſtatem habentes ipſorum,
benefici vocantur.

une femme vint à lui, lorsqu'il étoit à table, avec un vase d'albâtre, plein d'une huile odoriférante et de grand prix, qu'elle lui répandit sur la tête, ayant rompu le vase.

4. Et quelques-uns en furent indignés en eux-mêmes, et dirent : Pourquoi perdre ainsi ce parfum ?

5. Car on pouvoit le vendre plus de trois cents deniers, et les donner aux pauvres. Ainsi ils murmuroient contr'elle.

6. Mais Jésus leur dit : Laissez-la ; pourquoi lui faites-vous de la peine ? Elle a fait une bonne action à mon égard.

7. Car vous aurez toujours des pauvres parmi vous ; et toutes les fois que vous voudrez, vous pourrez leur faire du bien ; mais vous ne m'aurez pas toujours.

8. Elle a fait tout ce qui étoit en son pouvoir ; elle a embaumé par avance mon corps pour ma sépulture.

14. Alors l'un des douze, appelé Judas Iscariot, s'en alla vers les principaux Sacrificateurs,

15. Et leur dit : Que voulez-vous me donner, et je vous le livrerai ? Et ils convinrent de lui donner trente pièces d'argent.

16. Et depuis ce tems-là, il cherchoit une occasion propre pour le livrer.

17. Or, le premier jour de la fête des pains sans levain, les Disciples vinrent à Jésus et lui dirent : Où veux-tu que nous préparions pour manger la Pâque ?

18. Et il répondit : Allez dans le village chez un tel, et lui dites : Le Maître dit : Mon tems est proche ; je ferai la Pâque chez toi avec mes Disciples.

19. Et les Disciples firent comme Jésus leur avoit ordonné, et préparèrent la Pâque.

20. Quand le soir fut venu, il se mit à table avec les douze Apôtres.

24. Il arriva aussi une contestation entr'eux, pour savoir lequel d'entr'eux devoit être regardé comme le plus grand.

25. Mais il leur dit : Les Rois des nations les maitrisent ; et ceux qui usent d'autorité sur elles sont nommés bienfaiteurs.

having an alabaster-box of ointment of spikenard, very precious ; and she brake the box, and poured it on his head.

4 And there were some that had indignation within themselves, and said, Why was this waste of the ointment made ?

5 For it might have been sold for more than three hundred pence, and have been given to the poor. And they murmured against her.

6 And Jesus said, Let her alone, why trouble ye her ? she hath wrought a good work on me.

7 For ye have the poor with you always, and whensoever ye will, ye may do them good ; but me ye have not always.

8 She hath done what she could ; she is come aforehand to anoint my body to the burying.

14 Then one of the twelve called Judas Iscariot, went unto the chief priests,

15 And said unto them, What will ye give me, and I will deliver him unto you ? And they covenanted with him for thirty pieces of silver.

16 And from that time he sought opportunity to betray him.

17 Now, the first day of the feast of unleavened bread, the disciples came to Jesus, saying unto him, Where wilt thou that we prepare for thee to eat the passover ?

18 And he said, Go into the city to such a man, and say unto him, The Master saith, My time is at hand ; I will keep the passover at thy house with my disciples.

19 And the disciples did as Jesus had appointed them ; and they made ready the passover.

20 Now, when the even was come, he sat down with the twelve.

24 And there was also a strife among them, which of them should be accounted the greatest.

25 And he said unto them, The kings of the Gentiles exercise lordship over them ; and they that exercise authority upon them are called benefactors.

70

26 Ὑμεῖς δὲ ἐχ ὅτως· ἀλλ᾽ ὁ μείζων ἐν ὑμῖν, γενέσθω ὡς ὁ νεώτερ@· ἢ ὁ ἡγούμεν@, ὡς ὁ διακονῶν.

27 Τίς γὰρ μείζων, ὁ ἀνακείμεν@, ἢ ὁ διακονῶν; ἐχὶ ὁ ἀνακείμεν@; ἐγὼ δὲ εἰμι ἐν μέσῳ ὑμῶν ὡς ὁ διακονῶν.

2 Καὶ δείπνε γενομένε

4 Ἐγείρεται ἐκ τῇ δείπνε, ἡ τίθησι τὰ ἱμάτια· ἡ λαβὼν λέντιον, διέζωσεν ἑαυτόν.

* 5 Εἶτα βάλλει ὕδωρ εἰς τὸν † νιπτῆρα, ἡ ἤρξατο νίπτειν τὰς ποδας τῶν μαθητῶν, ἡ ‡ ἐκμάσσειν τῷ ‡ λεντίῳ ᾧ ἦν διεζωσμέν@.

6 Ἔρχεται ἐν πρὸς Σίμωνα Πέτρον· ἡ λέγει αὐτῷ ἐκεῖν@· Κύριε, σύ με νίπτεις τὰς ποδας;

7 Ἀπεκρίθη Ἰησῦς ἡ εἶπεν αὐτῷ· Ὃ ἐγὼ ποιῶ, σὺ ἐκ οἶδας ἄρτι, γνώσῃ δὲ μεθὰ ταῦτα.

8 Λέγει αὐτῷ Πέτρ@· Οὐ μὴ νίψῃς τὰς ποδας με εἰς τὸν αἰῶνα. Ἀπεκρίθη αὐτῷ ὁ Ἰησῦς· Ἐὰν μὴ νίψω σε, ἐκ ἔχεις μέρ@ μετ᾽ ἐμᾶ.

9 Λέγει αὐτῷ Σίμων Πέτρ@· Κύριε, μὴ τὰς ποδας με μόνον, ἀλλὰ ἡ τὰς χεῖρας ἡ τὴν κεφαλήν.

10 Λέγει αὐτῷ ὁ Ἰησῦς· Ὃ λελεμμέν@ ἐ χρείαν ἔχει ἢ τὰς ποδας νίψασθαι, ἀλλ᾽ ἔςι καθαρὸς ὅλ@· ἡ ὑμεῖς καθαροί ἐςε, ἀλλ᾽ ἐχὶ πάντες.

11 Ἤδει γὰρ τὸν παραδιδόντα αὐτόν· διὰ τῦτο εἶπεν· Οὐχὶ πάντες καθαροί ἐςε.

12 Ὅτε ἐν ἔνιψε τὰς ποδας αὐτῶν, ἡ ἔλαβε τὰ ἱμάτια αὐτῦ, ἀναπεσὼν πάλιν, εἶπεν αὐτοῖς· Γινώσκετε τί πεποίηκα ὑμῖν;

13 Ὑμεῖς φωνεῖτε με· Ὁ διδάσκαλ@· ἡ ὁ κύρι@· ἡ καλῶς λέγετε· εἰμὶ γάρ.

14 Εἰ ἐν ἐγὼ ἔνιψα ὑμῶν τὰς ποδας, ὁ κύρι@· ἡ ὁ διδάσκαλ@· ἡ ὑμεῖς ὀφείλετε ἀλλήλων νίπτειν τὰς ποδας.

15 Ὑπόδειγμα γὰρ ἔδωκα ὑμῖν, ἵνα καθὼς ἐγὼ ἐποίησα ὑμῖν, ἡ ὑμεῖς ποιῆτε.

16 Ἀμὴν, ἀμὴν, λέγω ὑμῖν, ἐκ ἔςι δῦλ@ μείζων τῦ κυρίε αὐτῦ, ἐδὲ ἀπόςολ@ μείζων τῦ πέμψαντ@ αὐτόν.

17 Εἰ ταῦτα οἴδατε, μακάριοί ἐςε ἐὰν ποιῆτε αὐτά.

---

26 Vos autem non sic: sed qui major in vobis, fiat sicut junior: & qui præcessor, sicut ministratur.

27 Quis enim major, recumbens, an ministrans? nonne recumbens? ego autem sum in medio vestrum sicut ministrans.

2 Et cœna facta,

4 Surgit à cœna, & ponit vestimenta: & accipiens linteum, præcinxit seipsum.

5 Deinde injicit aquam in pelvim, & cœpit lavare pedes discipulorum, & extergere linteo quo erat præcinctus.

6 Venit ergo ad Simonem Petrum: & dicit ei ille: Domine, tu meos lavas pedes?

7 Respondit Jesus & dixit ei: Quod ego facio, tu nescis modo, scies autem post hæc.

8 Dicit ei Petrus: Non lavabis pedes meos in æternum. Respondit ei Jesus: Si non lavero te, non habes partem cum me.

9 Dicit ei Simon Petrus: Domine, non pedes meos tantum, sed & manus & caput.

10 Dicit ei Jesus: Lotus non opus habet quam pedes lavare, sed est mundus totus: Et vos mundi estis, sed non omnes.

11 Sciebat enim tradentem se; propter hoc dixit: Non omnes mundi estis.

12 Postquam ergo lavit pedes eorum, & accepit vestimenta sua, recumbens iterum, dixit eis: Scitis quid fecerim vobis?

13 Vos vocatis me: Magister & Dominus: & pulchre dicitis: sum etenim.

14 Si ergo ego lavi vestros pedes, dominus & magister, &, vos debetis alii aliorum lavare pedes.

15 Exemplum enim dedi vobis ut quemadmodum ego feci vobis, & vos faciatis.

16 Amen, amen, dico vobis, non est servus major domino suo, neque legatus major mittente illum.

17 Si hæc scitis, beati estis si feceritis ea.

26. Il n'en doit pas être de même entre vous ; mais que celui qui est le plus grand parmi vous, soit comme le moindre ; et celui qui gouverne, comme celui qui sert.

27. Car qui est le plus grand, celui qui est à table, ou celui qui sert ? N'est-ce pas celui qui est à table ? Et cependant je suis au milieu de vous comme celui qui sert.

2. Et après le souper

4. Se leva du souper, et ôta sa robe ; et ayant pris un linge, il s'en ceignit.

5. Ensuite il mit de l'eau dans un bassin, et se mit à laver les pieds de ses Disciples, et à les essuyer avec le linge dont il étoit ceint.

6. Il vint donc à Simon Pierre, qui lui dit, Toi, Seigneur, tu me laverois les pieds !

7. Jésus répondit, et lui dit : Tu ne sais pas maintenant ce que je fais ; mais tu le sauras dans la suite.

8. Pierre lui dit : Tu ne me laveras jamais les pieds. Jésus lui répondit : Si je ne te lave, tu n'auras point de part avec moi.

9. Simon Pierre lui dit : Seigneur, non-seulement les pieds, mais aussi les mains et la tête.

10. Jesus lui dit : Celui qui est lavé, n'a besoin sinon qu'on lui lave les pieds, puis il est entièrement net. Or vous êtes nets, mais non pas tous.

11. Car il savoit qui étoit celui qui le trahiroit ; c'est pour cela qu'il dit : Vous n'êtes pas tous nets.

12. Après donc qu'il leur eut lavé les pieds, et qu'il eut repris sa robe, s'étant remis à table, il leur dit : Savez-vous ce que je vous ai fait ?

13. Vous m'appelez Maître et Seigneur, et vous dites vrai, car je le suis.

14. Si donc je vous ai lavé les pieds, moi qui suis le Seigneur et le Maître, vous devez aussi vous laver les pieds les uns aux autres.

15. Car je vous ai donné un exemple, afin que vous fassiez comme je vous ai fait.

16. En vérité, en vérité je vous dis : Que le Serviteur n'est pas plus que son Maître, ni l'Envoyé plus que celui qui l'a envoyé.

17. Si vous savez ces choses, vous êtes bienheureux, pourvu que vous les pratiquiez.

---

26 But ye *shall* not *be* so : but he that is greatest among you, let him be as the younger ; and he that is chief, as he that doth serve.

27 For whether *is* greater, he that sitteth at meat, or he that serveth ? *is* not he that sitteth at meat ? but I am among you as he that serveth.

2 And supper being ended,

4 He riseth from supper, and laid aside his garments ; and took a towel, and girded himself.

5 After that he poureth water into a bason, and began to wash the disciples' feet, and to wipe them with the towel wherewith he was girded.

6 Then cometh he to Simon Peter : and Peter saith unto him, Lord, dost thou wash my feet ?

7 Jesus answered, and said unto him, What I do, thou knowest not now ; but thou shalt know hereafter.

8 Peter saith unto him, Thou shalt never wash my feet. Jesus answered him, If I wash thee not, thou hast no part with me.

9 Simon Peter saith unto him, Lord, not my feet only, but also *my* hands and *my* head.

10 Jesus saith to him, He that is washed, needeth not, save to wash *his* feet, but is clean every whit : and ye are clean, but not all.

11 For he knew who should betray him ; therefore said he, Ye are not all clean.

12 So, after he had washed their feet, and had taken his garments, and was set down again, he said unto them, Know ye what I have done to you ?

13 Ye call me Master and Lord : and ye say well ; for *so* I am.

14 If I then, *your* Lord and Master, have washed your feet, ye also ought to wash one another's feet.

15 For I have given you an example, that ye should do as I have done to you.

16 Verily, verily, I say unto you, The servant is not greater than his lord : neither he that is sent, greater than he that sent him.

17 If ye know these things, happy are ye if ye do them.

71

21 Ταῦτα εἰπὼν ὁ Ἰησοῦς ἐ-
ταράχθη τῷ πνεύματι, καὶ ἐμαρτύ-
ρησε, καὶ εἶπεν Ἀμὴν, ἀμὴν, λέγω
ὑμῖν, ὅτι εἷς ἐξ ὑμῶν παραδώ-
σει με.

22 Ἔβλεπον οὖν εἰς ἀλλήλους
οἱ μαθηταὶ, ἀπορούμενοι περὶ τί-
νΘ- λέγει.

23 Ἦν δὲ ἀνακείμενΘ- εἰς τῶν
μαθητῶν αὐτοῦ ἐν τῷ κόλπῳ τοῦ
Ἰησοῦ, ὃν ἠγάπα ὁ Ἰησοῦς.

24 Νεύει οὖν τούτῳ Σίμων Πέ-
τρΘ- πυθέσθαι τίς ἂν εἴη περὶ
οὗ λέγει.

25 Ἐπιπεσὼν δὲ ἐκεῖνΘ- ἐπὶ
τὸ ςῆθΘ- τοῦ Ἰησοῦ, λέγει αὐτῷ·
Κύριε, τίς ἐςιν;

26 Ἀποκρίνεται ὁ Ἰησοῦς Ἐ-
κεῖνός ἐςιν ᾧ ἐγὼ βάψας τὸ ψωμίον ἐπιδώσω. Καὶ ἐμβάψας τὸ
ψωμίον, δίδωσιν Ἰούδᾳ Σίμωνος
Ἰσκαριώτῃ.

31 Ὅτε οὖν ἐξῆλθε, λέγει ὁ
Ἰησοῦς·

34 Ἐντολὴν καινὴν δίδωμι ὑμῖν,
ἵνα ἀγαπᾶτε ἀλλήλους· καθὼς ἠ-
γάπησα ὑμᾶς, ἵνα καὶ ὑμεῖς ἀγαπᾶτε ἀλλήλους.

35 Ἐν τούτῳ γνώσονται πάντες
ὅτι ἐμοὶ μαθηταί ἐςε, ἐὰν ἀγάπην
ἔχητε ἐν ἀλλήλοις.

31 Τότε λέγει αὐτοῖς ὁ Ἰησοῦς·
Πάντες ὑμεῖς σκανδαλισθήσεσθε ἐν
ἐμοὶ ἐν τῇ νυκτὶ ταύτῃ·

33 Ἀποκριθεὶς δὲ ὁ ΠέτρΘ-,
εἶπεν αὐτῷ· Εἰ καὶ πάντες σκανδα-
λισθήσονται ἐν σοὶ, ἐγὼ οὐδέποτε
σκανδαλισθήσομαι.

μετὰ σοῦ ἕτοιμός εἰμι καὶ εἰς φυλακὴν καὶ εἰς θάνατον πορεύεσθαι.

34 Ὁ δὲ εἶπε· Λέγω σοι,
Πέτρε, οὐ μὴ φωνήσει σήμερον
ἀλέκτωρ, πρὶν ἢ τρὶς ἀπαρνήσῃ
μὴ εἰδέναι με.

35 Λέγει αὐτῷ ὁ ΠέτρΘ-· Κἂν
δέῃ με σὺν σοὶ ἀποθανεῖν, οὐ μή
σε ἀπαρνήσομαι. Ὁμοίως καὶ πάντες
οἱ μαθηταὶ εἶπον.

36 Τότε ἔρχεται μετ᾽ αὐτῶν
ὁ Ἰησοῦς εἰς χωρίον λεγόμενον
Γεθσημανῆ καὶ λέγει τοῖς μαθηταῖς·
Καθίσατε αὐτοῦ, ἕως οὗ ἀπελθὼν
προσεύξωμαι ἐκεῖ·

---

21 Hæc dicens Jesus turba-
tus est spiritu, & protestatus est,
& dixit : Amen amen dico vobis, unus ex vobis tradet me.

22 Aspiciebant ergo ad invicem discipuli, hæsitantes de
quo diceret.

23 Erat autem recumbens u-
nus discipulorum ejus in sinu
Jesu, quem diligebat Jesus.

24 Innuit ergo huic Simon
Petrus percontari quis esset de
quo dicit.

25 Incumbens autem ille supra pectus Jesu, dicit ei : Domine, quis est ?

26 Respondit Jesus : Ille est
cui ego intingens buccellam de-
dero. Et intingens buccellam,
dat Judæ Simonis Iscariotæ.

31 Quum ergo exisset, dicit
Jesus :

34 Mandatum novum do vo-
bis, Ut diligatis invicem: sicut di-
lexi vos, ut & vos diligatis invicem.

35 In hoc cognoscent omnes
quia mei discipuli estis, si dilec-
tionem habueritis ad invicem.

31 Tunc dicit illis Jesus :
Omnes vos offendemini in me
in nocte istâ.

33 Respondens autem Petrus,
ait illi : Si & omnes scandalizati
fuerint in te, ego nunquam
scandalizabor.

tecum paratus sum & in
carcerem, & in mortem ire.

34 Ille autem dixit : Dico
tibi, Petre, non cantabit hodie
gallus, prius quam ter abneges,
nosse me.

35 Ait illi Petrus : Etiam si
oportuerit me cum te mori, non
te negabo. Similiter & omnes
discipuli dixerunt.

36 Tunc venit cum illis Jesus in villam dictam Gethse-
mani, & dicit discipulis : Se-
dete hic, usquequò vadens orem
illic.

21. Quand Jésus eut dit cela, il fut ému en son esprit, et il dit ouvertement : En vérité, en vérité je vous dis, que l'un de vous me trahira.

22. Et les Disciples se regardoient les uns les autres, étant en peine de qui il parloit.

23. Or il y avoit un des Disciples de Jésus, celui que Jésus aimoit, qui étoit couché vers son sein.

24. Simon Pierre lui fit signe de demander qui étoit celui de qui il parloit.

25. Lui donc s'étant penché sur le sein de Jésus, lui dit : Seigneur, qui est-ce ?

26. Jésus répondit : C'est celui à qui je donnerai un morceau trempé. Et ayant trempé un morceau, il le donna à Judas Iscariot, fils de Simon.

31. Quand il fut sorti, Jésus dit :

34. Je vous donne un commandément nouveau, que vous vous aimiez les uns les autres ; que comme je vous ai aimés, vous vous aimiez aussi les uns les autres.

35. C'est à cela que tous connoîtront que vous êtes mes Disciples, si vous avez de l'amour les uns pour les autres.

31. Alors Jésus leur dit : Je vous serai cette nuit à tous une occasion de chute :

33. Et Pierre prenant la parole, lui dit : Quand même tous les autres se scandaliseroient en toi, je ne serai jamais scandalisé. je suis tout prêt d'aller avec toi, et en prison et à la mort.

34. Mais Jésus lui dit : Pierre, je te dis que le coq ne chantera point aujourd'hui, que tu n'aies nié trois fois de me connoître.

35. Puis il leur dit : Lorsque je vous ai envoyés sans bourse, sans sac, et sans souliers, avez-vous manqué de quelque chose ? Et ils répondirent : De rien.

36. Mais maintenant, leur dit-il, que celui qui a une bourse la prenne, et de même celui qui a un sac ; et que celui qui n'a point d'épée vende sa robe, et en achète une.

---

21 When Jesus had thus said, he J. 13 was troubled in spirit, and testified, and said, Verily, verily, I say unto you, that one of you shall betray me.

22 Then the disciples looked one on another, doubting of whom he spake.

23 Now there was leaning on Jesus' bosom one of his disciples, whom Jesus loved.

24 Simon Peter, therefore, beckoned to him, that he should ask who it should be of whom he spake.

25 He then, lying on Jesus' breast, saith unto him, Lord, who is it?

26 Jesus answered, He it is, to whom I shall give a sop, when I have dipped it. And when he had dipped the sop, he gave it to Judas Iscariot, the son of Simon.

31 Therefore, when he was gone out, Jesus said,

34 A new commandment I give unto you, That ye love one another; as I have loved you, that ye also love one another.

35 By this shall all men know that ye are my disciples, if ye have love one to another.

31 Then saith Jesus unto them, M. 26 All ye shall be offended because of me this night:

33 Peter answered, and said unto him, Though all men shall be offended because of thee, yet will I never be offended.

I am ready to go with thee, both L. 22 into prison, and to death.

34 And he said, I tell thee, Peter, the cock shall not crow this day, before that thou shalt thrice deny that thou knowest me.

35 Peter said unto him, Though M. 26 I should die with thee, yet will I not deny thee. Likewise also said all the disciples.

36 Then cometh Jesus with them unto a place called Gethsemane, and saith unto the disciples, Sit ye here, while I go and pray yonder.

72

37 Καὶ παραλαβὼν τὸν Πέτρον κỳ τὸς δύο υἰὸς Ζεϐεδαίε ἤρξαῖο λυπεῖσθαι κỳ ἀδημονεῖν.

38 Τότε λέγει αὐτοῖς· Περίλυπός ἐςιν ἡ ψυχή με ἕως θανάτε· μείναῖε ὧδε, κỳ γρηγορεῖτε μετ' ἐμῦ.

39 Καὶ προελθὼν μικρὸν, ἔπεσεν ἐπὶ πρόσωπον αὐτῦ, προσευχόμενΘ·, κỳ λέγων· Πάτερ με, εἰ δυναῖόν ἐςι, παρελθέτω ἀπ' ἐμῦ τὸ ποῖήριον τῦτο. πλὴν ἐχ ὡς ἐγὼ θέλω, ἀλλ' ὡς σύ.

40 Καὶ ἔρχεῖαι πρὸς τὺς μαθηῖὰς, κỳ εὑρίσκει αὐτὺς καθεύδονῖας· κỳ λέγει τῷ Πέτρῳ· Οὕτως ἐκ ἰσχύσαῖε μίαν ὥραν γρηγορῆσαι μετ' ἐμῦ;

41 Γρηγορεῖτε κỳ προσεύχεσθε, ἵνα μὴ εἰσέλθηῖε εἰς πειρασμόν· τὸ μὲν πνεῦμα πρόθυμον, ἡ δὲ σὰρξ ἀσθενής.

42 Πάλιν ἐκ δευῖέρε ἀπελθὼν προσηύξαῖο, λέγων· Πάτερ με, εἰ ὀ δύναῖαι τῦτο τὸ ποῖήριον παρελθεῖν ἀπ' ἐμῦ, ἐὰν μὴ αὐτὸ πίω, γε͂ γθήτω τὸ θέλημά σε.

43 Καὶ ἐλθὼν εὑρίσκει αὐτὺς πάλιν καθεύδονῖας· ἦσαν γὰρ αὐτῶν οἱ ὀφθαλμοὶ βεϐαρημένοι.

44 Καὶ ἀφεὶς αὐτὺς, ἀπελθὼν πάλιν, προσηύξαῖο ἐκ τρίτε, τὸν αὐτὸν λόγον εἰπών.

45 Τότε ἔρχεῖαι πρὸς τὺς μαθηῖὰς αὐτῦ, κỳ λέγει αὐτοῖς· Καθεύδεῖε τὸ λοιπὸν, κỳ ἀναπαύεσθε·

Κεφ. ιή. 18.

1 Τ Αῦτα εἰπὼν ὁ Ἰησῦς, ἐξῆλθε σὺν τοῖς μαθηῖαῖς αὐτῦ πέραν τῦ χειμάρρε τῶν κέδρων, ὅπε ἦν κῆπΘ·, εἰς ὃν εἰσῆλθεν αὐτὸς κỳ οἱ μαθηῖαὶ αὐτῦ.

2 Ἤδει δὲ κỳ Ἰύδας, ὁ παραδιδὸς αὐτὸ, τὸν τόπον ὅτι πολλάκις συνήχθη ὁ Ἰησῦς ἐκεῖ μεῖὰ τῶν μαθηῖῶν αὐτῦ.

3 Ὁ ῦν Ἰύδας λαϐὼν τὴν σπεῖραν, κỳ ἐκ τῶν ἀρχιερέων κỳ φαρισαίων ὑπηρέτας, ἔρχεῖαι ἐκεῖ μεῖὰ φανῶν κỳ λαμπάδων κỳ ὅπλων.

---

37 Et assumens Petrum, & duos filios Zebedæi, cœpit contristari & graviffimè angi.

38 Tunc ait illis; Undique triftis est anima mea ufque ad mortem. Manete hic, & vigilate cum me.

39 Et progreffus pufillùm, procidit in faciem fuam, orans, & dicens: Pater mi, fi poffibile eft, tranfeat à me calix ifte, veruntamen non ficut ego volo, fed ficut tu.

40 Et venit ad difcipulos, & invenit eos dormientes: & dicit Petro: Sic non potuiftis una hora vigilare cum me?

41 Vigilate & orate, ut non intretis in tentationem: Quidem fpiritus promptus, verùm caro infirma.

42 Iterum ex fecundò abiens oravit dicens: Pater mi, fi non poteft hic calix tranfire à me, fi non illum bibam, fiat voluntas tua.

43 Et veniens invenit eos rurfus dormientes: erant enim eorum oculi gravati.

44 Et relinquens illos, abiens iterum, oravit ex tertio, eundem fermonem dicens.

45 Tunc venit ad difcipulos fuos, & dicit illis: Dormite cæterum, & requiefcite:

CAPUT XVIII.

1 HÆC dicens Jefus, egreffus eft cum difcipulis fuis trans torrentem Cedron, ubi erat hortus, in quem introivit ipfe, & difcipuli ejus.

2 Sciebat autem & Judas, tradens eum, locum, quia frequenter convenerat Jefus illuc cum difcipulis fuis.

3 Ergo Judas accipiens cohortem, & ex principibus Sacerdotum & Pharifæis miniftros, venit illuc cum laternis & facibus, & armis.

37. Et ayant pris avec lui Pierre et les deux fils de Zébédée, il commença à être fort triste, et dans une amère douleur.

38. Et il leur dit : Mon ame est saisie de tristesse jusqu'à la mort; demeurez ici, et veillez avec moi.

39. Et étant allé un peu plus avant, il se jeta le visage contre terre, priant et disant : Mon Père, que cette coupe passe loin de moi, s'il est possible ! Toutefois, *qu'il en soit*, non comme je le voudrois, mais comme tu le veux.

40. Puis il vint vers ses Disciples, et les trouva endormis ; et il dit à Pierre : Est-il possible que vous n'ayez pu veiller une heure avec moi ?

41. Veillez et priez, de peur que vous ne tombiez dans la tentation; car l'esprit *est* prompt, mais la chair *est* foible.

42. Il s'en alla encore pour la seconde fois, et pria, disant : Mon Père, s'il n'est pas possible que cette coupe passe loin de moi, sans que je la boive, que ta volonté soit faite !

43. Et revenant *à eux*, il les trouva encore endormis ; car leurs yeux étoient appesantis.

44. Et les ayant laissés, il s'en alla encore, et pria pour la troisième fois, disant les mêmes paroles.

45. Alors il vint vers ses disciples, et leur dit : Vous dormez encore, et vous vous reposez !

APRÈS que Jésus eut dit ces choses, il s'en alla avec ses Disciples au-delà du torrent de Cédron, où il y avoit un jardin dans lequel il entra avec ses Disciples.

2. Judas, qui le trahissoit, connoissoit aussi ce lieu-là, parce que Jésus s'y étoit souvent assemblé avec ses Disciples.

3. Judas ayant donc pris une compagnie *de soldats* et des sergens, de la part des principaux Sacrificateurs et des Pharisiens, vint là avec des lanternes, des flambeaux et des armes.

---

37 And he took with him Peter and the two sons of Zebedee, and began to be sorrowful and very heavy.

38 Then saith he unto them, My soul is exceeding sorrowful, even unto death : tarry ye here, and watch with me.

39 And he went a little farther, and fell on his face, and prayed, saying, O my Father, if it be possible, let this cup pass from me : nevertheless, not as I will, but as thou *wilt*.

40 And he cometh unto the disciples, and findeth them asleep, and saith unto Peter, What! could ye not watch with me one hour?

41 Watch and pray, that ye enter not into temptation : the spirit indeed *is* willing, but the flesh *is* weak.

42 He went away again the second time, and prayed, saying, O my Father, if this cup may not pass away from me, except I drink it, thy will be done.

43 And he came and found them asleep again : for their eyes were heavy.

44 And he left them, and went away again, and prayed the third time, saying the same words.

45 Then cometh he to his disciples, and saith unto them, Sleep on now, and take *your* rest :

CHAP. XVIII.
Judas betrayeth Jesus.

WHEN Jesus had spoken these words, he went forth with his disciples over the brook Cedron, where was a garden, into the which he entered, and his disciples.

2 And Judas also, which betrayed him, knew the place : for Jesus oft-times resorted thither with his disciples.

3 Judas then, having received a band *of men* and officers from the chief priests and Pharisees, cometh thither with lanterns, and torches, and weapons.

73

48 Ὁ δὲ παραδιδοὺς αὐτὸν, ἔδωκεν αὐτοῖς σημεῖον, λέγων· Ὃν ἂν φιλήσω, αυτός ἐςι· κρατήσατε αὐτόν.

48 At tradens eum, dedit illi signum, dicens: Quemcumque osculatus fuero, ipse est: prehendite eum.

49 Καὶ εὐθέως προσελθὼν τῷ Ἰησοῦ, εἶπε· Χαῖρε ῥαββί. Καὶ κατεφίλησεν αὐτόν.

49 Et confestim accedens ad Jesum, dixit: Gaude Rabbi. Et osculatus est eum.

50 Ὁ δὲ Ἰησοῦς εἶπεν αὐτῷ· Ἑταῖρε, ἐφ᾽ ᾧ πάρει; Τότε προσελθόντες ἐπέβαλον τὰς χεῖρας ἐπὶ τὸν Ἰησοῦν, ᾗ ἐκράτησαν αὐτόν.

50 At Jesus ait illi, Amice, in quo ades? Tunc accedentes injecerunt manus in Jesum, & prehenderunt eum.

4 Ἰησοῦς ἂν εἰδὼς πάντα τὰ ἐρχόμενα ἐπ᾽ αὐτὸν, ἐξελθὼν εἶπεν αὐτοῖς· Τίνα ζητεῖτε;

4 Jesus itaque sciens omnia ventura super se, exiens dixit eis: Quem quæritis?

5 Ἀπεκρίθησαν αὐτῷ· Ἰησοῦν τὸν Ναζωραῖον. Λέγει αὐτοῖς ὁ

5 Responderunt ei: Jesum Nazarenum. Dicit eis Jesus:

Ἰησοῦς· Ἐγώ εἰμι. Εἱστήκει δὲ ᾗ Ἰούδας ὁ παραδιδοὺς αὐτὸν μετ᾽ αὐτῶν.

Ego sum. Stabat autem & Judas ille tradens eum cum ipsis.

6 Ὡς ἂν εἶπεν αὐτοῖς· Ὅτι ἐγώ εἰμι, ἀπῆλθον εἰς τὰ ὀπίσω, ᾗ ἔπεσον χαμαί.

6 Ut ergo dixit eis: Ego sum, abierunt in ea quæ post, & ceciderunt humi.

7 Πάλιν ἂν αὐτὲς ἐπηρώτησε· Τίνα ζητεῖτε; Οἱ δὲ εἶπον· Ἰησοῦν τὸν Ναζωραῖον.

7 Iterum ergo eos interrogavit: Quem quæritis? At dixerunt: Jesum Nazarenum.

8 Ἀπεκρίθη ὁ Ἰησοῦς· Εἶπον ὑμῖν ὅτι ἐγώ εἰμι· εἰ ἂν ἐμὲ ζητεῖτε, ἄφετε τούτους ὑπάγειν.

8 Respondit Jesus: Dixi vobis, quia ego sum. si ergo me quæritis, sinite hos abire.

51 Καὶ ἰδὲ, εἷς τῶν μετὰ Ἰησοῦ, ἐκτείνας τὴν χεῖρα, ἀπέσπασε τὴν μάχαιραν αὐτοῦ ᾗ πατάξας τὸν δοῦλον τοῦ ἀρχιερέως, ἀφεῖλεν αὐτοῦ τὸ ὠτίον.

51 Et ecce unus eorum qui cum Jesu, extendens manum exemit gladium suum: & percutiens servum principis sacerdotum, amputavit ejus auriculam.

52 Τότε λέγει αὐτῷ ὁ Ἰησοῦς· Ἀπόστρεψόν σου τὴν μάχαιραν εἰς τὸν τόπον αὐτῆς· πάντες γὰρ οἱ λαβόντες μάχαιραν, ἐν μαχαίρᾳ ἀπολοῦνται.

52 Tunc ait illi Jesus, Converte tuum gladium in locum suum: omnes enim accipientes gladium, in gladio peribunt.

55 Ἐν ἐκείνῃ τῇ ὥρᾳ εἶπεν ὁ Ἰησοῦς τοῖς ὄχλοις· Ὡς ἐπὶ λῃστὴν ἐξήλθετε μετὰ μαχαιρῶν ᾗ ξύλων συλλαβεῖν με· καθ᾽ ἡμέραν πρὸς ὑμᾶς ἐκαθεζόμην διδάσκων ἐν τῷ ἱερῷ, ᾗ οὐκ ἐκρατήσατέ με.

55 In illa hora dixit Jesus turbis: Tanquam ad latronem existis cum gladiis & lignis, comprehendere me: quotidie apud vos sedebam docens in templo, & non prehendistis me.

Τότε οἱ μαθηταὶ πάντες, ἀφέντες αὐτὸν, ἔφυγον.

Tunc discipuli omnes relicto eo, fugerunt.

51 Καὶ εἷς τις νεανίσκος ἠκολούθει αὐτῷ, περιβεβλημένος σινδόνα ἐπὶ γυμνοῦ· ᾗ κρατοῦσιν αὐτὸν οἱ νεανίσκοι.

51 Et unus quidam juvenis sequebatur eum amictus sindone super nudo: & tenent eum juvenes.

52 Ὁ δὲ καταλιπὼν τὴν σινδόνα, γυμνὸς ἔφυγεν ἀπ᾽ αὐτῶν.

52 Ille autem relinquens sindonem, nudus profugit ab eis.

48. Et celui qui le trahissoit, leur avoit donné ce signal : Celui que je baiserai, c'est lui ; saisissez-le.

49. Et aussitôt s'approchant de Jésus, il lui dit : Maître, je te salue ; et il le baisa.

50. Et Jésus lui dit : Mon ami, pour quel sujet es-tu ici ?

4. Et Jésus qui savoit tout ce qui lui devoit arriver, s'avança, et leur dit: Qui cherchez-vous ?

5. Ils lui répondirent : Jésus de Nazareth. Jésus leur dit : C'est moi. Et Judas qui le trahissoit étoit aussi avec eux.

6. Et dès qu'il leur eut dit: C'est moi, ils reculèrent, et tombèrent par terre.

7. Il leur demanda encore une fois : Qui cherchez-vous ? Et ils répondirent : Jésus de Nazareth.

8. Jésus répondit : Je vous ai dit que c'est moi ; si donc c'est moi que vous cherchez, laissez aller ceux-ci.

Alors ils s'approchèrent, et jetèrent les mains sur Jésus, et le saisirent.

51. En même-tems, un de ceux qui *étoient* avec Jésus, portant la main à l'épée, la tira, et en frappa un serviteur du Souverain Sacrificateur, et lui emporta une oreille.

52. Alors Jésus lui dit : Remets ton épée dans le fourreau ; car tous ceux qui prendront l'épée, périront par l'épée.

55. En même-tems Jésus dit à cette troupe : Vous êtes sortis avec des épées et des bâtons, comme après un brigand, pour me prendre ; j'étois tous les jours assis parmi vous, enseignant dans le temple, et vous ne m'avez point saisi.

Alors tous les Disciples l'abandonnèrent et s'enfuirent.

51. Et il y avoit un jeune homme qui le suivoit, ayant le corps couvert *seulement d'un* linceul : et quelques jeunes gens l'ayant pris,

52. Il leur laissa le linceul, et s'enfuit nud de leurs mains.

---

48 Now he that betrayed him gave them a sign, saying, Whomsoever I shall kiss, that same is he: hold him fast.

49 And forthwith he came to Jesus, and said, Hail, Master, and kissed him.

50 And Jesus said unto him, Friend, wherefore art thou come?

4 Jesus, therefore, knowing all things that should come upon him, went forth, and said unto them, Whom seek ye?

5 They answered him, Jesus of Nazareth. Jesus saith unto them, I am *he*. (And Judas also, which betrayed him, stood with them.)

6 As soon then as he had said unto them, I am *he*, they went backward, and fell to the ground.

7 Then asked he them again, Whom seek ye? And they said, Jesus of Nazareth.

8 Jesus answered, I have told you, that I am *he*: if, therefore, ye seek me, let these go their way;

Then came they and laid hands on Jesus, and took him.

51 And, behold, one of them, which were with Jesus, stretched out *his* hand, and drew his sword, and struck a servant of the high priest, and smote off his ear.

52 Then said Jesus unto him, Put up again thy sword into his place: for all they that take the sword shall perish with the sword.

55 In that same hour said Jesus to the multitudes, Are ye come out, as against a thief, with swords, and staves for to take me? I sat daily with you teaching in the temple, and ye laid no hold on me.

56. Then all the disciples forsook him and fled.

51 And there followed him a certain young man, having a linen cloth cast about *his* naked *body*; and the young men laid hold on him:

52 And he left the linen cloth, and fled from them naked.

74

57 Οἱ δὲ κρατήσαντες τὸν
Ἰησῦν, ἀπήγαγον πρὸς Καϊά-
φαν τὸν ἀρχιερέα, ὅπυ οἱ γραμμαλεῖς, κ᾽ οἱ πρεσβύτεροι συνήχθησαν.

57 Illi verò tenentes Jesum,
adduxerunt ad Caipham principem Sacerdotum, ubi Scribæ, &
seniores convenerant.

* 15 Ἠκολύθει δὲ τῷ Ἰησῦ
Σίμων Πέτρ☉, κ᾽ ὁ ἄλλ☉ μα-
θητής. ὁ δὲ μαθητὴς ἐκεῖν☉ ἦν
γνωςὸς τῷ ἀρχιερεῖ, κ᾽ ‡ συνεισῆλ-
θε τῷ Ἰησῦ εἰς τὴν αὐλὴν τῦ
ἀρχιερέως.

15 Sequebatur autem Jesum
Simon Petrus, & alius discipulus. At discipulus ille erat notus principi Sacerdotum, & simul introivit Jesu in atrium
principis Sacerdotum.

16 Ὁ δὲ Πέτρ☉ εἱςήκει πρὸς
τῇ θύρᾳ ἔξω· ἐξῆλθεν ἦν ὁ μαθητὴς ὁ ἄλλ☉, ὃς ἦν γνωςὸς τῷ
ἀρχιερεῖ, κ᾽ εἶπε τῇ θυρωρῷ, κ᾽
εἰςήγαγε τὸν Πέτρον.

16 At Petrus stabat ad ostium
foris: Exivit ergo discipulus a-
lius, qui erat notus principi Sacerdotum, & dixit ostiariæ, &
introduxit Petrum.

18 Εἱςήκεισαν δὲ οἱ δῦλοι, κ᾽
οἱ ὑπηρέται ἀνθρακιὰν πεποιηκό-
τες, ὅτι ψύχ☉ ἦν, κ᾽ ἐθερμαί-
νοντο· ἦν δὲ μετ᾽ αὐτῶν ὁ Πέτρ☉
ἑςὼς κ᾽ θερμαινόμεν☉·

18 Stabant autem servi & ministri prunam facientes, quia
frigus erat, & calefaciebant se:
erat autem cum eis Petrus stans
& calefaciens se.

17 Λέγει ὖν ἡ παιδίσκη ἡ θυρωρὸς τῷ Πέτρῳ· Μὴ κ᾽ σὺ ἐκ τῶν
μαθηλῶν εἶ τῦ ἀνθρώπυ τύτυ;
Λέγει ἐκεῖν☉· Οὐκ εἰμί.

17 Dicit ergo ancilla ostiaria
Petro : Nunquid & tu ex discipulis es hominis istius? Dicit
ille : Non sum.

25 Ἦν δὲ Σίμων Πέτρ☉ ἑςὼς
κ᾽ θερμαινόμεν☉· εἶπον ὖν αὐτῷ·
Μὴ κ᾽ σὺ ἐκ τῶν μαθηλῶν αὐτῦ εἶ;
Ἠρνήσαλο ἐκεῖν☉, κ᾽ εἶπεν· Οὐκ
εἰμί.

25 Erat autem Simon Petrus
stans, & calefaciens se. Dixerunt ergo ei : Num & tu ex discipulis ejus es? Negavit ille, &
ait : Non sum.

26 Λέγει εἷς ἐκ τῶν δύλων
τῦ ἀρχιερέως, συγγενὴς ὢν ὗ ἀ-
πέκοψε Πέτρ☉ τὸ ‡ ὠτίον· Οὐκ
ἐγώ σε, εἶδον ἐν τῷ κήπῳ μετ᾽
αὐτῦ;

26 Dicit unus ex servis principis Sacerdotum, cognatus existens cujus absciderat Petrus auriculam : Non ego te vidi in
horto cum illo?

27 Πάλιν ὖν ἠρνήσαλο ὁ Πέ-
τρ☉, κ᾽ εὐθέως ἀλέκλωρ ἐφώνησεν.

27 Iterum ergo negavit Petrus, & statim gallus cantavit.

75 Καὶ ἐμνήσθη ὁ Πέτρ☉ τῦ
ῥήμαλ☉ τῦ Ἰησῦ, εἰρηκότ☉ αὐ-
τῷ· Ὅτι πρὶν ἀλέκλορα φωνῆσαι,
τρὶς ἀπαρνήσῃ με. Καὶ ἐξελθὼν
ἔξω, ἔκλαυσε πικρῶς. 26. †.

75 Et recordatus est Petrus
verbi Jesu, dicentis ei : Quod
ante gallum vociferari, ter ab-
negabis me. Et egressus foras,
flevit amarè.

19 Ὁ ὖν ἀρχιερεὺς ἠρώτησε
τὸν Ἰησῦν περὶ τῶν μαθηλῶν αὐτῦ, κ᾽ περὶ τῆς διδαχῆς αὐτῦ.

19 Ergo princeps Sacerdotum
interrogavit Jesum de discipulis
suis, & de doctrina ejus.

20 Ἀπεκρίθη αὐτῷ ὁ Ἰησῦς·
Ἐγὼ παρρησίᾳ ἐλάλησα τῷ κόσ-
μῳ· ἐγὼ πάντοτε ἐδίδαξα ἐν τῇ
συναγωγῇ κ᾽ ἐν τῷ ἱερῷ, ὅπυ
πάντοθεν οἱ Ἰυδαῖοι συνέρχονλαι,
κ᾽ ἐν κρυπλῷ ἐλάλησα ἐδέν·

20 Respondit ei Jesus : Ego
palam loquutus sum mundo :
ego semper docui in synagoga
& in templo, quo undique Judæi conveniunt, & in occulto
loquutus sum nihil.

57. Mais ceux qui avoient saisi Jésus, l'emmenèrent chez Caïphe le Souverain Sacrificateur, où les Scribes et les Sénateurs étoient assemblés.

57 And they that had laid hold on Jesus, led *him* away to Caiaphas the high priest, where the scribes and the elders were assembled.

15. Or, Simon Pierre, avec un autre Disciple, avoit suivi Jésus ; et ce Disciple étoit connu du Souverain Sacrificateur ; et il entra avec Jésus dans la cour *de la maison* du Souverain Sacrificateur.

16. Mais Pierre étoit *demeuré* dehors à la porte. Et cet autre Disciple qui étoit connu du souverain Sacrificateur, sortit, et parla à la portière, qui fit entrer Pierre.

18. Et les serviteurs et les sergens étoient là, et ayant fait du feu, parce qu'il faisoit froid, ils se chauffoient. Pierre étoit aussi avec eux, et se chauffoit.

15 And Simon Peter followed Jesus, and *so did* another disciple. That disciple was known unto the high priest, and went in with Jesus into the palace of the high priest.

16 But Peter stood at the door without. Then went out that other disciple, which was known unto the high priest, and spake unto her that kept the door, and brought in Peter.

18 And the servants and officers stood there, who had made a fire of coals, (for it was cold,) and they warmed themselves: and Peter stood with them, and warmed himself.

17. Et cette servante, qui étoit la portière, dit à Pierre : N'es-tu pas aussi des Disciples de cet homme ? Il dit : Je n'en suis point.

17 Then saith the damsel, that kept the door, unto Peter, Art not thou also *one* of this man's disciples? He saith, I am not.

25. Et Simon Pierre étoit là, et se chauffoit ; et ils lui dirent :

N'es-tu pas aussi de ses Disciples ? Il le nia, et dit : Je n'en suis point.

26. Et l'un des serviteurs du Souverain Sacrificateur, parent de celui à qui Pierre avoit coupé l'oreille, lui dit : Ne t'ai-je pas vu dans le jardin avec lui ?

27. Pierre le nia encore une fois ; et aussitôt le coq chanta.

25 And Simon Peter stood and warmed himself: they said, therefore, unto him, Art not thou also *one* of his disciples? He denied *it*, and said, I am not.

26 One of the servants of the high priest, (being *his* kinsman whose ear Peter cut off,) saith, Did not I see thee in the garden with him?

27 Peter then denied again; and immediately the cock crew.

75. Alors Pierre se souvint de la parabole de Jésus, qui lui avoit dit : Avant que le coq ait chanté, tu me renieras trois fois. Et étant sorti, il pleura amèrement.

75 And Peter remembered the words of Jesus, which said unto him, Before the cock crow, thou shalt deny me thrice. And he went out, and wept bitterly.

19. Et le souverain Sacrificateur interrogea Jésus touchant ses Disciples, et touchant sa doctrine.

20. Jésus lui répondit : J'ai parlé ouvertement à tout le monde, j'ai toujours enseigné dans la Synagogue et dans le Temple où les Juifs s'assemblent de toutes parts, et je n'ai rien dit en cachette.

19 The high priest then asked Jesus of his disciples, and of his doctrine.

20 Jesus answered him, I spake openly to the world; I ever taught in the synagogue, and in the temple, whither the Jews always resort; and in secret have I said nothing.

75

21 Τί με ἐπερωτᾷς; ἐπερώτησον τοὺς ἀκηκοότας, τί ἐλάλησα αὐτοῖς· ἴδε, οὗτοι οἴδασιν ἃ εἶπον ἐγώ.

22 Ταῦτα δὲ αὐτοῦ εἰπόντος, εἷς τῶν ὑπηρετῶν παρεστηκὼς ἔδωκε ῥάπισμα τῷ Ἰησοῦ, εἰπών· Οὕτως ἀποκρίνῃ τῷ ἀρχιερεῖ;

23 Ἀπεκρίθη αὐτῷ ὁ Ἰησοῦς· Εἰ κακῶς ἐλάλησα, μαρτύρησον περὶ τοῦ κακοῦ· εἰ δὲ καλῶς, τί με δέρεις;

21 Quid me interrogas? Interroga audientes, quid loquutus sim ipsis: ecce hi sciunt quæ dixerim ego.

22 Hæc autem eo dicente, unus ministrorum affistens dedit alapam Jesu, dicens: Sic respondes principi Sacerdotum?

23 Respondit ei Jesus: Si male loquutus sum, testare de malo: si autem bene, quid me cædis?

55 Οἱ δὲ ἀρχιερεῖς καὶ ὅλον τὸ συνέδριον ἐζήτουν κατὰ τοῦ Ἰησοῦ μαρτυρίαν, εἰς τὸ θανατῶσαι αὐτὸν, καὶ οὐχ εὕρισκον.

56 Πολλοὶ γὰρ ἐψευδομαρτύρουν κατ' αὐτοῦ, καὶ ἴσαι αἱ μαρτυρίαι οὐκ ἦσαν.

57 Καί τινες ἀναστάντες, ἐψευδομαρτύρουν κατ' αὐτοῦ, λέγοντες·

58 Ὅτι ἡμεῖς ἠκούσαμεν αὐτοῦ λέγοντος· Ὅτι ἐγὼ καταλύσω τὸν ναὸν τοῦτον τὸν χειροποίητον, καὶ διὰ τριῶν ἡμερῶν ἄλλον ἀχειροποίητον οἰκοδομήσω.

59 Καὶ οὐδὲ οὕτως ἴση ἦν ἡ μαρτυρία αὐτῶν.

60 Καὶ ἀναστὰς ὁ ἀρχιερεὺς εἰς τὸ μέσον, ἐπηρώτησε τὸν Ἰησοῦν, λέγων· Οὐκ ἀποκρίνῃ οὐδέν; τί οὗτοί σου καταμαρτυροῦσιν;

61 Ὁ δὲ ἐσιώπα, καὶ οὐδὲν ἀπεκρίνατο. Πάλιν ὁ ἀρχιερεὺς ἐπηρώτα αὐτόν, καὶ λέγει αὐτῷ· Σὺ εἶ ὁ Χριστὸς ὁ υἱὸς τοῦ εὐλογητοῦ;

55 At summi Sacerdotes, & omnis consessus quærebant adversus Jesum testimonium, ad morte afficiendum eum, & non inveniebant.

56 Multi enim testimonium falsum dicebant adversus eum, & paria testimonia non erant.

57 Et quidam surgentes falsum testimonium ferebant adversus eum, dicentes:

58 Quoniam nos audivimus eum dicentem: Quod ego dissolvam templum hoc manufactum, & per tres dies aliud non manufactum ædificabo.

59 Et nec sic par erat testimonium illorum.

60 Et exurgens summus Sacerdos in medium, interrogavit Jesum, dicens: Non respondes quicquam quid hi te adversum testantur?

61 Ille autem tacebat, & nihil respondit. Rursum summus Sacerdos interrogabat eum, & dicit ei: Tu es Christus filius benedicti?

Εἶπε δὲ αὐτοῖς· Ἐὰν ὑμῖν εἴπω, οὐ μὴ πιστεύσητε·

68 Ἐὰν δὲ καὶ ἐρωτήσω, οὐ μὴ ἀποκριθῆτέ μοι, ἢ ἀπολύσητε.

70 Εἶπον δὲ πάντες· Σὺ οὖν εἶ ὁ υἱὸς τοῦ Θεοῦ; Ὁ δὲ πρὸς αὐτοὺς ἔφη· Ὑμεῖς λέγετε, ὅτι ἐγώ εἰμι.

Ait autem illis:
Si vobis dixero non credetis.

68 Si autem & interrogavero, non respondebitis mihi, aut dimittetis.

70 Dixerunt autem omnes: Tu ergo es filius Dei? is autem ad eos ait: Vos dicitis, quia ego sum.

63 Ὁ δὲ ἀρχιερεὺς, διαρρήξας τοὺς χιτῶνας αὐτοῦ, λέγει· Τί ἔτι χρείαν ἔχομεν μαρτύρων;

64 Ἠκούσατε τῆς βλασφημίας· τί ὑμῖν φαίνεται; Οἱ δὲ

63 At summus Sacerdos disrumpens vestes suas, ait: Quid adhuc usum habemus testium?

64 Audistis blasphemiam; quid vobis videtur? Ii autem

21. Pourquoi m'interroges-tu ? Interroge ceux qui ont entendu ce que je leur ai dit : Ces gens-là savent ce que j'ai dit.

22. Lorsqu'il eut dit cela, un des sergens qui étoit présent donna un soufflet à Jésus, en lui disant : Est-ce ainsi que tu réponds au Souverain Sacrificateur ?

23. Jésus lui répondit : Si j'ai mal parlé, fais voir ce que j'ai dit de mal ; et si j'ai bien parlé, pourquoi me frappes-tu ?

55. Or les principaux Sacrificateurs et tout le Conseil cherchoient *quelque* témoignage contre Jésus pour le faire mourir ; et ils n'en trouvoient point.

56. Car plusieurs rendoient de faux témoignages contre lui ; mais leurs dépositions ne s'accordoient pas.

57. Alors quelques-uns se levèrent, qui portèrent un faux témoignage contre lui, disant :

58. Nous lui avons ouï dire : Je détruirai ce Temple, qui a été bâti par la main des hommes, et, dans trois jours, j'en rebâtirai un autre qui ne sera point fait de main d'*homme*.

59. Mais leur déposition ne s'accordoit pas non plus.

60. Alors le Souverain Sacrificateur se levant au milieu du *Conseil*, interrogea Jésus, et lui dit : Ne réponds-tu rien ? Qu'est-ce que ces gens déposent contre toi ?

61. Mais *Jésus* se tut et ne répondit rien. Le Souverain Sacrificateur l'interrogea encore, et lui dit : Es-tu le Christ, le Fils du *Dieu* béni ?

Et il leur répondit : Si je vous le dis, vous ne le croirez point :

68. Et si je *vous* interroge aussi, vous ne me répondrez point, ni ne me laisserez point aller.

70. Alors ils dirent tous : Es-tu donc le Fils de Dieu ? Et il leur dit : Vous le dites vous-mêmes : Je le suis.

63. Alors le Souverain Sacrificateur déchira ses vêtemens, et dit : Qu'avons-nous plus à faire de témoins ?

64. Vous avez entendu le blasphème ; que vous en semble ?

J. 18.

21 Why askest thou me? ask them which heard me, what I have said unto them : behold, they know what I said.

22 And, when he had thus spoken, one of the officers which stood by struck Jesus with the palm of his hand, saying, Answerest thou the high priest so ?

23 Jesus answered him, If I have spoken evil, bear witness of the evil ; but if well, why smitest thou me ?

Mk. 14

53 And they led Jesus away to the high priest ; and with him were assembled all the chief priests, and the elders, and the scribes.

55 And the chief priests, and all the council sought for witness against Jesus to put him to death ; and found none :

56 For many bare false witness against him, but their witness agreed not together.

57 And there arose certain, and bare false witness against him, saying,

58 We heard him say, I will destroy this temple that is made with hands, and within three days I will build another made without hands.

59 But neither so did their witness agree together.

60 And the high priest stood up in the midst, and asked Jesus, saying, Answerest thou nothing? what *is it which* these witness against thee.

61 But he held his peace, and answered nothing. Again the high priest asked him, and said unto him, Art thou the Christ, the Son of the Blessed ?

L. 22.

67. And he said unto them, If I tell you, ye will not believe :

68 And if I also ask *you*, ye will not answer me, nor let *me* go.

70 Then said they all, Art thou then the Son of God ? And he said unto them, Ye say that I am.

Mk. 14

63 Then the high priest rent his clothes, and saith, What need we any further witnesses ?

64 Ye have heard the blasphemy : what think ye ? And they

πάντες κατέκριναν αὐτὸν εἶναι
ἔνοχον θανάτε.
* 65 Καὶ ἤρξαντό τινες ‡ ἐμ-
πτύειν αὐτῷ, κ περικαλύπειν
τὸ πρόσωπον αὐτῦ, κ ‡ κολα-
φίζειν αὐτὸν, κ λέγειν αὐτῷ·
Προφήτευσον· κ οἱ ὑπηρέται ‡ ῥα-
πίσμασιν αὐτὸν ἔβαλλον.

omnes condemnaverunt eum
obnoxium esse mortis.
65 Et cœperunt quidam con-
spuere eum, & velare faciem
ejus, & colaphizare eum, &
dicere ei : Prophetiza, & ministri alapis eum impetebant.

* 28 Ἄγεσιν ἓν τὸν Ἰησῦν
ἀπὸ τῦ Καϊάφα εἰς τὸ πραιτώριον·
ἦν δὲ ‡ πρωΐα· κ αὐτοὶ ἐκ εἰσῆλθον εἰς τὸ ‡ πραιτώριον, ἵνα
μὴ ‡ μιανθῶσιν, ἀλλ' ἵνα φάγωσι
τὸ πάσχα.

28 Adducunt ergo Jesum à
Cajapha in prætorium; erat autem mane; & ipsi non introie-
runt in prætorium, ut non con-
taminarentur, sed ut manduca-
rent Pascha.

* 29 Ἐξῆλθεν ἓν ὁ Πιλάτ⊙·
πρὸς αὐτὸς, κ εἶπε· ‡ Τίνα
‡ κατηγορίαν φέρετε κατὰ τῦ ἀνθρώπε τύτυ;

29 Exivit ergo Pilatus ad eos,
& dixit: Quam accusationem af-
fertis adversus hominem hunc?

30 Ἀπεκρίθησαν κ εἶπον αὐ-
τῷ· Εἰ μὴ ἦν ὖτ⊙ κακοποιὸς,
ἐκ ἄν σοι παρεδώκαμεν αὐτόν.

30 Responderunt & dixerunt ei:
Si non esset hic malefactor, non
utique tibi tradidissemus eum.

31 Εἶπεν ἓν αὐτοῖς ὁ Πιλά-
τ⊙· Λάβετε αὐτὸν ὑμεῖς κ κατὰ τὸν νόμον ὑμῶν κρίνατε αὐτόν.
Εἶπον ἓν αὐτῷ οἱ Ἰουδαῖοι· Ἡμῖν
ἐκ ἔξεσιν ἀποκτεῖναι ἐδένα.

31 Dixit ergo eis Pilatus: Acci-
pite eum vos, & secundum legem vestram judicate eum. Dixerunt ergo ei Judæi: Nobis
non licet interficere quemquam.

33 Εἰσῆλθεν ἓν εἰς τὸ πραιτώριον πάλιν ὁ Πιλάτ⊙, κ ἐ-
φώνησε τὸν Ἰησῦν κ εἶπεν αὐ-
τῷ· Σὺ εἶ ὁ βασιλεὺς τῶν Ἰουδαίων;

33 Introivit ergo in prætori-
um iterum Pilatus, & vocavit
Jesum, & dixit ei: Tu es rex
Judæorum?

34 Ἀπεκρίθη αὐτῷ ὁ Ἰησῦς·
Ἀφ' ἑαυτῦ σὺ τῦτο λέγεις, ἢ
ἄλλοι σοι εἶπον περὶ ἐμῦ;

34 Respondit ei Jesus: A te-
metipso tu hoc dicis, an alii tibi
dixerunt de me?

35 Ἀπεκρίθη ὁ Πιλάτ⊙· Μήτι
ἐγὼ Ἰουδαῖός εἰμι; τὸ ἔθν⊙ τὸ
σὸν κ οἱ ἀρχιερεῖς παρεδωκάν σε
ἐμοί· τί ἐποίησας;

35 Respondit Pilatus: Numquid ego Judæus sum? Gens tua
& principes Sacerdotum tradi-
derunt te mihi: quid fecisti?

36 Ἀπεκρίθη ὁ Ἰησῦς· Ἡ βασιλεία ἡ ἐμὴ ἐκ ἔςιν ἐκ τῦ κόσμυ
τύτυ· εἰ ἐκ τῦ κόσμυ τύτυ ἦν
ἡ βασιλεία ἡ ἐμὴ, οἱ ὑπηρέται ἂν
οἱ ἐμοὶ ἠγωνίζοντο, ἵνα μὴ παρα-
δοθῶ τοῖς Ἰουδαίοις· νῦν δὲ ἡ βασιλεία ἡ ἐμὴ ἐκ ἔςιν ἐντεῦθεν.

36 Respondit Jesus: Regnum
meum non est de mundo hoc: si
ex mundo hoc esset regnum meum, ministri utique mei decer-
tarent, ut non traderer Judæis:
nunc autem regnum meum non
est hinc.

* 37 Εἶπεν ἓν αὐτῷ ὁ Πιλά-
τ⊙· † Οὐκῦν βασιλεὺς εἶ σύ;
Ἀπεκρίθη ὁ Ἰησῦς· Σὺ λέγεις
ὅτι βασιλεὺς εἰμι ἐγώ· ἐγὼ εἰς
τῦτο γεγέννημαι, κ εἰς τῦτο ἐλ-
ήλυθα εἰς τὸν κόσμον, ἵνα μαρ-
τυρήσω τῇ ἀληθείᾳ. Πᾶς ὁ ὢν ἐκ
τῆς ἀληθείας, ἀκούει μυ τῆς φωνῆς.

37 Dixit itaque ei Pilatus:
Num ergo rex es tu? Respondit
Jesus: Tu dicis, quia rex sum
ego: Ego in hoc natus sum, &
ad hoc veni in mundo, ut te-
ster veritati: omnis existens ex
veritate, audit meam vocem.

38 Λέγει αὐτῷ ὁ Πιλάτ⊙·
Τί ἐςιν ἀλήθεια; Καὶ τῦτο εἰπών, πάλιν ἐξῆλθε πρὸς τὰς Ἰυ-

38 Dicit ei Pilatus: Quid est
veritas? Et hoc dicens, iterum
exivit ad Judæos, & dicit eis:

δαίυς, κ λέγει αὐτοῖς· Ἐγὼ ἐδε-
μίαν αἰτίαν εὑρίσκω ἐν αὐτῷ.

Ego nullam causam invenio in
eo.

Alors tous le condamnèrent comme étant digne de mort.

65. Et quelques-uns se mirent à cracher contre lui, à lui couvrir le visage, et à lui donner des coups de poing, et ils lui disoient : Devine, *qui t'a frappé*. Et les Sergens lui donnoient des coups de leurs bâtons.

28. Ils menèrent ensuite Jésus, de Caïphe au Prétoire ; c'étoit le matin ; et ils n'entrèrent point dans le Prétoire, de peur de se souiller, et afin de pouvoir manger la Pâque.

29. Pilate donc sortit vers eux, et leur dit : Quelle accusation portez-vous contre cet homme ?

30. Ils lui répondirent : Si cet homme n'étoit pas un malfaiteur, nous ne te l'aurions pas livré.

31. Sur quoi Pilate leur dit : Prenez-le vous-mêmes, et le jugez selon votre Loi. Les Juifs lui dirent : Nous n'avons pas le pouvoir de faire mourir personne.

33. Pilate rentra dans le Prétoire et ayant fait venir Jésus, il lui dit : Es-tu le Roi des Juifs ?

34. Jésus lui répondit : Dis-tu ceci de ton propre mouvement, ou si d'autres te l'ont dit de moi ?

35. Pilate répondit : Suis-je Juif ? Ta nation et les principaux Sacrificateurs t'ont livré à moi ; qu'as-tu fait ?

36. Jésus répondit : Mon règne n'est pas de ce monde ; si mon règne étoit de ce monde, mes gens combattroient, afin que je ne fusse pas livré aux Juifs ; mais maintenant mon règne n'est point d'ici-bas.

37. Alors Pilate lui dit : tu es donc Roi ? Jésus répondit : Tu le dis ; je suis Roi, je suis né pour cela, et je suis venu dans le monde, pour rendre témoignage à la vérité. Quiconque est pour la vérité écoute ma voix.

38. Pilate lui dit : Qu'est-ce que cette vérité ? Et quand il eut dit cela, il sortit encore pour aller vers les Juifs, et leur dit : Je ne trouve aucun crime en lui.

all condemned him to be guilty of death.

65 And some began to spit on him, and to cover his face, and to buffet him, and to say unto him, Prophesy : and the servants did strike him with the palms of their hands, and it was early ; and they themselves went not into the judgment-hall, lest they should be defiled ; but that they might eat the passover.

29 Pilate then went out unto them, and said, What accusation bring ye against this man ?

30 They answered, and said unto him, If he were not a malefactor, we would not have delivered him up unto thee.

31 Then said Pilate unto them, Take ye him, and judge him according to your law. The Jews, therefore, said unto him, It is not lawful for us to put any man to death :

33 Then Pilate entered into the judgment-hall again, and called Jesus, and said unto him, Art thou the King of the Jews ?

34 Jesus answered him, Sayest thou this thing of thyself, or did others tell it thee of me ?

35 Pilate answered, Am I a Jew ? Thine own nation and the chief priests have delivered thee unto me. What hast thou done ?

36 Jesus answered, My kingdom is not of this world. If my kingdom were of this world, then would my servants fight, that I should not be delivered to the Jews : but now is my kingdom not from hence.

37 Pilate, therefore, said unto him, Art thou a King then ? Jesus answered, thou sayest that I am a king. To this end was I born, and for this cause came I into the world, that I should bear witness unto the truth. Every one that is of the truth heareth my voice.

38 Pilate saith unto him, What is truth ? And when he had said this, he went out again unto the Jews, and saith unto them, I find in him no fault at all.

* 5 Οἱ δὲ † ἐπίσχυον, λέ-
γοντες· Ὅτι ‡ ἀνασείει τὸν λαὸν,
διδάσκων καθ᾽ ὅλης τῆς Ἰουδαίας,
ἀρξάμεν۞ ἀπὸ τῆς Γαλιλαίας
ἕως ὧδε.

13 Τότε λέγει αὐτῷ ὁ Πιλά-
τ۞· Οὐκ ἀκύεις πόσα σου καλα-
μαρτυροῦσι,

6 Πιλάτ۞ δὲ ἀκύσας Γαλι-
λαίαν, ἐπηρώτησεν, εἰ ὁ ἄνθρω-
π۞ Γαλιλαῖός ἐςι

7 Καὶ ἐπιγνὼς ὅτι ἐκ τῆς
ἐξεσίας Ἡρώδου ἐ᾽ὶν, ἀνέπεμψεν
αὐτὸν πρὸς Ἡρώδην, ὄντα κỳ αὐτὸν
ἐν Ἱεροσολύμοις ἐν ταύταις ταῖς
ἡμέραις.

8 Ὁ δὲ Ἡρώδης, ἰδὼν τὸν Ἰησοῦν, ἐχάρη λίαν· ἦν γὰρ θέλων
ἐξ ἱκανῦ ἰδεῖν αὐτὸν, διὰ τὸ ἀ-
κούειν πολλὰ περὶ αὐτοῦ· κỳ ἤλ-
πιζέ τι σημεῖον ἰδεῖν ὑπ᾽ αὐτοῦ
γινόμενον.

9 Ἐπηρώτα δὲ αὐτὸν ἐν λό-
γοις ἱκανοῖς· αὐτὸς δὲ οὐδὲν ἀ-
πεκρίνατο αὐτῷ.

10 Εἱστήκεισαν δὲ οἱ ἀρχιερεῖς
κỳ οἱ γραμματεῖς εὐτόνως κατη-
γοροῦντες αὐτοῦ.

11 Ἐξουθενήσας δὲ αὐτὸν ὁ Ἡ-
ρώδης σὺν τοῖς ςρατεύμασιν αὐτῦ,
κỳ ἐμπαίξας, περιβαλὼν αὐτὸν
ἐσθῆτα λαμπρὰν, ἀνέπεμψεν αὐτὸν
τῷ Πιλάτῳ.

12 Ἐγένοντο δὲ φίλοι ὅ, τε
Πιλάτ۞ κỳ ὁ Ἡρώδης ἐν αὐτῇ τῇ
ἡμέρα μετ᾽ ἀλλήλων· προϋπῆρ-
χον γὰρ ἐν ἔχθρα ὄντες πρὸς ἑαυ-
τούς.

13 Πιλάτ۞ δὲ, ῦυγκαλεσά-
μεν۞ τοὺς ἀρχιερεῖς, κỳ τοὺς ἄρ-
χοντας, κỳ τὸν λαὸν,

14 Εἶπε πρὸς αὐτούς. Προσην-
έγκατέ μοι τὸν ἄνθρωπον τοῦτον,
ὡς ἀποςρέφοντα τὸν λαόν· κỳ ἰδϋ,
ἐγὼ ἐνώπιον ὑμῶν ἀνακρίνας, οὐδὲν
εὗρον ἐν τῷ ἀνθρώπῳ τούτῳ αἴτιον,
ὧν κατηγορεῖτε κατ᾽ αὐτῦ.

15 Ἀλλ᾽ οὐδὲ Ἡρώδης· ἀνέ-
πεμψα γὰρ ὑμᾶς πρὸς αὐτὸν, κỳ
ἰδοὺ, οὐδὲν ἄξιον θανάτου ἐςὶ πε-
πραγμένον αὐτῷ·

16 Παιδεύσας οὖν αὐτὸν ἀπολύσω.

---

5 Illi autem invalescebant,
dicentes : Quia commovet populum, docens per universam
Judæam, incipiens à Galilæa
usque huc.

13 Tunc dicit illi Pilatus :
Non audis quanta te contra tef-
tantur ?

6 Pilatus autem audiens Galilæam, interrogavit fi homo
Galilæus effet.

7 Et cognofcens quod de po-
teftate Herodis effet, remifit
eum ad Herodem, exiftentem
& ipfum in Hierofolymis, in
illis diebus.

8 At Herodes videns Jefum
gavifus eft valde : erat enim
volens ex multo videre eum,
propterea quod audiret multa
de eo : & fperabat aliquod fig-
num videre ab eo factum.

9 Interrogabat autem eum in
fermonibus multis : ipfe autem
nihil refpondebat illi.

10 Stabant autem principes
Sacerdotum & Scribæ conftan-
ter accufantes eum.

11 Nihil faciens autem illum
Herodes cum exercitibus fuis,
& illudens, amiciens eum veftem
fplendidam, remifit eum Pilato.

12 Facti funt autem amici
hicque Pilatus & Herodes hac
ipfa die cum invicem : præex-
titerant enim in inimicitia ex-
iftentes ad feipfos.

13 Pilatus autem convocans
principes facerdotum, & magi-
ftratus & populum,

14 Dixit ad illos : Obtuliftis
mihi hominem hunc, quafi a-
vertentem populum, & ecce ego
coram vobis interrogans, nullam
inveni in homine ifto caufam,
quorum accufatis adverfus eum.

15 Sed neque Herodes : re-
mifi enim vos ad illum, & ecce
nihil dignum morte eft factum
ei.

16 Caftigans ergo illum dimittam.

5. Mais ils insistoient encore plus fortement, en disant : Il soulève le peuple, enseignant par toute la Judée, ayant commencé depuis la Galilée jusqu'ici.

5 And they were the more fierce, saying, He stirreth up the people, teaching throughout all Jewry, beginning from Galilee to this place.

13. Alors Pilate lui dit : N'entends-tu pas combien de choses ils déposent contre toi ?

13 Then said Pilate unto him, Hearest thou not how many things they witness against thee?

6. Quand Pilate entendit parler de la Galilée, il demanda si Jésus étoit Galiléen.

6 When Pilate heard of Galilee, he asked whether the man were a Galilean.

7. Ayant appris qu'il étoit de la juridiction d'Hérode, il le renvoya à Hérode, qui étoit aussi alors à Jérusalem.

7 And as soon as he knew that he belonged unto Herod's jurisdiction, he sent him to Herod, who himself also was at Jerusalem at that time.

8. Quand Hérode vit Jésus, il en eut une grande joie ; car il y avoit long-tems qu'il souhaitoit de le voir, parce qu'il avoit ouï-dire beaucoup de choses de lui ;

8 And when Herod saw Jesus, he was exceeding glad: for he was desirous to see him of a long *season*, because he had heard many things of him; and he hoped to have seen some miracle done by him.

et il espéroit qu'il lui verroit faire quelque miracle.

9. Il lui fit donc plusieurs questions, mais Jésus-Christ ne lui répondit rien,

9 Then he questioned with him in many words; but he answered him nothing.

10. Et les principaux Sacrificateurs et les Scribes étoient-là, qui l'accusoient avec la plus grande véhémence.

10 And the chief priests and scribes stood, and vehemently accused him.

11. Mais Hérode, avec les gens de la garde, le traita avec mépris ; et pour se moquer de lui, il le fit vêtir d'un habit éclatant, et le renvoya à Pilate.

11 And Herod, with his men of war, set him at nought, and mocked *him*, and arrayed him in a gorgeous robe, and sent him again to Pilate.

12. En ce même jour, Pilate et Hérode devinrent amis, car auparavant ils étoient ennemis.

12 And the same day Pilate and Herod were made friends together: for before they were at enmity between themselves.

13. Alors Pilate ayant assemblé les principaux Sacrificateurs, et les Magistrats, et le peuple, leur dit :

13 And Pilate, when he had called together the chief priests, and the rulers, and the people,

14. Vous m'avez présenté cet homme comme soulevant le peuple ; et cependant l'ayant interrogé en votre présence, je ne l'ai trouvé coupable d'aucun des crimes dont vous l'accusez ;

14 Said unto them, Ye have brought this man unto me, as one that perverteth the people : and, behold, I, having examined *him* before you, have found no fault in this man, touching those things whereof ye accuse him :

15. Ni Hérode non plus ; car je vous ai renvoyés à lui, *et* on ne lui a rien fait *qui marque qu'il soit* digne de mort.

15 No, nor yet Herod: for I sent you to him; and, lo, nothing worthy of death is done unto him:

16. Ainsi, après l'avoir fait châtier, je le relâcherai.

16 I will, therefore, chastise him, and release *him*.

* under the Roman law *de seditiosis in crucem tol-lerd'is. Digest de poenis* L. 48. tit. 19. 6. 28.3 *capite ... tendi cum saepius seditiose et turbulentæ se gesserint, et aliquotiens reprehensi clementius eadem temeritate propositi perseveraverint.*

78

15 Κατὰ δὲ ἑορτὴν εἰώθει ὁ ἡγεμὼν ἀπολύειν ἕνα τῷ ὄχλῳ δέσμιον, ὃν ἤθελον.

16 Εἶχον δὲ τότε δέσμιον ἐπίσημον λεγόμενον Βαραββᾶν.

17 Συνηγμένων ὖν αὐτῶν, εἶπεν αὐτοῖς ὁ Πιλᾶτ۞· Τίνα θέλετε ἀπολύσω ὑμῖν; Βαραββᾶν, ἢ Ἰησοῦν τὸν λεγόμενον Χριστόν;

18 Ἤδει γὰρ ὅτι διὰ φθόνον παρέδωκαν αὐτόν.

19 Καθημένυ δὲ αὐτῦ ἐπὶ τῦ βήμα۞, ἀπέςειλε πρὸς αὐτὸν ἡ γυνὴ αὐτῦ, λέγυσα· Μηδέν σοι κỳ τῷ δικαίῳ ἐκείνῳ· πολλὰ γὰρ ἔπαθον σήμερον κατ᾿ ὄναρ δι᾿ αὐτόν.

20 Οἱ δὲ ἀρχιερεῖς κỳ οἱ πρεσβύτεροι ἔπεισαν τὺς ὄχλυς, ἵνα αἰτήσωνται τὸν Βαραββᾶν, τὸν δὲ Ἰησῦν ἀπολέσωσιν.

21 Ἀποκριθεὶς δὲ ὁ ἡγεμὼν, εἶπεν αὐτοῖς· Τίνα θέλετε ἀπὸ τῶν δύο ἀπολύσω ὑμῖν; Οἱ δὲ εἶπον, Βαραββᾶν.

22 Λέγει αὐτοῖς ὁ Πιλᾶτ۞· Τί ὖν ποιήσω Ἰησῦν, τὸν λεγόμενον Χριστόν; Λέγυσιν αὐτῷ πάντες· Σταυρωθήτω.

23 Ὁ δὲ ἡγεμὼν ἔφη· Τί γὰρ κακὸν ἐποίησεν; Οἱ δὲ περισσῶς ἔκραζον, λέγοντες· Σταυρωθήτω.

26 Τότε ἀπέλυσεν αὐτοῖς τὸν Βαραββᾶν· τὸν δὲ Ἰησῦν φραγελλώσας παρέδωκεν ἵνα ςαυρωθῇ.

27 Τότε οἱ ςρατιῶται τῦ ἡγεμόν۞, παραλαβόντες τὸν Ἰησῦν εἰς τὸ πραιτώριον, συνήγαγον ἐπ᾿ αὐτὸν ὅλην τὴν σπεῖραν.

* 29 Καὶ ‡ πλέξαντες ‡ ςέφανον ἐξ ἀκανθῶν, ἐπέθηκαν ἐπὶ τὴν κεφαλὴν αὐτῦ· κỳ κάλαμον ἐπὶ τὴν δεξιὰν αὐτῦ· κỳ ‡ γονυπετήσαντες ἔμπροσθεν αὐτῷ, ‡ ἐνέπαιζον αὐτῷ, λέγοντες· Χαῖρε ὁ βασιλεὺς τῶν Ἰυδαίων.

30 Καὶ ἐμπτύσαντες εἰς αὐτὸν, ἔλαβον τὸν κάλαμον, κỳ ἔτυπτον εἰς τὴν κεφαλὴν αὐτῦ.

* 31 Καὶ ὅτε ἐνέπαιξαν αὐτῷ, ἐξέδυσαν αὐτὸν τὴν ‡ χλαμύδα, κỳ ἐνέδυσαν αὐτὸν τὰ ἱμάτια αὐτῦ· κỳ ἀπήγαγον αὐτὸν εἰς τὸ ςαυρῶσαι.

---

15 Per autem festum consueverat præses absolvere unum vinctum turbæ, quem voluissent.

16 Habebant autem tunc vinctum insignem, dictum Barabbam.

17 Coactis ergo illis, dixit illis Pilatus: Quem vultis absolvam vobis? Barabbam, an Jesum dictum Christum?

18 Sciebat enim quod per invidiam tradidissent eum.

19 Sedente autem illo super tribunali, misit ad eum uxor ejus, dicens: Nihil tibi & justo illi: multa enim passa sum hodie per somnium propter eum.

20 At principes Sacerdotum & seniores persuaserunt turbis, ut peterent Barabbam, at Jesum perderent.

21 Respondens autem præses, ait illis: Quem vultis de duobus absolvam vobis? Illi verò dixerunt: Barabbam.

22 Dicit ergo illis Pilatus: Quid igitur faciam Jesum dictum Christum? dicunt ei omnes: Crucifigatur.

23 At præses ait: Quid enim mali fecit? Illi autem magis clamabant, dicentes: Crucifigatur.

26 Tunc absolvit illis Barabbam: At Jesum flagellans, tradidit ut crucifigeretur.

27 Tunc milites præsidis assumentes Jesum in prætorium, coëgerunt ad eum universam cohortem.

29 Et plectentes coronam de spinis, imposuerunt super caput ejus, & arundinem in dextera ejus: & genu flectentes ante eum, illudebant ei, dicentes: Gaude rex Judæorum.

30 Et inspuentes in eum, acceperunt arundinem, & percutiebant in caput ejus.

31 Et postquam illuserunt ei, exuerunt eum chlamydem, & induerunt eum vestimentis ejus: & abduxerunt eum ad crucifigendum.

15. Or le Gouverneur avoit accoutumé, à chaque fête de *Pâques*, de relâcher au peuple celui des prisonniers qu'ils vouloient.

16. Et il y avoit alors un prisonnier insigne, nommé Barabbas.

17. Comme ils étoient donc assemblés, Pilate leur dit : Lequel voulez-vous que je vous relâche ; Barabbas, ou Jésus qu'on appelle Christ ?

18. Car il savoit bien que c'étoit par envie qu'ils l'avoient livré.

19. Et pendant qu'il étoit assis sur le tribunal, sa femme lui envoya dire : N'aie rien à faire avec cet homme de bien ; car j'ai beaucoup souffert aujourd'hui en songe à son sujet.

20. Alors les principaux Sacrificateurs et les Sénateurs persuadèrent au peuple de demander Barabbas, et de faire périr Jésus.

21. Et le Gouverneur prenant la parole, leur dit : Lequel des deux voulez-vous que je vous relâche ? Et ils dirent : Barabbas.

22. Pilate leur dit : Que ferai-je donc de Jésus qu'on appelle Christ? Tous lui dirent : Qu'il soit crucifié.

23. Et le Gouverneur *leur* dit : Mais quel mal a-t-il fait ? Alors ils crièrent encore plus fort : Qu'il soit crucifié.

26. Alors il leur relâcha Barabbas, et après avoir fait fouetter Jésus, il le leur livra pour être crucifié.

27. Et les soldats du Gouverneur amenèrent Jésus au Prétoire, et ils assemblèrent autour de lui toute la compagnie *des soldats*.

29. Puis ayant fait une couronne d'épines, ils la lui mirent sur la tête, et lui mirent un roseau à la *main* droite, et s'agenouillant devant lui, ils se moquoient de lui, en lui disant : Je te salue, Roi des Juifs.

30. Et crachant contre lui, ils prenoient le roseau, et ils lui en donnoient des coups sur la tête.

31. Après s'être ainsi moqués de lui, ils lui ôtèrent le manteau, et lui remirent ses habits, et ils l'emmenèrent pour le crucifier.

15 Now at *that* feast the governor was wont to release unto the people a prisoner, whom they would.

16 And they had then a notable prisoner, called Barabbas.

17 Therefore, when they were gathered together, Pilate said unto them, Whom will ye that I release unto you? Barabbas, or Jesus, which is called Christ?

18 For he knew that for envy they had delivered him.

19 When he was set down on the judgment-seat, his wife sent unto him, saying, Have thou nothing to do with that just man : for I have suffered many things this day in a dream because of him.

20 But the chief priests and elders persuaded the multitude that they should ask Barabbas, and destroy Jesus.

21 The governor answered, and said unto them, Whether of the twain will ye that I release unto you? They said, Barabbas.

22 Pilate saith unto them, What shall I do then with Jesus, which is called Christ? *They* all say unto him, Let him be crucified.

23 And the governor said, Why, what evil hath he done? But they cried out the more, saying, Let him be crucified.

26 Then released he Barabbas, unto them ; and when he had scourged Jesus, he delivered *him* to be crucified.

27 Then the soldiers of the governor took Jesus into the common hall, and gathered unto him the whole band *of soldiers*.

29 And when they had platted a crown of thorns, they put *it* upon his head, and a reed in his right hand; and they bowed the knee before him, and mocked him, saying, Hail, king of the Jews!

30 And they spit upon him, and took the reed, and smote him on the head.

31 And after that they had mocked him, they took the robe off from him, and put his own raiment on him, and led him away to crucify *him*.

79

3 Τότε ἰδὼν Ἰούδας ὁ παραδιδοὺς αὐτὸν, ὅτι κατεκρίθη, μεταμεληθεὶς, ἀπέςρεψε τὰ τριάκοντα ἀργύρια τοῖς ἀρχιερεῦσι ϗ τοῖς πρεσβυτέροις,

4 Λέγων· Ἥμαρτον, παραδοὺς αἷμα ἀθῶον. Οἱ δὲ εἶπον· Τί πρὸς ἡμᾶς; σὺ ὄψει.

* 5 Καὶ ῥίψας τὰ ἀργύρια ἐν τῷ ναῷ, ‡ ἀνεχώρησε· ϗ ἀπελθὼν, † ἀπήγξατο.

6 Οἱ δὲ ἀρχιερεῖς λαβόντες τὰ ἀργύρια, εἶπον· Οὐκ ἔξεςι βαλεῖν αὐτὰ εἰς τὸν κορβανᾶν· ἐπεὶ τιμὴ αἵματός ἐςι.

* 7 Συμβούλιον δὲ λαβόντες, ‡ ἠγόρασαν ἐξ αὐτῶν τὸν ἀγρὸν τοῦ ‡ κεραμέως, εἰς † ταφὴν τοῖς ‡ ξένοις.

8 Διὸ ἐκλήθη ὁ ἀγρὸς ἐκεῖνος, ἀγρὸς αἵματος, ἕως τῆς σήμερον.

26 Καὶ ὡς ἀπήγαγον αὐτὸν, ἐπιλαβόμενοι Σίμωνός τινος Κυρηναίου τοῦ ἐρχομένου ἀπ' ἀγροῦ, ἐπέθηκαν αὐτῷ τὸν ςαυρὸν, φέρειν ὄπισθεν τοῦ Ἰησοῦ.

27 Ἠκολούθει δὲ αὐτῷ πολὺ πλῆθος τοῦ λαοῦ ϗ γυναικῶν, αἳ ϗ ἐκόπτοντο ϗ ἐθρήνουν αὐτόν.

28 Στραφεὶς δὲ πρὸς αὐτὰς ὁ Ἰησοῦς, εἶπε· Θυγατέρες Ἱερουσαλὴμ, μὴ κλαίετε ἐπ' ἐμέ, πλὴν ἐφ' ἑαυτὰς κλαίετε, ϗ ἐπὶ τὰ τέκνα ὑμῶν·

29 Ὅτι ἰδοὺ, ἔρχονται ἡμέραι ἐν αἷς ἐροῦσι· Μακάριαι αἱ ςεῖραι,

ϗ κοιλίαι αἳ οὐκ ἐγέννησαν, ϗ μαςοὶ οἳ οὐκ ἐθήλασαν.

30 Τότε ἄρξονται λέγειν τοῖς ὄρεσι· Πέσετε ἐφ' ἡμᾶς· ϗ τοῖς βουνοῖς· Καλύψατε ἡμᾶς.

* 31 Ὅτι εἰ ἐν τῷ † ὑγρῷ ξύλῳ ταῦτα ποιοῦσιν, ἐν τῷ ξηρῷ τί γένηται;

32 Ἤγοντο δὲ ϗ ἕτεροι δύο κακοῦργοι σὺν αὐτῷ ἀναιρεθῆναι.

---

3 Tunc videns Judas qui tradens [fuit] eum, quod damnatus esset, pœnitens, retulit triginta argenteos principibus Sacerdotum, & senioribus,

4 Dicens, Peccavi, tradens sanguinem innoxium. Illi verò dixerunt, Quid ad nos? tu videris.

5 Et projiciens argenteos in templo, recessit: & abiens se strangulavit.

6 At principes Sacerdotum accipientes argenteos, dixerunt: Non licet injicere eos in corbanam: quia pretium sanguinis est.

7 Consilium autem sumentes mercati sunt ex illis agrum figuli in sepulturam peregrinis.

8 Quapropter vocatus est ager ille, Ager sanguinis, usque hodie.

26 Et quum abducerent eum, apprehendentes Simonem quendam Cyrenæum venientem ab agro, imposuerunt illi crucem, ut ferret post Jesum.

27 Sequebatur autem illum multa turba populi, & mulierum, quæ & plangebant, & lamentabantur eum.

28 Conversus autem ad illas Jesus, dixit: Filiæ Hierusalem, ne flete super me, sed super vos ipsas flete, & super filios vestros.

29 Quoniam ecce venient dies, in quibus dicent: Beatæ steriles,

& ventres qui non genuerunt, & ubera quæ non lactaverunt.

30 Tunc incipient dicere montibus: Cadite super nos: & collibus: Operite nos.

31 Quia si in viridi ligno hæc faciunt, in arido quid fiet?

32 Ducebantur autem & alii duo malefici ut cum eo tollerentur

3 Then Judas which had betrayed him, when he saw that he was condemned, repented himself, and brought again the thirty pieces of silver to the chief priests and elders,

4 Saying, I have sinned, in that I have betrayed the innocent blood. And they said, What is that to us? see thou to that.

5 And he cast down the pieces of silver in the temple, and departed, and went and hanged himself.

6 And the chief priests took the silver pieces, and said, It is not lawful for to put them into the treasury, because it is the price of blood.

7 And they took counsel, and bought with them the potter's field, to bury strangers in.

8 Wherefore that field was called, The field of blood, unto this lay.

5. Alors Judas, qui l'avoit trahi, voyant qu'il étoit condamné, se repentit, et reporta les trente pièces d'argent aux principaux Sacrificateurs et aux Sénateurs;

4. Disant : J'ai péché en trahissant le sang innocent. Mais ils dirent · Que nous importe? tu y pourvoiras.

5. Alors après avoir jeté les pièces d'argent dans le temple, il se retira, et s'en alla, et s'étrangla.

6. Et les principaux Sacrificateurs ayant pris les pièces d'argent, dirent : Il n'est pas permis de les mettre dans le trésor sacré ; car c'est le prix du sang.

7. Et ayant délibéré, ils en achetèrent le champ d'un potier, pour la sépulture des étrangers.

8. C'est pourquoi ce champ-là a été appelé jusqu'à aujourd'hui : Le champ du sang.

26 And, as they led him away, they laid hold upon one Simon, a Cyrenian, coming out of the country, and on him they laid the cross, that he might bear it after Jesus.

27 And there followed him a great company of people, and of women, which also bewailed and lamented him.

28 But Jesus, turning unto them, said, Daughters of Jerusalem, weep not for me, but weep for yourselves, and for your children.

29 For, behold, the days are coming, in the which they shall say, Blessed are the barren, and the wombs that never bare, and the paps which never gave suck.

30 Then shall they begin to say to the mountains, Fall on us; and to the hills, Cover us.

31 For if they do these things in a green tree, what shall be done in the dry?

32 And there were also two others, malefactors, led with him to be put to death.

26. Et comme ils le menoient au supplice, ils prirent un homme de Cyrène, nommé Simon, qui revenoit des champs, et le chargèrent de la croix, pour la porter après Jésus.

27. Et une grande multitude de peuple et de femmes le suivoient, qui se frappoient la poitrine, et se lamentoient.

28. Mais Jésus se tournant vers elles, leur dit : Filles de Jérusalem, ne pleurez point sur moi, mais pleurez sur vous-mêmes et sur vos enfans.

29. Car les jours viendront auxquels on dira : Heureuses les stériles, les femmes qui n'ont point enfanté, les mamelles qui n'ont point allaité !

30. Alors ils se mettront à dire aux montagnes : Tombez sur nous; et aux côteaux, couvrez-nous.

31. Car si l'on fait ces choses au bois vert, que fera-t-on au bois sec.

32. On menoit aussi deux autres hommes qui étoient des malfaiteurs, pour les faire mourir avec lui.

80

17 Καὶ βαςάζων τὸν ςαυρὸν αὐτῦ ἐξῆλθεν εἰς τὸν λεγόμενον Κρανίε τόπον, ὃς λέγεlαι Ἑβραϊςὶ Γολγοθᾶ.

18 Ὅπε αὐτὸν ἐςαύρωσαν, κỳ μετ᾽ αὐτῦ ἄλλες δύο, ἐντεῦθεν κỳ ἐντεῦθεν, μέσον δὲ τὸν Ἰησῦν.

19 Ἔγραψε δὲ κỳ τίτλον ὁ Πιλάτ⟨Θ⟩, κỳ ἔθηκεν ἐπὶ τῦ ςαυρῦ ἦν δὲ γεγραμμένον· ΙΗΣΟΥΣ Ο ΝΑΖΩΡΑΙΟΣ Ο ΒΑΣΙΛΕΥΣ ΤΩΝ ΙΟΥΔΑΙΩΝ.

* 20 Τῦτον ἒν τὸν ‡ τίτλον πολλοὶ ἀνέγνωσαν τῶν Ἰεδαίων, ὅτι ἐγγὺς ἦν τῆς πόλεως ὁ τόπ⟨Θ⟩

ὅπε ἐςαυρώθη ὁ Ἰησῦς· κỳ ἦν γεγραμμένον Ἑβραϊςὶ, ‡ Ἑλληνιςὶ, ‡ Ῥωμαϊςὶ.

21 Ἔλεγον ἒν τῷ Πιλάτῳ οἱ ἀρχιερεῖς τῶν Ἰεδαίων· Μὴ γράφε· Ὁ βασιλεὺς τῶν Ἰεδαίων· ἀλλ᾽ ὅτι ἐκεῖν⟨Θ⟩ εἶπε· Βασιλεύς εἰμι τῶν Ἰεδαίων.

22 Ἀπεκρίθη ὁ Πιλάτ⟨Θ⟩· Ὃ γέγραφα, γέγραφα.

* 23 Οἱ ἒν ςρατιῶται, ὅτε ἐςαύρωσαν τὸν Ἰησῦν, ἔλαβον τὰ ἱμάτια αὐτῦ, (κỳ ἐποίησαν τέσσαρα μέρη, ἑκάςῳ ςρατιώτῃ μέρ⟨Θ⟩·) κỳ τὸν χιτῶνα· ἦν δὲ ὁ ‡ χιτὼν † ἄρρα⟨Θ⟩, ἐκ τῶν ‡ ἄνωθεν † ὑφανὸς δι᾽ ὅλε.

24 Εἶπον ἒν πρὸς ἀλλήλες· Μὴ σχίσωμεν αὐτόν, ἀλλὰ λάχωμεν περὶ αὐτῦ, τίν⟨Θ⟩ ἔςαι.

39 Οἱ δὲ παραπορευόμενοι ἐβλασφήμεν αὐτόν, κινῦνἰες τὰς κεφαλὰς αὐτῶν,

40 Καὶ λέγονlες· Ὁ καlαλύων τὸν ναὸν κỳ ἐν τρισὶν ἡμέραις οἰκοδομῶν, σῶσον σεαυτόν· εἰ υἱὸς εἶ τῦ Θεῦ, κατάβηθι ἀπὸ τῦ ςαυρῦ.

41 Ὁμοίως δὲ κỳ οἱ ἀρχιερεῖς, ἐμπαίζονlες μετὰ τῶν γραμμαlέων κỳ πρεσβυlέρων, ἔλεγον·

42 Ἄλλες ἔσωσεν, ἑαυτὸν ἒ δύναlαι σῶσαι· εἰ βασιλεὺς Ἰσραὴλ ἐςι, καlαβάτω νῦν ἀπὸ τῦ ςαυρῦ, κỳ πιςεύσομεν αὐτῷ.

43 Πέποιθεν ἐπὶ τὸν Θεόν· ῥυσάσθω νῦν αὐτόν, εἰ θέλει αὐτόν· εἶπε γάρ· Ὅτι Θεῦ εἰμι υἱός.

17 Et portans crucem fuam, exivit in dictum Calvariæ locum, qui dicitur Hebraice Golgotha.

18 Ubi eum crucifixerunt, & cum eo alios duos, hinc & hinc, medium autem Jefum.

19 Scripfit autem & titulum Pilatus, & pofuit fuper crucem. Erat autem fcriptum : JESUS NAZARENUS REX JUDÆORUM.

20 Hunc ergo titulum multi legerunt Judæorum : quia prope erat locus civitatem ubi crucifixus eft Jefus. Et erat fcriptum Hebraice, Græce, Romane.

21 Dicebant ergo Pilato principes Sacerdotum Judæorum : Ne fcribe : Rex Judæorum : fed quia ipfe dixit : Rex fum Judæorum.

22 Refpondit Pilatus : Quod fcripfi, fcripfi.

23 Ergo milites quum crucifixiffent Jefum, acceperunt veftimenta ejus, (& fecerunt quatuor partes, unicuique militi partem,) & tunicam : Erat autem tunica inconfutilis, ex iis quæ defuper contexta per totum.

24 Dixerunt ergo ad invicem : Non fcindamus eam, fed fortiariur de illa, cujus erit.

39 At prætereuntes blafphemabant eum, moventes capita fua,

40 Et dicentes : Diffolvens templum, & in tribus diebus ædificans, ferva teipfum. Si filius es Dei, defcende de cruce.

41 Similiter verò & principes Sacerdotum illudentes cum Scribis, & fenioribus, dicebant :

42 Alios fervavit, feipfum non poteft fervare : Si rex Ifraël eft, defcendat nunc de cruce, & credemus ei.

43 Confidit in Deo, liberet nunc eum, fi vult eum ; dixit enim : Quia Dei fum filius.

17. Et Jésus, portant sa croix, vint au lieu appelé le Calvaire, qui se nomme en hébreu, Golgotha ;

18. Où ils le crucifièrent, et deux autres avec lui, *l'un* d'un côté, et *l'autre* de l'autre, et Jésus au milieu.

19. Pilate fit aussi faire un écriteau, et le fit mettre au-dessus de la croix ; et on y avoit écrit :

JESUS DE NAZARETH, ROI DES JUIFS.

20. Plusieurs donc des Juifs lurent cet écriteau, parce que le lieu où Jésus étoit crucifié étoit près de la ville, et il étoit écrit en Hébreu, en Grec, et en Latin.

21. Et les principaux Sacrificateurs des Juifs dirent à Pilate : N'écris pas, Le Roi des Juifs ; mais qu'il a dit : Je suis le Roi des Juifs.

22. Pilate répondit : Ce que j'ai écrit, je l'ai écrit.

23. Après que les soldats eurent crucifié Jésus, ils prirent ses habits, et ils en firent quatre parts, une part pour chaque soldat ; *ils prirent* aussi la robe ; mais la robe étoit sans couture, d'un seul tissu, depuis le haut jusqu'au bas.

24. Ils dirent donc entr'eux : Ne la mettons pas en pièces, mais tirons au sort à qui l'aura ;

39. Et ceux qui passoient par là, lui disoient des outrages, branlant la tête ;

40. Et disant : toi qui détruits le temple, et qui le rebâtis en trois jours, sauve-toi toi-même ; si tu es le Fils de Dieu, descends de la croix.

41. De même aussi les principaux Sacrificateurs, avec les Scribes et les Sénateurs, disoient en se moquant :

42. Il a sauvé les autres et il ne se peut sauver lui-même : s'il est le Roi d'Israël, qu'il descende maintenant de la croix et nous croirons en lui.

43. Il se confie en Dieu ; que *Dieu* le délivre maintenant, s'il lui est agréable ; car il a dit : Je suis le Fils de Dieu.

J. 19

17 And he, bearing his cross, went forth into a place called *the place* of a skull, which is called in the Hebrew, Golgotha ;

18 Where they crucified him, and two others with him, on either side one, and Jesus in the midst.

19 And Pilate wrote a title, and put it on the cross. And the writing was, JESUS OF NAZARETH, THE KING OF THE JEWS.

20 This title then read many of the Jews : for the place where Jesus was crucified was nigh to the city : and it was written in Hebrew, *and* Greek, *and* Latin.

21 Then said the chief priests of the Jews to Pilate, Write not, The King of the Jews ; but that he said, I am King of the Jews.

22 Pilate answered, What I have written, I have written.

23 Then the soldiers, when they had crucified Jesus, took his garments, and made four parts, to every soldier a part, and also *his* coat : now the coat was without seam, woven from the top throughout.

24 They said, therefore, among themselves, Let us not rend it, but cast lots for it, whose it shall be :

Mt. 27

39 And they that passed by reviled him, wagging their heads,

40 And saying, Thou that destroyest the temple, and buildest *it* in three days, save thyself. If thou be the Son of God, come down from the cross.

41 Likewise also the chief priests mocking *him*, with the scribes and elders, said,

42 He saved others ; himself he cannot save. If he be the King of Israel, let him now come down from the cross, and we will believe him.

43 He trusted in God ; let him deliver him now, if he will have him : for he said, I am the Son of God.

81

39 Εἷς δὲ τῶν κρεμασθέντων
κακούργων ἐϐλασφήμει αὐτὸν, λέ-
γων· Εἰ σὺ εἶ ὁ Χριϛὸς, σῶσον
σεαυτὸν κ̄ ἡμᾶς.
40 Ἀποκριθεὶς δὲ ὁ ἕτερ@·
ἐπέϊμα αὐτῷ, λέγων· Οὐδὲ φοϐῇ
σὺ τὸν Θεὸν, ὅτι ἐν τῷ αὐτῷ
κρίμαλι εἶ;
41 Καὶ ἡμεῖς μὲν δικαίως·
ἄξια γὰρ ὧν ἐπράξαμεν ἀπολαμ-

39 Unus autem pendentium
maleficorum blasphemabat e-
um, dicens: Si tu es Christus,
serva temetipsum & nos.
40 Respondens autem alter
increpabat eum, dicens: Neque
times tu Deum, quod in eadem
damnatione es?
41 Et nos quidem juste: digna enim eorum quæ fecimus

ϐάνομεν· ὗτ@· δὲ οὐδὲν ἄτοπον
ἔπραξε.

recipimus: hic vero nihil in-
solens egit.

---

34 Ὁ δὲ Ἰησῦς ἔλεγε· Πάτερ,
ἄφες αὐτοῖς· ὐ γὰρ οἴδασι τί
ποιῦσι.

34 At Jesus dicebat: Pater,
dimitte illis: non enim sciunt
quid faciunt.

---

25 Εἰϛήκεισαν δὲ παρὰ τῷ
ϛαυρῷ τῦ Ἰησῦ ἡ μήτηρ αὐτῦ κ̄
ἡ ἀ᾿ελφὴ τῆς μηϐρὸς αὐτῦ, Μαρία
ἡ τῦ Κλωπᾶ, κ̄ Μαρία ἡ Μαγϐα-
ληνή.
26 Ἰησῦς ὖν ἰδὼν τὴν μηϐέρα,
κ̄ τὸν μαθηϐὴν παρεϛῶτα, ὃν ἠ-
γάπα, λέγει τῇ μηϐρὶ αὐτῦ. Γύ-
ναι, ἴϐε ὁ υἱός σε.
27 Εἶτα λέγει τῷ μαθηϐῇ· Ἰϐὲ
ἡ μήτηρ σε. Καὶ ἀπ᾿ ἐκείνης
τῆς ὥρας· ἔλαϐεν αὐτὴν ὁ μαθηϐὴς
εἰς τὰ ἴδια.

25 Stabant autem juxta crucem Jesu, mater ejus & soror
matris ejus, Maria Cleopæ, &
Maria Magdalene.
26 Jesus ergo videns matrem
& discipulum adstantem, quem
diligebat, dicit matri suæ: Mulier, ecce filius tuus.
27 Deinde dicit discipulo:
Ecce mater tua. Et ex illa hora
accepit eam discipulus ille in
propria.

---

46 Περὶ δὲ τὴν ἐνάτην ὥραν
ἀνεϐόησεν ὁ Ἰεσοὺς φωνῇ μεγάλη,
λέγων· Ἠλὶ, Ἠλὶ, λαμὰ σαϐαχ-
θανί; τῦτ᾿ ἔϛι, Θεέ μκ, Θεέ μκ,
ἱνατί με ἐγκατέλιπες;
47 Τινὲς δὲ τῶν ἐκεῖ ἑϛώτων
ἀκύσαντες, ἔλεγον· Ὅτι Ἠλίαν
φωνεῖ ὗτ@·.
48 Καὶ εὐθέως δραμὼν εἷς ἐξ
αὐτῶν, κ̄ λαϐὼν ϯ σπόγγον, πλή-
σας τε ὄξυς, κ̄ ϯ περιθεὶς καλάμῳ,
κ̄ ϯ ἐπότιζεν αὐτόν.
49 Οἱ δὲ λοιποὶ ἔλεγον· Ἄφες
ἴδωμεν εἰ ἔρχεϐαι Ἠλίας σώσων
αὐτόν.
50 Ὁ δὲ Ἰησῦς, πάλιν κρά-

46 Circa vero nonam horam
clamavit Jesus voce magna, dicens: Eli, Eli, lama sabachthani? hoc est, Deus meus, Deus
meus, ut quid me dereliquisti?
47 Quidam autem illic stan-
tium, audientes, dicebant, Quod
Eliam vocat iste.
48 Et continuo currens unus
ex eis, & accipiens spongiam,
implensque aceti, & circumpo-
nens arundini potabat eum.
49 Verum cæteri dicebant:
Sine, videamus an veniat Elias
liberaturus eum.
50 At Jesus iterum cla-

ξας φωνῇ μεγάλη, ἀφῆκε τὸ
πνεῦμα.

mans voce magna, emisit spiritum.

---

55 Ἦσαν δὲ ἐκεῖ γυναῖκες
πολλαὶ, ἀπὸ μακρόθεν θεωρῦσαι·
αἵτινες ἠκολύθησαν τῷ Ἰησῦ ἀπὸ
τῆς Γαλιλαίας, διακονῦσαι αὐτῷ.
56 Ἐν αἷς ἦν Μαρία ἡ Μαγ-
ϐαληνὴ, κ̄ Μαρία ἡ τῦ Ἰακώϐε
κ̄ Ἰωσῆ μήτηρ, κ̄ ἡ μήτηρ τῶν υἱῶν
Ζεϐεϐαίε.

55 Erant autem ibi mulieres
multæ à longè spectantes, quæ
sequutæ erant Jesum à Galilæa,
ministrantes ei:
56 In quibus erat Maria
Magdalene, & Maria Jacobi &
Jose mater, & mater filiorum
Zebedæi.

39. L'un des malfaiteurs qui étoient crucifiés, l'outrageoit aussi, en disant : Si tu es le Christ, sauve-toi toi-même, et nous aussi.

40. Mais l'autre le prenant, lui dit : Ne crains-tu point Dieu, puisque tu es condamné au même suplice.

41. Et pour nous, *nous le sommes* avec justice; car nous souffrons ce que nos crimes méritent; mais celui-ci n'a fait aucun mal.

34. Mais Jésus disoit : Mon père, pardonne-leur : car ils ne savent ce qu'ils font.

25. Or, la Mère de Jésus, et la sœur de sa Mère, Marie, *femme de Cléopas*, et Marie Magdelaine, se tenoient près de sa croix.

26. Jésus donc voyant sa Mère, et près d'elle, le Disciple qu'il aimoit, dit à sa Mère : Femme, voilà ton Fils.

27. Puis il dit au Disciple : Voilà ta Mère : Et dès cette heure-là, ce Disciple la prit chez lui.

46. Et environ la neuvième heure, Jésus s'écria à haute voix, disant : Eli, Eli, lamma sabachthani ? C'est à-dire, mon Dieu, mon Dieu, pourquoi m'as-tu abandonné !

47. Et quelques-uns de ceux qui étoient présens, ayant ouï cela, disoient : il appelle Elie.

48. Et aussitôt quelqu'un d'entr'eux courut et prit une éponge, et l'ayant remplie de vinaigre, il la mit au bout d'une canne, et lui en donna à boire.

49. Et les autres disoient : attendez, voyons si Elie viendra le délivrer.

50. Et Jésus ayant encore crié à haute voix, rendit l'esprit.

55. Il y avoit aussi là plusieurs femmes, qui regardoient de loin, et qui avoient suivi Jésus, depuis la Galilée, en le servant;

56. Entre lesquelles étoient Marie-Magdeleine, et Marie, mère de Jacques et de Joses, et la mère des fils de Zébédée.

39 And one of the malefactors, *L. 23.* which were hanged, railed on him, saying, If thou be Christ, save thyself and us.

40 But the other, answering, rebuked him, saying, Dost not thou fear God, seeing thou art in the same condemnation?

41 And we indeed justly; for we receive the due reward of our deeds: but this man hath done nothing amiss.

34 Then said Jesus, Father, forgive them; for they know not what they do.

25 Now there stood by the cross *J. 19* of Jesus, his mother, and his mother's sister, Mary the *wife* of Cleophas, and Mary Magdalene.

26 When Jesus, therefore, saw his mother, and the disciple standing by whom he loved, he saith unto his mother, Woman, behold thy Son!

27 Then saith he to the disciple, Behold thy mother! And from that hour that disciple took her unto his own *home*.

46 And about the ninth hour, *M. 27.* Jesus cried with a loud voice, saying, Eli, Eli, lama sabachthani? that is to say, My God, my God, why hast thou forsaken me?

47 Some of them that stood there, when they heard *that*, said, This *man* calleth for Elias.

48 And straightway one of them ran, and took a spunge, and filled *it* with vinegar, and put *it* on a reed, and gave him to drink.

49 The rest said, Let be, let us see whether Elias will come to save him.

50 Jesus, when he had cried again with a loud voice, yielded up the ghost.

55 And many women were there, beholding afar off, which followed Jesus from Galilee, ministering unto him:

56 Among which was Mary Magdalene, and Mary the mother of James and Joses, and the mother of Zebedee's children.

82

31 Οἱ οὖν Ἰουδαῖοι, ἵνα μὴ μείνῃ ἐπὶ τοῦ σταυροῦ τὰ σώματα ἐν τῷ σαββάτῳ, ἐπεὶ παρασκευὴ ἦν, (ἦν γὰρ μεγάλη ἡ ἡμέρα ἐκείνη τοῦ σαββάτου) ἠρώτησαν τὸν Πιλάτον ἵνα κατεαγῶσιν αὐτῶν τὰ ‡ σκέλη, καὶ ἀρθῶσιν.

32 Ἦλθον οὖν οἱ στρατιῶται, καὶ τοῦ μὲν πρώτου κατέαξαν τὰ σκέλη, καὶ τοῦ ἄλλου τοῦ συσταυρωθέντος αὐτῷ.

33 Ἐπὶ δὲ τὸν Ἰησοῦν ἐλθόντες, ὡς εἶδον αὐτὸν ἤδη τεθνηκότα, οὐ κατέαξαν αὐτοῦ τὰ σκέλη·

34 Ἀλλ' εἷς τῶν ‡ στρατιωτῶν † λόγχῃ αὐτοῦ τὴν ‡ πλευρὰν † ἔνυξε, καὶ ‡ εὐθὺς ἐξῆλθεν αἷμα καὶ ὕδωρ.

38 Μετὰ δὲ ταῦτα ἠρώτησε τὸν Πιλάτον ὁ Ἰωσὴφ ὁ ἀπὸ Ἀριμαθαίας, (ὢν μαθητὴς τοῦ Ἰησοῦ, κεκρυμμένος δὲ διὰ τὸν φόβον τῶν Ἰουδαίων) ἵνα ἄρῃ τὸ σῶμα τοῦ Ἰησοῦ· καὶ ἐπέτρεψεν ὁ Πιλάτος· ἦλθεν οὖν καὶ ἦρε τὸ σῶμα τοῦ Ἰησοῦ.

39 Ἦλθε δὲ καὶ Νικόδημος (ὁ ἐλθὼν πρὸς τὸν Ἰησοῦν νυκτὸς τὸ πρῶτον) φέρων † μίγμα ‡ σμύρνης καὶ ἀλόης· ὡσεὶ λίτρας ἑκατόν.

40 Ἔλαβον οὖν τὸ σῶμα τοῦ Ἰησοῦ, καὶ ἔδησαν αὐτὸ ‡ ὀθονίοις μετὰ τῶν ‡ ἀρωμάτων, ‡ καθὼς ‡ ἔθος ἐστὶ τοῖς Ἰουδαίοις ‡ ἐνταφιάζειν.

41 Ἦν δὲ ἐν τῷ τόπῳ ὅπου ἐσταυρώθη, κῆπος, καὶ ἐν τῷ κήπῳ μνημεῖον καινόν, ἐν ᾧ οὐδέπω οὐδεὶς ἐτέθη.

42 Ἐκεῖ οὖν ἔθηκαν τὸν Ἰησοῦν.

καὶ προσκυλίσας λίθον μέγαν τῇ θύρᾳ τοῦ μνημείου, ἀπῆλθεν.

---

31 Ergo Judæi, ut non remanerent in cruce corpora in Sabbato, quoniam Parasceve erat, (erat enim magnus dies ille Sabbati) rogaverunt Pilatum ut frangerentur eorum crura, & tollerentur.

32 Venerunt ergo milites, & quidem primi fregerunt crura: & alterius concrucifixi ei.

33 Ad autem Jesum venientes, ut viderunt eum jam mortuum, non fregerunt ejus crura.

34 Sed unus militum lancea ejus latus fodit, & continuo exivit sanguis & aqua.

38 Post hæc rogavit Pilatum Joseph ab Arimathæa (existens discipulus Jesu, occultus autem propter metum Judæorum) ut tolleret corpus Jesu: & permisit Pilatus: Venit ergo & tulit corpus Jesu.

39 Venit autem & Nicodemus (ille veniens ad Jesum nocte primum) ferens mixturam myrrhæ & aloës, quasi libras centum.

40 Acceperunt ergo corpus Jesu, & ligaverunt illud linteis cum aromatibus, sicut mos est Judæis sepelire.

41 Erat autem in loco, ubi crucifixus est, hortus, & in horto monumentum novum, in quo nondum quisquam positus erat.

42 Ibi ergo posuerunt Jesum, . . . & . . . volvens lapidem m . . . . abiit.

31. Or, les Juifs, de peur que les corps ne demeurassent sur la croix le jour du Sabbat (car c'en étoit la préparation, et ce Sabbat étoit un jour fort solennel), prièrent Pilate de leur faire rompre les jambes, et qu'on les ôtât.

32. Les soldats vinrent donc, et rompirent les jambes au premier, et ensuite à l'autre qui étoit crucifié avec lui.

33. Mais lorsqu'ils vinrent à Jésus, voyant qu'il étoit déjà mort, ils ne lui rompirent point les jambes.

34. Mais un des soldats lui perça le côté avec une lance, et aussitôt il en sortit du sang et de l'eau.

38. Après cela, Joseph d'Arimathée, qui étoit Disciple de Jésus, mais en secret, parce qu'il craignoit les Juifs, pria Pilate qu'il pût ôter le corps de Jésus; et Pilate le lui permit. Il vint donc et emporta le corps de Jésus.

39. Nicodème qui, au commencement, étoit venu de nuit vers Jésus, y vint aussi, apportant environ cent livres d'une composition de myrrhe et d'aloës.

40. Ils prirent donc le corps de Jésus, et l'enveloppèrent de linges, avec des drogues aromatiques, comme les Juifs ont accoutumé d'ensevelir.

41. Or, il y avoit un jardin au lieu où il avoit été crucifié, et dans ce jardin un sépulcre neuf, où personne n'avoit été mis.

42. Ils mirent donc là Jésus, et ayant roulé une grand pierre à l'entrée du sépulcre, il s'en alla.

31 The Jews, therefore, because it was the preparation, that the bodies should not remain upon the cross on the sabbath-day, (for that sabbath-day was an high day,) besought Pilate that their legs might be broken, and that they might be taken away.

32 Then came the soldiers, and brake the legs of the first, and of the other which was crucified with him.

33 But when they came to Jesus, and saw that he was dead already, they brake not his legs:

34 But one of the soldiers with a spear pierced his side, and forthwith came thereout blood and water.

38 And after this, Joseph of Arimathea, (being a disciple of Jesus, but secretly for fear of the Jews,) besought Pilate that he might take away the body of Jesus: and Pilate gave him leave. He came therefore, and took the body of Jesus.

39 And there came also Nicodemus, (which at the first came to Jesus by night and brought a mixture of myrrh and aloes, about an hundred pound weight.

40 Then took they the body of Jesus, and wound it in linen clothes with the spices, as the manner of the Jews is to bury.

41 Now, in the place where he was crucified, there was a garden; and in the garden a new sepulchre, wherein was never man yet laid.

42 There laid they Jesus,

60. and rolled a great stone to the door of the sepulchre, and departed.

83

This facsimile reproduction of the Jefferson Bible
was published by Smithsonian Books in November 2011
on the occasion of the conservation and exhibition of the Jefferson Bible
by the National Museum of American History,
Smithsonian Institution.

SMITHSONIAN BOOKS

Carolyn Gleason, Director

Christina Wiginton, Project Editor

Jefferson Bible pages photographed by Hugh Talman,
National Museum of American History

Images prepared for publication by Marie Koller, Smithsonian Media

Edited by Duke Johns

Designed by Robert L. Wiser

Illustration credits:

Jacket and frontispiece—
Collection of the New-York Historical Society, Accession No. 1867.306

Page 18—Thomas Sully, Benjamin Rush, ca. 1813, oil on canvas,
the Trout Gallery at Dickinson College, Carlisle, PA

Page 21—Monticello, Thomas Jefferson Foundation, Inc.

Page 22—American Philosophical Society

Page 29—Gift of Mrs. Robert Homans,
image courtesy National Gallery of Art, Washington

Page 32—Smithsonian Institution Archives, Cyrus Adler, ca. 1890.
Record Unit 95 Box 1, Folder 21. Image # SIA2011–0921

Conservation photography by
Laura A. Bedford, Emily S. Rainwater, and Hugh Talman

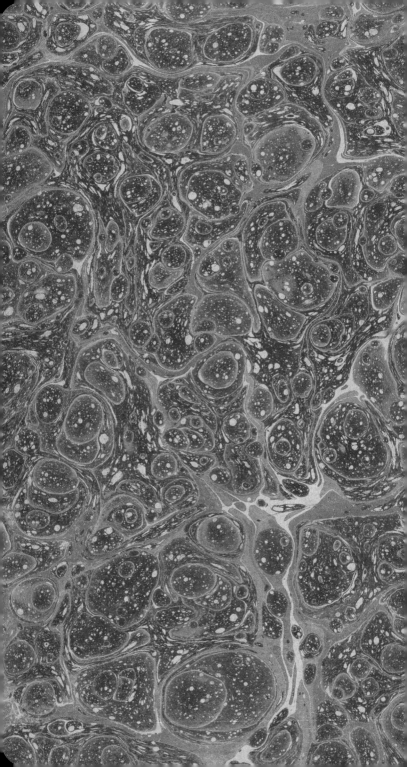